MAPPING DETROIT

GREAT LAKES BOOKS

A complete listing of the books in this series can be found online at wsupress.wayne.edu

EDITOR
Charles K. Hyde, *Wayne State University*

ADVISORY EDITORS

Jeffrey Abt, *Wayne State University*

Fredric C. Bohm, *Michigan State University*

Sandra Sageser Clark, *Michigan Historical Center*

Brian Leigh Dunnigan, *Clements Library*

De Witt Dykes, *Oakland University*

Joe Grimm, *Michigan State University*

Richard H. Harms, *Calvin College*

Laurie Harris, *Pleasant Ridge, Michigan*

Thomas Klug, *Marygrove College*

Susan Higman Larsen, *Detroit Institute of Arts*

Philip P. Mason, *Prescott, Arizona, and Eagle Harbor, Michigan*

Dennis Moore, *Consulate General of Canada*

Erik C. Nordberg, *Michigan Humanities Council*

Deborah Smith Pollard, *University of Michigan–Dearborn*

Michael O. Smith, *Wayne State University*

Joseph M. Turrini, *Wayne State University*

Arthur M. Woodford, *Harsens Island, Michigan*

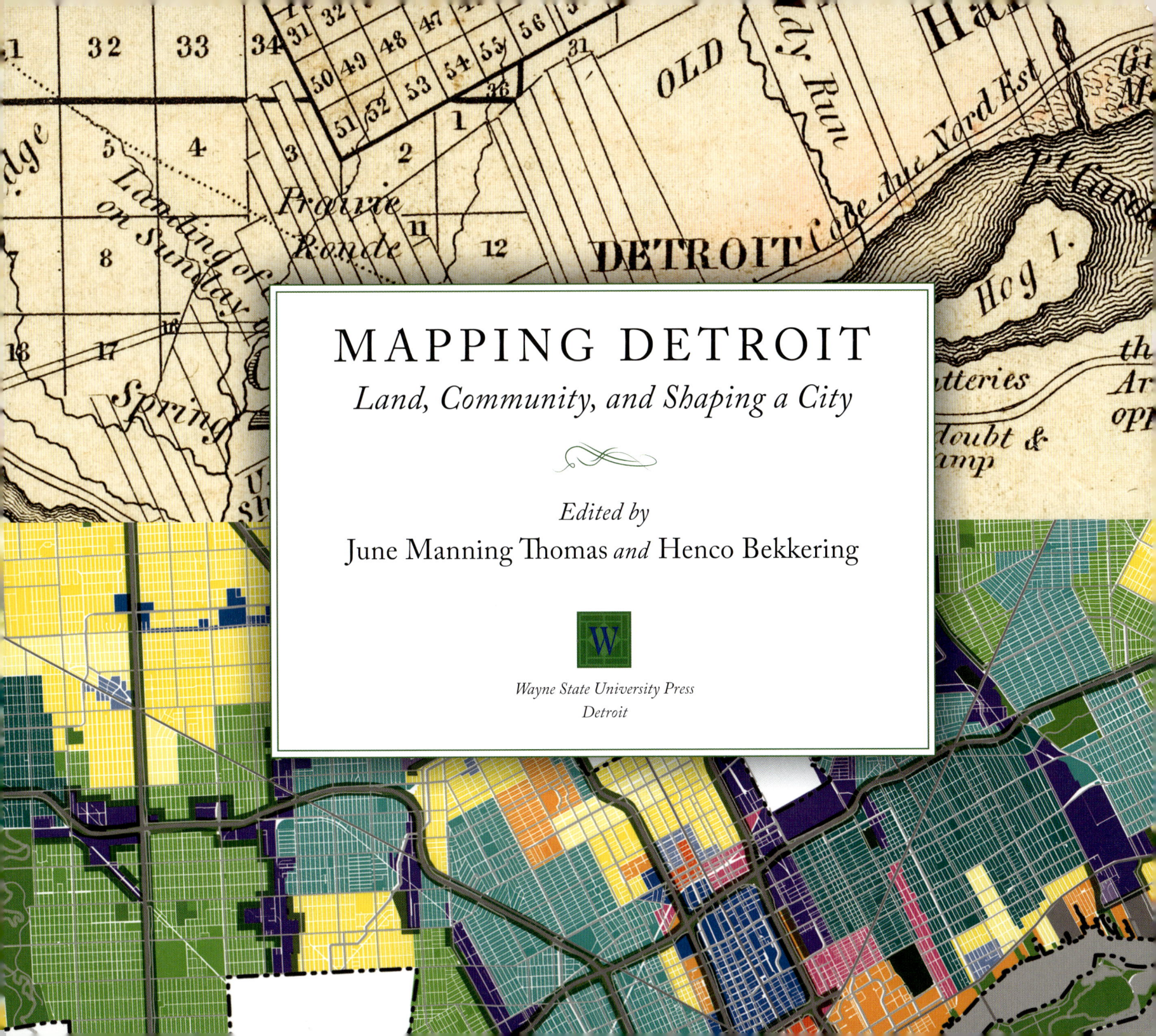

MAPPING DETROIT

Land, Community, and Shaping a City

Edited by

June Manning Thomas *and* Henco Bekkering

Wayne State University Press
Detroit

© 2015 by Wayne State University Press, Detroit, Michigan 48201.
All rights reserved. No part of this book may be reproduced without formal permission.
Manufactured in the United States of America.

20 19 18 17 16   6 5 4 3 2

ISBN 978-0-8143-4026-4 (paperback)
ISBN 978-0-8143-4027-1 (e-book)

Library of Congress Control Number: 2014947712

∞

Designed and typeset by Bryce Schimanski
Composed in Adobe Caslon Pro

CONTENTS

Foreword by Monica Ponce de Leon vii

Preface ix

Introduction: Land and Change in Detroit 1
June Manning Thomas and Henco Bekkering

PART I
EVOLVING DETROIT: PAST TO PRESENT

1. Charting the Shape of Early Detroit: 1701–1838 17
   Brian Leigh Dunnigan

2. Mapping Detroit: "The City of Holes" 27
   Henco Bekkering and Yanjia Liu

3. Redevelopment in Detroit: Spatial Evolution 51
   June Manning Thomas

PART II
PORTIONS OF THE CITY

4. Detroit: Linear City 77
   Robert Fishman

5. Comparing People and Places with Transportation Accessibility in Metropolitan Detroit 101
   Joe Grengs

6. Mapping Delray: Understanding Changes in a Southwest Detroit Community 115
   María Arquero de Alarcón and Larissa Larsen

7. Remaking Brightmoor 143
   Margaret Dewar and Robert Linn

PART III
UNDERSTANDING CONTEMPORARY SPACE AND POTENTIAL

8. Mapping the Urban Landscape: Revealing the Archipelago 169
   Lars Gräbner

9. Redesigning Community with Propinquity: Fragments of Detroit's Region 189
   June Manning Thomas

Epilogue: *Detroit Future City* 209
Toni L. Griffin and June Manning Thomas

Contributors 233

Index 237

FOREWORD

I am very pleased to write the foreword to this book, which offers an array of critical insights into the spatial evolution and present conditions of the city of Detroit. The perspectives range from simple historical accounts to analyses of key topics and subareas to innovative presentations envisioning possible alternative futures. Several of the authors have been associated with the University of Michigan's Taubman College of Architecture and Urban Planning, as current or previous faculty members or, in two cases, as former students. We in the college highly value our long-standing relationships with Detroit and our history of efforts to help envision a better city and region. This book's collection of unique, beautifully illustrated insights into the spatial dynamics of that important city is just one facet of these efforts. Detroit belongs to a unique cadre of American cities in which determination and ingenuity led to a distinctive identity known throughout the world. As an industrial and cultural pioneer, Detroit played a pivotal role in transforming the infrastructure and social fabric of cities worldwide. The cars, trucks, and other vehicles assembled there have helped to speed up the processes of urbanization, and the urban form of cities worldwide reflects the influence of motor vehicles and the economic opportunities they have brought. Detroit's role in shaping urban areas worldwide cannot be overstated. However, the city itself has proven to be a precursor for the consequences of many challenges, such as those resulting from overdependence on the manufacture of vehicles and other durable goods. Detroit has experienced negative environmental effects, fluctuating business cycles, manufacturing decline, the spatial decentralization of the metropolis, and diminishing population and tax bases in the central city. Yet it also offers many opportunities for innovation and adaptation.

This book presents compelling illustrations of the history and evolving land use patterns of Detroit, as well as clear explanations of pivotal issues and potentialities. The issues covered include land vacancy, redevelopment, industries' location policies, neighborhood development in two key areas, and lack of transportation access for all citizens. The potentialities include opportunities to recognize and support informal land development strategies in abandoned neighborhoods, enhance regional cooperation and connection, reuse vacant land, unearth ancient waterways, and create a better future city of Detroit. These are tangible, attainable visions that in some cases have gained widespread attention and in other cases have not. The circumstances of Detroit make it ripe for such innovative ideas and proposals.

All the authors of this volume present descriptive and historical maps and images but then build upon these by offering analytic observations about people, places, and institutions. The areas of author expertise include history, architecture, archival maps, landscape architecture, land use planning, redevelopment policy, transportation, and urban design. Thus the orientation of this book is definitely toward land use and spatial dynamics. However, sociopolitical insights are provided as well, with chapter topics such as changing redevelopment policy, social inequity in transportation access, and residents' responses to vacant land or industrial intrusions in their neighborhoods.

I think you will find this to be an exciting volume, filled with knowledge and stimulating to the senses and the imagination. Each chapter offers its own insights into some fascinating aspect of Detroit. The interdisciplinary collection of authors captures the incredible challenges and opportunities of Detroit, a city that has exemplified unprecedented transformation over the past three centuries.

Monica Ponce de Leon

PREFACE

Henco Bekkering first proposed, to several Michigan colleagues, the idea of creating a book concerning "mapping Detroit." Bekkering's original idea for this project emerged during a sabbatical semester in the fall of 2009, when he served as Netherlands Visiting Professor at the A. Alfred Taubman College of Architecture and Urban Planning, part of the University of Michigan. The initial proposal was to generate a series of drawn maps, consistent as to area, scale, orientation, and legend, that showed the history of growth and decline of the city of Detroit, Michigan.

Such a series did not exist, though the research done by the Greek architect/planner Constantinos A. Doxiadis, internationally known urbanist and planning consultant, came close. The Detroit Edison Company, a utility firm, commissioned and published Doxiadis's three-volume work on Detroit in 1966, 1967, and 1970, part of what originally was intended to be a ten-volume series. The series was named *Emergence and Growth of an Urban Region: The Developing Urban Detroit Area.* Its purpose, in part, was to help the utility company understand future electric needs in the Detroit metropolitan area, but it also aimed to project future patterns of growth for a wider audience. Doxiadis's work was an amazing image of the natural integration of the broader Detroit metropolitan area in terms of its environment, society, and infrastructure. It showed the power of linked bird's-eye portraits of places fragmented by serendipitous political boundaries. His maps were riveting displays of information at the time but are now more than forty years old.

We added to the project's original vision, which focused on a series of consistent maps as an exercise in visual documentation, design, and understanding of the city as it is now. This book uses maps to help make clear specific land-related issues of concern such as vacancy, redevelopment, industrial change, transportation, and neighborhood development in Detroit. The maps were used for the research, and help make these issues more visible to the reader.

The change in book purpose came in part because of the emergence of a partnership, in the form of the editing team of Bekkering and longtime Detroit observer, June Manning Thomas. The joining together of Bekkering, urban designer and creator of informative maps, and Thomas, planner and observer of urban community life, resulted in a unique trans-Atlantic collaboration that brought many benefits to the project. At the same time, however, the true heart of the book comes from the diverse set of authors of the various chapters, described in some detail in the Introduction.

In the context of contemporary political and fiscal crises, during a time when population flight remains a real concern, it may take a special sense of acuity to focus on land and its relationship to community in the shaping of a city. Yet the physical landscape interconnects with everything else, and this is a part of the overall context of social and economic change. This is, indeed, a very important part, as the state of the land and its buildings confronts every school child, resident, business or nonprofit organization, and government worker practically every day.

This book goes beyond discussing the physical landscape, however, for good reason. As we go to press, backers have announced a major proposal to clear out all of the physical "blight" in the city of Detroit, which means taking down the tens of thousands of vacant houses and buildings found to exist throughout the city. The estimates of the costs of such a deconstruction initiative add up to at least $2 billion. The implication, in some minds, may be that taking down the physical markers of decline will solve many of the city's problems and allow it to create more livable neighborhoods, commercial and industrial districts, and institutional areas.

Yet, as we note in the Introduction, the reasons so many abandoned houses and buildings exist are complex. The process of physical abandonment speeded up in the early 2000s, because of the effects of the foreclosure crisis, but began decades before because of governmental, corporate, institutional, and finally individual household decisions. Simply tearing down the buildings left behind does not address why those buildings were left behind, and doesn't stop the process of abandonment. Needed is a view that acknowledges the devastation but recognizes the roots of the problem and takes action to help create a better future long after the derelict buildings come down. Strategic plans, such as *Detroit Future City*, may help, as we note in the Epilogue, but such foundation-funded initiatives are not and cannot be systemic in the sense of addressing fundamental dilemmas of disinvestment and deindustrialization. The conversation needs to open up to issues of governance, since regional sprawl and fragmentation are at the core of Detroit's abandonment; physical infrastructure, since several such systems (for example highway networks) have contributed to the exodus; as well as deep social problems of racial estrangement, concentration of poverty, and the inability of many able-bodied adults to find accessible work that pays a living wage. This conversation would have to open up in a more fundamental way to the concept of community, at both the neighborhood and regional level.

We use maps to show the historical and physical "shaping" of an exceptional city within its region, but also to chart the changing landscape of industry; the evolving fortunes of specific neighborhoods and their residents; the pathways of inequality of access; and visions of a reconfigured

Detroit that embraces, with new definitions and configurations, various forms of vacancy. We use narrative to flesh out these ideas or in some cases to discuss both relevant issues and vexing dilemmas, "mapping" possible solutions in conceptual ways. We describe communities to show what happens to people in the places they live when many aspects of the city make everyday life challenging. While we make no claim to resolve problems, we do aim to link issues of land to issues of community in ways that help us think about and visualize new ways of understanding the past and future shaping of Detroit.

June Manning Thomas and Henco Bekkering
May 30, 2014

INTRODUCTION

Land and Change in Detroit

JUNE MANNING THOMAS AND HENCO BEKKERING

Some areas of Detroit are thriving, and the city has many assets—social, cultural, and economic. However, Detroit currently faces many dilemmas; one of these is the status of existing land. This dilemma presents itself as large swaths of vacant land and decaying residential properties, neglected or shuttered parks and community facilities, abandoned or marginalized retail stores, and empty factory buildings. This situation is the visible result of large-scale population loss and industrial decline. A remarkable change in the physical landscape has followed the post–World War II decline in numbers of people, families, neighborhoods, and firms. The rate of this decline increased during the decade leading up to 2010, when the city lost 25 percent of its 2000 population size, a remarkable drop in the context of the world's cities.

The resulting change in land usage offers particular challenges. The status of the land and its buildings lasts a long time, because rapid changes in how people use land are difficult. Palliative reforms can do little to rebuild large city sections already torn down or crumbling—areas that one of our chapters refers to as "holes" in the urban fabric—because of sheer scale. A 2009 survey showed the number of vacant residential lots in Detroit to be 91,488 (Detroit Data Collaborative 2010), a situation due in great part to low market demand. Another challenge is that land use difficulties reflect deep social fissures, such as the gap between affluent, mobile people and the isolated disadvantaged left behind in the central city. Detroit's land vacancy imposes huge burdens on residents and government in the central city and, to a lesser extent, in the region. This situation also requires a new set of decisions. Prominent among these are what to do with vacant land, how to decide which areas to target for government redevelopment dollars, how to improve access to jobs and services for non-mobile residents left stranded in a poorly serviced city, how to help residents in neighborhoods with dwindling populations adjust to the changing landscape, how to use urban design as a tool for viewing a different future, where to concentrate investment and where to let land lie fallow, and, for regional actors, whether to support the central city in its struggle or to remain aloof.

This book aims to contribute to the dialogue about these necessary decisions. Such decisions and related reforms will, of course, need extensive discussion on many levels for years to come. They will need fundamental reforms in several levels of government and their policies—deep reforms well beyond the pale of any report or book. Research and planning are merely tools helpful in analyzing problems and exploring potential solutions. A foundation-funded initiative that yielded *Detroit Future City* (2012), a strategic framework plan report, provided some of the necessary research and suggested both realistic and visionary ways to reconfigure Detroit's land base. It also initiated a series of conversations about Detroit's future, creating a framework for action. Much work remains to be done, however.

This book offers another part of the required arsenal of tools necessary to understand Detroit current situation. By exploring background information, in text and visually through mapping, the book helps provide a clearer view of both the past and the potential future. Discussing this issue of land and its use in a depopulating or "legacy"[1] central city requires rethinking several concepts; at least one definition is in order. By "land usage" we mean the general condition of the city's land and its uses, but with a different approach than the typical urban planning focus on "land use" as land categorization and regulation.[2] This book actually addresses very little about land categorization, except to discuss, at times, the important role of transportation networks, redevelopment projects, or industrial placement. Instead we aim to understand and address some of the historical causes and contemporary effects of conditions of vacancy and inaccessibility in Detroit, a city that by 2010 had lost three-fifths of its 1950 population and a large portion of its housing units.

Each of the social, economic, and political factors leading to Detroit's present situation is complex. Detroit's population loss, for example, came in great part because of the steady and increasing dominance of surrounding suburbs. This phenomenon is well entrenched in U.S. life. The tendency for middle-class or prosperous families to move to outer neighborhoods and then suburbs was evident in U.S. cities as soon as the early nineteenth century and well established by the beginning of the twentieth century. Each advancement in transportation technology led to more decentralization, with the automobile serving as a primary driver for movement outward.

U.S. federal policy, to be sure, played a significant role in this. The Revenue Act of 1913, which set up the current form of federal income taxes on individual earnings, allowed several deductions that reduced taxable income. One allowable deduction was for "consumer interest," including the interest on loans. At that time, only a small percentage of upper-income U.S. taxpayers benefited from this deduction. Although not originally intended for this purpose, this tax write-off for interest payments turned out to be a major boost for home ownership, as more families obtained mortgage loans in the following decades, and thus this provision supported suburbanization (Ventry 2009). In the 1930s new federal mortgage insurance programs—sponsored by the Federal Housing Administration (FHA) and Veterans' Administration (VA)—reduced the level of down payment necessary to get a mortgage and made home purchase much more affordable for qualified families. Racial prejudice was built into this system: neighborhoods that FHA/VA underwriters approved for mortgages were often all white, and early FHA/VA policies explicitly favored mortgages in racially homogeneous neighborhoods, a policy that all but guaranteed racial segregation (Thomas and Ritzdorf 1996).³ The policies also did not favor multi-family units or rentals, thus handicapping central cities in the competition for new families. After World War II, the federal government boosted suburban development even more by subsidizing an interstate highway construction program that pierced through older cities and literally laid the groundwork for an exodus of mobile people and jobs.

In Detroit, local conditions greatly magnified these national trends, particularly during and after World War II. Ford Motor Company's suburban Willow Run plant, located twenty-eight miles west of Detroit, manufactured air bombers during World War II; over 42,000 people worked there in 1943, and they needed housing in surrounding areas in order to be able to get to work (Thomas 2013). Chapter 4 by Robert Fishman shows that location decisions by individual automobile companies, particularly Ford Motor Company, furthered the tendency for auto-related firms to move outward. Another key event was construction of the nation's first major shopping mall of hub design, anchored by the Hudson's Department Store (the flagship department store for Detroit's central business district); the suburban Hudson's branch opened in 1953. Other suburban retail malls soon sprang up, sucking retail business and eventually flagship stores themselves from the central city's central business district. No national or Michigan state policies regulated these trends, and suburban governments supported retail development located on vast tracts of vacant or agricultural land (green fields) that Detroit did not have available at that time.

Detroit's transportation systems played a major role in depopulation as well. Owners shut down Detroit's extensive streetcar system in the mid-1950s. Aggressive highway construction, funded in part by the federal Highway Act of 1956, which encouraged highways but not rail-based commuter systems, gave Detroit a strong network of limited-access roads or expressways. Most of these roadways passed into or near the central business district. Detroit's expressway network, however, was arguably too extensive, and it facilitated decentralization to an unusual degree, because—unlike many other major U.S. cities—Detroit lacked a subway or light-rail system of any substance. Three decades after the postwar suburban exodus had begun, the city government did launch a project to build a monorail system using grants won beginning in 1976. But this Detroit People Mover monorail system did not open for fare-based service until 1987 because of construction delays and severe cost overruns. This expensive and underused system was originally intended to be a part of a larger commuter rail system, but it never materialized due to lack of regional support for a metropolitan network. The People Mover ended up as a 2.9-mile long loop that simply circled part of the central business district and served little practical purpose for the city's or region's commuters (Tadi and Dutta 1997).

Employment systems and governmental fragmentation mattered as well. Central-city industrial jobs collapsed in Detroit more than in other places, in part because of Detroit's overdependence on automobile manufacturing as its single most important export-based industry. Assembly line manufacturing required increasingly larger tracts of land, more easily obtainable in suburbs; manufacturers sought cheaper labor, available first in the U.S. South and then increasingly abroad (Thomas 2013). Racial segregation gained extra momentum in Detroit in part because of strong union roots. Major battles over union or skilled-trade membership and access to industrial jobs, a history of white neighborhood protectionism that sometimes turned violent, and failed efforts to promote non-discrimination in housing in both public and private residential areas all contributed to the city's high degree of racial isolation (Sugrue 1996). Compounding the effects of these trends was the governance system. Local governments in the Detroit area were particularly fragmented compared to other places because Michigan's stringent state policies discouraged central-city annexation of nearby places and enabled suburban governments to incorporate easily as independent entities (Jacobs 2009). Racial bifurcation became reflected in the political map.

At first, many of those who left the central city were white, because only white people were freely able to move into most of Detroit's suburbs. But over time some middle-class families of other races were able to move as well. Open-housing legislation in the 1960s enabled some such movement for blacks, the last racial or ethnic group to remain in high numbers in the central city, and the phenomenon of middle-class exodus among all races and ethnicities was clearly visible by 2010. These movers carried with them significant chunks of the city's population and tax base. They also set off a chain reaction that affected the land usage we describe in this book.

When movers could not sell or rent out their houses, or pay their mortgages, these houses often reverted back to financial institutions, which also could not sell unmarketable housing units. When private or institutional owners failed to pay property taxes owed, these residential buildings reverted to state, county, or local governments through a long and complicated process that left many structures in limbo for an extended period of time. Some observers note that much of the housing stock was not particularly sturdy to begin with because inexpensive construction wood framing, and wood siding deteriorated quickly in damp weather (Gallagher 2010). Houses in various states of decline, without residents or visible owners, created more blight at best and threats to public safety at worst. Public safety threats included the appropriation of vacant houses by drug dealers, the threat to children and other passersby by criminals who lurked in the empty buildings, and the collapse of the structures—sometimes on city fire fighters sent to battle all-too-frequent acts of arson. Thieves desperate for cash sometimes removed metals such as copper pipes from vacant or unsecured houses and buildings, making rehabilitation more expensive and less likely. Such actions brought down surrounding property values and made marketability even more difficult. These circumstances led to increasing abandonment and vacancy, more in some neighborhoods than in others; eventually some neighborhoods all but disappeared.

Much of the resulting vacancy was a purposeful emptiness created as the city government condemned and demolished dangerous empty buildings and thus extracted physical sources of decay. Demolitions cleared some of the empty units, but often left vacant land with unclear ownership titles, which complicated resale or reuse. The result of more demolition than construction—demolition permits far outnumbered building permits for several years leading up to 2012 (Gallagher 2012)—is visual evidence of increasing abandonment of a once-mighty city in a once-centralized metropolitan area.

At first, the pull of the suburbs caused population exodus, particularly in the two decades just after World War II when federal action boosted suburban life. As the pull of the suburbs continued, the push outward came as people left because of personal and financial circumstances, but also because of a perceived lower quality of life in the central city. Push factors seemed to escalate after the civil disorders of 1967, which caused loss of life and property and escalated fears of the city. The role of these disorders in Detroit's social and economic decline is sometimes overemphasized: problems existed long before then and oppressive conditions fostered rebellion. Nevertheless, the fact that observers bring these incidents up again and again is indicative of the psychological effect of these events. This is particularly true of the region's whites, many of whom blame the civil disorders of the 1960s for Detroit's decline, steadfastly ignoring all other causative factors. Palliative attempts to build racial unity within the region since the 1960s have been persistent but have had only limited effect (Darden, Hill, Thomas, and Thomas 1987; Darden and Thomas 2013).

The problem was more complicated than racial disunity, however. The waves of domestic automobile manufacturing crises beginning in the 1970s caused even more auto plant closures and undercut the locational advantage of living in city neighborhoods, many of which had nestled closely to industrial jobs in earlier eras. A reputation for crime was sometimes exaggerated, but poverty and persistent lack of opportunity did contribute to desperation and illegal activity. By the end of the twentieth century, declining public service levels in the city of Detroit co-existed with much higher property tax rates compared to surrounding municipalities, an imbalance only partially offset by lower property values in the city. Detroit's public school system experienced chronic funding difficulties and uneven or substandard performance for students. Increasing proportions of Detroit's low-income children lacked a family background that made school performance easier, a problem that federally subsidized school lunches helped only a little. Catholic elementary and secondary schools diminished in number, giving middle-class families with children even more incentive to leave or not move into Detroit.

These and other difficulties drove more people away. Remaining citizens' dropping income levels led to less revenue for the city government, which depended on both property and income taxes, as well as on declining sources of revenue from the state. Times of economic downturn proved particularly difficult. Tens of thousands of homes that survived up until the mid-2000s were lost after the post-2007 foreclosure crisis led to more abandonment and physical devastation than was already underway. Short- and long-term expenses mounted, leading the state's governor to appoint an emergency financial manager. Even with this financial management, the city government teetered on the edge of bankruptcy, and then succumbed.

Several observers have written about social, economic, and political trends in the city during the post–World War II era (Darden, Hill, Thomas, Thomas 1987; Darden and Thomas 2013, Farley, Danziger, and Holzer 2000; Jacobs 2009; Sugrue 1996; Thomas 2013). A side effect of these trends that has received less attention, with few exceptions (*Detroit Future City* 2012; Dewar and Thomas 2013; Gallagher 2010), is the land usage dilemma we address in this book. This particular dilemma is a result of the broader social and economic trends that we have only touched upon but that others have described very well; it is, in fact, the visible legacy of disinvestment.

The physical condition of the city has many implications for residents and their neighborhoods, people who live or work in the city, business and corporations, public and private institutions, and municipal government. The challenge is obvious when one drives through the city and sees the crazy-quilt patchwork that now exists. Some areas are filled with residential buildings and businesses, or with strong institutions such as hospitals or universities and associated commercial areas, as in Midtown and certain neighborhoods. Other parts of the city resemble an urban prairie and offer very little evidence of a past history that included populated neighborhoods and busy commercial strips. Faltering or shuttered commercial and industrial buildings lined along major roads, remnants of an era of neighborhood commerce and employment since vanished, now detract from surrounding residential areas. The city's neighborhoods might change from year to year—one year displaying a fairly healthy row of well-kept houses, the next year showing a few shuttered or burned out houses here and there, and the next year or two or ten showing major gaps—much as an old man's mouth might as one tooth after another decays and falls out. In some places, neighborhood as community remains intact. In others, newly constructed housing developments, often subsidized with federal dollars, have brought new residents, but these places are not the norm.

At the same time, much hope exists in this city and even in the region for adjustment and modified renewal. We are writing this book at a particular snapshot in time, characterized by yawning contradictions. On the one hand, the city has lost the highest percentage of people in its history and faces both fiscal and land usage dilemmas of enormous magnitude. On the other hand, the city is by no means empty—the 2010 census counted over 700,000 people—and renewed efforts are being made to rectify its fiscal condition, make its political system more effective, and envision a future city based on a realistic assessment of its smaller size and great potential. Because of these efforts, it is more difficult than usual to predict where this mix of events negative and positive will end up. The drama continues, but it does so with wrenching twists and turns, fervent disjuncture, and dizzying prospects. Obviously, we can only explain what is possible to see now. As circumstances evolve, future scholars will need to offer new and updated observations.

The maps and descriptions of various aspects of Detroit and its region that we have made and selected for this book are an attempt to make sense of today's transformed landscape and to help chart some aspects of what once was and of what is now—even what might be in the future. Detroit is one of the great mysteries of modern urban life: a once-mighty city whose fame spread around the world, both because of its major industrial product (predominantly motor vehicles) and because of its musical innovations (particularly Motown), and yet at the same time one of the most dramatic examples of what happens when people and resources located in one place disperse far past municipal boundaries. Here we see what can happen when a large city loses its main industrial purpose and a major portion of its population because of a series of human-made actions rather than natural disasters. We see a vibrant metropolis turning into a devastated physical envelope, in many ways too big for its remaining contents and haunted by a sense of vacancy and emptiness. We see as well what happens when the residents and institutions associated with that city "hang tough," refusing to give up hope, making modest improvements in some important areas of the city, seeking alternatives, and charting a course for a realistic, better future. These efforts range from the highly visible (such as long-term initiatives designed to buttress the Midtown area and its institutions, or to enhance the central business district and riverfront, or to create a fifty-year strategic land use plan) to the almost invisible (such as residents' efforts to reuse abandoned land in neighborhoods such as Brightmoor, or to travel to work in a city that does not support accessibility).

COMPARISONS WITH OTHER CITIES

Detroit is not the only city in the United States or in the world that has lost population. Cities all over the world have experienced this phenomenon, as demonstrated in the *Atlas of Shrinking Cities*, a publication of German origin that showed cities and their population loss on several continents (Oswalt and Rieniets 2006). Yet in this atlas's great tally of the world's large and small cities that have shrunk, only a few (that it could measure) had reached at least one million people by the middle of the twentieth century but contracted in numbers of people by the year 2000. Berlin lost 30 percent of its population between its peak year of 1940 and the year 1983 but grew substantially thereafter; Moscow expanded robustly after 1950 and dipped only slightly in the 1990s. Romania's Bucharest lost 17 percent of its peak population by 2000, comparable to losses in Hungary's Budapest, but Great Britain's Birmingham lost only 9 percent, regaining much of that by 2000. Japan's Kobe and Nagoya experienced only short-term losses from peak population and then continued to grow; Canada's Montreal dropped 18 percent during the 1970s but added numbers of people since; Italy's Naples lost 22 percent of its peak population between 1970 and 2000 but ended up with pretty much the same number of people it had in 1950, just over a million. Chicago lost 23 percent between 1950 and 1990 but then gained a few tens of thousands in 2000, losing a relatively modest 6.9 percent again between 2000 and 2010, when the U.S. Census tallied 2.7 million people. In stark contrast to all of those, Detroit between 1950 and 2000 fell in population size by 49 percent, from a high of at least 1.85 million; in the decade following, Detroit's population fell to 39 percent of its 1950 peak (U.S. Census 2010).

Among the 400 worldwide cities listed in this atlas, the only other city included that had ever reached over one million in population and that had losses similar to Detroit's was Glasgow, which fell 48 percent from its peak. Yet these two cities are vastly different. Glasgow, Scotland's largest city, emerged when cities were relatively compact; although surrounded by suburbs and new towns, its municipal boundaries in 2000 included 68 square miles, serving 584,000 people (Oswalt and Rieniets 2006). Detroit in 2000 had perhaps 30 percent more people, 951,000 (reduced in 2010 to 713,777, or 22 percent more people than Glasgow), but it was spread over 139 square miles, much of this pockmarked by large areas of vacant land. Vacancy is a relatively rare phenomenon in Glasgow except in eastern and northern portions (City of Glasgow 2011a), and the city grew in population size by a few hundred people each year between 2000 and 2006 (City of Glasgow 2011b).

One important trend that could influence such results is reduction in household size. Large families may become small ones because of housing opportunity, or children may eventually leave their parents behind and move to other locales. Reduction in number of households, therefore, is a truer indication of loss related to tax base and land use than is population decline. The U.S. Census equates number of households with number of occupied housing units, and so household numbers can help illuminate demand for residential land. Large U.S. cities that consistently lost population in both the 1980s and 1990s make up a set of municipalities that Robert Beauregard has called the "persistent twelve" (Beauregard 2009). Three U.S. cities lost at least 38 percent of their peak year households by 2010. These are Cleveland, Ohio; St. Louis, Missouri; and Detroit. Table I.1 shows population numbers for these three. By 2010, Detroit's population had declined by 1.1 million people (61.4 percent) since its 1950 population peak year, and over half a million households (47.7 percent) since its 1960 household peak year. By 2010 the number of households lost since their

CITY/YEAR	CHANGE IN POPULATION FROM PREVIOUS DECADE (%)	CHANGE IN HOUSEHOLDS FROM PREVIOUS DECADE (%)
Cleveland		
2010	−17.1	−12.1
2000	−5.4	−4.6
1990	−11.9	−8.5
Detroit		
2010	−25	−19.9
2000	−7.5	−10.1
1990	−14.6	−13.7
St. Louis*		
2010	−8.3	−3.4
2000	−12.2	−10.8
1990	−12.4	−7.4

*In 1980 St. Louis had lost 17.4 percent of its households compared to 1970.

TABLE I.1 Change in population and number of households from peak years as of 2010 in three cities.
Source: Data from U.S. Census Bureau, various years.

peak years had also declined in the two other cities, falling by 37.9 percent in Cleveland and 45 percent in St. Louis. Detroit's 2000 to 2010 drop was the steepest of the three; the city's population fell by 25 percent, and the number of households dropped by 19.9 percent (Table I.2). In contrast, Cleveland lost 12.1 percent of its households for that decade, and St. Louis lost only 3.4 percent. Furthermore, subsequent years' estimates revealed that Detroit's population continued to drop after 2010.

INTRODUCTION: Land and Change in Detroit 7

CITY	2010 POPULATION (IN THOUSANDS)	POPULATION CHANGE FROM PEAK* (IN THOUSANDS)	POPULATION CHANGE PERCENTAGE	HOUSEHOLD CHANGE FROM PEAK* (OCCUPIED UNITS, IN THOUSANDS)	HOUSEHOLDS CHANGE PERCENTAGE
Cleveland	396.8	−518.0	−56.6	−102.4	−37.9
Detroit	713.8	−1,135.9	−61.4	−514.8	−47.7
St. Louis	319.3	−537.5	−62.7	−116.1	−45.0

*Peak decennial years for Cleveland according to the U.S. Census were 1950 for population, 1960 for households; for Detroit, 1950 for population, 1960 for households; for St. Louis, 1950 for both.

TABLE 1.2 Population and household change, three decades, three cities. *Source: Data from U.S. Census Bureau, various years.*

Poverty remained a problem as well. In 2010 Detroit's families were experiencing a 32.8 percent poverty rate, up from the year 1999 rate of 21.7 percent; Cleveland's families were similarly stressed, with 2010 estimates of 30.4 percent, worse than 1999 levels of 22.9 percent. St. Louis's families were 21 percent in poverty in 2010, about the same as in the year 1999, so its poverty level had not increased during that decade.[4] The poverty brought complicated changes. Decreasing numbers of middle-class children in neighborhoods and schools jeopardized the educational experience of remaining students and drove even more middle-class families away. Increasing proportions of residents unable to afford automobiles suffered from the growing inadequacy of public transportation and did not have access to public services such as parks and to commercial facilities such as grocery stores. Businesses died for lack of customers with disposable income. Inadequate opportunities for a poorly educated labor pool stranded in an increasingly technological world fostered an underground economy that included, among other things, drug traffic. Simple home repair and upkeep became too expensive for many.

Detroit Future City argued that parts of Detroit were really not much less dense, counted as people per square mile, than other major cities such as Denver and Atlanta (*Detroit Future City* 2012, p. 94). Even this document, however, recognized that conditions were different in Detroit than in such cities. Denver, for example, contained vast portions never developed or developed with low-density housing; but only small portions had experienced the wrenching reversal of fortune of Detroit, where vast tracts of land once hosting houses or factories now contained empty hulks or, eventually, land cleared with sporadic government grants. Other cities were not experiencing exodus rates rapidly increasing as city services rapidly declined, as did Detroit. Their economies had not plummeted.

Detroit is somewhat of a special case in the nation and in the world, and its region has experienced continued flight away from the center as well (Orfield and Luce 2003). The outward movement of people and commerce away from the city has affected Detroit's inner-ring suburbs even as these trends had affected the central city itself. Warren, for example, is a suburban municipality just north of Detroit's northern boundary, Eight Mile Road. Warren's 34.5 square miles housed only 42,653 people in 1940, but by 1970 it had 179,260 people, 99.5 percent of whom were white. After 1970 its population began to drop as people moved to even farther suburbs

(Ernsten, Moceri, et al. 2009); by 2000 it had 138,247 people, a 33 percent decline from 1970, and in 2010 it had 134,056 people, another drop.[5]

The major population drop in the Detroit metropolitan area, however, was in the central city. In 1940, Detroit was the fourth largest city of the United States. In 2009, the U.S. Census estimated that it ranked eleventh, but the Census Bureau had overestimated Detroit's population size for 2005–09 (Okrent 2009; U.S. Census 2010, 2011). The official ranking in 2011 was eighteenth in the United States, with El Paso and Memphis expected to exceed Detroit in size in the near future (Tanner 2012). The drop in 2010 population numbers of 25 percent compared to 2000 was a shock to many observers, but simply continued a trend of decentralization that had been taking place for some time.

This trend had changed in one important way, however. Not dissimilar to a development noticeable in other major U.S. metropolitan areas (Frey 2011), blacks were leaving the central city of Detroit, going to nearby suburbs such as Warren. During 2000–10, the black central-city population dropped by 185,546 people or 16.5 percent, compared to a low 0.3 percent decline during the 1990s. This was the largest drop in raw numbers for central-city blacks for any major U.S. city during that decade (Frey 2011, p. 8), and left 590,226 blacks living in the city in 2010. A 3 percent increase in the city's relatively small Hispanic (of any race) base during that decade—to a total of 48,679—was not nearly enough to offset this drop citywide, although the Hispanic presence helped stabilize southwest Detroit's neighborhoods. Non-Hispanic whites as a proportion of Detroit's population fell during the decade by 35 percent, more than the black drop-off rate, but their presence was already relatively small. In 2010 the city contained only 75,758 non-Hispanic whites. Suburbanization patterns remained bifurcated, as many suburbs, especially on the outer fringes, remained predominately white.

Given such levels of industrial job loss, population decline, decrease in occupied housing units, increase in poverty levels of remaining families, and racial division—all in the metropolitan context of suburbs that acted like magnets and central-city conditions that had the opposite effect—it is not surprising that the city of Detroit faced major challenges in land usage. This is particularly visible in many of its residential neighborhoods, which could not benefit from Detroit's most visible areas of growth and development, such as some parts of the central business district and the nearby Midtown area. Too soon perhaps, some observers declared that the city had "collapsed." One article in Time magazine proclaimed:

> The story of Detroit is not simply one of a great city's collapse. It is also about the erosion of the industries that helped build the country we know today. The ultimate fate of Detroit will reveal much about the character of America in the 21st century. . . . The city itself with its elm-lined streets [is] where [people] lived idyllic 1950's lives. . . . The city of homeowners, some called it, a city with endless miles of owner occupied bungalows and half-capes and modest mock Tudors that were the respectable legacy of five decades of the auto industry's primacy in the American economy and Detroiters' naive faith that the industry would never run out of gas. (Okrent, 2009)

As we will see, Detroit had not so much "collapsed" as contracted into what was becoming a new and different urban form. But over its history it had undergone many shifts in form before, at both small and large scale, as had its region. This was merely the latest and perhaps the most painful transition.

THE ORGANIZATION OF THE BOOK

Three major parts of the book frame our discussion. Part 1 offers a firm background for understanding key features of the spatial evolution of Detroit to its present condition. From its early beginnings, like many other cities, Detroit grew in accordance with its needs for fortification, economic growth, and provision of services and housing for its citizens. In chapter 1, Brian Leigh Dunnigan reviews the period from 1701 to 1838 by describing the city's physical evolution under the influence of agriculture, trade, and military fortification. He surveys not only the physical routes that made up the early structure of the city, but also the art of map making as this applies to early Detroit.

In chapter 2, Henco Bekkering and Yanjia Liu comment on historical evolution as well, but then carry us to contemporary times. The physical evolution of the city was based on certain key characteristics such as rivers, means of land division, and transport lines. But with population and industrial changes, the deconstruction of the city left major holes or gaps in the city's physical fabric. To show this, they have created two series of maps, one showing the evolution of the city from its earliest creation, and the other the region. These authors use the construction of sequential maps to isolate the main spatial systems critical for the formation of Detroit's morphology, and they offer critical comments about the city's contemporary spatial evolution. In chapter 3, the final chapter of part 1, June Manning Thomas discusses attempts by the city's leaders to reshape the central portion of Detroit through federally enabled redevelopment. She notes the problems with government-sponsored redevelopment but explains that such projects historically created stable nodes of development and protected key medical and educational institutions. Most recently, however, the redevelopment strategy has inevitably lost focus, as illustrated through a mapping of wider and wider "target areas," and has not been able to overcome endemic problems of population and economic decline.

In part 2, we address how specific land-related systems or neighborhoods have evolved in recent decades, with particular emphasis on the roles of social and economic change. First is Robert Fishman's innovative analysis in chapter 4 of the evolution of industrial corridors in the Detroit region from the perspective of the theory of linear cities. As he shows, much of the twentieth-century development in Detroit's industrial corridors actually followed the outlines of what some urban theorists thought would be the ideal city formation: a linear configuration, with factories organized by major corridors of infrastructure and bordered by houses and commercial facilities. He describes lost opportunities for the automobile industry to settle more permanently within city borders, or at least next to rail-served corridors. Industrial plants could have served as the focal points of multi-use neighborhoods, as they once did; instead, they scattered in ever-widening rings of abandonment and isolated suburban location. His chapter does much to help explain that the amount of vacant industrial land in the central city has been due in part to purposeful decisions made decades ago by industrial leaders.

This air of lost opportunity also characterizes chapter 5 by Joe Grengs, who looks at accessibility through maps representing two racial groups' access to jobs and other key services such as banks and major grocery stores. His chapter illustrates the effects of limited access to everyday needs (because of inadequate public transportation and low levels of car ownership) on Detroit's majority-black residents. This account refutes the simplicity of much of the literature about jobs and transportation; Grengs demonstrates that spatial accessibility, as measured by distance to jobs, is actually quite good within the Detroit central city but that this means little to the transit-hampered unemployed. His is a sobering tale that reveals that, even though much central-city land is devoted to roads and highways, and thus ostensibly to transportation land use, this does not provide social equity in transportation access.

Part 2 continues by looking at specific areas of the city and their struggles to adapt to changing landscapes. In chapter 6, María Arquero de Alarcón and Larissa Larsen examine Southwest Detroit's Delray neighborhood, offering a microcosmic view of this critical portion of Detroit. This is a dramatic story of a neighborhood that first hosted waves of immigrants but fought against suffocating industrial and municipal utility pollution as well as studied city government discouragement of residential living. They reveal some of the challenges that face residents who were left behind in the shadow of industrial plants when their neighbors left. The authors not only offer a perceptive historical perspective, but they also give us insight into contemporary challenges facing the community, particularly in light of proposals to build a new international bridge that would essentially be based in the middle of the neighborhood. Chapter 7, by Margaret Dewar and Robert Linn, offers critical insights into Brightmoor, a particularly challenged city neighborhood with a high degree of abandonment. What is particularly unique about the approach of Dewar and Linn is that they accept the resulting landscape as it is, and then describe how the residents who remain use land that has become vacant. They argue that the actions of many people and organizations have creatively produced a changed physical fabric and a new landscape without anyone purposefully planning for this. Their series of maps shows, perhaps, a vision of future adaptability to large-scale vacancy; they suggest supporting these indigenous efforts because sometimes people are able to develop their own pragmatic solutions.

Part 3 of the book offers additional suggestions for creating a different and better future built on both the existing spatial fabric and on recognition of the challenges of cohesion and thus community. In chapter 8, Lars Gräbner reviews the ecological subsystem underlying Detroit, as well as patterns of vacancy, and explores the potential to remake Detroit in a way that increases its environmental sustainability as well as makes use of its vacant land. Using much of the same raw material as several authors used in earlier portions of the book, particularly concerning the location of vacant land and structurally unsound houses, he overlays these locations on top of historic rivers and streams and proceeds to outline potential areas for intervention. Drawing from European and U.S. examples, he suggests day-lighting streams and creating associated landscapes devoted to recreation and to the cultivation of energy-producing crops. More of a visionary exercise in imagination than a plan, his discussion and maps nevertheless present a certain spatial logic and draw on many ideas and plans that others, ranging from city-hired consultants to local journalists, are proposing for possible reuse of Detroit's landscape. The fact that he developed these visions individually, writing his chapter draft independently of the process leading to *Detroit Future City,* is particularly noteworthy. This shows that a savvy individual—aware of trends in other parts of the world that are dealing with vacant land in cities—could discern the major features of necessary land usage changes, changes which foreshadowed proposals made in the heavily funded *Detroit Future City.* In some ways Gräbner presents different ideas from those of the official consultants, however. For example, Gräbner's view that land changes must start in part by charting ancient streams, and his visual representation of this proposal, is a unique contribution to current discussions of Detroit's future in terms of "blue infrastructure," and very different from *Detroit Future City's* street-system-based proposal for waterways.

A chapter on parts of the region, chapter 9 by June Manning Thomas, revisits the situation of the city of Detroit's profound disengagement from the region as a challenge to the possibilities of community, which she defines using sociological terms. Short descriptions of five area municipalities in addition to Detroit show that life circumstances vary greatly depending upon locale. Several suburban places, for example, have suffered because of industrial decline; others have prospered nonetheless. The region's political, social, and racial fragmentation make meaningful cooperation difficult to imagine, much less implement, and yet such cooperation will be necessary for simple matters such as building a regional transit system or enhanced regional land use planning. She calls for stronger commitment to overcoming barriers and addressing the profound inequity that exists, such as by broadening the experiences of those places that have managed to retain diverse populations.

The epilogue offers a brief synopsis of the major concepts and ideas involved in the 2012 *Detroit Future City* report. Written by Toni L. Griffin, the lead planning consultant for this initiative, and June Manning Thomas, this epilogue illustrates the principle that nothing stands still in time; people and institutions strive to reimagine positive changes for the city even in the midst of historic, traumatic change. The epilogue provides highlights of this planning effort, which delineated Detroit's considerable assets yet simultaneously acknowledged its many challenges. Designed as a long-range fifty-year strategy, the *Detroit Future City* strategic framework plan has already attracted a great deal of media, professional, and scholarly attention, for it approaches the concept of a shrinking or legacy city as a unique opportunity to lay out a new set of strategies. Detroit-based corporations, foundations, governments, and neighborhood groups have begun to study the framework plan's recommendations, and some efforts have been made to support its implementation—in part, if not in whole.

The authors of these chapters include a map librarian, a historian, several urban designers and architects, urban planners, and demographers. These professions are disparate, yet we admit that the book itself is heavily tilted toward urban planning and design. However, the individual approaches are so unique, and some of the perspectives so refreshing, that we feel the reader will find within these pages numerous insights worth pondering. In the book's second chapter, map historian Dunnigan notes that "The first and most important fact that is necessary to know about any individual map or plan is the purpose of its author. The purpose will determine what is shown and influence the level of detail; the purpose sometimes reveals biases . . . ." Although he was speaking about historical hand-drawn maps, which varied much according to perspective and purpose, his observations hold true today. We have "mapped" or otherwise described specific features of a region's landscape that reflect evolving patterns of land use; but, at the same time, an important purpose of this book is to explore various forms of spatial and social connections, whether these are historical, existing, or visionary.

NOTES

We would like to acknowledge the many graduate assistant students who helped with various phases of whole-book production over the course of the preparation for this book. These have included Jared Enriquez, Angela Fortino, Payton Heins, Pete McGrath, Michael Vos, Terra Reed, and Pam Schaeffer. In addition, three students who are now chapter co-authors or map editors offered support to the whole book at times as well: Robert Linn, Yanjia Liu, and Scott Pitera. Many thanks are due these assistants! In some chapters, footnotes also mention other helpers for the appropriate chapter.

1. "Legacy city" is a term that the 2011 American Assembly, a group of varied leaders of thought from throughout the nation, adopted as a descriptor for cities experiencing large-scale population loss under conditions of duress and yet containing great assets. See Mallach (2012).
2. The term "land use" in most writing about urban planning often means the categorization of land into such categories as residential, commercial, and institutional. Urban planners may make recommendations in comprehensive plans concerning the layout of these uses and then give these recommendations legal force through zoning ordinances or related municipal regulations. Here we use the term "land usage" to mean the condition or use of land and its buildings in a specific situation: that of a city that has evolved from a frontier metropolis laid out simply to a city facing massive depopulation and property abandonment in many of its neighborhoods.
3. Several passages in underwriters' manuals made intentions for racial segregation clear. For a summary of key provisions in FHA regulations, see the appendix in Thomas and Ritzdorf (1996).
4. See Table QT-P35 (U.S. Census 2000) for 1999 poverty figures from and Table S1702 for 2010 poverty figures.
5. Racial diversity had increased somewhat, however. In 2000 91.3 percent of its residents were white; by 2010 only 78.4 percent of Warren's residents were white, with 13.5 percent black residents and 4.6 percent Asian.

REFERENCES

Beauregard, R. (2009). Urban population loss in historical perspective: United States, 1820–2000. *Environment and Planning A, 41,* 514–29.

City of Glasgow. (2011a). *City Plan 2. Web-based plan with discussion and maps.* Retrieved from www.glasgow.gov.uk/en/Business/CityPlan/Part2_DevStratPP/Environment/fenvironment.htm

City of Glasgow. (2011b). *2011 Key Statistics.* Retrieved from https://www.glasgow.gov.uk/CHttpHandler.ashx?id=17543&p=0

Darden, J., Hill, R. C., Thomas, J. M., and Thomas, R. (1987). *Detroit: Race and uneven development.* Philadelphia, PA: Temple University Press.

Darden, J., and Thomas, R. W. (2013). *Detroit: Race riots, racial conflicts, and efforts to bridge the racial divide.* East Lansing: Michigan State University Press.

Detroit Data Collaborative. (2010). *Detroit residential parcel survey.* Retrieved from www.detroitparcelsurvey.org

Detroit future city: 2012 Detroit strategic framework plan. (2012). Detroit, MI.

Dewar, M., and Thomas, J. M. (Eds.). (2013). *The city after abandonment.* Philadelphia: University of Pennsylvania Press.

Ernsten, C., Moceri, T., et al. (2009). Warren special report. From crisis to project. *Archis, 2,* 65–84.

Farley, R., Danziger, S., and Holzer, H. (2000). *Detroit divided.* New York, NY: Russell Sage Foundation.

Frey, W. (2011, May). *Melting pot cities and suburbs: Racial and ethnic change in metro America in the 2000s.* State of Metropolitan American Report. Washington, DC: Brookings Institute.

Gallagher, J. (2010). *Reimagining Detroit: Opportunities for redefining an American City.* Detroit, MI: Wayne State University Press.

Gallagher, J. (2012, April 1). Wide open Detroit. *Detroit Free Press,* p. 19A.

Jacobs, J. (2009). Embedded contrasts in race, municipal fragmentation, and planning. *Journal of Urban Affairs, 31,* 147–72.

Mallach, A. (Ed.). (2012). *Rebuilding America's legacy cities: New directions for the industrial heartland.* New York, NY: Columbia University, American Assembly.

Okrent, D. (2009, October 5). Notown. *Time,* pp. 26–35.

Orfield, M., and Luce, T. (2003). *Michigan metropatterns: A regional agenda for community and prosperity in Michigan.* Minneapolis, MN: Ameregis, Metropolitan Area Research Corporation.

Oswalt, P., and Rieniets, T. (Eds.). (2006). *Atlas of shrinking cities.* Ostfildern, Germany: Hatje Cantz.

Sugrue, T. (1996). *The origins of the urban racial crisis: Race and inequality in postwar Detroit.* Princeton, NJ: Princeton University Press.

Tadi, R., and Dutta, U. (1997). Detroit downtown people mover: Ten years after. In W. Sproule, E. Neumann, and S. Lynch (Eds.), *Automated people movers VI: Creative access for major activity centers: Proceedings of the sixth international conference: Las Vegas, Nevada, April 9–12* (pp. 134–42). Reston, VA: American Society of Civil Engineers.

Tanner, K. (2012, June 28). Detroit keeps ranking as 18th biggest city. *Detroit Free Press.* Retrieved from www.freep.com/article/20120628/NEWS05/206280514/Detroit-keeps-ranking-as-18th-biggest-city-Census-Bureau-says

Thomas, J. M. (2013). *Redevelopment and race: Planning a finer city in postwar Detroit* (2nd ed,). Detroit, MI: Wayne State University Press.

Thomas, J. M., and Ritzdorf, M. (Eds.). (1996). *Urban planning and the African American community: In the shadows.* Philadelphia, PA: Temple University Press.

U.S. Bureau of the Census. (2010). *Census of population, various estimated and decennial statistics, by city.* Retrieved from American Factfinder, http://factfinder2.census.gov.

U.S. Bureau of the Census. (2011). *Incorporated places with 175,000 inhabitants in 2009. Table 27.* Retrieved from www.census.gov/compendia/statab/2011/tables/11s0027.pdf

Ventry, D. (2009). The accidental deduction: A history and critique of the tax subsidy for mortgage interest. *Law and Contemporary Problems, 73,* 233–84.

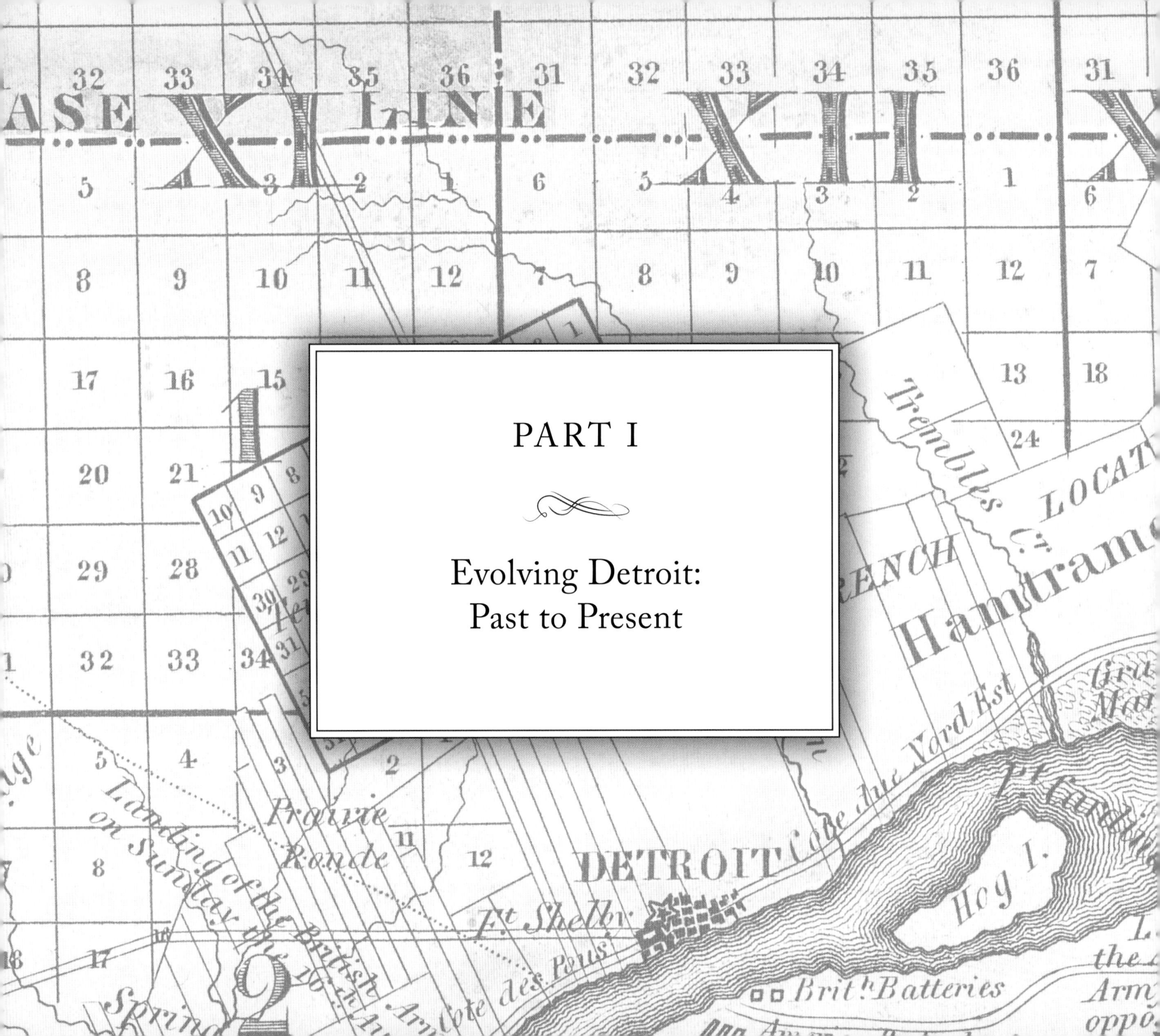

PART I

Evolving Detroit:
Past to Present

I

CHARTING THE SHAPE OF EARLY DETROIT
1701–1838

BRIAN LEIGH DUNNIGAN

Most people know the city of Detroit for its glory days as the center of the global automotive industry and, more recently, for its tragic slide into economic and urban decay. A reference to "old" Detroit is likely to conjure up visions of Model T's rolling off an early twentieth-century assembly line or smoke and fire belching from the chimneys of the River Rouge industrial complex. Less known is the fact that by the time the first of Henry Ford's automobiles rolled out of his Highland Park plant in 1902, Detroit had just concluded the celebration of its bicentennial, and many residents were justly proud that their city was only a quarter century younger than Philadelphia or Charleston and much older than many other towns of the eastern United States and Canada.

The French had, in fact, established Detroit in 1701 as an outpost of their colony of New France. Despite the trauma of warfare, economic hardship, and conflagration, the place has been continuously occupied since that time. The reasons for establishing a settlement in Detroit at the dawn of the eighteenth century were far different from its later industrial purpose, however. Beginning as an agricultural colony and fur-trading post, the place grew slowly through the eighteenth century and then blossomed in the nineteenth as an early political, manufacturing, and transportation center before making its name on the world stage as an example of industrial productivity and innovation. Throughout this time, the shape of the town that came to be known as Detroit was documented in maps and plans as it constantly changed and developed. Many of these visual sources survive in public and private collections, and, for the era prior to the introduction of photography, they are of particular importance for understanding the early urban form of Detroit and nearby hinterlands that the growing city would ultimately absorb.

The purpose of this chapter is to discuss the pre-photographic cartographic record of Detroit and suggest some of the ways in which these sources can be of use to urban historians, planners, and designers. The period covered here is 1701 to 1838, a span of years during which the town grew from a simple, stockade village to a more substantial fortified town and then shed its defenses as it developed the nucleus of its modern street plan. During this time, Detroit passed successively through the political control of France, Great Britain, and the United States until, by 1838 and the eve of the introduction of photography, the city had become the capital of the newly established state of Michigan. This discussion is based on summary points from a comprehensive, pre-photographic iconography of Detroit presented in the book *Frontier Metropolis: Picturing Early Detroit, 1701–1838* (Dunnigan 2001), published in 2001 on the occasion of the city's tercentennial.

FRENCH COLONIAL PERIOD

A number of factors influenced the establishment of Detroit and the reasons for its location on the right (north) bank of the Detroit River, the strait connecting Lake St. Clair with Lake Erie. First among these was a strategic and imperial concern of France at a time of developing colonial rivalries on the North American continent. French commercial and missionary activity had drawn fur traders, Jesuit priests, and soldiers to the upper Great Lakes since the mid-seventeenth century. During this time, the French colonists of Canada and their Native American allies engaged in chronic warfare with the five nations of the Iroquois Confederacy, and, after 1689, with their English allies in the colony of New York. Although Canadian traders and military garrisons were officially withdrawn from the western regions in 1697, a French officer and opportunist named Antoine Laumet de la Mothe Cadillac was able to obtain official sanction to establish a settlement on the Detroit River. Among his strongest arguments was that a post there would block Iroquois and English access to the upper Great Lakes and ultimately protect French fur-trading interests.

A fortified post on the Detroit River placed that critical water transportation link under the control of France and preserved it for the use of that country's commerce. Cadillac's broader plan for the settlement aimed to enhance this trading advantage to the utmost by inviting diverse Native American nations of the West to establish their own villages along the strait, where they could reside within the French trading orbit and also under the influence of colonial officials and missionaries. To encourage cross-cultural assimilation, Cadillac insisted on introducing a population of French-Canadian farmers, whose agricultural activity, with that of the Native American groups, would provide a solid foundation for a vigorous colony. Ultimately, despite occasional periods of violence and disruption, four Native American nations would maintain permanent villages near the French fort as late as the 1760s–70s, and the population of colonial farmers would grow steadily and establish strong agricultural and cultural roots. It was the agricultural emphasis that set Detroit apart from other French forts of the Great Lakes, which were primarily fur-trading stations, and agriculture greatly influenced the development of the settlement and its town.

These political, military, and social factors influenced the selection of the site where Detroit would grow. Arriving with soldiers, farmers, and workmen in July 1701, Cadillac explored the length of the strait, seeking the most favorable location for his fort and colony (see Figure 1.1). Among his requirements was fertile land with adequate space to accommodate his farmers and whatever Native American groups might be enticed to settle nearby. Fortunately, the soil along both sides of the river was suitable, and the climate was temperate enough to permit the cultivation of European crops, such as wheat, as well as the maize and other crops that supported Native American populations.

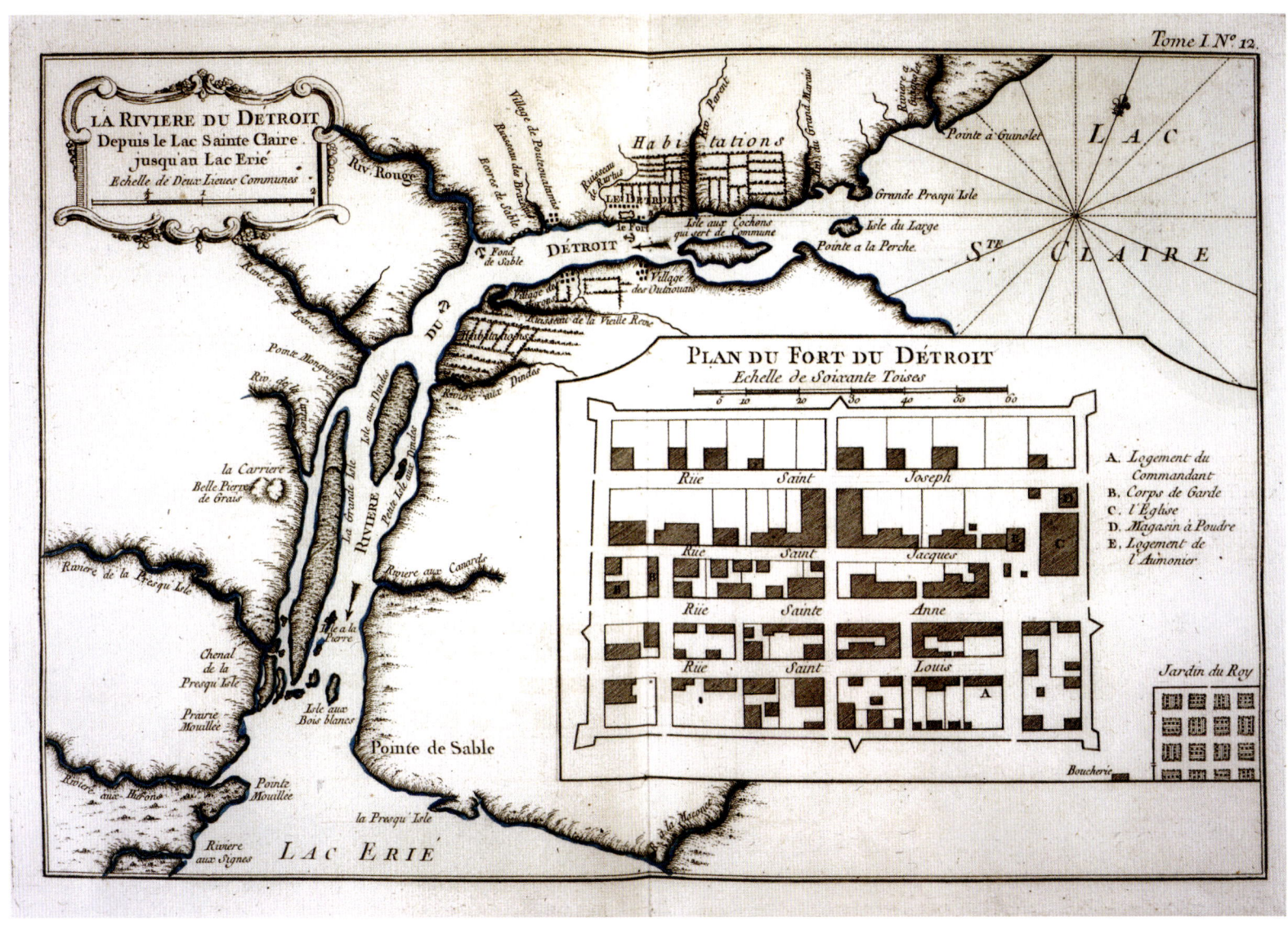

FIGURE 1.1 Gaspard-Joseph Chaussegros de Léry's *Plan du Fort du Détroit* was inset on his map of the Detroit River published in *Le Petit Atlas Maritime* by J. N. Bellin (1764). This is often cited as representing Detroit as it was during Pontiac's siege of 1763. In fact, the plan was engraved from Léry's survey of 1749, at which time the outline of the town was quite different.
Source: William L. Clements Library, University of Michigan.

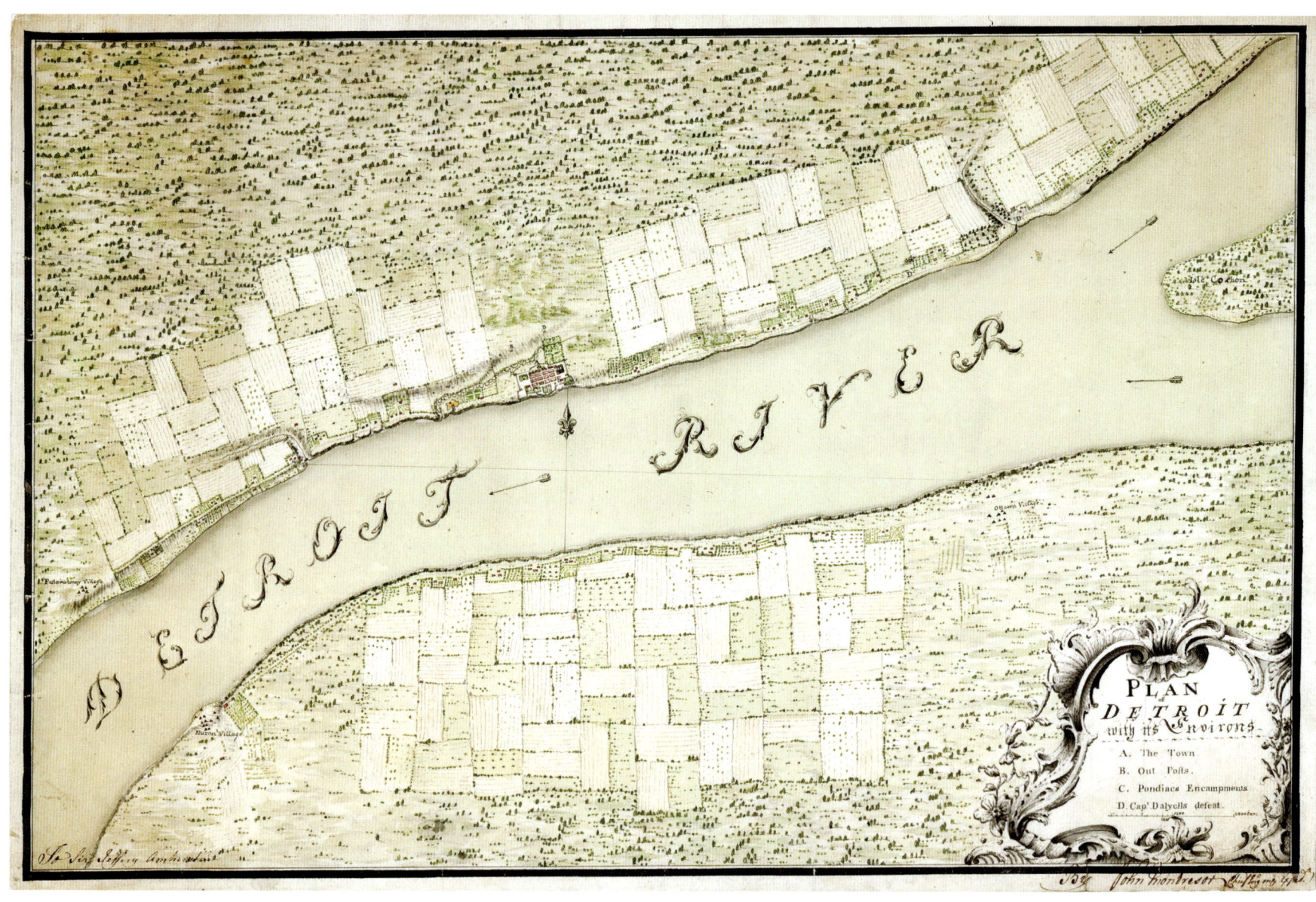

FIGURE 1.2 British engineer John Montrésor drafted his "Plan of Detroit with its Environs" in 1764. His intention was to accurately depict the local topography and the form of the town and its defenses as it was during Pontiac's siege of 1763. *Source: William L. Clements Library, University of Michigan.*

Because either side of the strait would be conducive to agriculture, the deciding factor for selecting a location for a fort was defensibility. Cadillac accordingly chose a stretch of high riverbank about equidistant between Belle Isle and the great bend below the site of the modern Ambassador Bridge, where the east-west flowing strait turns sharply to the south. The position, which Cadillac believed to be at the narrowest part of the river, was elevated and unobstructed by islands, and observers at the fort could see all water traffic. He selected the site for the stockade for tactical reasons as well. The top of the bank had sufficient space for a fortified village and its future expansion. A creek with a broad, shallow valley ran parallel to the water before turning to join it a few hundred yards farther west, and separated the bank from higher ground to the north (inland). The Huron (later called Savoyard) Creek thus provided a natural ditch to protect the north side of the French fort. The presence of higher ground north of the creek was a minor disadvantage that was of less importance in Cadillac's time, but would later be addressed during the American Revolution when Fort Lernoult was established there. These critical topographical features are no longer readily apparent, having been obscured or eliminated by the growth of the nineteenth-century city.

No sooner had the stockade been raised than Cadillac's men began to clear land for planting wheat. Again, the proximity of the river influenced the development of the land as they laid out and platted farm lots. Ultimately, most parcels were long, narrow "ribbons" of two to four arpents (a French unit of measurement[i]) in width and forty or so in depth. Each farmer thus gained water frontage, and the farmhouses were located in close proximity to each other in the pattern of the French settlements of the St. Lawrence River valley. Although parcels set aside for Indian villages and cornfields initially disrupted the regularity of this arrangement, the entire north bank and most of the south would eventually be laid out in ribbon farms. As a result, when nineteenth-century Detroit began to outgrow its original boundaries, it expanded along the river to the east and

FIGURE 1.3 Patrick McNiff carefully recorded the distinctive ribbon farms along the Michigan bank of the Detroit River in 1796 at the behest of newly installed United States authorities. The surveyor identified the proprietor of each plot. This panel, one of five that make up a complete map of the river, includes the town and fort in the broad ribbon of the "public land."
Source: *William L. Clements Library, University of Michigan.*

west, incorporating the narrow ribbons one after another. Many streets perpendicular to the river still bear the names of owners of the long-vanished farms along whose boundaries they run (see Figures 1.2 and 1.3).

CHARTING THE SHAPE OF EARLY DETROIT 21

In the eighteenth and early nineteenth centuries, the town expanded within a similar but much broader ribbon of land that Cadillac originally granted to himself. (After he left the colony, this area became the king's "domain" and later, under the Americans, the "public" land.) This parcel provided ground for the periodic expansion of the town and for compensating victims of a major fire in June 1805 with "donation lots" within the new city plan. The east and west boundaries of the domain became those of the rebuilt town. The urban Detroit of 1701–1838 was located within this area.

FORTIFICATIONS

Of particular importance in understanding the development of the early town of Detroit is the fact that, for the first 125 years of its existence, fortifications both protected and confined the town. Detroit was, in the parlance of the time, a "fortified place," similar, on a miniature scale, to the hundreds of fortress towns scattered across Europe. As such, it enclosed a population of civilians and their properties but also supported a garrison of soldiers. From 1701 until 1805 the town was entirely within a stockade wall, accessible only through gateways guarded by soldiers. Between 1806 and 1826, the town was more open but still had in its midst a large earthen fort and adjacent military reserve that interrupted the street plan and kept a large part of the town from development. These fortifications were a necessity, however, because Detroit was a dangerous place. During the first half of the eighteenth century, it withstood no fewer than four organized assaults by Native Americans, and it was not until the late 1730s that any of the French settlers resided in farmhouses outside the town walls. The fifth attack, Pontiac's attempt of 1763, led to the longest siege ever conducted by Native Americans. Detroit had to be protected during the colonial conflicts of the early eighteenth century, the Seven Years' War, the American Revolution, and the Ohio Indian wars of the 1780s–90s. In the War of 1812, the British bombarded and captured the town, and then occupied it for fourteen months. During these years prior to 1826, the fortifications provided security but also impeded the growth of the town and the movements of its inhabitants and placed them within the line of fire of any attack, as in 1763 and 1812.

Until 1805 the presence of fortifications guided the form of the town plan and controlled its expansion. Ste. Anne Street, the primary east-west thoroughfare, had a gate at each end, while some of the cross lanes led to smaller portals on the waterside. Opportunities to enlarge the town generally corresponded with the need, every eight to ten years or so, to replace the rotted pickets of its stockade. When the fortified area expanded dramatically in 1782 to incorporate Fort Lernoult to the north, the guns of the fort were situated to both protect the length of the stockade and cover the cross streets of the town against potential penetration by the enemy or insurrection by the inhabitants. These military constraints contributed to the building density, which allowed the 1805 fire to quickly spread and virtually destroy eighteenth-century Detroit (see Figure 1.4).

DETROIT AFTER 1805

The subsequent reconstruction of the town based on territorial judge Augustus B. Woodward's imaginative but ultimately impracticable plan threw off many of the constraints of fortification. To use walls of defense in the new design would not be economical, and military activity from 1806 until 1826 thus centered on Fort Detroit (the former Fort Lernoult, renamed in 1805 and then known after 1813 as Fort Shelby). Originally constructed in 1778 to occupy the higher ground to the north of the town, the fort was badly situated to fire upon the river, from which attacks might come, because many private buildings stood in between. This defect, combined with the changing strategic situation in the aftermath of the War of 1812 and the army's continued occupation of valuable real estate, contributed to the decision to abandon Fort

Shelby and open its site for urban development. In 1826 the era of fortified Detroit came to an end.

The 1805 fire had a significant impact on the use of early maps for studying the growth of Detroit, as the destruction resulted in a nearly complete disconnect of the pre-1805 street plan from that which replaced it. All but one of the buildings of the town were consumed; the only significant surviving landmark was the earthen fort, which was far enough removed from the civilian area to escape destruction. As such, Fort Detroit (Fort Shelby after 1813) provides an important benchmark for linking maps of the eighteenth century with those drawn after 1805. Fort Shelby appears on plans of Detroit as late as 1825, and its documented relationship to the streets of the Woodward trace can assist in pinpointing other parts of the pre-1805 town. Archaeological discoveries have confirmed that the fortification occupied the area of the intersection (appropriately enough) of Fort and Shelby streets.

Plans of post-1805 Detroit are more easily compared with the modern street grid, which was laid over the site of the incinerated town and took in additional area to the east and to the north. These plans chart the development of the nineteenth-century city through the 1830s, including the abandonment of the Woodward street plan and expansion beyond the 1806 boundaries of the old domain as the city incorporated the first of the ribbon farms to the east and to the west. The first published plan of the town was printed in 1825 (Dunnigan 2001, p. 172). Although it has numerous large and small differences from the actual street plan that developed, it is the cartographic foundation of the modern city and, through its inclusion of Fort Shelby, provides a tenuous link with the pre-1805 colonial town.

CARTOGRAPHIC RECORD

The cartographic and visual record for pre-1838 Detroit is quite rich, although it possesses a number of unfortunate gaps. The iconography for *Frontier Metropolis* (Dunnigan 2001) was assembled from some 225 images

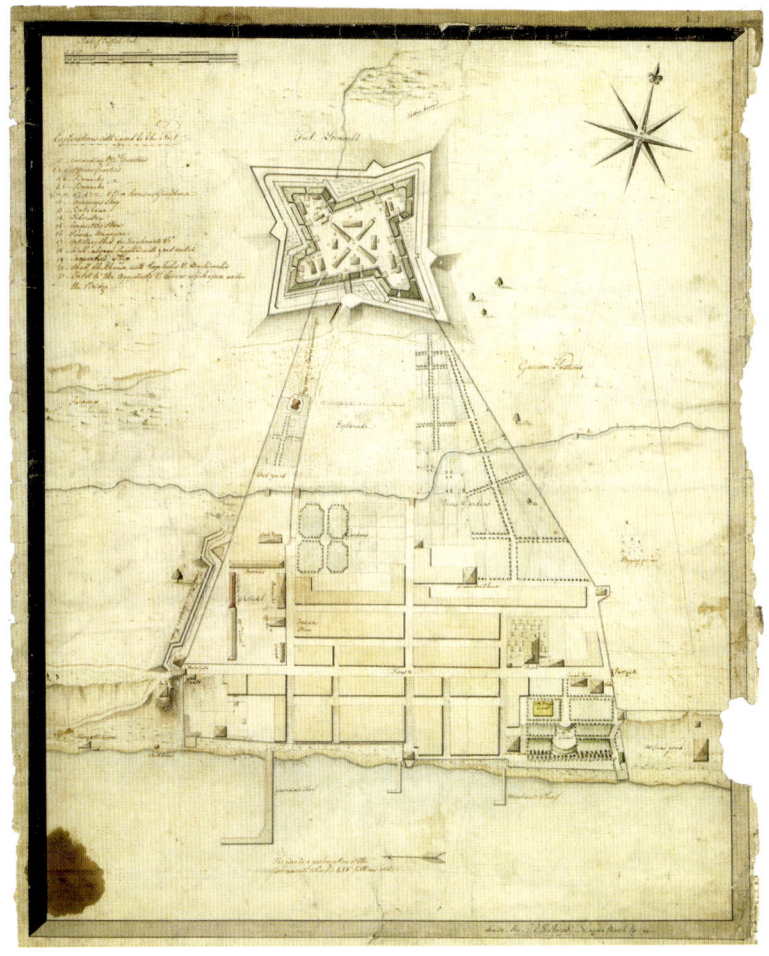

FIGURE 1.4 The fortified town that burned in June 1805 had taken on its distinctive triangular ground plan by 1782. Fort Lernoult (Fort Detroit) is at the apex, separated from the civilian area by a broad open space of parade grounds and pasture. This firebreak saved the fort from the conflagration. The purpose of Major John J. U. Rivardi's untitled map of 1799 was to show the fortifications in great detail. *Source: William L. Clements Library, University of Michigan.*

of all sorts, ranging from detailed maps and plans to sketches, drawings, prints, carvings, and even designs on wampum belts and ceramics. Each contributes in its own way to documenting the appearance of Detroit and the surrounding area during its first 137 years. Most useful for charting the form of the colonial town and budding American city are the maps and plans that represent the street grid in its entirety or show significant portions of it. A total of forty-one maps of this category survive, as far as we know, providing snapshots of the town's layout at twenty-three separate times between 1702 and 1837. Many other plans show smaller portions of the town or its fortifications. These provide useful details but do not contribute as much to our understanding of the form of the overall street plan. The surviving plans present a record of slow but steady expansion of the town and its fortifications until 1805 and then development along the Woodward design and its post-1818 replacement.

These cartographic materials are primary-source historical documents and, as such, must be considered critically and used with care and with the corroboration of other drawn, written, or printed sources. One must remember that, although maps and plans project the appearance of reliability and accuracy, they are completely subjective, and a mapmaker or engraver can err, lie, or distort the facts just as easily as the author of a written account. The author may add, delete, or project at whim and in accordance with his or her own purpose. Furthermore, the cartographic record is incomplete, and the availability of maps of Detroit for any given time period is dependent upon their survival and their correctly identification. One of the chief purposes of *Frontier Metropolis* (Dunnigan 2001) was to locate, identify, and document images of Detroit wherever they might be found—in archives, private collections, local institutions, and government agencies. Although few discoveries of previously unknown imagery of early Detroit have been made in the years since 2001, it is inevitable that more will be uncovered in the future, and these will strengthen and expand the early cartographic record of the city.

The first and most important fact that is necessary to know about any individual map or plan is the purpose of its author. The purpose will determine what is shown and influence the level of detail; the purpose sometimes reveals biases that might have influenced the composition. A cadastral map produced by a surveyor, for instance, is likely to focus on the size and shape of properties, their relationship to the street plan, and the names of their owners while ignoring the shapes and positions of buildings. General maps of the fortifications often show only the blocks of the town and might not even have buildings scaled accurately, as their purpose was to show the relationship of the town to its defenses. Plans may also reflect proposed changes that might not have been accomplished in the manner depicted.

Accuracy of scale may also vary widely according to the purpose of the map or plan. A plan of the French fort drafted in 1732 by post commandant Captain Henri-Louis Deschamps de Boishébert (Dunnigan 2001, p. 31) bears all the signs of having been carefully scaled and measured; it provides details as minute as the placement of doors and windows in the houses. Boishébert's purpose was to record a recent restoration of the long-neglected town and its stockade. A plan drawn by British Lieutenant Diedrich Brehm in 1760 (Dunnigan 2001, p. 52) focuses on the fortifications but carefully represents the community—including the shapes of individual buildings. Brehm recorded the town for the British commander in chief in North America at the time it passed from French to British control, and he was interested in both military and civil details. A plan of the town as it was after 1782, by Captain David William Smith, was intended only to show the general form of the fortifications and the arrangement of blocks of buildings within the town, so we cannot rely on it for precise measurements.

We must also consider the actual date of creation and depiction of each work. Many manuscript plans of Detroit are first-generation documents, drawn at the time they depict. Some are even accompanied by letters of transmission identifying the purpose of the plan, its intended recipient, and the exact date of its creation. Competent engineers and draftsmen could copy such maps with ease, however, and surviving manuscript plans may be duplicates of the original made at a somewhat later time. These are usually exact copies, though they might include minor changes. We must use printed maps with great care, for they often reflect the appearance of the place at a considerably earlier time than their date of publication. The crisp and business-like rendering of the French fort published in Jacques-Nicolas Bellin's *Le Petit Atlas Maritime* (Bellin 1764; Dunnigan 2001, p. 40) has often been reproduced and described as the town of Pontiac's 1763 siege. In reality, the source material used was a manuscript plan drawn by Ensign Gaspard-Joseph Chaussegros de Léry in 1749, and the town had undergone at least two substantial expansions and changes to the outline of its stockade by the time of Pontiac's War and the publication of Bellin's map in 1764 (see Figure 1.1).

Once we know the context and purpose of the early plans of Detroit, we can use these documents to explain the developing form of the colonial town and its early nineteenth-century replacement. They show a place that grew in area through the natural increase of its population and the changing needs of its defense. The tiny stockade of Cadillac's day went through at least eleven significant expansions before the possibility of attack during the American Revolution caused the construction of Fort Lernoult in 1778 and its connection to the town in 1782. This greatly expanded the overall enclosed area, though the streets and blocks of the civilian precinct remained essentially unchanged after the 1760s.

Only two interruptions occur in the cartographic documentation of this progression, though, unfortunately, they come at critical times. No known plan of Detroit covers the period between Cadillac's drawing of 1702 (Dunnigan 2001, p. 24) and that made by Boishébert exactly thirty years later (Dunnigan 2001, p. 31). During the intervening years, the orientation of the town and its stockade changed from the small square of Cadillac's design to a rectangular form with its long axis parallel to the river, and the arrangement of the houses changed from a compact cluster to a more military-style grid of east-west streets punctuated by north-south lanes. The second major gap is for the period from 1765 to 1782, during which the town plan remained relatively unchanged but the trace of the fortifications expanded dramatically. Otherwise, the early cartographic record of Detroit is essentially complete through the end of the decade of the 1830s and the development of the form of the city was continuous.

In studying the changing form of Detroit through time, maps provide urban historians, planners, and designers with the most comprehensive and complete sources available for the years before the introduction of photography in the 1840s–50s. Although they must be critically analyzed and used with care, these visual documents depict the ways in which space was organized and utilized within a growing frontier settlement and town long before it began to develop the industrial base that would result in a sprawling twentieth-century metropolis. For historians, planners, and designers, this visual, cartographic chronology allows the connection of the form of the city with its commercial, residential, and military functions and purposes, and it places the historical and social events of the place within a physical context. Early Detroit, especially the pre-1805 town, may seem far removed from the city of today, but it formed the core of the modern city and established some of the characteristics that have contributed to its distinctive form and personality.

NOTES

1. Each arpent is about 0.85 of a modern acre. The term *arpent* also refers to a unit of length. See U.S. Department of Interior (2012).

REFERENCES

Bellin, J. N. (1764). *Le petit atlas maritime.* Paris, France: Jacques Nicolas Bellin.
Dunnigan, B. L. (2001). *Frontier metropolis: Picturing early Detroit, 1701–1838.* Detroit, MI: Wayne State University Press.
U.S. Department of Interior. (2012). *Public land survey system.* Retrieved from http://nationalatlas.gov/articles/boundaries/a_plss.html

2

MAPPING DETROIT
"The City of Holes"

HENCO BEKKERING AND YANJIA LIU

And how can [the general] knowledge [of the territory] be obtained so readily as from a correct map?
Orange Risdon in the *Detroit Gazette,* September 10, 1824, on the need of
the *Map of the Surveyed Part of the Territory of Michigan* that he made in 1825.

The introduction to this book gives a background on the origins of this chapter about Detroit as a "city of holes" (Smithson 1997). As explained there, the mapping work of Constantinos A. Doxiadis, in particular, inspired co-author Bekkering's desire to create an updated series of maps concerning the evolution of the city of Detroit. Also prompting this research plan was an article written by Professor Marcel Smets of the University of Leuven, Belgium, published in the Dutch journal *Architecture, Urbanism and Visual Arts: Archis 3 1996,* entitled "Detroit als wegwerpstad. Beeld van een company town / Detroit—A disposable town. Picture of a company town" (Smets 1996). Marcel Smets very tellingly characterized the urban process in Detroit at that moment as the reverse of an American dream. The article presented four figure-ground drawings of the downtown area, published in the magazine *Architecture* (Plunz 1996) in the same year by Professor Richard Plunz, then of Columbia University in New York. The drawings are of varying origin.[1] At the time, Richard Plunz had invited Marcel Smets to serve on the jury assessing students' work in his Detroit studio at Columbia—reason for both of them to look into Detroit. Giorgia Daskalakis republished the four drawings in *Stalking Detroit* (Daskalakis, Waldheim, and Young 2001). A fifth drawing of downtown, showing the situation in 2004 (see Figure 2.1), appeared in a published report of work generated in conjunction with one of the charettes or workshops on the future of Detroit which the University of Michigan's Taubman College held annually at that time (Kelbaugh et al. 2007). When we checked, the map of 2009 did not show relevant differences from that of 2004. The series, however, covered only downtown. Therefore, the

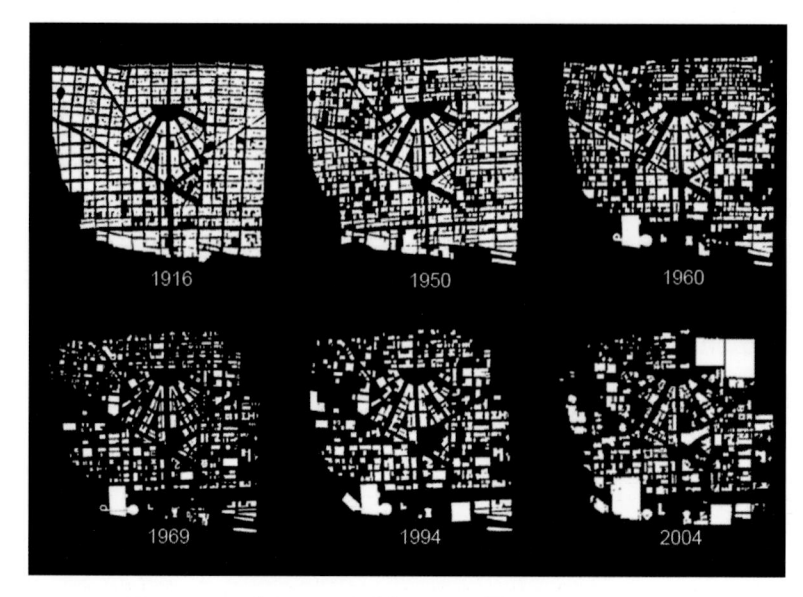

FIGURE 2.1 Figure-ground drawings of downtown Detroit.
Sources: 1916, 1950, 1960, and 1969 drawings: courtesy of DTE Energy, from Doxiadis, C. A. (1970). A concept for future development. Emergence and growth of an urban region: The developing urban Detroit area *(Vol. 3). Detroit, MI: Detroit Edison Co., p. 157. 1994 drawing: Plunz (1996), pp. 2012–2013. 2004 drawing: Kelbaugh et al. (2007).*

modern record of maps seemed episodic and incomplete, offering an incentive for this project. We intend this chapter to provide further information about the historical evolution of urban space in the Detroit city and region, determining in particular what spatial features in the city's landscape appeared to be most important in forming and changing Detroit's urban morphology, but also to comment on the challenging process of mapping itself, a discussion already initiated in chapter 1.

OUTPLACEMENT OF THE AUTOMOBILE FACTORIES

During co-author Bekkering's third visit to Detroit, in 1997, the first results were visible of the revitalization of Woodward Avenue, one of the main structuring elements of the city and a corridor that had previously showed a severe decline. At the same time, however, a specific and new episode of the outplacement of automobile factories was taking place, and this was destructive to the city, as it had been in previous eras.

At least four phases characterize the spatial development of the automobile industry and related effects on the planning and development of the city. The first phase started with the construction of the first automobile plant in 1900. This plant, which produced Oldsmobiles, burned in 1901. The owner moved his activities back to Lansing, but ties to foundries and machine shops remained. The Ford Motor Company opened in 1903, and soon other companies such as Packard, General Motors (GM), Chevrolet, and Chrysler opened (Larsen et al. 2006; Woodford 2001). In the beginning of the automobile industry in Detroit, up to about 1910, many small, privately owned workshops were dispersed all over the city as it existed at the time, and these shops produced materials and parts for the large factories—which, even then, were close in character to assembly plants. The first true assembly line, however, was not installed until 1913, in the Ford Motor Company plant in Highland Park. The factory was designed by the highly respected and very productive architect Albert Kahn, as described in chapter 4.

In the second phase, big companies incorporated more and more individual workshops, merging them into their own operations, necessitating larger factory buildings. This still occurred inside or very close to the then built-up area of the city, in what is now its center. "In 1925 the city was home to 3,000 manufacturing plants, 37 automobile manufacturing plants, and 250 automobile accessory plants. Factories employed over 300,000 people" (Martin 1993, p. 4). Trying to ride this tide, the city government, together with the captains of industry, wanted to create a second office and commercial node called New Center, around the intersection of Woodward Avenue and West Grand Boulevard, about three miles north of the central business district (CBD). Because of the Great Depression, the New Center was not fully developed

FIGURE 2.2 Aerial photographs of downtown Detroit in 2006.
Source: Inside cover and page 1 of Kelbaugh, D. S., Strickland, R., Dueweke, E., et al. (2007). 5D: Adding three dimensions to downtown Detroit (Detroit Design Workshop 2007). Ann Arbor: A. Alfred Taubman College of Architecture and Urban Planning, The University of Michigan. Aerial photography by Jim Rogers.

as planned, although some great buildings were realized. These include the General Motors Building (now Cadillac Place, constructed in 1922), built as GM's headquarters, and the Fisher Building (constructed in 1928). Both were designed by Albert Kahn, although they were very different in character and style. Because of the economy, the Fisher Building as actually constructed was much smaller than originally proposed. Between the CBD and the small New Center area, a big gap was left that was never really filled.

Another example of the over-estimation of the urban potential by the city government and the railroad company is the very large Michigan Central Station built in 1913; it was designed for rail passengers by Warren & Wetmore and Reed & Stem, the architects of Grand Central Station in New York. Though situated close to Michigan Avenue, one of the main radial avenues of the city, and located less than two miles from downtown, the station never attracted the number of travelers intended. The station includes a large amount of office space, and the five highest office floors have never been occupied. The entire building has been out of use and empty since rail passenger service ceased in 1988, and it has become the striking and frightening (though very photogenic) physical symbol of the decline of Detroit. Passengers now use a small Amtrak station located near New Center, less than a mile north of the great cultural institutions of the Detroit Institute of Arts (one of the important art museums of the United States) and the Detroit Public Library.

The third phase of the development of the automobile industry involved further decentralization. Because automotive factories as well as offices continued to leave the city, and because of population flight from urban areas to suburban areas where more space was more easily available at lower costs (and racially exclusionary), after the 1950s the physical fabric of the city began to show holes: brown fields that lay fallow, partly polluted, and vacant housing lots. Once-lively buildings, including dozens of downtown buildings (among which were skyscrapers), were left completely empty and fell into severe disrepair, sometimes having lost all of their glass. With a few exceptions, no market existed that warranted purchase and reconstruction of such buildings (see Figure 2.2). The great Packard Automobile Manufacturing Plant of 1907 was designed by Albert Kahn, is 0.6 miles (1 km) long, is located just 2.5 miles (4 km) east of New Center, and has been empty and deteriorating since 1956.

By the early 1980s, it was obvious that the automobile industry of the "Big Three"—Ford, GM, and Chrysler—had entered a fourth phase of decentralization. In 1981, the GM Detroit-Hamtramck Assembly Plant was built through a joint public-private initiative, showing that major investment in assembly operations in the central city would take place only with significant public incentives (Thomas 2013). Otherwise, automotive firms were placing their operations at ever-greater distances from the city and its suburbs. They established factories in towns tens and hundreds of miles away in all directions, partly to other states and other countries.

SETUP OF THE RESEARCH

To gain insight into the land use aspects of urban development in Detroit's evolution, our research composed and used a series of maps spanning time and scale. (For a more detailed description of the mapping itself, see Appendix 2.A.) The history of Detroit starts in 1701 with the establishment of a French fortified village called Fort Pontchartrain, as described in chapter 1. The first map that depicts this fort is dated 1702 (Dunnigan 2001, p. 24).

Wayne State University Press published a collection of the early maps of Detroit—from that first fort map until the beginnings of photography—in the thoroughly researched and beautifully crafted *Frontier Metropolis: Picturing Early Detroit, 1701–1838* (Dunnigan 2001) by Brian Leigh Dunnigan, associate director and curator of maps at the William L. Clements Library at the University of Michigan. This book has been extremely useful for our research. We have selected from it the maps that as a series show the successive major changes in the structure of the city up to 1838 (see Appendix

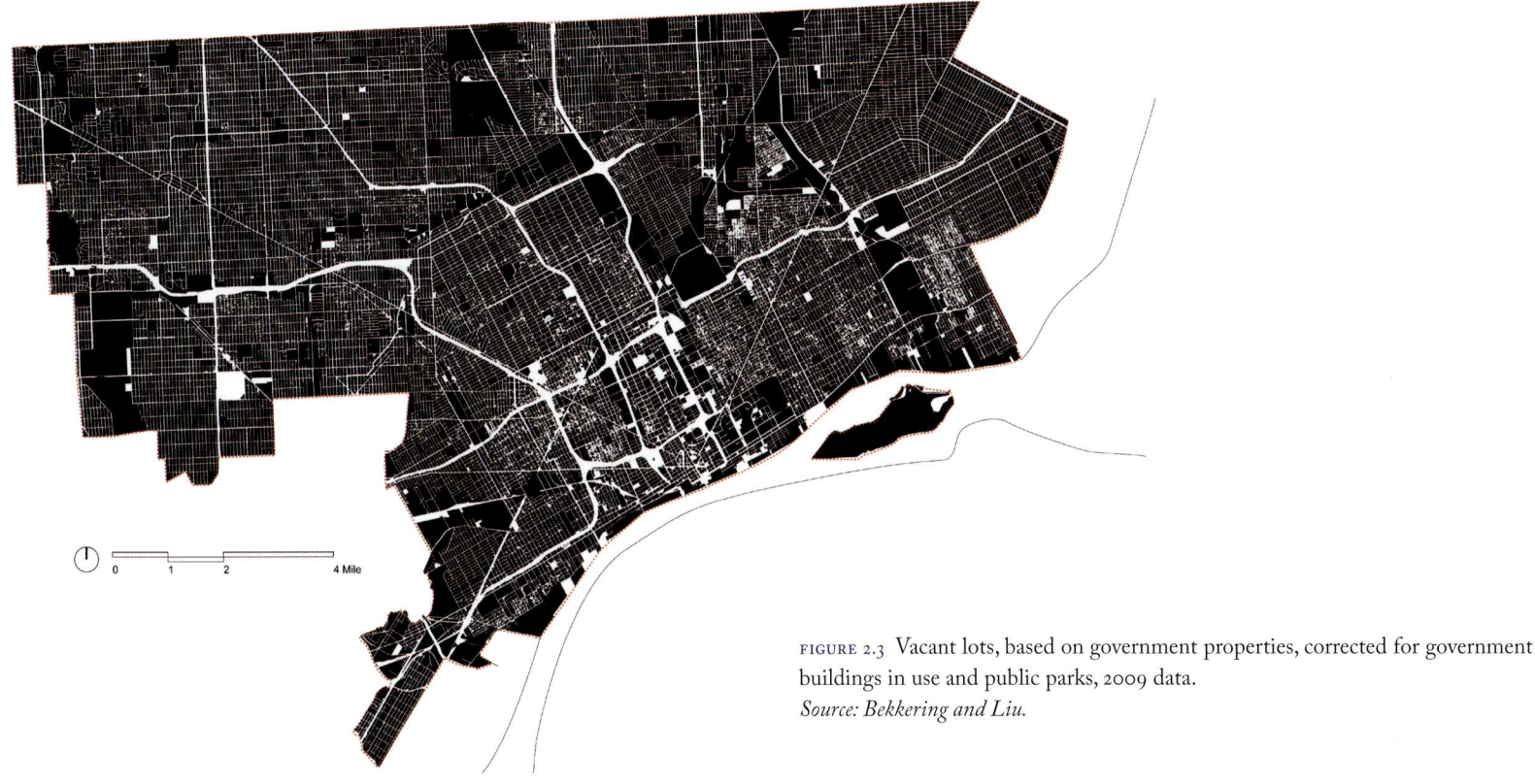

FIGURE 2.3 Vacant lots, based on government properties, corrected for government buildings in use and public parks, 2009 data.
Source: Bekkering and Liu.

2.B). We redrew these maps to the same scale and with a consistent, strongly reduced legend, trying at the same time to find the correct or most probable topographical position in relation to the present map of the city.

With the assistance of map librarian Karl Longstreth, we made a second selection from the significant collection located in the Harlan Hatcher Graduate Map Library of the University of Michigan (hereafter Hatcher Library), covering the period from 1838 until now. We used both the scale of within the city limits, which were enlarged several times during the city's history, and the scale of the metropolitan area (see Appendix 2.C). The metropolitan area has no definitive border; the U.S. Census Bureau, focused on county borders, has in fact redefined the standard metropolitan area several times over the last few decades. For reasons of density of built-up areas and of infrastructure on the most recent maps, we include Mount Clemens in the east, Ann Arbor in the west, Waterford in the north, and Trenton in the south: 54 by 42 miles (87 by 68 km). We found additional maps, necessary to create a consistent series, in commercial road atlases and in the Detroit Public Library (see Appendix 2.C).

HOUSING VACANCIES

At the time of a 2009 field survey, the areas of Detroit surveyed had 91,488 vacant lots where houses once stood, or 27 percent of the 343,849 surveyed residential properties (Detroit Data Collaborative 2010).[2] This high level of vacancy was due not only to deindustrialization, but also to demographic trends, housing abandonment, tax delinquencies, and mortgage foreclosures. Clearance of vacant buildings for the sake of public safety left vacant land where buildings once stood. We show the location of vacant lots in Figure 2.3, which we will discuss later in this chapter. (See also chapters 7 and 8.)

In some American cities with high levels of vacancy, the ownership goes to a public land bank that tries to put the lots or rehabilitated homes on the market and uses the money thus recouped to help at-risk homeowners keep their homes or restart in different locations. Such banks also develop and build infill projects attempting to repair neighborhoods, and—if no other solution is found—demolish buildings. In Detroit, at least two land banks are in operation, at the city and county levels, with differing processes and portfolios. In contrast, the Genesee County Land Bank, operating in and around Flint, Michigan, is a more unified effort. This county land bank is one of the pioneering models for addressing large-scale vacancy and has become an important support system for Flint (Beckley 2009). Detroit and Wayne County are still refining their land bank initiatives. The goal of these institutions should be to maintain and create sustainable neighborhoods in urbanized areas and to promote and practice smart growth principles in newly developed areas.

The high total amount of vacant residential lots examined at the time of the 2009 parcel survey—91,488—resulted in the image of an "urban prairie" in some parts of the city. To this should be added at least 30,806 empty single-family residential structures found, with another 2,721 possibly vacant single-family houses, according to these surveyors of major (not all) portions of the city. Of a total of 343,849 residential lots surveyed, at least 122,294 were vacant or contained vacant houses: 35.6 percent. The percentage of vacant residential units or parcels in particular neighborhoods climbed well above 60 percent.

These numbers are available only because of the Detroit Residential Parcel Survey, carried out in August and September 2009. The Detroit Office of Foreclosure Prevention and Response proposed this very significant project, with fieldwork directed by the local organization Data Driven Detroit. Local residents and students of the University of Michigan—recruited by its Edward Ginsberg Center, which enhances learning through community services—spent many days collecting this data. The *Detroit Free Press* published summaries of the report, and a web page provides full detail (Detroit Data Collaborative 2010). The impetus for the extensive research came in part from a few foundations' shared concern about the present state and the future of the city. This led to a combined effort under the name of the Detroit Data Collaborative, which the Ford Foundation and Living Cities supported financially. The collaborative aimed to collect a new and updated inventory in order to create more reliable maps, which would in turn inform decision making about necessary local strategies. The maps of this survey are aggregated in GIS by census block group and the data is collapsed into quartile or quintile categories. Thus the maps are more abstract and less topographical than our map of "The City of Holes." They convey different kinds of information. Unfortunately, it was impossible to translate the survey's data into our type of map.

We also had available, as a data source, the digital information in GIS format of the ownership of all 387,000 lots of Detroit within city limits; this data was researched by a group of University of Michigan students in the fall of 2006. According to Professor Margaret Dewar, who led the students' research, due to the inadequately staffed city government (for doing regular field visits) and the lack of municipal systems in 2006 (for sharing data), too many errors in the original data of the 2006 research exist to allow for a meaningful comparison of the then-indicated government owned lots with the more recent map of vacant residential parcels.

Missing at the moment are maps that would show the successive phases of spatial dispersion of the automobile industry. No doubt this is a very im-

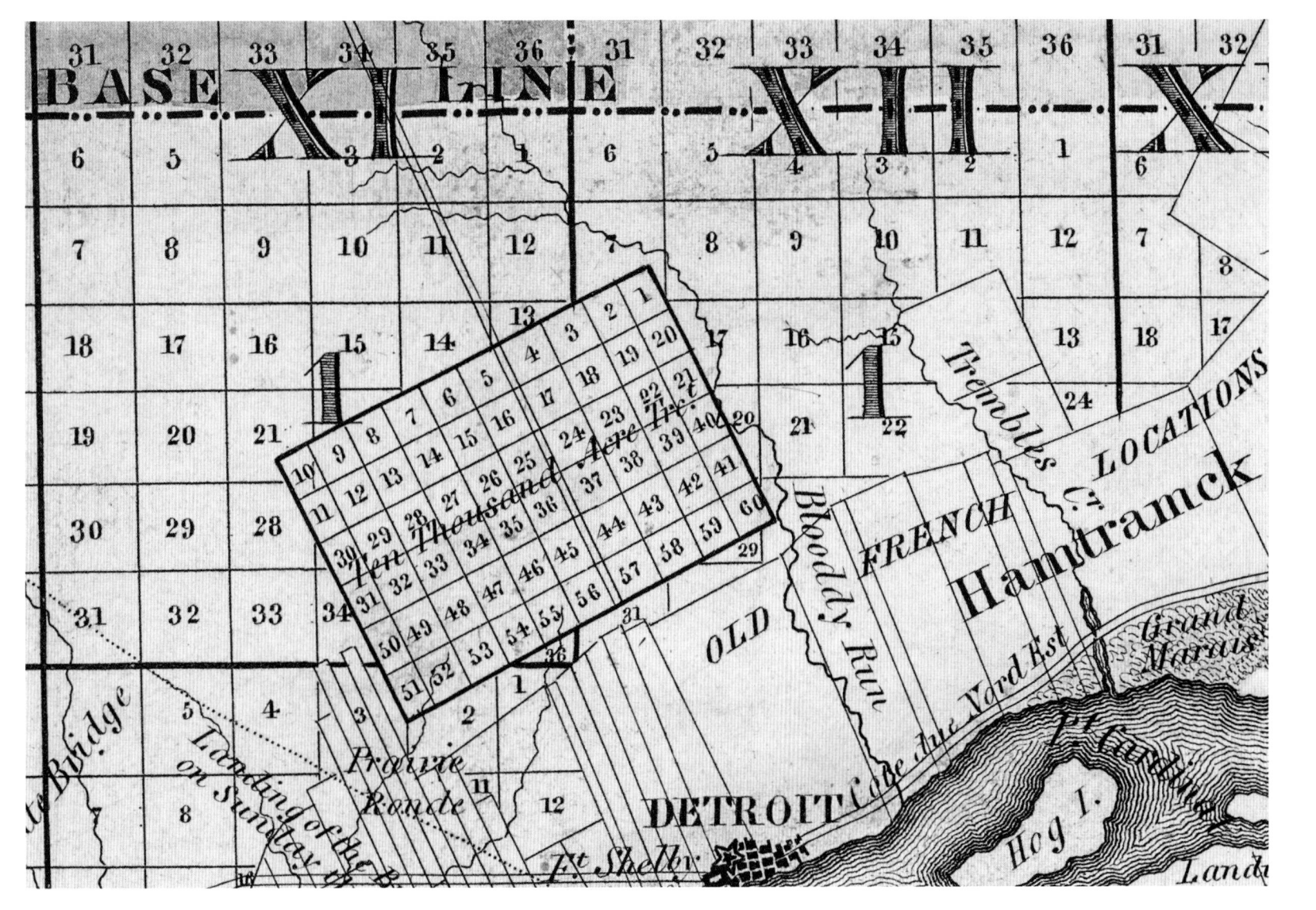

FIGURE 2.4 Detail of the Map of the Surveyed Part of the Territory of Michigan by Risdon, 1825, showing the Ten Thousand Acres Grid (*upper middle*).

Source: William L. Clements Library, University of Michigan.

portant part of the complete story of the growth and decline of Detroit. Such a series would require, however, research in cooperation with other disciplines besides urbanism and much more time than we had available. So far, there is apparently no geographical overview of the outplacement of the automobile industries. Non-geographic sources describing some aspects of such change, of course, exist in several places, including Sugrue (1996) and Darden, Hill, Thomas, and Thomas (1987). The authors strongly recommend complementary historical and cartographic research describing these changes.

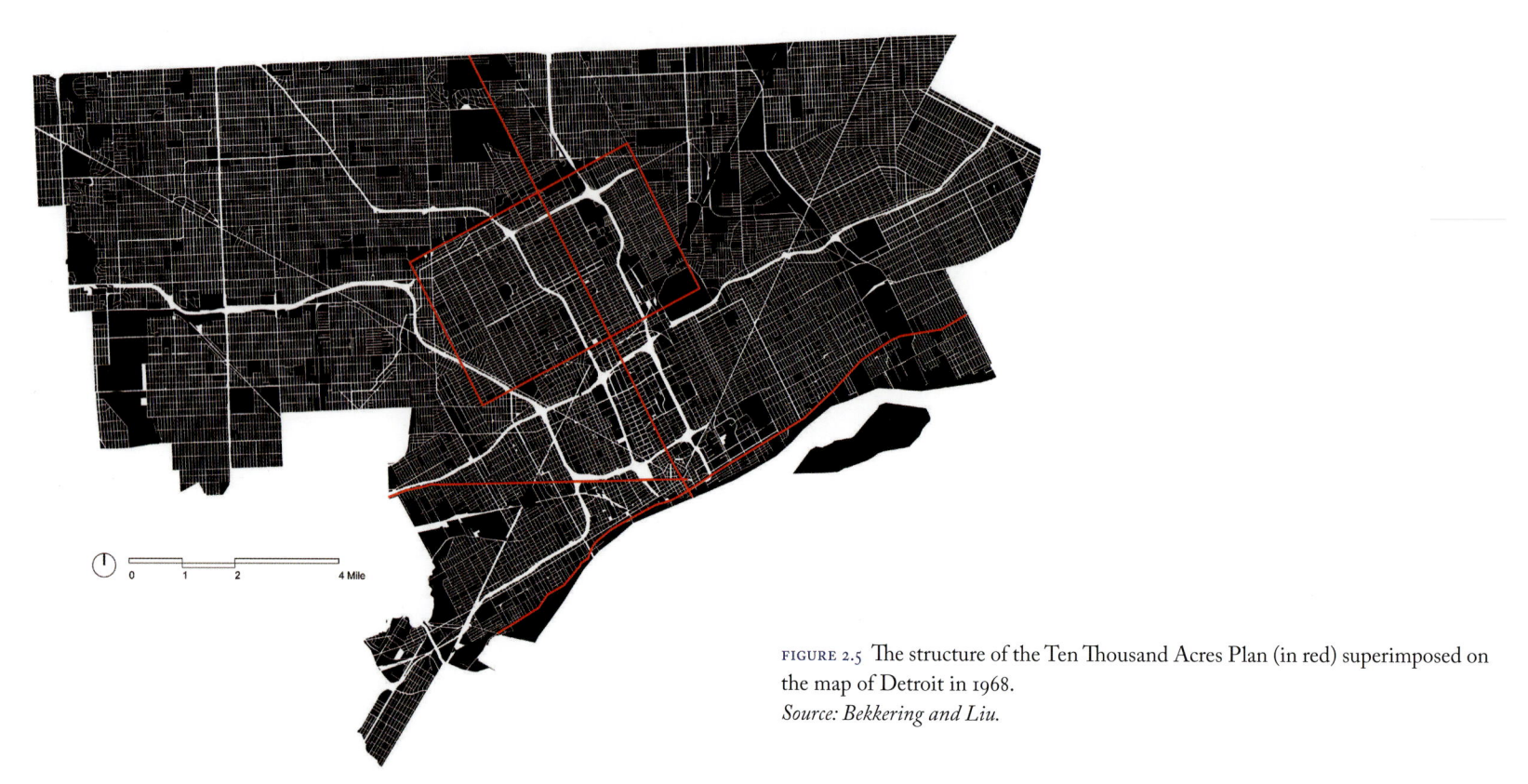

FIGURE 2.5 The structure of the Ten Thousand Acres Plan (in red) superimposed on the map of Detroit in 1968.
Source: Bekkering and Liu.

HISTORY FIXED IN PLACE

The map of Detroit and surroundings in 1825, depicting the so-called "Ten Thousand Acre Grid" surrounded by the larger-scale standard American Jefferson Grid,[3] also shows several sets of double lines, most probably representing pre-existing Indian trails (see Figure 2.4). We were able to fix three of the four corners of the Ten Thousand Acre Grid to existing street corners on the 2009 map of Detroit and found complete correspondence between the double lines in the historical map and the present course of Woodward Avenue. (Located next to Second Street and Third Street, Woodward Avenue is apparently the missing First Avenue.) To match the course of Jefferson Avenue and the bank of the Detroit River, we had to deform the map, shortening the distance between grid and river. This is probably due to a mistake in the 1825 map. After this correction, the somewhat irregular course of Michigan Avenue fits as well (see Figure 2.5). According to our interpretation, the old Indian trails have transformed into Woodward, Michigan, and Jefferson Avenues. This legacy held out even in the reconstruction of the city after the great fire of 1805 that left only one house standing. As is so often the case in the history of cities, the original structure of the city has proven to be as good as permanent. This structure also survived the changes in government: after the French rule from 1702 to 1770, the area became British, and in 1793 the United States government took over. Because Cobo Hall was built right over and across Jefferson Avenue, this huge building

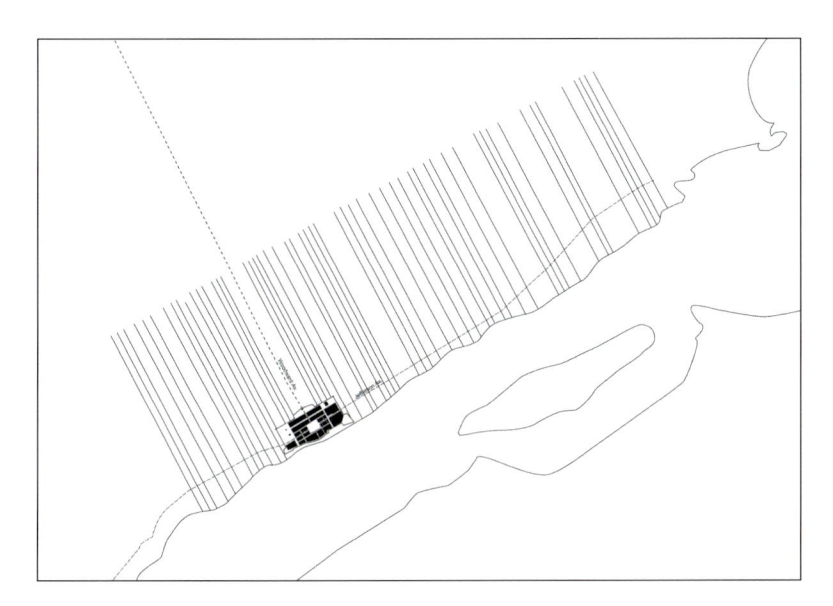

FIGURE 2.6 Map of the agricultural strip farms as layed out by the Franch, based on Carte de La Riviere du Detroit depuis le Lac Erie jus'ques au Lac Ste Claire by C.E. Hickman in 1952 after Lieutenant Gaspard-Joseph Chaussegros de Léry, 1752.
Source: Bekkering and Liu. Original image from William L. Clements Library, University of Michigan

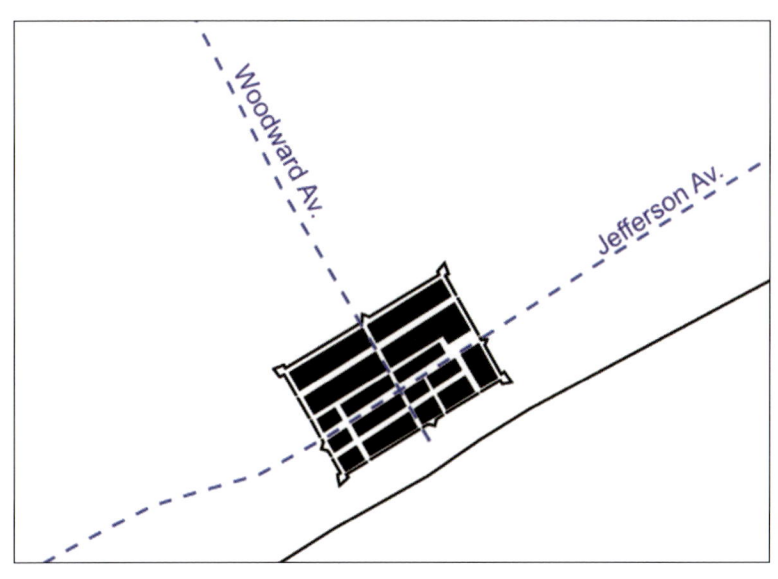

FIGURE 2.7 Rendering of the enlarged Fort at Detroit, based on *Plan du fort du Détroit* by Ensign Gaspard-Joseph Chaussegros de Léry, 1749.
Source: Bekkering and Liu. Original image from William L. Clements Library, University of Michigan

complex regrettably impedes the visual perception of the basic historical urban structure in this part of the city.

From this, we reasoned backward in time once again. The orientation of the Ten Thousand Acres Grid is derived from the French agricultural parceling that initially used narrow strips of land more or less perpendicular to the bank of the river, resulting in the so-called "ribbon farms," (described in chapter 1; see Figure 1.3) apparent in Figure 2.6. The central crossing in the urban structure of Detroit between Woodward and Jefferson Avenues was already present in the different stages of the forts that preceded the city; each had a central crossing, as military forts tend to have (see Figures 2.7 and 2.8). The enlarged forts even show the beginnings of the urban pattern that is still recognizable in the small-scaled building blocks of downtown today. It made sense to situate the first French Fort Pontchartrain on the crossing of the Indian trails, because this meant that it was relatively easy to reach from larger distances and to explain its location to first visitors.

An interesting attempt at such a reconstruction of the history of the city in a map was published as a single sheet dating 1796 titled "The Old Town of Detroit. A Map Showing its Exact Location on the Site of the City of Detroit, Interesting Statistics and Leading Political and Historical Events" (see Figure 2.9). The map on the sheet shows the later Fort Lernoult, after 1813 called Fort Shelby, located further away from the riverbank, and a pattern of building blocks in the area in between that is very close to the pattern of the second enlarged fort shown in Figure 2.8. Then it shows a very small shaded form representing this same fort

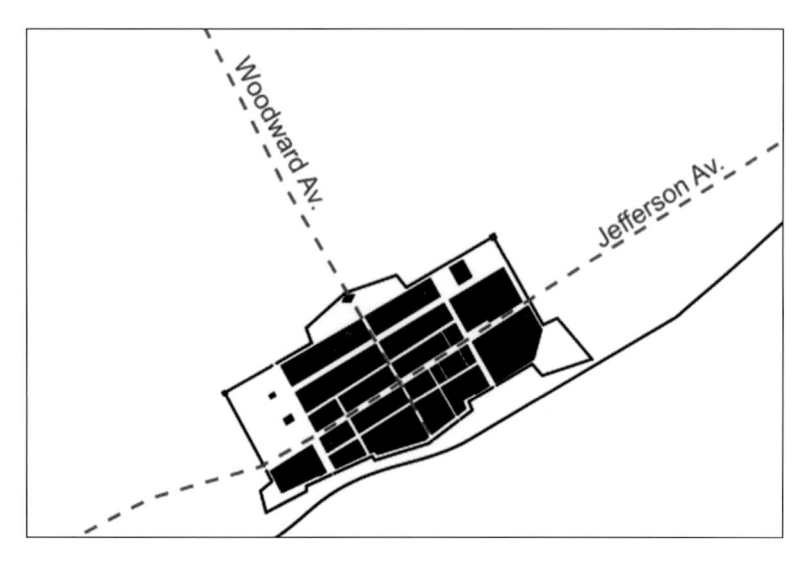

FIGURE 2.8 Rendering of the further enlarged Fort at Detroit, based on *Plan of the Fort at Detroit, 1760* by Diedrich Brehmm, 1761.
Source: Bekkering and Liu. Original image from William L. Clements Library, University of Michigan.

near the river. Obviously this is impossible; a serious mistake in scale had been made.

ATTEMPTS TO (RE)DESIGN THE CITY

Although the fire that razed the city of Detroit in 1805 was devastating, the built-up portion of the city was very small at that point, containing perhaps three hundred residential, commercial, and industrial buildings in total (Dunnigan 2001; Farmer 1884). Nevertheless, rather than simply allow rebuilding on the existing footprint, the territorial governor appointed Judge Augustus B. Woodward to lead the redevelopment. He had a plan made that he intended to resemble Pierre-Charles L'Enfant's layout of Washington D.C., defining large lots and granting one to every adult resident or couple after the fire (see Figure 2.10). This

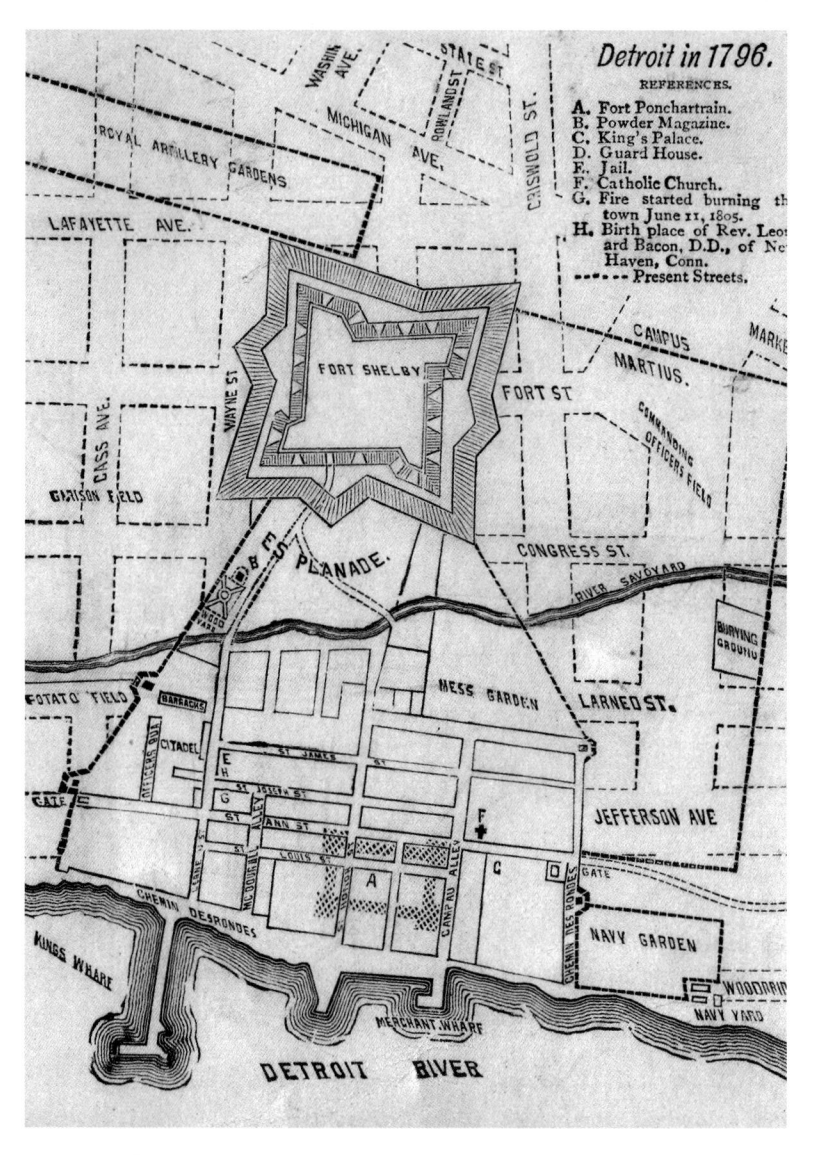

FIGURE 2.9 Detail of *Detroit in 1796*, depicting the location of the old town of Detroit within the city. Map compiled by R. F. Roberts after Thomas Smith and Lieutenant Ralph Willett Adye, 1880.
Source: William L. Clements Library, University of Michigan.

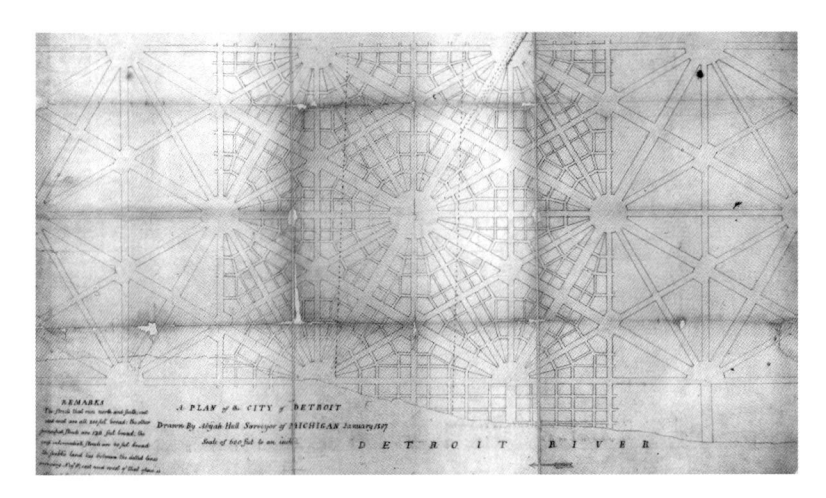

FIGURE 2.10 *A Plan of the City of Detroit.* Drawn By Albijah Hull, surveyor of Michigan, January 1807. Depicts the Woodward Plan of 1806.
Source: Courtesy of the Burton Historical Collection, Detroit Public Library.

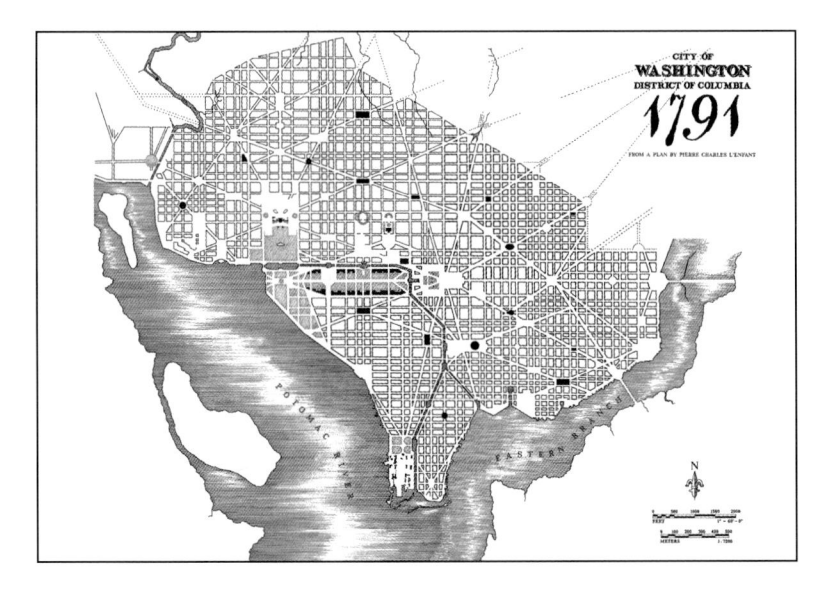

FIGURE 2.11 Plan of Washington, D.C., by Pierre-Charles L'Enfant, 1791.
Source: Library of Congress, Prints and Photographs Division, HABS, Reproduction number HABS DC, WASH, 612 (sheet 2 of 32).

is the start of Detroit as the city still is, made of freestanding single-family homes rather than the row houses that dominated several other American cities of the time, such as Boston, Philadelphia, and New York. The Woodward Plan as a whole was abandoned by 1818 (Larsen et al. 2006). It is indeed an inadequate urban design, as it results in lots with mostly non-rectangular borders on the small scale and endless repetition without recognizable hierarchy on the larger scale. It would have resulted in a city in which it would have been impossible to find one's way around. This is almost the opposite of L'Enfant's plan of Washington D.C., which does have hierarchy and an easily recognizable urban form and pattern (see Figure 2.11).

One very interesting aspect of the Woodward Plan, however, has been a determining factor for the urban form of Detroit. The plan appears to have found inspiration in and made use of the original pattern of the crossing of Woodward Avenue—supposedly not named after the Judge, but as an avenue running *towards* the great *woods* of Michigan north of the city—and Jefferson Avenue together with the diagonal course of Michigan Avenue. The plan added new radial avenues to these to create the regular hexagonal pattern. In the downtown area, we see this idea retained in the street pattern as it was finally executed, though in reality the pattern is not entirely regular: the avenues do not convene in one point. As Figure 2.12 shows, the city planners aimed for this regularity, even retaining four plazas from which avenues radiate outward, of which only two are present in the city's street plan as it is now: Campus Martius and Grand Circus. This has resulted in the double patte d'oie (three-pronged road structure) in two opposite directions of downtown today. This plan also shows the irregular position and form of the most central plaza, Campus Martius, even though in this map the three avenues—Woodward, Michigan/Grand, and what is now Monroe Street—do cross in one point. Earlier plans of Detroit

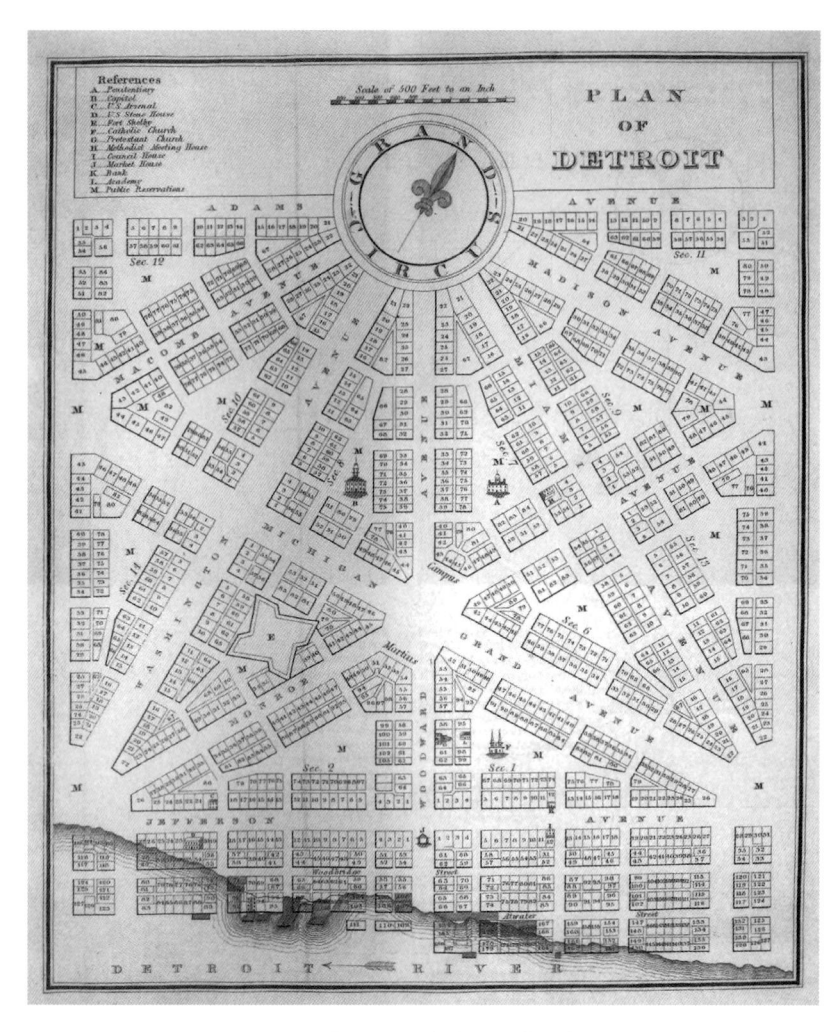

FIGURE 2.12 *Plan of Detroit*, 1824. Engraving by James Otto Lewis, 1825.
Source: *William L. Clements Library, University of Michigan.*

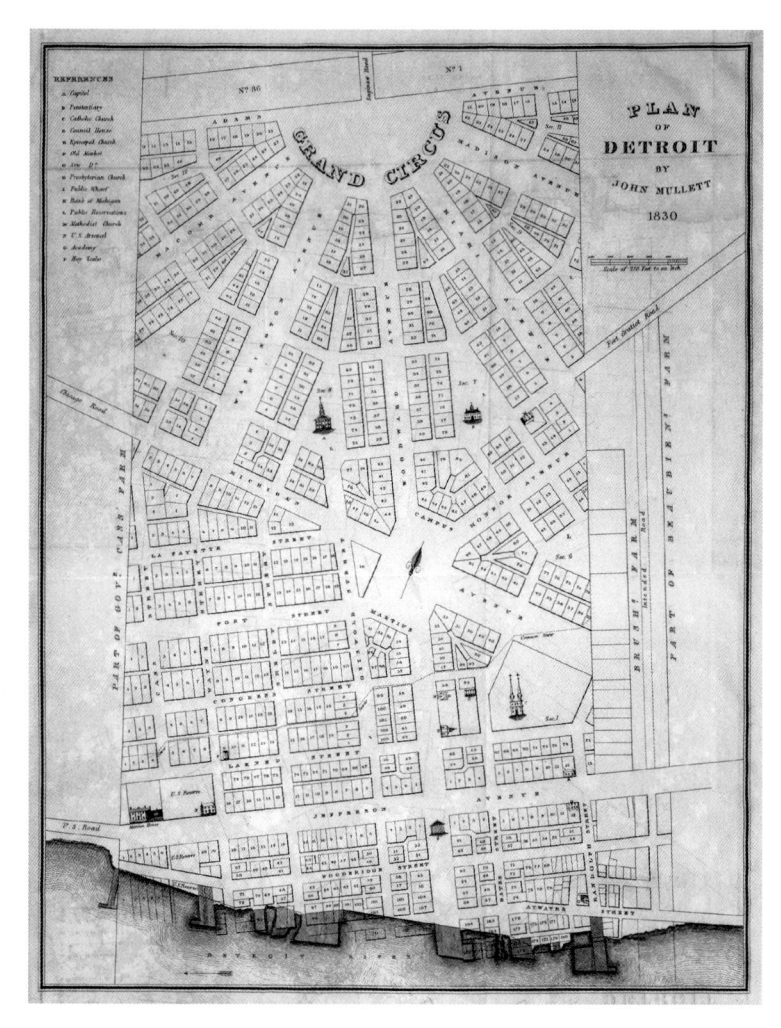

FIGURE 2.13 *Plan of Detroit by John Mullett*, 1830. Engraved and published by James Otto Lewis, 1830.
Source: *William L. Clements Library, University of Michigan.*

do not show an explanation for this irregularity. Figure 2.13 shows how still-existing lots and streets in the southeastern part of downtown that date back to the pre-urban pattern of the early, enlarged forts on this location are pragmatically incorporated (see Figures 2.12 and 2.13).

Though the old course of Michigan Avenue, stemming from an Indian trail, led to the addition of Grand River Avenue west of Woodward, east of Woodward only one radial avenue was implemented: Gratiot. In reality, the radiating pattern of these great avenues of Detroit is not only asymmetrical, but also confusing; as mentioned previously, they do not cross at one point, and this makes the pattern around Campus Martius relatively hard to understand. Fort Street, more or less parallel to the much older Jefferson Avenue, has been added to form the base line of the patte d'oie, but it crosses Woodward at a distance from the others, on the south side of Campus Martius. Campus Martius itself was never a spatially well-defined place. Not only were its borders irregular, and the intersection of diagonal streets confusing, this intended plaza had very little spatial definition because so many buildings surrounding it had only a narrow façade toward the plaza. The character of the place up to the 1950s was largely determined by the many streetcar tracks crossing there, resulting in a space busy with traffic and people. Some buildings built since the mid-1990s, furthermore, do not relate well to Campus Martius because of their orientations and setbacks. However, the city government spearheaded major renovations of the site and the surrounding streets as a project associated with the city's 2001 celebration of its 300th birthday. The newly designed Campus Martius Park, with its first phase completed in 2004, has won national design awards for Rundell Ernstberger Associates. Landscaping, sculptures, a fountain, a restaurant, and features such as café-style outdoor seating have made it into a pleasant space in itself that will benefit in the future from the seclusion offered by the then-grown trees around it.

NINE SPATIAL SYSTEMS

From this part of the research, analyzing the historical and our reconstructed maps, we conclude that nine spatial systems have determined the morphological structure of the city of Detroit as it is today (see Figure 2.14).

1. The Detroit River is the reason for Detroit to be where it is, as the city was originally dependent to a large degree on open water for transport. The riverbank has been changed considerably over time because of landfill and harbor constructions. The tributaries have largely disappeared from view. (See chapter 8.)

2. The early forts fixed the central crossing of the urban structure of Detroit and one of the radial avenues: Woodward, Jefferson and Michigan Avenues, all three probably stemming from old Indian trails. The extensions of the forts formed the first small-scale urban pattern of the downtown area that is still recognizable today.

3. The French ribbon farms set the orientation of the central urban grid, more or less perpendicular to the riverbank.

4. The Ten Thousand Acres Grid, taking over the orientation of the ribbon farms, remains in the city plan as the area between Tireman Avenue/West Grand Boulevard in the south, Conant Avenue in the east, the railroad track north of Oakman Boulevard in the north, and Ironwood Avenue and Nardin Street in the west. The northwestern corner has been cut off by Livernois Avenue.

5. The Jefferson Grid determined the orientation of the rest of the urban grid: north-south and east-west. It is reflected in the successive Mile Roads that cross the city from west to east.

6. The great radial avenues break through the relative regularity of the grids: Woodward, Michigan, Grand River, and Gratiot Avenues.

7. The block grids within the area of the original ribbon farms and the Ten Thousand Acres Grid are oriented parallel to the Detroit River, longer from east to west. Outside this area, they are mainly oriented according to the Jefferson Grid and are generally longer from north to south.

8. The railroads were largely in place before urbanization, so they have been more or less incorporated in the urban pattern by pragmatic adjustments of the grids.

9. The later installment of the highway system in the 1950s and 60s in the existing urban tissue has been much more destructive. As

1. Rivers 2. Early Fort 3. Ribbon Farms
4. Ten Thousand Acres Grid 5. Jefferson Grid 6. Radial Avenues
7. Street Grids 8. Railroads 9. Highways

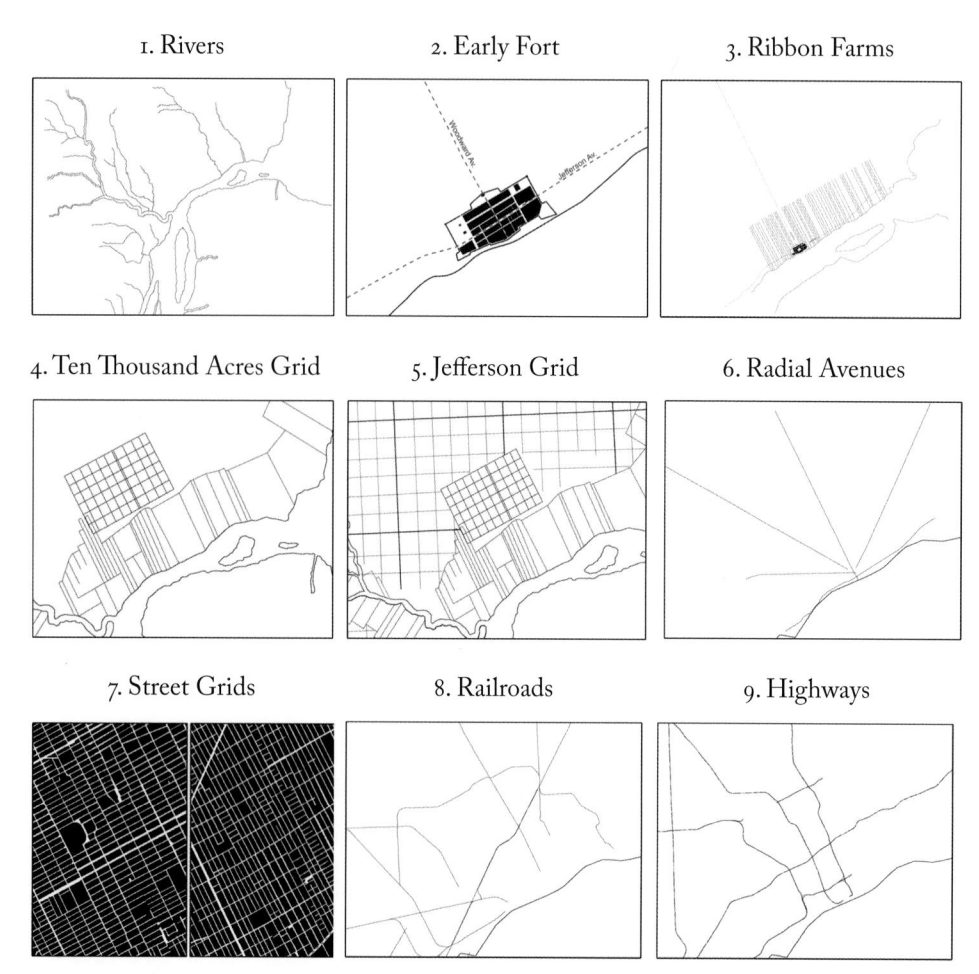

FIGURE 2.14 The nine systems that characterize the morphology of Detroit's development, missing only the effects of the city's redevelopment policies. *Source: Bekkering and Liu.*

partial construction below grade, which necessitated extensive excavations much wider than the highways themselves, results in destruction of existing homes and streets of areas as wide as two or three blocks, and near downtown Hastings Street, a historic African American commercial sector, has been obliterated all together (Thomas 2013, p. 21) (see Figure 2.15).

In addition to these nine structuring systems, the many plans for redevelopment of older or physically deteriorated neighborhoods, particularly those located in the central portion of the city and near key institutions, form together a tenth influence on the form of the city. As the city government generally conceived these redevelopment plans for different parts of the city over a series of decades, with some of the projects not finished according to plan, it is not possible to show their effects in one schematic drawing. However, Thomas elaborates on this system and describes its evolution in chapter 3, offering a partial mapping of several such efforts. (See also Thomas 2013.)

Another determining system for the morphology of the city that deserves some attention here is the streetcar system—though it largely followed existing street patterns, was eliminated in 1956, and has left almost no visible traces

in many American cities, the highways demolished some areas of the city that were low income and thus cheaper to buy; areas where residents had no clout, such as high-minority neighborhoods; and places where the main criteria was road efficiency rather than neighborhood preservation. In the case of Detroit, the

in the city. The horse-drawn streetcars were replaced by electricity-powered cars in 1893 (Larsen et al. 2006; Schramm 2006). The plan of the streetcar lines at their peak shows the importance of the combination of the grid, which allowed for easily implemented loops, and the diagonal avenues, which allowed for fast long-distance services to what were then the outskirts of the city (see Figure 2.16). Some sources have suggested that the automobile companies deliberately put the streetcar lines out of business. Regardless

FIGURE 2.15 Early aerial photograph of the building of John C. Lodge Expressway, now State Highway MI-10, 1950.
Source: Michigan State Highway Department, Bentley Historical Museum, University of Michigan, LeRoy Barnett photograph collection, Box 1, image b1004014.

of whether they did try to do so, suburbanization, the availability of automobiles, and highway construction reduced the system's use to the point where its functionality became compromised, especially so when more and more of the factories were out of reach of the streetcar system (Schramm 2006). Even when the need for public transport grew with the size of the city and the increase of the low-income and elderly portion of the inhabitants who could not afford a car or drive a car, respectively, the metropolitan area did not develop a regional light-rail public transportation system. As Detroit became a segregated region, a majority black city surrounded by majority white suburbs, political battles over regional concerns often succumbed to race baiting and local parochialism. A regional transit system was, for a long time, a casualty of this political dynamic: a key proposal emerged in 1972, but lack of metropolitan cooperation—as required for federal funds—killed it; and a 2002 proposal failed because outgoing Governor John Engler refused to sign the legislation into law. After a 2011 proposal, a Regional Transit Authority for metropolitan Detroit was finally enabled by state law in 2012 and established in 2013. Meanwhile, automobiles and the highway system remained the dominant form of transportation.

GROWTH AND DECLINE ON THE SCALE OF THE CITY

The morphology of the city and how this developed in time can be examined using the two series of maps that follow; one series is on the scale of the city and the other is on the scale of the metropolitan area. The time

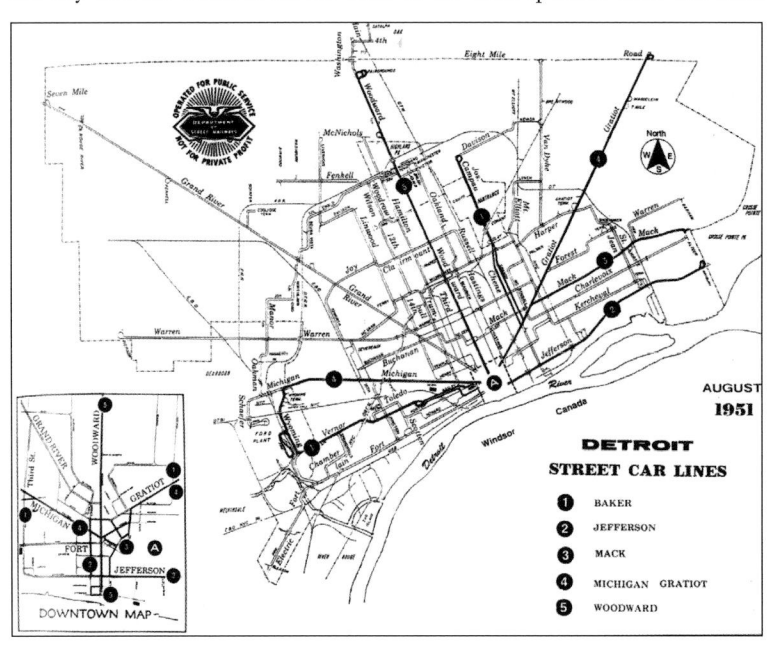

FIGURE 2.16 The streetcar system in 1951.
Source: Schramm, K. (2006). Detroit's street railways: Images of rail. Chicago, IL: Arcadia Publishing, p. 79. (Detroit Street Railways Commission)

MAPPING DETROIT: "The City of Holes" 41

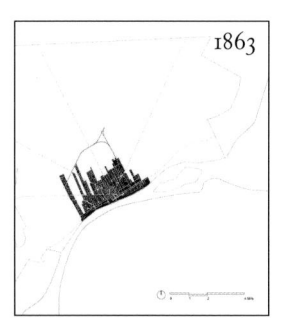

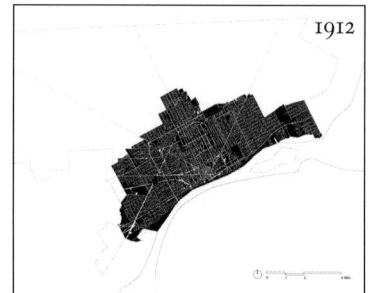

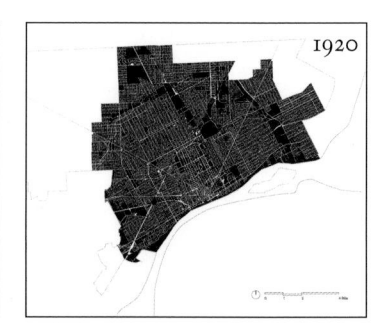

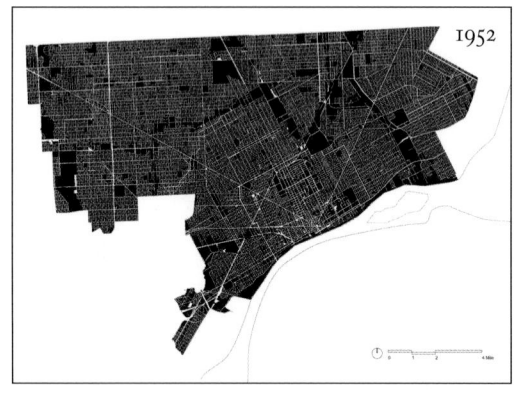

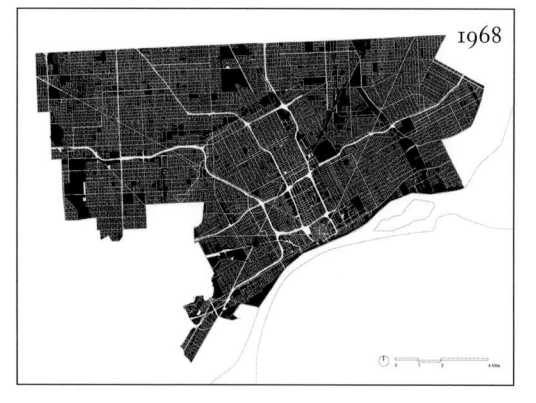

periods of the maps in the series on the scale of the city (see Figure 2.17) were selected based partly on major changes in size and morphology of the city, and partly on the availability of historical maps in the three University of Michigan map libraries. The series starts at the end of the period covered by *Frontier Metropolis*, with the redrawing of a map by John Farmer dated 1835 found in the Detroit Public Library.

The first maps of the growth of the city show a small town that measured in 1835 less than 1 by 2 miles (1.6 by 3.2 km), clearly based on the double patte d'oie structure, with almost all of the present downtown laid out and eastern and western extensions on several of the former ribbon farms. In 1863, this pattern had extended to an area of about 2 by 4 miles (3.2 by 6.4 km). The urban area had become at least five times as big in less than thirty years, and maps show the first railroads, largely outside the city. In 1895 the area within

FIGURE 2.17 Series of maps on the scale of the city between 1835 and 2009. This series of maps shows the progression up until the present situation of holes in the urban fabric.
Source: Bekkering and Liu.

the city limits of that moment is filled to the brim: approximately 3 by 6 miles (4.8 by 9.7 km). Urban growth is very strong during this period. The same is true for the situation in 1912, when the distances from downtown to the city limits in the east and the west, and from the river to the north, are more than 6 miles (almost 10 km). As mentioned before, developed areas would lie outside the city limits during this time period, offering reasons for enlarging these political boundaries soon after. (For this overflow, compare the series of maps on the metropolitan scale, from 1921 on, in Figure 2.18.) By 1920 the city had reached more than half of its present size. Thirty-two years later, in 1952, all of the area within the present city limits was filled up: 139 square miles (357 km²), 29 miles (47 km) east to west, and 13 miles (21 km) north to south. From that moment on, the morphology of the city did not change, except for the destruction caused by the installment of the highway system in the ten years between 1958 and 1968, the redevelopment plans, and the large sports stadia and casinos built downtown. The lack of city boundary expansion was due directly to state annexation and home rule laws, which froze the city limits of Detroit and made it impossible to annex surrounding territory (Thomas 2013). The interstate highways fragmented the city and isolated the downtown area from the surrounding neighborhoods. Some highways were built below ground level, similar to open-air tunnels, meaning that the floor of the city could relatively easily be continued across the highways by building additional bridges or bridging over larger stretches in the future, but the current structure severely distances neighborhoods from each other.

The final map in Figure 2.17, of 2009, shows The City of Holes (see also Figure 2.3): black portions are the built-up parts of the urban blocks (not the buildings, but the lots with buildings in use on them); white portions are, in addition to public open space, the great many vacant lots spread all over the city. Relative concentrations of vacancies are in the neighborhoods east and west of downtown and New Center, around West Grand Boulevard and around the well-to-do Indian Village subdivision east of downtown; south and east of Coleman A. Young International Airport; in the far southeast just north of Jefferson Avenue; and in the far north just west of Interstate Highway 75. These are the areas where the negative effects of vacancy are most apparent, often with dilapidated or partially demolished buildings still more or less standing and posing a real danger to their surroundings. The visual impact ranges from surreal, where the municipality or neighbors have taken some action to tidy things up, to flat-out frightening, where the scene resembles cities after destructive acts of war, with empty and burned-out buildings and buildings literally falling apart. Private citizens and companies own many of these properties, but the city's efforts to force the owners to maintain them have seriously faltered, in large part because of insufficient funds to maintain accurate records and to hire enforcement staff for such a large territory. Even where the city has taken the trouble to break down the dilapidated buildings that have fallen into public ownership, and where it has flattened out the lots, sown grass, and regularly had it mowed—which are difficult tasks, given the city's financial state—the images take away one's breath. It is hard to imagine how this spatial disruption can be repaired within one or even two generations. It is indeed hard to decide whether repair would be advisable: certainly not to reconstruct the city as it was. Such would be impossible because of the severely diminished economic base for the city at the moment. It is probably also not desirable, because problems include its spatial form and endless repetition of small freestanding homes on endless straight streets—a format that was doomed for decline—and because of environmental issues will be even more doomed in the future.

GROWTH ON THE SCALE OF THE METROPOLITAN AREA

On the metropolitan scale, we chose time periods for the series of maps illustrating increasing urbanization in order to demonstrate major changes. However, the availability of historical maps somewhat limited this choice. (See Appendices 2.A and 2.C.) As indicated earlier, we defined the metropolitan area of today as stretching from Mount Clemens to Ann Arbor, and from Waterford to Trenton (see Figure 2.8).

In 1921 the urban area extended somewhat beyond the city limits in the east and in the north. There were no suburbs away from the city, as some other American cities had by this time. One might say that Detroit did not need them (yet), as the city had been built throughout with freestanding homes with their own gardens. The growth between 1921 and 1935, as shown by the successive maps, is almost too hard to believe. The built-up area more than

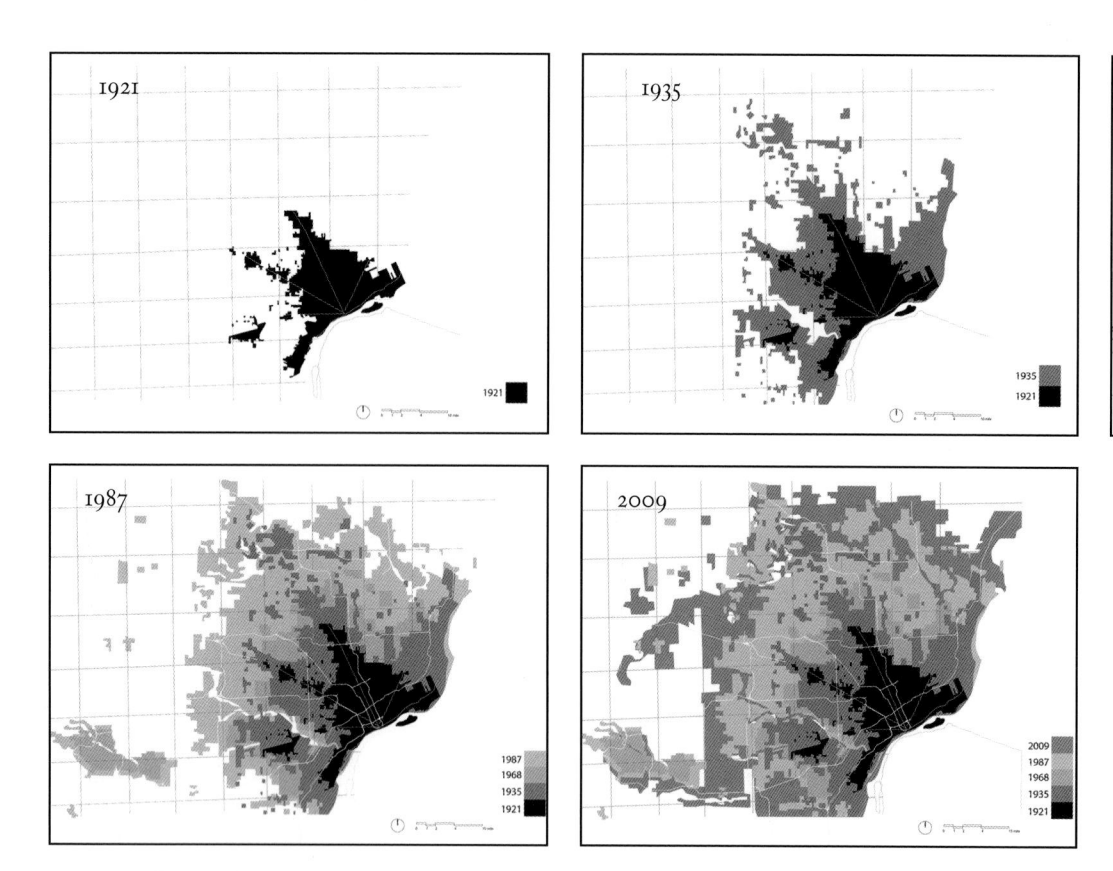

FIGURE 2.18 Series of maps on the scale of the metropolitan area between 1921 and 2009.
Source: Bekkering and Liu.

doubled in less than eight years in a period that included the Great Depression. A comparable doubling of the built-up area occurred between 1935 and 1987, in fifty-two years. Since then, the growth of the urbanized area has continued, as the 2009 map shows. So, even if the excessive consumption of land had its high point in the first quarter of the twentieth century, the spreading out of the metropolitan area continues until today and will not be stopped very soon, as the United States has no effective urban containment or regional planning system, and the state of Michigan does not have systems in place to regulate urban sprawl. The frightening specter of the Greater Detroit in Doxiadis's plans threatens to become reality, as drawn in his 1970 map "Where the Detroit Area Is Going" (Doxiadis 1970). It shows an amoeba that extends beyond Jackson to Battle Creek in the east, beyond Flint to Bay City in the north, beyond Monroe to Toledo, Ohio in the south and into Canada, but population growth does not warrant this much use of land (see Figure 2.19).

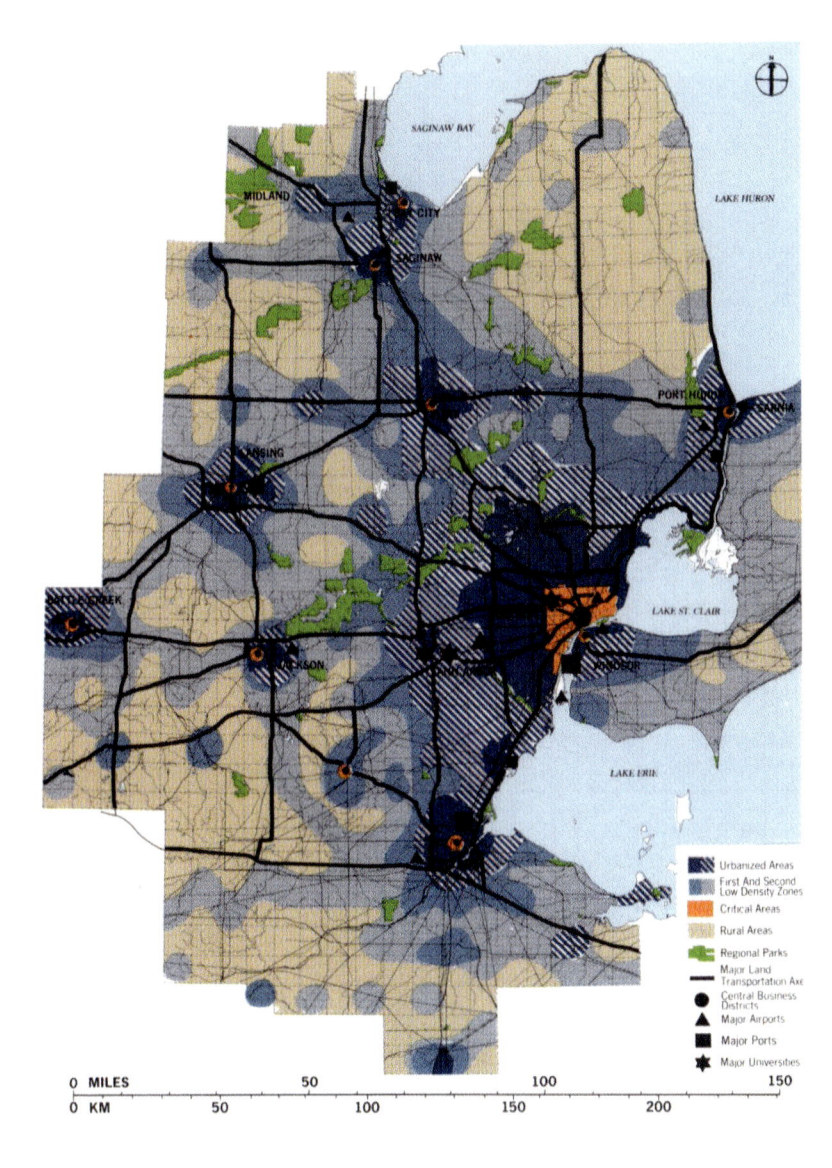

FIGURE 2.19 Where the Detroit area is going.
Source: Courtesy of DTE Energy, from Doxiadis, C. A. (1970). A concept for future development. Emergence and growth of an urban region: The developing urban Detroit area (Vol. 3). Detroit, MI: Detroit Edison Co., p. 113.

APPENDIX 2.A: THE MAPPING PROCESS AND TECHNIQUE

Fitting the Maps to Each Other

It was expected and immediately apparent that the historical maps collected do not fit exactly with recent maps or, for that matter, each other. We obviously needed a base map for the series; we derived this from the United States Geographical Survey Map of the Detroit area of 2009. The level of aggregation was digitally raised from the individual parcel to the urban block to create the pattern of streets or rather public space, and blocks of private lots. We needed to impose some deformations in order to fit the historical maps to the base map because of the inaccuracy that was inevitable at the time of the drawing of these maps in the eighteenth and nineteenth centuries, and because of differences in cartographical projection, as more recent aerial photographs (e.g., Google) and maps do not fit exactly either. So, by necessity, the series of maps produced holds interpretations and knowledgeable guesses by the authors.

The Legend

The legend used to redraw the maps was explicitly intended to result in maps that are readable when printed on normal book or magazine pages in black and white. The obvious choice might seem to have been figure-ground maps, not only because of the status they have in the discipline of urbanism, going back to Giambattista Nolli's *Nova Pianta di Roma* of 1748, but also in keeping with the series of maps of downtown Detroit by Doxiadis/Smets/Plunz/Kelbaugh (see Figure 2.1). For several reasons, this approach was not feasible, causing us to choose street pattern drawings instead of figure-ground drawings. These actually appear to be figure-ground drawings at a larger level of scale, thus strongly reducing the information and focusing on the morphology of the city.

MAPPING DETROIT: "The City of Holes" 45

Limitations

The way in which we produced the series of maps in this research has limitations and contains assumptions. The most important limitation appears in the series showing the growth of the city up to the area within the present city limits. Of course, Detroit, as all other major cities, is part of a much larger metropolitan area where the different parts have a certain inner coherence and, to a large degree, depend on each other. It was necessary for us to choose, again for reasons of producing readable maps, to make the two series separate: we created the first relatively more detailed series on the level of scale of the city and then a second with further-reduced detail on the scale of the metropolitan area. This second series depicts built-up areas and only the very basic infrastructure of (the extensions of) the avenues radiating from downtown and the highway system.

A second limitation for the mapping is that the city limits have changed several times. Around the moments of change, the area within the former city limits was fairly well filled up (which is why it was necessary to enlarge city boundaries), and areas of new construction certainly extended beyond the city limits of that moment. Our maps on the scale of the city from 1921 on do not show this overflow; those on the metropolitan scale do.

A next point to be mentioned is that the two municipalities of Highland Park and Hamtramck are completely surrounded by the city of Detroit. As they are obviously part of the urban system around them, we have included the graphic information for their areas in our maps. Also, we have given the highway system of the city graphical representation as what it is: a veritable spider web of elongated holes in the city, not just lines without dimensions.

We had available, as a data source, the digital information in GIS format of the ownership of all 387,000 lots of Detroit within city limits, researched by a group of University of Michigan students in the fall of 2006.[4] The students' map shows parcels owned by the government (the City of Detroit, Wayne County, and the State of Michigan), excluding public parks, police and fire stations, public schools and libraries, city hall, and other still-functioning public institutions. As the map shows no difference between vacant lots and lots with vacant or partly demolished buildings still standing, it gives a more complete impression of "the holes in the city" formed by about 52,000 publicly owned properties. This information we superimposed on the base map to create our map of The City of Holes (see Figure 2.3).

Digital Manipulation in Redrawing the Historical Maps

To transform maps with different projections into a series of consistent maps with the same projection, scale, and orientation was a challenging task, needing the help of rather advanced graphic computer techniques. As explained before, the historical maps do not fit exactly to the recent maps.

For the series of maps on the scale of the city, we dealt with this problem by deducting, as far as we could do so, the urban growth of a certain period from the most recent map with standard projection, which was our base map. With the help of the staff of the division of the Spatial and Numerical Data Services Lab of the University of Michigan at A. Alfred Taubman College (hereafter SAND Lab North),[5] we were able to work with the U.S. Geological Survey parcel-based GIS data for the Greater Detroit Area of 2009. This data is on the scale of taxable parcels and thus includes a lot of information irrelevant for our maps. SAND Lab North helped us to aggregate parcels into urban building blocks using the GIS toolbox. The new maps show the islands of the building blocks in black and the network of public and other open space in white: the simplest legend possible, referring to the black and white of figure-ground drawings but not the same. We placed the historical maps of the selected years over the base map, and adjusted these in scale and orientation. They cannot be perfectly matched to each other, but it is not difficult to relate specific parts and spots in different maps to each other. By reducing the built-up urban areas of the 2009 building block map through referring to the lesser built-up areas in the historical maps, introducing distortion where necessary, we generated the maps going back in time until 1968, the earliest map showing the completed highway system. We used a 1952 map to add the many blocks that were torn down for the construction of the highways, as shown in the 1968 map. With this new base map of 1952, we reconstructed the maps backward until 1835 following the same procedure. This was necessary because, to our regret, and contrary to our expectation, almost no U.S. Geographical Survey maps for the metropolitan area are digitally accessible. The Hatcher Library only had the 1968 part of the series digitized as a central measuring moment for the urban development of the area, including the then-finished highway system. In some cases, individual sheets of the Geographical Survey map of the area at a specific year of redrawing are missing. These seem to have never been produced.

The Metropolitan Scale

We generated the series of maps of the metropolitan urban system separately from the series of the city scale, and from different sources. We found most in the Map Department of the Hatcher Library at the University of Michigan, but some are from standard commercial road atlases (see Appendix 2.C). Some had the same scale, but many did not. For the railroads and highways on the maps we used GIS data of the transportation system provided by the Southeast Michigan Council of Governments (SEMCOG). Again with the help of SAND Lab North, we transformed these into vector files that can be manipulated. The maps show the growth and development of the suburbs. Built-up areas were defined by drawing by hand on top of the different maps according to visual assessment of the density of built-up areas and of streets and roads. We scanned and then transformed these sketches to the same scale and digital format as the other maps. Because these maps only show built-up areas, and do not include any detailed information on geographical elements or the transportation networks, the distortion due to different projections is less apparent.

APPENDIX 2.B: MAPS SELECTED FROM *FRONTIER METROPOLIS*

1702: Fort Pontchartrain
Plan du fort du Détroit construit par le sieur de la Mothe du Cadillac. Author: probably Captain Antoine Laumette, dit de Lamothe Cadillac. Collection: Centre des Archives d'Outre-mer, Aix-en Provence, Archives Nationales, France (Dunnigan 2001, p. 24).

1749: Fort (enlarged)
Plan du fort du Détroit. Scitué a Six Lieux de Lentre de La rivière du détroit, Par les 42 Degres 12. minutes 24. Secondes a La Coste du Nord de la dite Rivière. Author: Ensign Gaspard-Joseph Chaussegros de Léry. Collection Centre des Archives d'Outre-mer, Aix-en Provence, Archives Nationales, France (Dunnigan 2001, p. 38).

1749: Agricultural Strips
Carte de La Riviere du detroit depuis Le Lac Erie jus'ques au Lac Ste Claire. Author: C.E. Hickman after Lieutenant Gaspard-Joseph Chaussegros de Léry. Date of map ca. 1930 after a work of 1752 with a notation postdating 1755. Collection: Clements Library, University of Michigan, Ann Arbor (Dunnigan 2001, p. 45).

1760: Fort (further enlarged)
Plan of the fort at Detroit 1760. Author: Lieutenant Diedrich Brehm. Burton Historical Collection: Detroit Public Library (Dunnigan 2001, p. 52).

1796: The Old Town of Detroit
The Old Town of Detroit. A Map Showing Its Exact Location on the Site of the City of Detroit. Interesting Statistics and Leading Political and Historical Events. Single sheet publication, compiled by R.F. Roberts

after Thomas Smith and Lieutenant Ralph Willett Adye. Collection: Clements Library, University of Michigan, Ann Arbor (Dunnigan 2001, p. 94).

1807: New Plan for the City of Detroit
A Plan of the City of Detroit. Drawn by Albijah Hull, Surveyor of Michigan, January 1807. Collection: Detroit Public Library (Dunnigan 2001, p. 117).

1825: Ten Thousand Acre Grid
Map of the Surveyed Part of the Territory of Michigan. Author: O. Risdon. Collection: Clements Library, University of Michigan, Ann Arbor (Dunnigan 2001, p. 175).

1835: City of Detroit in the State of Michigan
City of Detroit in the State of Michigan by John Farmer, District Surveyor. Author: John Farmer, lithograph by C. B. and J. R. Graham. Collection: Detroit Public Library (Dunnigan 2001, p. 194).

APPENDIX 2.C: ADDITIONAL MAPS USED

Rivers
Map of the Surveyed Part of the Territory of Michigan. Author: Orange Risdon. Collection: Clements Library, University of Michigan, Ann Arbor (Dunnigan 2001, p. 175).

Railroads and Highways
Current Transit Routes Southeast Michigan, 2009. Retrieved from GIS map data from Southeast Michigan Council of Governments, www.semcog.org/MapCatalog_Transportation.aspx

City Scale Series
1863
Map in the collection of the University of Michigan Harlan Hatcher Graduate Map Library (hereafter Hatcher Library).

1895
Map in the collection of the Hatcher Library.

1912
Map of the City of Detroit 1912, showing streets with house numbers; street car lines; and the location of the principal industrial, educational and religious buildings, drawn and published by Sauer Bros 7 Frydrych. Collection: Hatcher Library.

1921
Wm. Sauer's Maps. Exclusively sold by Sanders-Burridge Co. 1921. Collection: Hatcher Library.

1952
Authentic Map of Detroit and Environs, copyright National Lithograph Co., Detroit, MI. Collection: Hatcher Library.

1968
Nine combined geological survey maps, mapped, edited, and published by the U.S. Geological Survey in Cooperation with State of Michigan agencies, control by USGS, USC&GS, U.S. Lake Survey and City of Detroit, planimetry by photogrammetric methods from aerial photographs, topography by planet surveys 1938, revised from aerial photographs taken in 1967. Collection: Hatcher Library.

2009
U.S. Geological Survey map, parcel information of Detroit, data provided by SAND LAB of the University of Michigan.

Metropolitan Scale Series

1921
Wm. Sauer's Maps. Exclusively sold by Sanders-Burridge Co. 1921. Collection: Hatcher Library.

1935
Hearne Brother's Map of Greater Detroit 1935, Polyconic Projection. Copyright by Hearne Brothers. Collection: Burton Library.

1968
Nine combined geological survey maps, mapped, edited, and published by the United States of America Geological Survey in Cooperation with State of Michigan agencies, control by USGS, USC&GS, U.S. Lake Survey and City of Detroit, planimetry by photogrammetric methods from aerial photographs, topography by planet surveys 1938, revised from aerial photographs taken in 1967. Collection: Hatcher Library.

1987
Delorme Michigan Atlas 1987. Collection: Burton Library.

2009
Delorme Michigan Atlas 2009. Personal collection of Professor Henco Bekkering.

NOTES

Each of the following has contributed in her or his way to the ideas in this research: Bob Beckley, Margaret Dewar, Eric Dueweke, Robert Fishman, Joseph Grengs, Larissa Larsen, Jonathan Levine, Roy Strickland, and June Manning Thomas, all of the A. Alfred Taubman College of Architecture and Urban Planning, University of Michigan; Jen Green and Nicole Scholtz of the staff of the Spatial and Numerical Data Services Lab of the University of Michigan at Taubman College (SAND Lab North); Karl Longstreth of the Harlan Hatcher Graduate Map Library at the University of Michigan; and Brian Dunnigan of the Clements Library, also at the University of Michigan.

1. Editor's note: In late 2013–14, a well-funded Blight Removal Task Force carried out a new survey of properties in the city; this data is not referenced in this chapter. Their 2014 report is available at http://report.timetoendblight.org.
2. The first three of these drawings (1916, 1950, and 1960) had been published by Constantinos A. Doxiadis in his three-volume series (Doxiadis 1970, p. 157). Smets and Plunz, omitting the original 1969 drawing, added one of 1994, made according to Marcel Smets by Plunz or his students. Smets's article gave a concise description of the growth and decline of Detroit up to that time, but did not include any other maps.
3. In 1785 Thomas Jefferson, president of the United States, created and implemented the subdivision of the Western Territories in squares of one mile in both directions, orientation north-south and east-west. This simple but powerful system continues to affect the spatial order of the country to this day. In Detroit it shows as the main grid pattern of the roads and streets. Previously, under French rule, there was a similar but smaller system: the Ten Thousand Acres Grid. This system was installed beyond the strips for agrarian allotments on the Detroit River, taking its orientation from these strips. The grid runs parallel to Jefferson Avenue and the Detroit River.
4. The class was taught by Professor Margaret Dewar and Eric Dueweke of the Urban and Regional Planning Program in Taubman College, University of Michigan.
5. We'd like to thank staffers Jen Green and Nicole Scholtz.

REFERENCES

Beckley, B. (2009). Planning, management and disposition [PowerPoint slides]. Genesee Land Bank. Darden, J., Hill, R. C., Thomas, J. M., and Thomas, R. W. (1987). *Detroit: Race and uneven development.* Philadelphia, PA: Temple University Press.

Darden, J., Hill, R. C., Thomas, J. M., and Thomas, R. (1987). *Detroit: Race and uneven development*. Philadelphia, PA: Temple University Press.

Daskalakis, G., Waldheim, C., and Young, J. (Eds.). (2001). *Stalking Detroit*. Barcelona, Spain: Actar.

Detroit Data Collaborative. (2010). *Detroit residential parcel survey.* Retrieved from www.detroitparcelsurvey.org

Doxiadis, C. A. (1970). A concept for future development. *Emergence and growth of an urban region: The developing urban Detroit area* (Vol. 3). Detroit, MI: Detroit Edison.

Volume 1: Analysis, 1966

Volume 2: Future Alternatives, 1967

Volume 3: A Concept for Future Development, 1970

Dunnigan, B. L. (2001). *Frontier metropolis: Picturing early Detroit, 1701–1838*. Detroit, MI: Wayne State University Press.

Farmer, S. (1884). *The history of Detroit and Michigan*. Detroit, MI: S. Farmer & Co.

Kelbaugh, D. S., Strickland, R., Dueweke, E., et al. (2007). *5D: Adding three dimensions to downtown Detroit*. Detroit Design Workshop 2007. Ann Arbor, MI: A. Alfred Taubman College of Architecture and Urban Planning, University of Michigan.

Larsen, L., Leinberger, C., et al. (2006). *Planning for the strategic development of downtown Detroit, Michigan*. A University of Michigan Interdisciplinary Graduate Student Capstone Project, December 2006. Ann Arbor: A. Alfred Taubman College of Architecture and Urban Planning, University of Michigan.

Martin, E. A. (1993). *Detroit and the great migration 1916–1929*. Ann Arbor: Bentley Historical Library Printing Services, The University of Michigan. Bentley Bulletin no. 40.

Plunz, R. (1996, April). Detroit is everywhere. *Architecture, 85*(4), 55–61.

Schramm, K. (2006). *Detroit's street railways. Images of rail*. Chicago, IL: Arcadia Publishing.

Smets, M. (1996). Detroit als wegwerpstad. Beeld van een company town / Detroit—a disposable town. *Archis, 3*, 66–80.

Smithson, A. (1997). The center city full of holes. *Architectural Association Quarterly, 9*(2/3), 4–23.

Sugrue, T. J. (1996). *The origins of the urban crisis: Race and inequality in postwar Detroit*. Princeton, NJ: Princeton University Press.

Thomas, J. M. (2013). *Redevelopment and race: Planning a finer city in postwar Detroit* (2nd ed). Detroit, MI: Wayne State University Press.

Woodford, A. M. (2001). *This is Detroit: 1701–2001*. Detroit, MI: Wayne State University Press.

3

REDEVELOPMENT IN DETROIT
Spatial Evolution

JUNE MANNING THOMAS

Not only did physical, environmental, and social changes affect the city of Detroit and its evolution; so too did public-sector efforts. Much of the change taking place after the middle twentieth century was well beyond the reach of such efforts, because larger forces such as metropolitan decentralization and industrial decline prevailed, but nevertheless city leaders made several attempts to counteract dominant trends. For example, through planning and redevelopment staff, city leaders directed reconstruction of specific parcels of land, usually made up of dozens of acres. Although these efforts were not successful in their intent of allowing the city to survive as a vibrant and growing metropolis, they nonetheless had a decided influence on the city's morphology. They also created at least some form of social and economic stability in selected parts of the city.

Detroit's redevelopment agenda was no different from the agendas of other large U.S. cities. What was unusual about Detroit was that its public and private leaders only fitfully succeeded in accomplishing their goals. Typically, in other cities, local political and economic powers joined forces to buttress key areas for growth and redevelopment. Urban regimes—fairly stable, long-term coalitions between public sector and private interests that transcended local political administrations—supported such initiatives (Mossberger and Stoker 2001; Orr and Stoker 1994; Stone 1989). Detroit, however, lacked a strong enough urban regime to support sustained growth or to reverse the city's contracting fortunes. Its "pro-growth coalition," a broad label for the collection of politicians, developers, civic leaders, journalists, and others who often promote civic growth (Logan and Molotch 1987), was fragmented and sporadic. Furthermore, Detroit's redevelopment operated in a metropolitan context of unusually high racial conflict, government support for suburbanization, and deindustrialization.

This situation undergirds this chapter's overview of city planning and development efforts from the 1930s to 2013. These efforts did not reverse the flow of people and capital outward to suburban areas, but they created islands of relative prosperity and activity that turned out to be very important for the welfare of the city and its residents. Rather than judge city redevelopment by its ability to meet goals dating from the mid-twentieth century, such as eliminating "slums" and "blight"—out-of-fashion terms used at that time to denote dilapidated housing and areas failing to remain economically viable—it may be more useful to judge such efforts by looking at the presence and impact of their targeted projects. From this perspective, the original redevelopment projects were remarkable in many ways, in part because of the great political, economic, and social odds against success that faced them.

Development efforts in the early part of the twenty-first century built on earlier projects, whether located in the central business district (CBD) or near institutional venues such as the Detroit Medical Center or the Detroit Institute of Arts. However, some of the city's more recent redevelopment efforts have not always made a physical or economic difference in the city's fortunes. This is true because of the nature of changing federal legislation and of general urban conditions, but also because of social and political considerations. It became increasingly difficult to target waning community development resources effectively, for reasons both logistical and political. Logistical challenges included the large areas of city need compared with relatively modest resources; political dilemmas included the nature of local decision making, continuing racial and class disunity, and metropolitan fragmentation. One tentative resolution of these dilemmas was to move leadership for redevelopment away from local government and into the corporate, nonprofit, and foundation realms, a strange twist for a weak-regime city. A part of this solution most recently has been to focus investment in the "greater downtown" area, including the CBD, Midtown, and riverfront—a strategy that left much of the rest of the city weakly tended and, in some ways, both alleviated and aggravated racial tension.

We will review redevelopment during four major periods defined by national urban programs and by local political events. The first period was the public housing era, beginning in the late 1930s. The urban renewal era covers redevelopment enabled under legislation from 1949 until approximately 1974, as well as the Model Cities (later known as Model Neighborhoods) program from 1966 to 1974. The third period started in 1974 with launching of the Community Development Block Grant (CDBG) program and the inauguration of Mayor Coleman Young (1974–94). The fourth period started in 1994 with the inauguration of Mayor Dennis Archer and Detroit's successful winning of Empowerment Zone (EZ) designation. This section will end in the year 2013. It is quite possible that, in the future, historians will note that a new period of time in the evolution of the city's redevelopment began in 2013, for several reasons.[1]

The urban renewal period, from 1949 until 1974, coincides roughly with an era of pervasive population loss for the largest U.S. cities (Beauregard 2009). Between 1950 and 1980, forty out of the fifty largest U.S. central cities lost population. (From 1980 to 2000, only eighteen of the top fifty declined in population size.) Detroit was among the eighteen that struggled during this time, and its population loss was relatively large compared to many other cities in its size category.

By 2010, Detroit had less than two-fifths its 1950 population size and much loss of tax base, but still contained 139 square miles. This situation required Detroit's leaders to consider such options as shutting down portions of the city from services or development support. In light of such circumstances, our claim that Detroit's postwar redevelopment agenda was partially successful seems quite ironic, if not delusional. However, as we will describe, the redevelopment did succeed in some ways, due partially to conditions that no longer exist, and haven't for a long time.

LOW-COST FAMILY HOUSING

The first phase of Detroit's redevelopment involved public housing, meaning housing built and managed by local governmental housing authorities. Detroit set up a housing commission first funded by a 1933 grant from the Federal Emergency Housing Corporation (Conot 1974). The commission's first director, Josephine Gomon, only served for two years but set the direction for a housing and redevelopment program that was visionary and far reaching (Thomas 2009).

At first, laudatory newspaper articles cheered the rehousing initiative, launched in splendid fashion by Eleanor Roosevelt's presence at the 1935 groundbreaking for the first project, Brewster Homes. The newspapers openly derided city council members who opposed the new housing. But soon squabbles arose over racial characteristics of the complexes, weakening the fragile local coalition. As in other cities, public housing became a tool for racial segregation. The city government built Brewster Homes for blacks only because Gomon realized that opposition by the Wider Woodward Association, white business owners located on the city's main thoroughfare, would kill the project if it were not segregated. Gomon gave black leaders the choice of either racially segregated housing or none at all; they chose segregation. When she left office, less well-connected program leaders replaced her (Thomas 2009). The commission's 1942 attempt to place the black residents of the Sojourner Truth housing project in a resistant white neighborhood led to violent repercussions by whites and contributed to the bloody 1943 race riots (Capeci 1984).

The first public housing developments, Brewster Homes for blacks and Jeffries Homes for whites, reflected progressive thinking about the spatial arrangements necessary to protect the neighborhood purpose of such housing (Bauman 1987). The first set of units included clusters of townhouses and low-rise walk-up apartment buildings, appropriate for families with children, as well as playgrounds, all located close to convenient commercial facilities (Thomas 2009, 2013a). As conservative opposition in the U.S. Congress increasingly constrained funding, however, much U.S. public housing morphed into austere high-rise towers with insufficient elevators; such buildings were ripe environments for crime and gave families with children little outside access (Newman 1996). A national trend of loosened resident admission policies in the 1960s resulted in the destitute poor replacing the working poor in public housing buildings, and Detroit's units further ostracized the low-income, minority families that increasingly lived there as whites moved out. Surrounding neighborhoods did not benefit from those project sites, which were themselves sources of blight.

After the initial years, no sustained coalition of political or economic interests supported Detroit's public housing program. Instead local political leaders such as Albert Cobo, mayor from 1950 to 1957, attacked public housing and labor unions alike (Conot 1974; Sugrue 1996). The public housing program continued to expand fitfully, but, as elsewhere, maintenance funding did not keep pace with needs. By 1980 Mayor Coleman Young, Detroit's first black mayor, told an interviewer that the city's public housing units, which he numbered at 10,000, had outlived their purpose and that city government should not have to maintain them. Young actually began to dismantle the system and appointed a string of directors with no previous experience in housing (Shaw 2009). From 1979 until 1997 the U.S. Department of Housing and Urban Development designated Detroit's housing authority as "severely troubled" (Shaw 2009, p. 96). Residents' efforts to fight for their housing rights led to conflict and protests, apparent throughout the 1970s, 1980s, and early 1990s, but yielded little social change in low-income families' favor, except for a few efforts such as the 250 townhouses that the city government built in 1994 to replace the original Brewster Homes (City of Detroit 2012).

In 1992, the federal government created HOPE VI, a program designed to redevelop the nation's most troubled public housing projects into mixed-income housing. By 2009, the Detroit Housing Commission had used HOPE VI to rehabilitate or build new housing in complexes such as Woodbridge Estates (formerly Jeffries Homes), The Villages at Parkside (formerly Parkside), and Gardenview Estates (formerly Herman Gardens) (City of Detroit 2009a). However, these clusters of impressive new townhouses and apartments required demolition of much older housing stock that was affordable to low-income people. By 2009 the commission supported 5,800 families in a federal voucher program that placed families in non-housing-authority buildings in any of five counties (City of Detroit 2009a). Some older project sites stood vacant and un-rehabilitated for years, such as the Douglass Homes high-rise towers and townhouses located immediately north of the CBD.

The total number of existing housing authority units is unclear, but simple addition of published numbers suggests perhaps 2,500 units in 2012, some of them vacant (City of Detroit 2012); see Figure 3.1.

The public housing program has faced many barriers and setbacks throughout its long history. Other programs picked up some of the slack. The federal Low Income Housing Tax Credit program (LIHTC), for example, provided subsidies through tax credits to private and nonprofit developers who met certain conditions. From 1987 to 2007, LIHTC supported construction or rehabilitation of over 10,000 low-income rental housing units (Deng 2013), but the program did not always support positive neighborhood development (Deng 2013; Thomas 2013b). The city's LIHTC inventory dwarfed the functional public housing stock, much of which was devoted to the elderly.

SLUMS, BLIGHT, AND TARGETING: 1949–74

Redevelopment as defined by the Housing Acts of 1949 and 1954 (which first used the nomenclature "urban renewal") and by the Model Cities program, under the Demonstration Cities and Metropolitan Development Act in 1966, required cities to apply for funds and then to use them in specific targeted areas. Whereas urban renewal addressed mainly physical demolition and rehabilitation, the Model Cities funding assisted a much broader socioeconomic agenda. Together, these programs made an indelible mark on the city.

In both 1944 and 1947 Detroit issued redevelopment plans that targeted key areas of the city, particularly the largely black community to the east of the CBD. According to city planners' reports, property values in this area had fallen to the point that the city government incurred high service costs not recouped by tax revenue. Merchants in the nearby CBD,

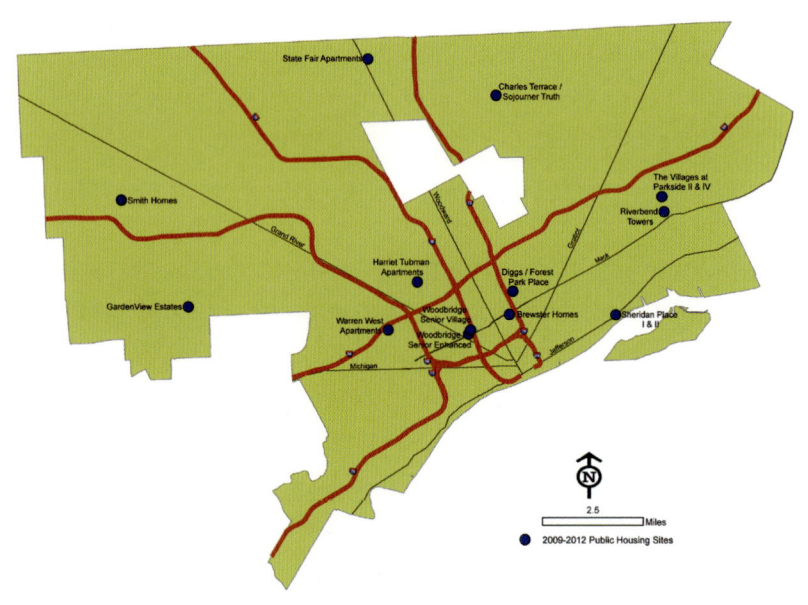

FIGURE 3.1 Public housing developments around downtown Detroit in 2012. *Source: Detroit Housing Commission, 2012. (Rob Linn and Terra Reed, Map Editors)*

furthermore, were concerned about the proximity of a black ghetto, which could not provide a middle-class white customer base for their businesses. These business interests formed an identifiable pro-growth contingent that urged the city government to act to clear the slums.

In 1947 the city government planned to use general funds for this purpose; it would recoup costs through increased tax revenues on land reconfigured for higher-value uses. Detroit aimed to reconstruct 100 acres a year, for a total of 10,000 acres in 100 years (City of Detroit 1947; Thomas 2013a). This acreage equals just under sixteen square miles, or 12 percent of city land. In order to accomplish this goal, the rest of the city would have to remain intact without public intervention.

Title I of the Housing Act of 1949 provided federal money for redevelopment, so the city government did not have to depend solely on local funding to support its plans. The city's first project, east of the CBD, was known initially as the Gratiot project (later renamed Lafayette Park). Nearby contiguous projects emerging in phases included Elmwood I, Elmwood II, and Elmwood III, for a total of 500 acres, all to the east of the CBD. To the west of the CBD was the industrial project Corktown, which cleared out largely white ethnic groups. The location of these two first projects confirms their important role in buttressing the economic security of CBD businesses.

The federal urban renewal program was flawed in several ways, and one of these was poor handling of resident displacement, a problem that emerged in Detroit as well. For its first phase, the city government removed 1900 families from the Gratiot site. The resulting dislocation drove existing residents into overcrowded nearby housing, caused emotional and psychological damage, and devastated many black-owned businesses. As in other cities, because federal relocation allowances were woefully inadequate, and because housing segregation left an insufficient number of units open to displaced black families, Detroit's urban renewal process led to a great deal of suffering and resentment on the part of the black community (Thomas 2013a).

Even so, the white development community was not anxious to rebuild on cleared "slum" land. The redevelopment initiative lacked strong support from area real estate developers and other potential pro-growth coalition members, and these projects took much longer to complete than anyone had anticipated. Whereas postwar leaders had thought they could clear 100 acres a year, many years of reconstruction completed much less than that amount. Private developers doubted that the market justified building housing for middle-class families on urban renewal land, and that market did indeed turn out to be limited. Low-income housing was limited as well, as only in later years was federal money available to build such housing on cleared sites. For the Lafayette Park project, over 1000 families had moved off the cleared land by 1952, but groundbreaking was delayed until 1956 (Thomas 2013a). Elmwood III, the last phase of this cluster of projects, gained federal approval for planning in 1965, and received federal commitment of funds in 1969 (Ernecq 1972), but the city government's brochure offering parcels for sale is dated 1974 (City of Detroit 1974). Elmwood III eventually filled out in the 1990s and 2000s using federal funding sources such as LIHTC, but some cleared parcels had sat vacant for years.

Lafayette Park is a mixed-use superblock project designed according to neighborhood unit principles. It contains modernist townhouses and towers, a well-landscaped linear park (Lafayette Plaisance) around which residential units cluster, shared parking lots for automobiles, and car-free pedestrian access to commercial facilities and an elementary school. Its overall design has stood the test of time, grounded as it is by the work of architect Mies van der Rohe and his design colleagues Ludwig Hilberseimer and Alfred Caldwell. The difficulty of carrying out this project, however, was characteristic of the national experiment in cleared-site redevelopment. Selecting sites involved targeting heavily populated and often minority-race residential areas in a time

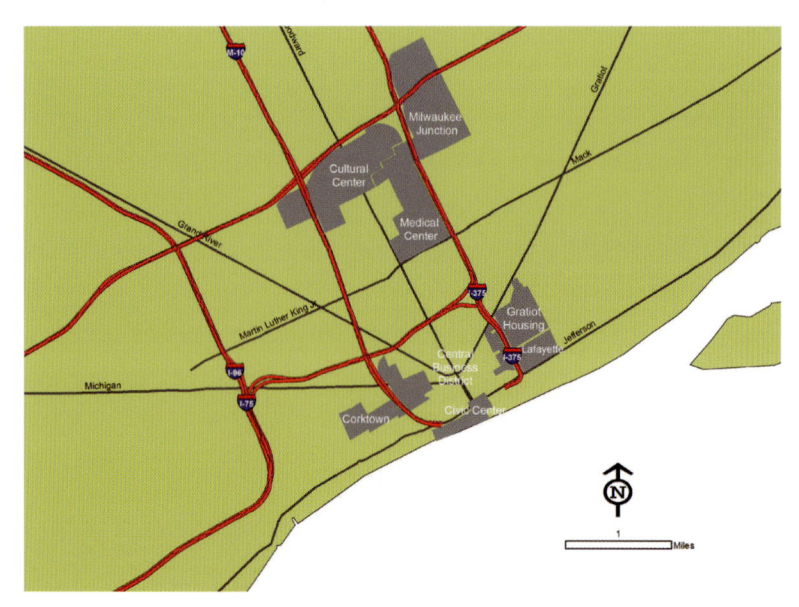

FIGURE 3.2 Redevelopment target areas in 1956. These were the areas that planners targeted for expenditure of urban renewal funds for clearance and redevelopment; shown are a mixture of residential, commercial, and industrial projects.
Source: Parkins, M. (1958). Neighborhood conservation: A pilot study. Detroit, MI: Detroit Plan Commission in cooperation with U.S. Housing and Home Finance Agency, p. 193. (Scott Pitera, Map Editor)

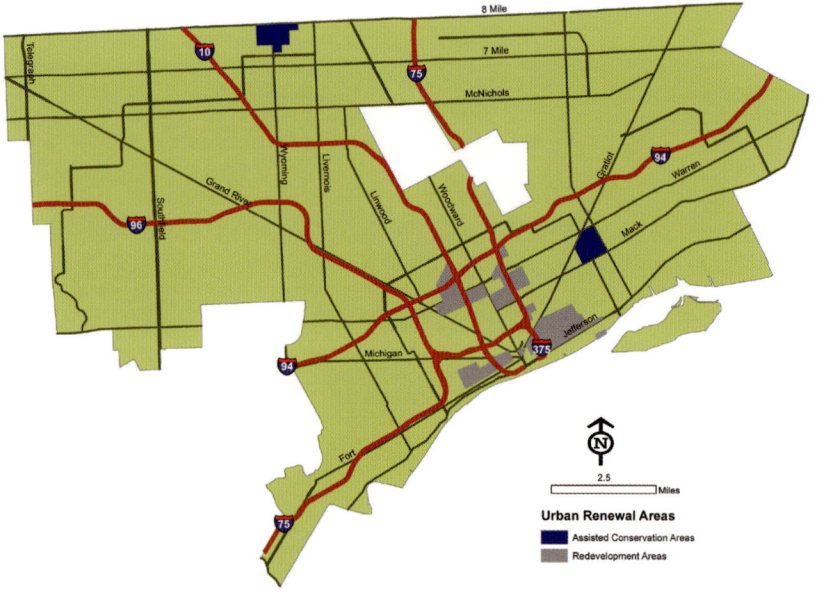

FIGURE 3.3 Urban renewal areas, 1966.
Source: City of Detroit (1966), Summary report: Detroit, the new city. Detroit, MI: Community Renewal Program. (Robert Linn, Map Editor)

of housing scarcity. Not until the early 1970s did federal legislation reform relocation procedures, improving monetary compensation for families and businesses. Many residents witnessed their neighborhoods bulldozed, only to see them lie fallow for many years, belying claims of "renewal."

However, in many ways this project cluster managed to accomplish what the city government intended. In particular, the first portion, Lafayette Park, cleared out housing units considered to be deteriorated and of little tax value; it replaced these with middle-class housing assumed to offer a stronger customer base for the nearby CBD and it anchored future redevelopment efforts extending to the east. As in many other U.S. cities during this era, the city government extended its renewal efforts to other housing, commercial, and industrial redevelopment sites as well. Only when it successfully engaged key institutions, however, such as the Detroit Medical Center and Wayne State University (originally part of the Cultural Center), did the city government gain strong partners. See Figure 3.2, a close-up of the central portion of the city, for an overview of these sites in 1956. Although boundary lines changed, this map shows the first phase of Detroit's redevelopment projects. Figure 3.3 shows how redevelopment project sites had changed by 1966, and includes as well assisted neighborhood conservation project areas.

Most noticeable about both maps is how consistent they are with how the city actually developed in project areas, replacing older, pre–World War II spatial fabric with newer streets, site design, and buildings, a process described in detail by Brent Ryan (2008). Those portions of central Detroit that contain intact areas not pockmarked with major vacancies are often former urban renewal sites. The exceptions include the Corktown industrial project, which never filled out as anticipated, and the Milwaukee Junction industrial project, which also faltered for many years (although another site just northeast of it now includes the Detroit-Hamtramck GM assembly plant constructed in the 1980s). The expressways sketched out were built, and the projects labeled Gratiot Housing and Lafayette Housing transformed rather directly into the Lafayette Park and Elmwood projects. The city government financed much of its civic center with its own funds or municipal bonds, but urban renewal paid for much of the other CBD projects, on sites that are now headquarters for such major businesses as Michigan Blue Cross Blue Shield.

Was Detroit's urban regime during this era functional? Some scholars suggest not, because of weak private-sector partners (Orr and Stokes 1994). The CBD did not contain any of the Big Three auto firms, and CBD project sites were disconnected and fragmented; one project focused on a utility company on the west side, and another on Blue Cross on the east, but with no connections. No major corporations arose to push forward a strong central business initiative. CBD merchants, active in the 1940s and 1950s, soon fled to suburban shopping centers, aiding decentralization of the city's residents and capital.

Nevertheless, during this period of time, a pro-growth coalition—weaker than that in many cities, and by no means as strong as an urban regime—did exist, if we take into account the nonprofit institutions that benefited from urban renewal. Leaders of the Detroit Institute of Arts, the Detroit Medical Center, and Wayne State University were particularly important boosters, working with a succession of mayors and planning staff to redevelop their surroundings. The Cultural Center, portrayed as one monolithic mass in Figure 3.2, became a bifurcated project with two parts: (1) Wayne State University and nearby University City residential areas located west of Woodward Avenue, and (2) the Cultural Center (later renamed Art Center) project, including a museum district and nearby residential areas, located east of Woodward Avenue.[2] The Detroit Medical Center housed not just the four hospitals that were originally envisioned as needing expansion, but also a number of other medical institutions and businesses. The resulting complex is now one of the major employers in the city, with more than 10,000 workers at any given time.

Detroit's urban renewal was therefore somewhat successful in what it set out to do (although it occurred at a glacial pace and brought a great deal of human misery along the way). The city government's aim was to replace deteriorated housing and businesses in low-income, minority-race areas with new housing, white middle-class residents, industries, and institutional buildings. The details of how this was done project by project are not as important as the overall scheme: exchanging so-called slums and blight for tax-generating land uses of more economic value and, at the same time, reclaiming portions of the black ghetto.

Despite the partial success and the positive aim of the Detroit renewal projects, they could never achieve the wide and long-lasting effects desired. Even if we ignore the nagging dilemma of flawed social equity for blacks unable to relocate into suitable housing they could afford (Thomas 2013a), other dilemmas lurked. The first was that the city government was not truly operating with a stable urban regime that would support downtown development or a major corporate presence. Episodic pro-growth coalitions arose to support Wayne State University, the Detroit Medical Center, the Art Center, and pieces of the CBD, but the results were fragmented.

The second problem was demographic trends. Redevelopment was supposed to take place in a city that remained an important political, economic, and social center within its region. This era's city leaders and planners did not anticipate the massive population outflow, which was apparent as early as the 1960 census and continued unabated through the 2010 census and

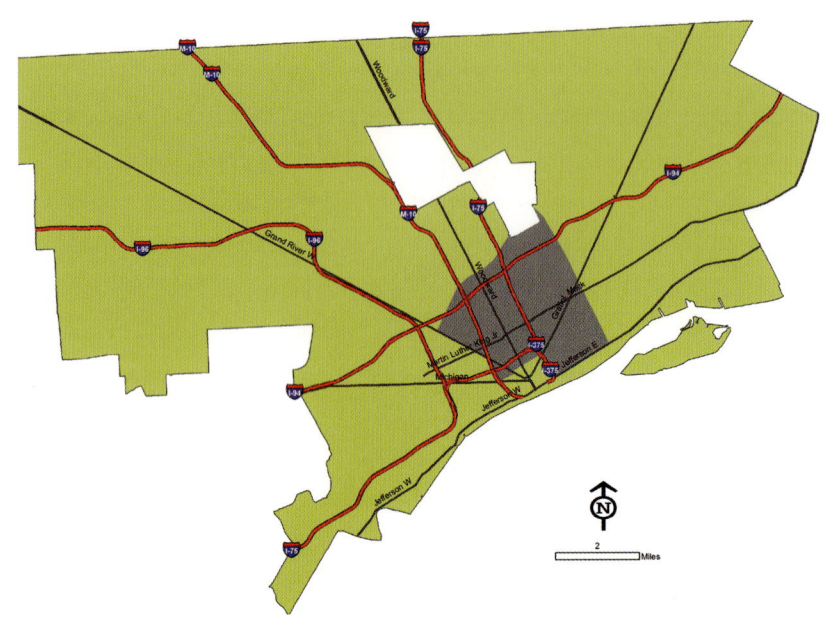

FIGURE 3.4 Detroit Model City neighborhoods in 1970. The city of Detroit's Model Cities areas, subsequently called Model Neighborhoods, included many former urban renewal sites as well as additional neighborhoods.
Source: City of Detroit, Planning Department. (Scott Pitera, Map Editor)

beyond. The city government's 1951 master plan aimed to complement what the planners assumed would be the consolidation of the social, economic, and physical fabric of the city, organized around existing neighborhoods within the larger framework of 139 square miles, all held together by elongated sectors of operational industrial plants (City of Detroit 1951).

Largely because of racial conflict dating back several decades, but exacerbated by estrangement during the post–World War II period and then by black civil rebellions in the 1960s, Detroit lost the battle for white residents. Sociologists could measure the attitudinal phenomenon (Farley, Danziger, and Holzer 2000), and historians could explain its relationship to the battle for jobs and turf (Sugrue 1996): most whites were unwilling to live in neighborhoods where even a few blacks lived, setting up

constant residential turmoil and decentralization as tolerant whites faced increasingly black neighborhoods when less tolerant whites fled (Farley et al. 2000). Falling income and public service levels and the increasing racial conflict and crime pushed families out of Detroit as well. In the increasingly atomized suburbs, mobile families saw opportunities, and they took them; white families were the most mobile, because they did not face racial discrimination in housing and bank financing, and because of higher socioeconomic status in general. The city government's redevelopment planners attempted neighborhood rehabilitation programs, starting in the 1950s with conservation initiatives, but these more modest approaches to neighborhood enhancement could not stop neighborhood socioeconomic decline (City of Detroit 1966; Parkins 1958; Thomas 2013a).[3] For example, former conservation planner and Detroit Councilman Mel Ravitz theorized that the conservation program of the 1950s failed because whites were unwilling to invest even in home repair in racially changing central-city neighborhoods when they could so easily leave (Ravitz 1955).

The city also lost industrial jobs as the automobile industry left the central city (and later the region), a trend that had begun well before this era. Industrial plants had actually served as neighborhood anchors in earlier decades, as workers lived nearby and walked or used streetcars to get to work; these workers also patronized nearby businesses. The industrial sector was one of the first to decentralize, in part because of taxes, the spatial requirements for production, and the difficulty of inner-city expansion, issues cited in industrial surveys in the 1940s (Thomas 2013a). Industrial decentralization was also due to what chapter 4 explains were flawed policies by industrial leaders; for example, Henry Ford built a self-sustained, de-urbanizing industrial campus in Dearborn. All of the Big Three automotive companies scattered operations throughout the region. Even special projects in the central city launched by industrial leaders, such as the Renaissance Center boosted by Henry Ford's grandson Henry Ford II in the aftermath of the 1960s civil rebellions, represented fragments rather than the heart of industrial and corporate wealth in the city. Plant closings further weakened the fabric of existing neighborhoods, industrial districts, and commercial sectors, to the point that they could no longer support and protect the borders and hinterland extending beyond the focal redevelopment projects. Those redevelopment sites had been designed to serve as complements, not substitutes for normally functioning city neighborhoods and districts. Redevelopment projects eventually were often left standing, surrounded by empty land as the city lost people and buildings.

If social trends had indeed supported the planners in their visions, perhaps observers would now praise these redevelopment projects as trend-setting initiatives. The Detroit Medical Center complex succeeded in anchoring the expanding medical industry in ways far beyond the wildest dreams of the 1950s (Detroit Medical Center Citizens Committee 1958). Wayne State University, now the third-largest university in Michigan, employs thousands and continues to build new buildings in and near the area designated in the 1956 map as the city's Cultural Center.[4]

Federal policy changed again in the late 1960s. When the citizen outcry against the clearance aspects of the urban renewal program forced reconsideration of that agenda both nationwide and locally, the federal government set up a program popularly known as Model Cities but soon renamed with a more modest moniker: Model Neighborhoods. Detroit, identified early as a potential candidate for the initiative, successfully applied for those funds (Frieden and Kaplan 1975). Model Neighborhoods focused on one targeted area, illustrated in Figure 3.4, and hosted a more multidimensional program of action than was possible under urban renewal. The program supported social and economic initiatives in addition to physical, and included a much stronger role for citizen decision making.

In some ways, however, this was a continuation of the same agenda. Comparing Figures 3.4 and 3.3, we see that Detroit's Model Neighborhood included many of the core urban renewal project sites left over from an earlier era, building upon and reinforcing the previous redevelopment agenda. Within the boundaries apparent in Figure 3.4 are Lafayette Park, Elmwood, Wayne State University, Cultural Center, Medical Center, and even the Milwaukee Junction Industrial urban renewal project areas.

Residents living in the Model Neighborhood area had more say in the program than had residents in urban renewal areas. They chose representatives for an overall governing board, which could select from an array of programs and guide implementation. Hiring many locals, the Detroit Model Neighborhood program provided temporary employment and opened up new career ladders, helped address educational needs in local elementary schools, and put in place a public health care delivery system. In addition, specific subsections of the Model Neighborhood area developed their own redevelopment initiatives. This is evident in the citizen-driven plans for the neighborhood immediately north of the Elmwood III project, Model Neighborhood D-I, in a neighborhood subsequently known as McDougall-Hunt. This area is now best known as the location of the Heidelberg Project, a permanent art installation located on Heidelberg Street and based on creative decoration of numerous vacant lots and houses with found objects such as discarded shoes and dolls. In the early 1970s, however, vacant lots or houses were relatively few. Consultants' plans (Parkins/Rogers & Associates 1972) suggested repurposing the few vacancies that existed into alternative uses (Figure 3.5) and implementing a neighborhood plan (Figure 3.6) that complemented the urban renewal project to the south, Elmwood III, without clearing out existing homes. Similar plans emerged for other subsections, such as Model Neighborhood C-III, an area known as Forest Park, which evolved into a collection of townhouse developments (Christopher Wzacny & Associates 1972).

Local evaluation reports from the era indicated a number of Model Neighborhood accomplishments, not the least of which was a sense of involvement by local residents in determining their area's future, in stark

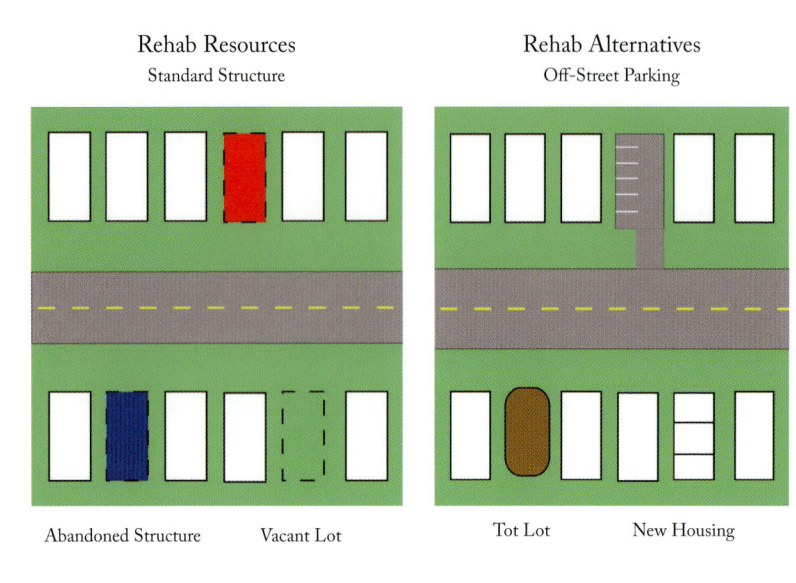

FIGURE 3.5 Example of Model Neighborhood resource alternatives in (1972. Left: Rehab resources; right: rehab alternatives. This shows how neighborhood residents of this subsection of Model Neighborhoods envisioned necessary ways of handling vacant lots and substandard areas in this neighborhood north of Elmwood III.
Source: Based on Parkins/Rogers and Associates. (1972). Development plan: Model Neighborhood D-1 area development corporation, p. 14.

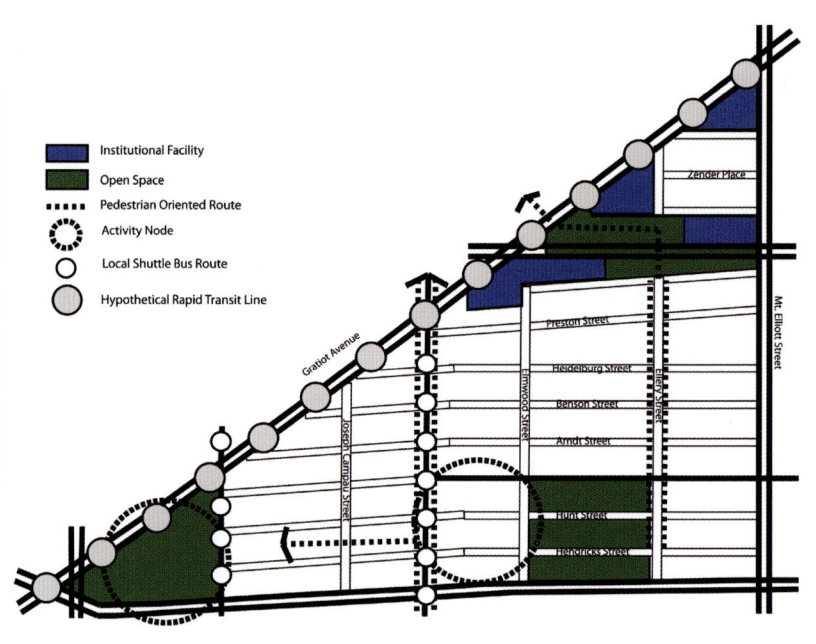

FIGURE 3.6 Example of model neighborhood circulation and open space plan from 1972. This shows how neighborhood residents of this subsection of Model Neighborhoods and their planning consultant envisioned traffic flow in this neighborhood north of Elmwood III.
Source: Based on Parkins/Rogers and Associates. (1972). Development plan: Model Neighborhood D-1 area development corporation, p. 23.

contrast to previous years (Detroit Model Neighborhood Agency 1975). Comparison of census tract demographics with those of Cleveland's target area also suggested some progress because of Model Neighborhoods or the sum of several redevelopment projects in its area of service (Thomas 1996). But the program began at a very difficult time, because the City applied for its planning grant just before 1967, a year of renewed racial conflict. Model Neighborhoods helped to calm the waters ruffled as a result of civil disorders of the mid-1960s, and then settled into a gentler, more participatory support role for urban renewal. Those citizens who worked to improve target neighborhoods redefined development in a more social and economic direction that the old redevelopment practices, but their expectations and needs far outweighed resources (Thomas 1996). For several reasons, new allocations for federal support for the Model Neighborhood program ended, nationwide, in 1974 (Frieden and Kaplan 1975).

Other programs during this era, from 1949 to 1974, included several low-income housing programs, anti-poverty initiatives, and other community development efforts, but urban renewal and the Model Neighborhood program had the greatest influence on Detroit. Looking from the vantage point of the twenty-first century, we see the footprint of their efforts quite clearly. Included within the original urban renewal and Model Neighborhood boundaries are not only the institutions previously named, but also a number of multifamily housing developments—mostly townhouses—many of them subsidized with federal funds such as LIHTC. Former dreams of massive redevelopment under one program or another, however, died in the next phase of constrained and reconfigured federal funding.

REFOCUS: 1974–94

Detroit lost uneven proportions of population from 1970 to 2000: 20.5 percent lost during the 1970s, 14.6 percent during the 1980s, and 7.5 percent during the 1990s. The drop was racially selective; blacks were only 44.5 percent of city population in 1970, but they were 63 percent by 1980 and 76 percent by 1990 (Detroit Free Press 2001). Varying theories about the large population drop in the 1970s include reactions to the 1967 civil rebellions, white residents' hostility toward Coleman Young's tenure, a divisive school integration/busing case, the cumulative effects of racially exclusionary suburbanization, and the impact of the economic recession of the early 1970s. None of these explanations is quite satisfying by itself, but all (plus more) probably played a role. Our focus is not on demographic explanation but rather on redevelopment in 1974–94, in the midst of this persistent drop in households. Redevelopment trends included continued support for existing urban renewal redevelopment areas and attempts to branch out to additional nearby areas; additional efforts to support neighborhoods in the city at large; and focus on key economic development projects, particularly in the CBD, riverfront, and industrial sectors. All of these initiatives, however, depended on reduced federal funding and a much weaker pro-growth coalition than existed in previous decades, in an era of escalating deindustrialization and white flight.

Federal support for redevelopment changed in 1974 when the U.S. Congress launched Community Development Block Grants (CDBG). CDBG's provisions were less inclined to target distressed cities or to encourage cities to target specific identifiable areas within their borders than previous redevelopment programs. CDBG also vastly expanded the number of eligible communities compared to previous redevelopment programs. Cities such as Detroit had to share the overall allocation of federal funding with large suburban communities as well as with much smaller and less distressed cities throughout the state and country.

Cities could use CDBG to complete or build on urban renewal projects. In a 1974 prospectus, the City of Detroit offered 19 parcels for development in Elmwood III, which contained a total of 188 acres and could accommodate more than 2000 dwelling units. At that time, Lafayette Park housed approximately 5,000 residents, and Elmwood I provided housing for 1,200 middle and upper income families, while Elmwood II housed predominately low and moderate income families (City of Detroit 1974).[5] Between 1975 and 1982, the city government put higher-than-average CDBG expenditures in sections of the city close to or including urban renewal projects, such as the Jefferson-Chalmers neighborhood to the far southeast, designated as an urban renewal area in 1971 (Ernecq 1972); the CBD; and the East Central sector, which included Elmwood I, II, and III (Darden, Hill, Thomas, and Thomas 1987). Furthermore, the city government maintained funding support for citizen district councils, advisory groups mandated under the state's urban renewal enabling legislation. Table 3.1 gives a list of the citizen district councils in existence between 1991 and 1993, and indicates which ones were in or adjacent to urban renewal projects from the 1960s. These councils' existence confirmed the continuity of the urban renewal agenda. This continuity showed in other ways as well, as in the city's 1992 master plan, which continued to refer to priority urban renewal projects, even though the federal "urban renewal" program had long before died (City

FIGURE 3.7 Major development areas in 1993. This map shows that by the early 1990s, for its report to the U.S. Department of Housing and Urban Development, the city of Detroit was still focused on central areas of the city and Jefferson-Chalmers neighborhood to the east.
Source: City of Detroit. (1991–92). Comprehensive housing affordability strategies performance report, *p. 42. (Scott Pitera, Map Editor)*

of Detroit 1992). The 1992 sites portrayed on Figure 3.7 do not include all urban renewal projects, some of which were completed by then, but show some of these projects' nearby successors; we list most of these in Table 3.1.

The second redevelopment trend evident in this era was city government's effort to spread community development funding beyond formal redevelopment projects, but this yielded both greater reach and reduced focus. Detroit's planning activities were split between the executive and

TABLE 3.1 Citizen district councils in relation to urban renewal areas, 1991–93.
Sources: Determined from comparison of map in City of Detroit (1991–92), Comprehensive housing assistance strategy performance report, *p. 43. See also City of Detroit (1992–93),* Comprehensive housing assistance strategy performance report, *p. 94; and City of Detroit (1966),* Community Renewal Program, summary report: Detroit, the new city, *p. 12.*

CITIZEN DISTRICT COUNCIL	SPATIAL RELATIONSHIP TO 1966 URBAN RENEWAL PROJECT	1966 URBAN RENEWAL PROJECT LABEL
1. Art Center	North of	Cultural Center
2. Ash-Myrtle-Humboldt	None	
3. Brush Park	South of / North of	Detroit Medical Center / Central Business District
4. Cork Town	Same as	Corktown
5. Downtown	Same as	Central Business District
6. Eight Mile-Wyoming	Not yet designated	(same as conservation area)
7. Elmwood Park No. 3	Same as	Elmwood Park III
8. Forest Park	East of	Detroit Medical Center
9. Hubbard-Richard	West of	Corktown
10. Jefferson-Chalmers	Same as	Jefferson-Chalmers
11. Kercheval-McClellan	None	
12. Medical Center	Same as	Medical Center
13. McDougall-Hunt	North of	Elmwood Park III
14. Mid-City	West of	Cultural Center
15. Southeast	Same as	Lafayette Park, Elmwood I and II
16. University City	Same as	Wayne State University area
17. Virginia Park	None	
18. West Jefferson	None	(south of conservation area)
19. Wholesale	North of / South of	Lafayette Park / Detroit Medical Center
20. Woodbridge	None	

*Parentheses in third column refer to the conservation program, funded under urban renewal, which often used rehabilitation instead of clearance.

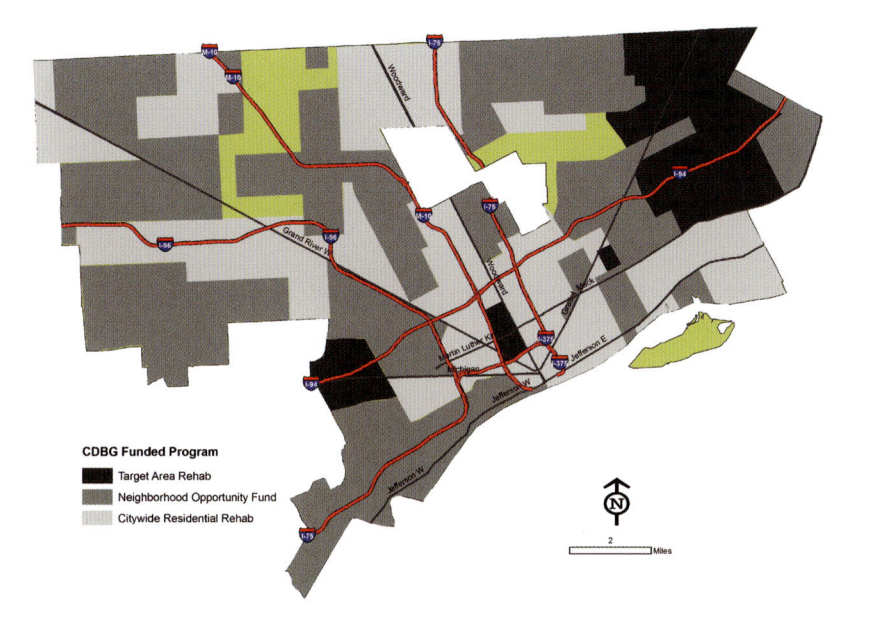

FIGURE 3.8 CDBG funded program areas. This map illustrates the difficulty in finding a targeting strategy for the Community Development Block Grant program, in part because of distribution of the Neighborhood Opportunity Fund.
Source: City of Detroit. (1991–92). Comprehensive housing affordability strategies performance report, p. 42. (Scott Pitera, Map Editor).

FIGURE 3.9 Major development focus areas from 1956 to 1993. This map overlays many development focus areas over the years to show an overall pattern up until 1993. It includes two major assisted automobile plant sites for GM and Chrysler.
Source: City of Detroit. (1991–92). Comprehensive housing affordability strategies performance report, p. 42; Parkins, M. (1958). Neighborhood conservation: A pilot study. Detroit, MI: Detroit Plan Commission in cooperation with U.S. Housing and Home Finance Agency. (Scott Pitera, Map Editor)

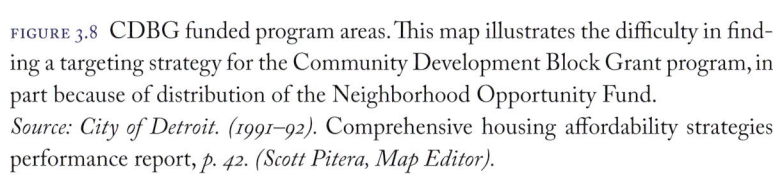

the legislative branches of city government,[6] and both spent CDBG funds. The Detroit city council's decision to establish a CDBG-funded program called the Neighborhood Opportunity Fund (NOF), with allocations based on applications from various community-based organizations, meant that many community groups received NOF funds. However, the council did not necessarily favor groups with proven ability to carry out major initiatives. Not all funds were distributed in this way, as the mayor's executive branch pursued more large-scale CDBG-funded projects. Over the years, the complex pattern of expenditures made it difficult to discern critical mass or overall impact of CDBG expenditures. See Figure 3.8 for a map published in a 1991–92 performance report, which shows in symbolic terms the wide distribution of these funds.

The third trend was the tendency for the city government to concentrate redevelopment efforts in the CBD, riverfront, and industrial areas. During the first phase of the CDBG allocations, from 1975 to 1982, the city invested 16.2 percent of $154 million in the CBD (Darden et al. 1987, p. 194). Projects built there included the Joe Louis Arena, the Millender Center located across from the Renaissance Center, and apartment towers on the western riverfront. The city government likewise invested in the riverfront east of the CBD, creating the first pieces of a linked parks system expected to attract residential development, and prepared sites for two new auto plants: the General Motors (GM) Detroit-Hamtramck assembly plant and Chrysler assembly plant located on East Jefferson Avenue. Figure 3.9 includes previous redevelopment target areas as well as the sites for GM and Chrysler automobile plants.

These projects greatly expanded the geographic reach of the city's publicly assisted efforts but, with few exceptions, the city government pushed for them with almost no help from the private sector. Researchers who interviewed top private-sector and nonprofit interest groups found that they were too distrustful of city government—particularly of Mayor Young, a former union activist and staunch defender of black self-determination—to allow

FIGURE 3.10 Detroit Empowerment Zone borders (1993). With the Empowerment Zone (EZ) application, the city broke out of previous areas of concentration, following guidance specified by the U.S. Department of Housing and Urban Development for selecting EZ target areas. The shape of the zone reflects, in part, the input of specific community development corporations.
Source: City of Detroit, Planning Department. (Scott Pitera, Map Editor)

for a long-lasting collaborative relationship that might have yielded more tangible results (Orr and Stoker 1994). By the end of Mayor Young's term in 1994, his built-environmental legacy in the CBD, riverfront, and industrial sector was clear, but critical mass was lacking, and non-targeted commercial and residential areas continued to decline in marketability and population. The 1992 Master Plan of Policies offered general goals that covered all areas of the city, but did not clarify the city's priorities for the future.

The oil crises of 1973 and 1979, along with the ascendancy of strong Asian competitors, meant that the automobile industry lost market share and needed to reduce production costs. Closing down old, labor-intensive automobile plants such as those in the city of Detroit, which increasingly did not meet environmental protection laws at any rate, was one way automotive companies reduced costs. Industrial construction, such as at the new GM Detroit-Hamtramck assembly plant, provided only a fraction of the historic automobile job base at great monetary cost to the state of Michigan and the city, which had provided a major portion of the supportive infrastructure and used eminent domain powers to clear the sites of existing residents, churches, and other buildings.

The City of Detroit was using its thinly stretched resources to focus on large, expensive projects and to support, to a lesser extent, community-based initiatives. However, these efforts were not making a substantial difference in halting continual decline in population, jobs, and businesses. Population fell in the twenty years between 1970 and 1990 by 32 percent, from 1.51 million to 1.03 million, as people continued to flee, and Detroit became a majority-black city. The relationship between Detroit and its suburbs became one of racial estrangement and political/economic distance.

EMPOWERMENT AND SHRINKAGE: 1994–2013

In 1994 Mayor Dennis Archer succeeded Coleman Young. Archer advisers helped him pursue two courses of action: successful application for designation as a federal EZ—a new ten-year program that promised to inject $100 million plus more in winner cities' target zones—and creation of a new land-use plan. Although both of these initiatives led to several positive results, by the end of the ten-year period it was clear that they had limited effect. The city also leveraged a federal Renewal Communities designation, which provided fewer benefits than had the EZ but offered tax credits to businesses and corporations in order to spur economic development. Then the city government began a search for a targeted strategy that could respond to the city's continued contraction.

Figure 3.10 shows the Detroit EZ, a zone created by linking census tracts that met the federal government's requirements for social and economic distress. As a requirement for winning funds in 1994, the city had to focus on the areas already suffering from various problems, including a high rate of poverty—a strategy that did not build on strengths but targeted weaknesses. The zone looks different than the urban renewal and Model City project areas previously mapped because of the EZ program's different criteria, but its peculiar shape is due also to the participation of community-based organizations that urged the inclusion of areas they served. This federal program provided $100 million in federal social services funds over ten years to winning cities, including Detroit, as well as other funds and incentives for Zone businesses to hire local residents; in return the city could support economic development, public safety, housing and community development, transportation, and other critical needs in a ten-year plan. The federal grant was actually quite modest, but the city's application included pledges of support from numerous corporations and financial institutions. Even though these funds added up to more than $2 billion, much of that was in the form of lenders' pledges for targeted loans (City of Detroit 1994). The EZ program assumed that a modest place-based, multi-faceted strategy could alleviate conditions caused by demographic and economic trends that were already strongly established; in hindsight, this was overly optimistic.

The U.S. Department of Housing and Urban Development (HUD) lists, at its webpage, annual Detroit EZ reports for the years 1998 to 2005, just after the required ten-year plan ended (U.S. Department of Housing and Urban Development 2010a). These reports list several accomplishments, ranging from providing bonding authority for the redevelopment of the downtown Book Cadillac Hotel to creating a small neighborhood park. For a sobering assessment of the limited power of the EZ program nationwide to make substantive changes in the social and economic status of targeted EZ tracts, however, we can turn to studies carried out by independent scholars. Although these used different methods and results varied somewhat (Oakley and Tsao 2006; Rich and Stoker 2010), the overall conclusions were that some indicators

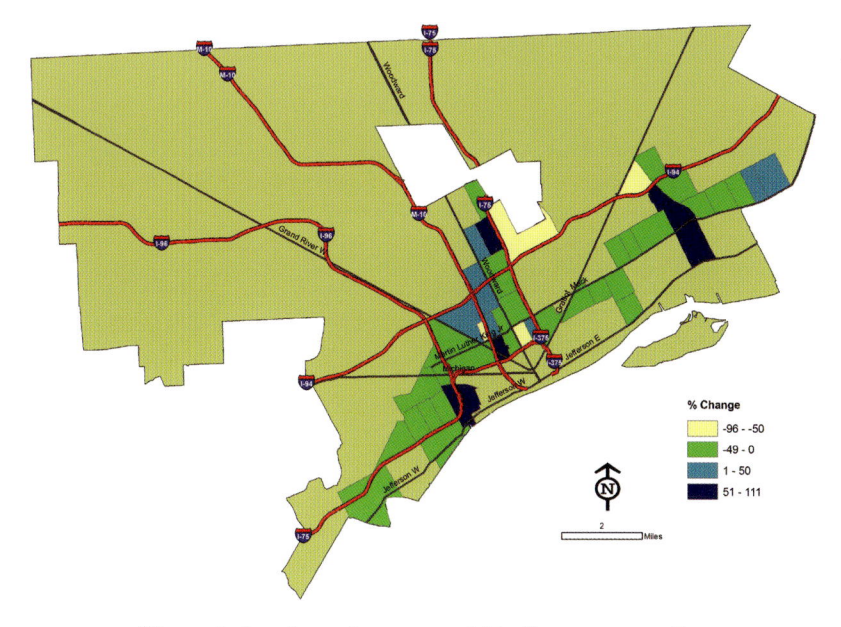

FIGURE 3.11 Change in housing unit vacancy within Empowerment Zone, 1990–2000. This shows that the designated Zone experienced some decline in housing vacancy during this decade, which included the first portion of EZ's ten-year plan; most EZ allocations ended in 2005.
Sources: City of Detroit, Planning Department; U.S. Census Bureau. (Scott Pitera, Map Editor)

REDEVELOPMENT IN DETROIT: Spatial Evolution   65

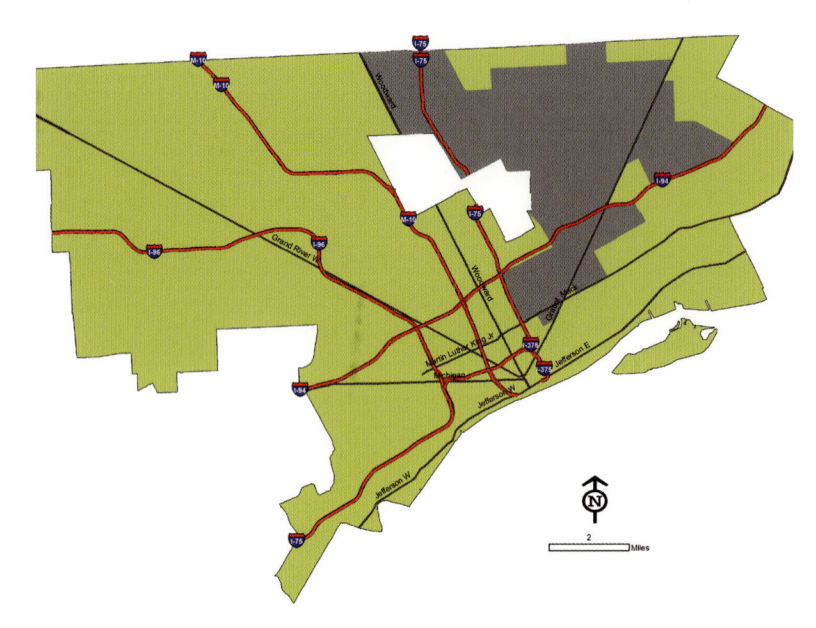

FIGURE 3.12 Renewal Community borders. The Renewal Community, successor to EZ, included much fewer monetary and programmatic benefits than EZ, but encompassed a larger and different area of the city.
Source: City of Detroit, Planning Commission. (Scott Pitera, Map Editor)

improved in Detroit's EZ census tracts compared to comparable census tracts, but not enough to generate significant neighborhood improvement. See Figure 3.11 for one example of trends in Detroit's EZ: this shows that the number of housing units dropped in most EZ census tracts between 1990 and 2000.

Detroit also received support from the Michigan Renaissance Zone Act and the Michigan Neighborhood Enterprise Zone Act. Detroit's 1996 Renaissance Zone eliminated many state and local taxes in a designated 1,345 acres, a small fraction of the area covered by the city's EZ. This state program gave tax breaks for an industrial park on the east side near the GM Detroit-Hamtramck plant as well as other industrial sites. The Neighborhood Enterprise Zone funded specific housing projects to provide an investment savings for new home builders (City of Detroit 1997a). In addition, in 2002 the city became a designee of the federal Renewal Community (RC) program (Figure 3.12), under which it offered tax benefits for employers; again, it was a much more modest agenda than that of the EZ program (U.S. Department of Housing and Urban Development 2010b).

By the mid-1990s it became very difficult to trace the city's CDBG expenditures (City of Detroit 1997b). A 2000 report on economic development provides a compendium of many projects built, those supported by public funds as well as others (City of Detroit 2000). Although the colorful report reads like promotional literature, its charts, maps, and graphs show that development had not stopped. Accomplishments listed included 2,100 new and renovated housing units between 1994 and 1999, and 50 completed economic development projects related to industrial and manufacturing entities, 70 percent of which were located in Detroit's special zones, either EZ or Renaissance. The map showing commercial development, except for some efforts along the East riverfront, revealed widely scattered, small commercial projects.

Mayor Archer's 1994 Mayor's Land Use Task Force led to a citywide visioning initiative labeled the Community Reinvestment Strategy (CRS), with residents developing priorities and strategies for ten clusters in the city. Each cluster's committee produced one of ten volumes of the city's CRS strategy, but these led to no noticeable results besides the adoption of the boundaries of the ten clusters and ideas partially transferred to several subsequent master plan drafts. Each cluster document overwhelms the reader with the large scale of it all. For example, in cluster three, the east side neighborhood of Jefferson Chalmers and its three census tracts fairly drown in its mapped-out territory, which extends to the west and north (City of Detroit 1997c). Cluster three included 16.5 square miles and 124,000 people according to the 1990 census. Vacancy maps showed large splotches of vacant land in several key areas of the cluster. Smaller, more viable neighborhoods such as Jefferson-Chalmers retained sturdy housing stock as well as new low-income and market-rate housing projects subsidized by programs such as urban renewal, Section 235, and LIHTC, yet the mixed-income riverfront neighborhood still needed focused improvements. Jefferson-Chalmer's needs paled in comparison to those of its larger cluster. Implementing even a fraction of the indicated CRS strategies, which included a wide range of business development, housing, entrepreneurial, transportation, environmental, and youth programs, would have required an enormous amount of public funding and continued support by an almost-invisible private sector.

All of this seemed to be an impossible task. The city council did not adopt these CRS volumes as official documents, leaving citizens who worked on the 1997 volumes with no resolution or substantive implementation, but with a lingering sense of betrayal. Even when the master plan adopted aspects of CRS in 2009, the gap in years was long and citizens involved in CRS had no way of knowing this had happened (Bernstein et al. 2012, p.17).

Mayor Archer served for two four-year terms. The next administration, headed by Kwame Kilpatrick (2002–08), Detroit's third black mayor, faced numerous issues related to political ethics and fiscal responsibility. Before its fall in a flurry of scandal-ridden court cases, the Kilpatrick administration supported key projects in the CBD and riverfront, such as the reconstruction of the Westin Book Cadillac Hotel, but its strategy for addressing increasing vacancy in other parts of the city relied on spotty demolition of abandoned housing. The closest thing to an official city designation of consistent target areas was the Next Detroit Neighborhood Initiative (NDNI), which lasted only a few years and faced limited resources. A broader vision had not emerged since the EZ application and CRS plans. Several organizations established their own areas of service, such as the Skillman Foundation, with its focus on community schools in specific neighborhoods; such initiatives selected their own target areas. Draft revisions of the master plan prepared in 2004 and 2005 by the mayor's executive branch failed to be adopted by the Detroit city council, as required by the city's charter. When in 2009 the council finally replaced the 1992 plan by adopting a new master plan, this was almost devoid of fresh citizen input, and instead relied on citizens' twelve-year-old input into CRS.

When the economic crisis of 2007 hit the United States, many cities were desperate for assistance with escalating foreclosure rates and housing abandonment. As part of a stimulus package, the federal government created a phased Neighborhood Stabilization Program (NSP) but required some indication of target areas the cities aimed to improve. After Kilpatrick's administration collapsed because of his forced resignation in 2008, Council President Kenneth Cockrel, Jr., governed for a few months, in transition to Mayor David Bing. Cockrel authorized the 2009 application for the first round of NSP funds. For its request, the city government designated huge swatches of land as "target areas," portrayed in Figure 3.13, even though such a large territory could offer little ability to

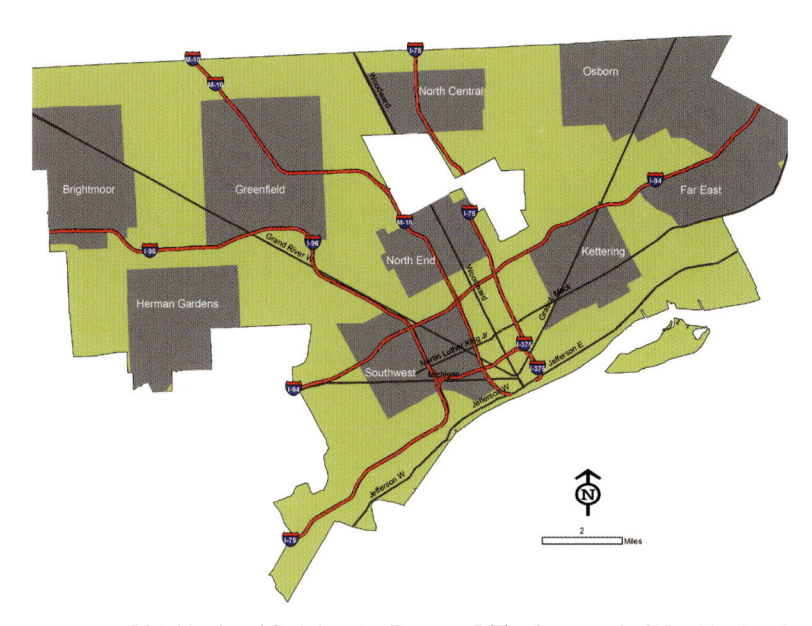

FIGURE 3.13 Neighborhood Stabilization Program I. The first round of Neighborhood Stabilization Program (NSP) money was distributed widely, dampening impact.
Source: City of Detroit, Planning Commission. (Scott Pitera, Map Editor)

REDEVELOPMENT IN DETROIT: Spatial Evolution 67

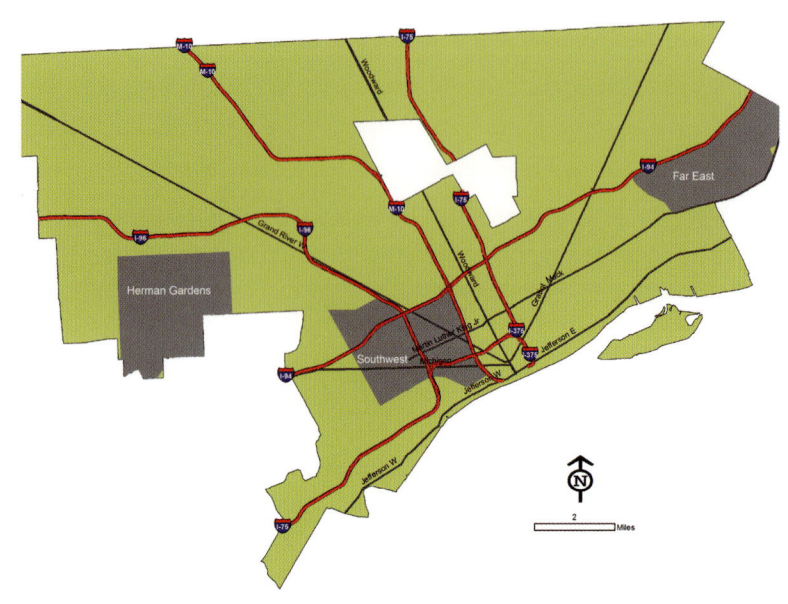

FIGURE 3.14 Neighborhood Stabilization Program II. At the urging of HUD, NSP II and the subsequent NSP III, were more targeted.
Source: City of Detroit, Planning Commission. (Scott Pitera, Map Editor)

ensure visible results with the $47 million that the city requested (City of Detroit 2009b). The city scaled back for second-round requests, selecting only three areas, mapped in Figure 3.14, for targeted action; these pictured were later scaled back in size as well. With the city's allocation focused on demolishing vacant housing units, areas not chosen for targeting simply had fewer vacant buildings torn down. With the third round of NSP funding, Detroit chose much smaller target areas, mostly in the city's outer rim.

Although many problems characterized this last era, new housing construction continued often under the federal LIHTC program. Some housing fit squarely within development areas identified in the early 1990s, such as Art Center and other areas listed in Table 3.1. Both private sector developers and nonprofit housing development corporations built many of these units, most of which were rental, but these were sometimes interspersed with market-rate or Habitat for Humanity houses built for homeowners. These developments provided a major portion of new construction in the city during the 1990s and 2000s (Deng 2013; Thomas 2013b).

Throughout this era, some development took place in the CBD. Projects included Comerica Park in 2000 and Ford Field in 2002, serving baseball and football fans, but requiring government funds for surrounding infrastructure. Sports stadia are not sufficient to support a downtown area, but nevertheless these eventually created a revenue stream and anchored a small tourist industry. Three casinos became self-contained venues that did little to add to street life or to nearby businesses but provided important sources of revenue for city coffers.

Perhaps most notable, however, is that soon the nature of redevelopment began to change. Building on the gestational matrix established by urban renewal funds, major nonprofit institutions began to grow on their own, expanding and collaborating—a trend most notable in the Midtown area, anchored by the strong "eds and meds" of the Detroit Medical Center, Henry Ford Hospital System, Wayne State University, the College for Creative Studies, and associated institutions and businesses, as well as cultural facilities such as the Detroit Institute of Arts. These organizations and their ancillaries built new buildings and expanded or rehabilitated old ones, in some cases creating their own mini land-use plans for expansion and consolidation, and attracting nearby housing development (some financed by LIHTC or tax subsidies). Detroit Midtown, Inc., a nonprofit based in this area, played a particularly important role in stoking partnerships and knitting together stakeholders, seeking funds from foundations, and attracting residents, including whites. Tri-county voters, in 2012, supported a ten-year property tax millage for the Detroit Institute of Arts in exchange for free admission for tri-county residents. The area began to show a form of redevelopment much less dependent on city or federal government redevelopment funds than in previous decades.

The nature of redevelopment changed as well in the CBD. After the building of the casinos and stadia, other projects began to pull different partners together to use urban design as a way to change the nature of street life in the CBD. For example, the city government helped support creation of a gem of an urban park in the middle of the CBD, Campus Martius, named in 2010 as the first-ever winner of the Urban Land Institute's new Amanda Burden award for U.S. urban open spaces (Urban Land Institute 2010). Sheltered by the nearby Compuware office building, this park that intersects Woodward Avenue also anchors a small island of new office development and recreational uses.

The Illitch family had modeled the idea of buying several buildings in the theater district and leveraging these into a connected venue, but starting in 2010 Dan Gilbert (founder and chairman of Quicken Loans, a prosperous on-line mortgage company) took this idea to a new level. His firm, Rock Ventures, began buying up buildings in Detroit's CBD and renovating them for lease and resale, seizing an investment opportunity that lent a decidedly private slant to downtown renewal. The city government, particularly through the quasi-public Detroit Economic Growth Corporation, continued to assist and invest in nearby projects, such as the Westin Book Cadillac However, the Westin was an enormously expensive undertaking for the developer and a city government with few resources and an escalating fiscal crisis, even with the infusion of resources such as government workers' pension funds. Gilbert was able to move much faster and had much more money for such ventures, which continue to evolve and expand as we write this chapter, and Rock Ventures began to promulgate its own vision of the CBD. Allied development such as pop-up retail stores (those open for limited periods of time) emerged, along with a renewed housing market for condos and apartments in newly renovated buildings. The CBD became an area with prospects.

It became increasingly clear that the corporate sector and foundations were interested in certain portions of Detroit, as they knit together a new form of growth coalition. In some cases, this involved creating or supporting organizations that took over certain traditional functions of city government. The Detroit Riverfront Conservancy, for example, which was formed as a nonprofit in 2003, leveraged support from the city government as well as from foundations and GM (which donated its Renaissance Center riverfront plaza) to build on the riverfront-linked parks idea and create a linear parkway, well designed and well used. The Conservancy supervised projects such as the bike and pedestrian route Dequindre Cut, heading north along abandoned rail lines extending from the riverfront to a refurbished Detroit Eastern Market; this demonstrated the possibility of a future based on anchor areas, comparable to urban amenities in other parts of the country. A light rail project proposed for Woodward Avenue emerged, faltered, but reemerged with a combination of private, foundation, and federal dollars. The report *7.2 Square Miles* (Hudson-Webber Foundation 2013) boasted of market potential and changed demographics in "greater downtown," an area defined by the consortium of report writers to include just a portion of the city's 139 square miles, focusing particularly on Midtown, the CBD, the Eastern Market district, Corktown, the Woodbridge and Lafayette Park neighborhoods, and the riverfront, in a data-gathering exercise that staked out defended territory.

Such initiatives were impressive, coming after a long dry period of decline in all sectors, but they buttressed only portions of the city: those areas important for the professional classes. The vast hinterland of Detroit's ordinary residential neighborhoods experienced varying fates, depending in part on socioeconomic status. Many fell into increasing decay and abandonment. Amazingly, in a city that had bemoaned its shrinking status, the few white professionals who moved into areas such as Midtown and Corktown sometimes elicited cries of gentrification, a multi-faceted term that was less likely to refer to physical removal than to a perceived form of cultural displacement and marginalization. Although the media hailed Gilbert and his investment in downtown, some others viewed this as yet another stage in the marginalization of low-income black populations, because the connection between the development of the Greater Downtown and the revival of neighborhoods and job opportunities for low-income residents was not clear (Elliott 2012; Williams 2013). This was a sign of underlying socioeconomic and racial tensions that had never been resolved (Darden and Thomas 2013).

By 2010, according to the census, the city's population had declined by 25 percent since 2000, in its biggest ten-year drop yet. Whites had continued to leave in large numbers, but so had middle-class blacks, whose numbers dropped by 16.5 percent during those ten years (compared to 0.3 percent in the 1990s), although they still made up 83 percent of the city's shrunken population. Widely taxed public services continued to decline in quality, in areas ranging from public schools and parks to police and fire protection. Mayor David Bing determined that approaches to land use planning needed to be more aggressive than the traditionally oriented 2009 master plan had suggested. He worked together with foundations, particularly Kresge, to help launch a major new planning initiative, Detroit Works. This had a well-publicized start characterized by excellent technical assistance from consultants but a somewhat contentious public engagement process and detachment from the internal workings of city government. Major overhauls in 2011 led to much-improved public engagement and a necessary division of labor between city staff and outside consultants.

The resulting long-term framework plan for land use, *Detroit Future City*—which we will describe in more detail in the epilogue—aimed to use Detroit's shrinking size as a spur to reenvisioning the city's economy, neighborhoods, infrastructure, and landscape, despite the logistical and strategic difficulties posed in a city with shrinking population. But the city government's perilous fiscal circumstances, born of a decentralizing tax base and escalating costs for a static but increasingly vacant land mass, loomed as a major barrier to positive action as city government tumbled into bankruptcy. Leaders of new redevelopment efforts within the city would necessarily have to include new and possibly shifting coalitions of leaders and organizations—not just the large and visible organizations mentioned here, but also thousands of households, block clubs, associations, alliances, activists, and visionaries, the only ones in many parts of the city with the motivation to act. As chapter 7 on Brightmoor shows, ordinary residents were already remaking the city's land usage in practical ways large and small, but whether they could help remake the city in the plan's ambitious vision remained to be seen. The challenges would become, in many ways, even more daunting than before, in great part because none of these developments and plans and initiatives addressed the fundamental problem of massive bifurcation within the region, with social, economic, and even political institutions having long since abandoned the central city of Detroit (Galster 2012). A new mayor, Mike Duggan, took office in 2014 and began a renewed effort to halt a process of decline that had threatened to engulf the city; he pledged to give particular attention to neighborhood blight.

CONCLUSION

Detroit's government-driven redevelopment agenda had important but limited effects. The public housing era highlighted endemic problems of racial segregation and might actually have reduced the quality of some neighborhoods because of the nature of built housing units. The urban renewal era led to the most visible imprint of public policy upon the land. That modernist agenda, however, required considerable displacement and was impossible to sustain for social and political reasons. After 1974, CDBG, urban renewal's replacement, could have worked very well in a city where the private market sustained the city's viability, but the modestly-funded program faltered in the context of widespread decentralization. An EZ program launched in 1994 aimed to assist low-income residents living in a specific distressed zone, but it was not able to improve local conditions measurably. (Subsequent efforts are still in process but may focus on only a portion of the city, such as "greater downtown," although more widely spread strategies have promise.)

A modest pro-growth coalition existed at various times in Detroit's history but was too weak and compromised to reverse the city's forces. A small pro-growth coalition built several important projects between 1974 and 1994, particularly in the CBD and industrial sector, but also faced major problems of mistrust and fragmentation. More recently, foundations selected their own planning initiatives, such as neighborhood-based approaches, the riverfront, and the Detroit Works initiative, with results yet to be fully realized. *Detroit Future City,* a fifty-year framework plan designed to reconceptualize the city's land use, drew major foundation support, but it will take time to assess its initial phases (see epilogue). The year 2013 proved to be a particularly important landmark in the city's evolution. In addition to the more visible or well-publicized changes—such as the appointment of an emergency financial manager, the election of a new mayor, and bankruptcy—other less visible changes emerged as well. Foundations paid for the hiring of an implementation staff for *Detroit Future City.* A major effort emerged to recount the number of vacant and dilapidated buildings and to "eliminate blight"; the city began to beef up the Detroit Land Bank's staff resources. Rock Ventures, the umbrella organization for Dan Gilbert's companies, including Quicken Loans, revealed its own vision of the CBD based on the purchase of dozens of CBD buildings and lots. The Illitch family steadily worked on its own plans for a massive redevelopment project surrounding the site of a new hockey arena, just north of the traditional CBD. Bankruptcy spurred the creation of a new form of pro-growth coalition, this time aimed toward saving the Detroit Institute of Arts as a regional cultural institution; the launching of a light rail system connecting the CBD and New Center had generated corporate support as well. It appeared that the city was entering a new phase of redevelopment, one which future scholars will need to analyze, as results have not yet counteracted decades of neglect.

This chapter by necessity recounted strategies and difficulties in the past rather than prospects for the future. It focused largely on mayors, visible leaders with varying talents for leadership. We've given less emphasis to the larger political system within the city, and little or none to the outside political system. Both venues provided major barriers to any attempt to remake Detroit, but the external barriers were particularly fierce. Detroit's spatial, social, and economic isolation within the region is the main reason redevelopment efforts faltered. Such efforts took place in the middle of a severely fragmented metropolitan area, where suburban governments were free to operate autonomously, with little sense of cooperation with or commitment to the city of Detroit. The industrial sector funneled ever more people and capital outward, contributing to the massive decentralization of the city. The lack of a strong pro-growth coalition was due in part to suburbanization of key economic interests. The guardians of an increasingly shrinking city tried to attract back the people that continued to flee, along with tax base, industries, corporations, retail outlets, and even grocery stores. As resources fled the city, the city became increasingly less viable as a residential or business location—except for a few favored spots—generating yet more exodus by those able to leave. Redevelopment was never meant to counteract such massive forces of decentralization and fragmentation, but rather to clean up pockets of "slums and blight" here and there. The David of central-city redevelopment in Detroit could not, under these circumstances, slay the Goliath.

NOTES

Scott Pitera was the initial editor for all of the maps and figures for this chapter.

1. The year 2013 was in some sense a landmark because Gov. Rick Snyder appointed Kevin Orr as emergency financial manager for the city of Detroit in that year. Critical events that took place in 2013 related to redevelopment included the

January release of the 2012 *Detroit Future City*, the establishment of an implementation office for that strategic plan, the creation of several highly visible efforts to eliminate "blight" in the city including its neighborhoods, and the increasingly obvious scale of entrepreneur Dan Gilbert's vision for the acquisition and remaking of the CBD. In addition, citizens elected a new mayor, Mike Duggan, who promised to make major reforms even under the shadow of an emergency financial manager and in the context of bankruptcy.

2. The Art Center project is the current Development Plan area, as of 2010; this includes residential streets northeast of the Detroit Institute of Arts. See http://www.detroitmi.gov/Departments/PlanningDevelopmentDepartment/Planning/LongRangeandCommunityPlanning/UrbanRenewalDevelopmentPlansPA344/tabid/1991/Default.aspx

3. Chapter 4 of Thomas (2013a) is devoted to the fitful efforts of the conservation program to stop neighborhood decline and racial turnover.

4. The number of employees at Wayne State University varies, but the *Chronicle of Higher Education* indicated in its 2010 survey of best colleges and universities to work for (Great Colleges to Work For, 2012) that Wayne State had 4,794 administrators, full and part-time faculty members, and professional staff.

5. Ernecq (1972, p. 21) indicates that the original number of housing units on the Elmwood II site was 1,947, and the anticipated number, at the time he wrote his report, was 893.

6. The charter approved by voters in 1973 established two separate planning operations, in the executive branch and in the legislative branch. The planners in the executive branch, under the mayor's leadership, handled most development activities, but planners associated with the city's planning commission operated separately. See Thomas (2013a).

REFERENCES

Bauman, J. (1987). *Public housing, race, and renewal: Urban planning in Philadelphia, 1920 to 1974*. Philadelphia, PA: Temple University Press.

Beauregard, R. (2009). Urban population loss in historical perspective: United States, 1820–2000. *Environment and Planning A, 41*, 514–28.

Bernstein, E., et al. (2012). *Engagement works, planning with citizens for Detroit's future*. Ann Arbor, MI: Urban and Regional Planning Program, University of Michigan. Retrieved from http://sitemaker.umich.edu/urpoutreachreports/capacity_building__b_/da.data/0000c0a8de10000007d51b050000139d3b6ef19833f4545/ReportFile/engagement_works_report.pdf

Capeci, D. J. (1984). *Race relations in wartime Detroit: The Sojourner Truth housing controversy*. Philadelphia, PA: Temple University Press.

Christopher Wzacny & Associates, and Parkins/Rogers & Associates. (1972). Development Plan: Model Neighborhood C-III Area Community Corporation. Detroit, MI.

City of Detroit. (1947, February). *The Detroit plan*. Detroit, MI: City Plan Commission.

City of Detroit. (1951). The Detroit master plan: The official comprehensive plan for the development and improvement of Detroit as approved by the Mayor and the Common Council. Detroit, MI: City Plan Commission.

City of Detroit. (1966). *Summary report: Detroit, the new city*. Detroit, MI: Community Renewal Program.

City of Detroit. (1974). *Elmwood III: A prospectus for an offering of land*. Detroit, MI: Community and Economic Development Department.

City of Detroit. (1991–92). *Comprehensive housing assistance strategy performance report*. Detroit, MI: City of Detroit.

City of Detroit. (1992). *Revised master plan of policies*. Detroit: City Plan Commission. Detroit, MI: City of Detroit.

City of Detroit. (1992–93). *Comprehensive housing assistance strategy annual plan*. Detroit, MI: City of Detroit.

City of Detroit. (1994). *Jumpstarting the motor city*. (Application/strategic plan for Empowerment Zone funds). Detroit, MI: Empowerment Zone (EZ) Coordinating Council, Planning and Development Department.

City of Detroit. (1997a, May). *Overall economic development program report*. Detroit, MI: City of Detroit.

City of Detroit. (1997b). *Community development block grant, grantee performance report* (Vols. 1–3). Detroit, MI: City of Detroit.

City of Detroit. (1997c, December). *Detroit community reinvestment strategy final report: Cluster 3*. Detroit, MI: Planning and Development Department.

City of Detroit. (2000). *Detroit: A world class city III. A progress report on economic development in the city of Detroit*. Detroit, MI: City of Detroit.

City of Detroit. (2009a). *Annual report: A new beginning*. Detroit, MI: Housing Commission. Retrieved from www.dhcmi.org/uploads/page/annual_report2009.pdf

City of Detroit. (2009b). *Neighborhood Stabilization Program plan*. Detroit, MI: Planning and Development Department. Retrieved from www.Detroitmi.gov/DepartmentsandAgencies/PlanningDevelopmentDepartment/NeighborhoodStabilizationPlan.aspx

City of Detroit. (2012). *About development.* Detroit, MI: Housing Commission. Retrieved from www.dhcmi.org/development.aspx

Conot, R. (1974). *American odyssey.* New York, NY: William Morrow & Company.

Darden, J., Hill, R. C., Thomas, J. M., and Thomas, R. (1987). *Detroit: Race and uneven development.* Philadelphia, PA: Temple University Press.

Darden, J., and Thomas, R.W. (2013). *Detroit: Race riots, racial conflicts, and efforts to bridge the racial divide.* East Lansing: Michigan State University Press.

Deng, L. (2013). Building affordable housing in cities after abandonment. In M. Dewar and J. Thomas (Eds.), *The city after abandonment* (pp. 41–63). Philadelphia: University of Pennsylvania Press.

Detroit Free Press. (2001). *The Detroit almanac: 300 years of life in the motor city.* Detroit, MI: Detroit Free Press.

Detroit Medical Center Citizens Committee. (1958). The Detroit Medical Center: A proposal for the reuse of land cleared under the federal and city urban renewal program. Detroit, MI: City of Detroit.

Detroit Model Neighborhood Agency. (1975). Final local evaluation of model cities program: Detroit, Michigan 1969–1975. Detroit, MI: Detroit Model Neighborhood Agency.

Detroit future city: 2012 Detroit strategic framework plan. (2012). Detroit, MI.

Elliott, M. (2012, January 10). Planning appropriately for our future. *The Huffington Post.* Retrieved from www.huffingtonpost.com/meagan-elliott/detroit-gentrification_b_1194534.html

Ernecq, J. M. (1972). *Urban renewal history of Detroit: 1946–1970.* Detroit, MI: Wayne State University Press.

Farley, R., Danziger, S., and Holzer, H. (2000). *Detroit divided.* New York, NY: Russell Sage Foundation.

Frieden, B., and Kaplan, M. (1975). *The politics of neglect: Urban aid from model cities to revenue sharing.* Cambridge, MA: Massachusetts Institute of Technology Press.

Galster, G. (2012). *Driving Detroit: The quest for respect in the Motor City.* Philadelphia: University of Pennsylvania Press.

Great colleges to work for. (2010, July 25). *The Chronicle of Higher Education.* Retrieved from http://chronicle.com/article/Great-Colleges-to-Work-For/65724

Hudson-Webber Foundation, Detroit Economic Growth Corporation, and partners. (2013). *7.2 Sq. Miles: A Report on Greater Downtown Detroit.* Retrieved from www.detroitsevenpointtwo.com

Logan, J., and Molotch, H. (1987). *Urban fortune: The political economy of place.* Berkeley: University of California Press.

Mossberger, K., and Stoker, G. (2001). The evolution of urban regime theory: The challenge of conceptualization. *Urban Affairs Review, 36,* 810–35.

Newman, O. (1996). Creating defensible space. U.S. Department of Housing and Urban Development. Retrieved from www.huduser.org/publications/pdf/def.pdf

Oakley, D., and Tsao, H. (2006). A new way of revitalizing distressed urban communities? Assessing the impact of the federal EZ program. *Journal of Urban Affairs, 28*(5), 443–71.

Orr, M., and Stoker, G. (1994). Urban regimes and leadership in Detroit. *Urban Affairs Review, 30,* 48–69.

Parkins, M. (1958). *Neighborhood conservation: A pilot study.* Detroit, MI: Detroit Plan Commission in cooperation with U. S. Housing and Home Finance Agency.

Parkins/Rogers & Associates. (1972). Development plan: Model Neighborhood D-1 area development corporation. Detroit, MI: Parkins/Rogers & Associates.

Ravitz, M. (1955). Urban renewal faces critical roadblocks. *Journal of the American Institute of Planners, 21,* 17–21.

Rich, M., and Stoker, R. (2010). Rethinking empowerment: Evidence from local Empowerment Zone programs. *Urban Affairs Review, 45,* 775–90.

Ryan, B. (2008). The restructuring of Detroit: City block form change in a shrinking city, 1900–2000. *Urban Design International, 13,* 156–68.

Shaw, T. (2009). *Now is the time! Detroit black politics and grassroots activism.* Durham, NC: Duke University Press.

Stone, C. (1989). *Regime politics: Governing Atlanta, 1946–88.* Lawrence: University Press of Kansas.

Sugrue, T. (1996). *The origins of the racial crisis: Race and inequality in postwar Detroit.* Princeton, NJ: Princeton University Press.

Thomas, J. M. (1996). Model Cities revisited: Issues of race and empowerment. In J. M. Thomas and M. Ritzdorf (Eds.), *Urban planning and the African American community: In the shadows* (pp. 143–65). Thousand Oaks, CA: Sage.

Thomas, J. M. (2009, October). Josephine Gomon's public housing as Detroit redevelopment strategy. Paper read to the Association of Collegiate Schools of Planning.

Thomas, J. M. (2013a). *Redevelopment and race: Planning a finer city in postwar Detroit.* (2nd ed.). Detroit, MI: Wayne State University Press.

Thomas, J. M. (2013b). Targeting strategies of three Detroit CDCs. In M. Dewar and J. M. Thomas (Eds.), *The city after abandonment* (pp. 197–225). Philadelphia: University of Pennsylvania Press.

Urban Land Institute. (2010, April 16). *Urban space that is changing the face of Detroit*. Retrieved from www.campusmartiuspark.org

U.S. Department of Housing and Urban Development (HUD). (2010a). *Annual report for Detroit, Michigan empowerment zone*. Retrieved from www5.hud.gov/urban/tour/showReport.asp?community=Detroit&state=mi&ID=26169800001

U.S. Department of Housing and Urban Development. (2010b). *Detroit renewal community map*. Retrieved from www.hud.gov/offices/cpd/economicdevelopment/programs/rc/tour/mi/DetroitRC

Williams, M. (2013). *Listening to Detroit: Perspectives on gentrification in the Motor City* (Undergraduate honors thesis). Department of Afroamerican and African Studies, University of Michigan.

PART II

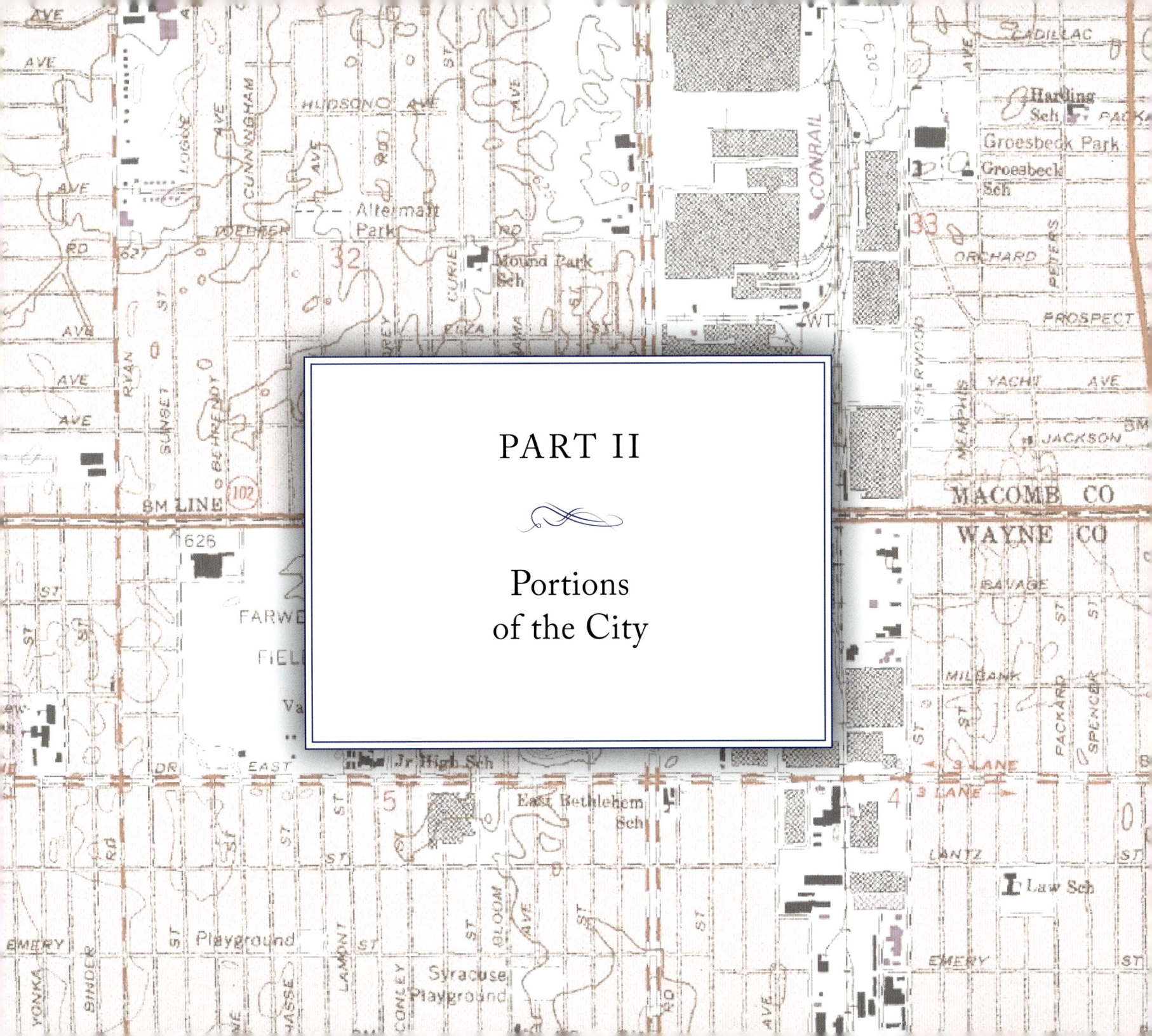

Portions of the City

4

DETROIT
Linear City

ROBERT FISHMAN

In the early 1930s, the Soviet architect and planner Nikolai Miliutin published designs for a "linear city" that he claimed would realize Marx and Engels's utopian hopes for the "gradual abolition of the distinction between town and country" (Marx and Engels 1988 [1848], p. 15) and at the same time provide the most efficient sites for Soviet industrialization under Stalin's Five Year Plan. Miliutin's concept was to decentralize industry by moving large factories out of the crowded factory districts of older cities to exurban and rural sites along parallel rail and highway corridors. The linear city would be defined by this set of parallel lines: first the rail line itself; then a linear "factory zone" bordered on one side by the rail line and on the other side by an arterial highway; then a landscaped greenbelt; and finally a linear zone of workers' housing, schools, and public buildings merging into agricultural land and peasant villages (see Figure 4.1). Located between the highway and rail lines, factories would benefit from direct freight service without the congestion of the older cities. Workers too would escape urban crowding while living just across the greenbelt from the factories where they were employed (Miliutin 1974 [1930]).

In the early 1940s, Le Corbusier (without acknowledging Miliutin or earlier linear city theorists like Arturo Soria y Mata) adopted the linear city form as one of his "three human establishments" (Collins, 1959a and 1959b). With his customary clarity, Le Corbusier divided human settlements in the industrial era into (1) "radiocentric" urban centers for trade, culture, and administration; (2) "radiant farms" for agriculture; and (3) the linear cities of industry, running between the radiocentric cities (Boesiger and Girsbirger 1967, p. 119) (see Figure 4.2). As in Miliutin's plan, factories would be adjacent to highway and rail lines, and separated from worker's

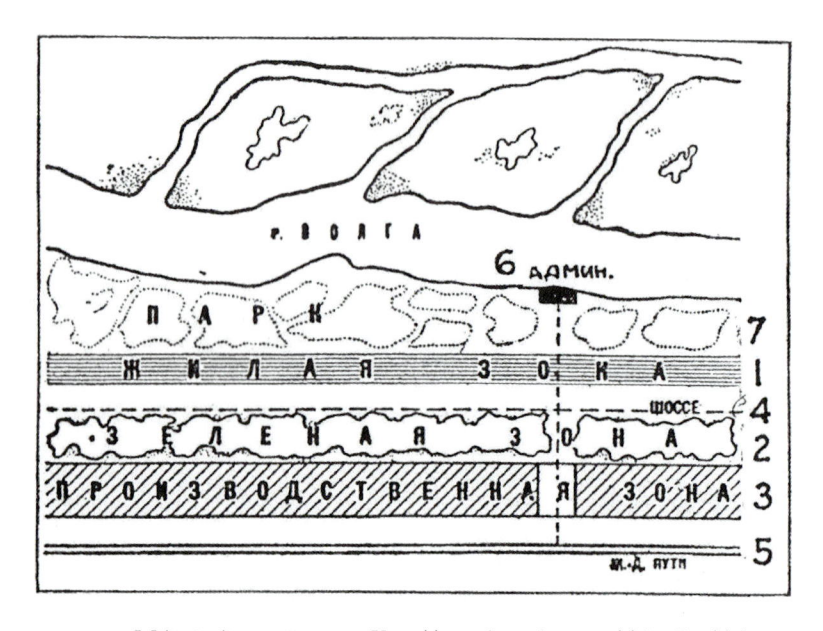

FIGURE 4.1 Miliutin linear city, 1930. Key: (1) residential zones, (2) buffer, (3) heavy industry, (4) highway, (5) rail line, (6) river, and (7) park with peasant village.
Source: Courtesy of MIT Press. From Miliutin, N. (1974). Sotsgorod: The problem of building socialist cities. Transl. A. Sprague. Prepared for publication by G. Collins and W. Alex. Cambridge, MA: MIT Press, p. 42. Originally published in 1930.

housing by a greenbelt. Unlike Miliutin's modest low-rise workers' cooperatives, Le Corbusier's favored housing for workers was high-rise Unités—a large raised slab of housing with facilities—in a landscaped setting.

What neither Miliutin nor Le Corbusier realized was that a powerful version of the linear city they imagined as a quasi-utopian form for industrial production was actually being built in the 1930s and 1940s—in Detroit. (See Figure 4.3) Here it proved to be the very real and indeed most effective setting for industrial production under corporate capitalism. As both Miliutin and Le Corbusier understood theoretically, the linear city was unmatched in its potential to enable massive industrial plants to function efficiently, as well as to provide convenient locations for workers' housing. Linear cities arose where a major rail line at the still-undeveloped rural fringe of the Detroit metropolitan area ran parallel to a major arterial highway, with ample space between for the largest automobile assembly plants of the period and their major suppliers.

The archetypal example is the Mound Road linear city that took shape during World War II. It begins at the northern edge of Detroit and runs north through neighboring Warren where a Michigan Central Railroad line bisects Mound Road and Van Dyke Avenue (both broad arterials).

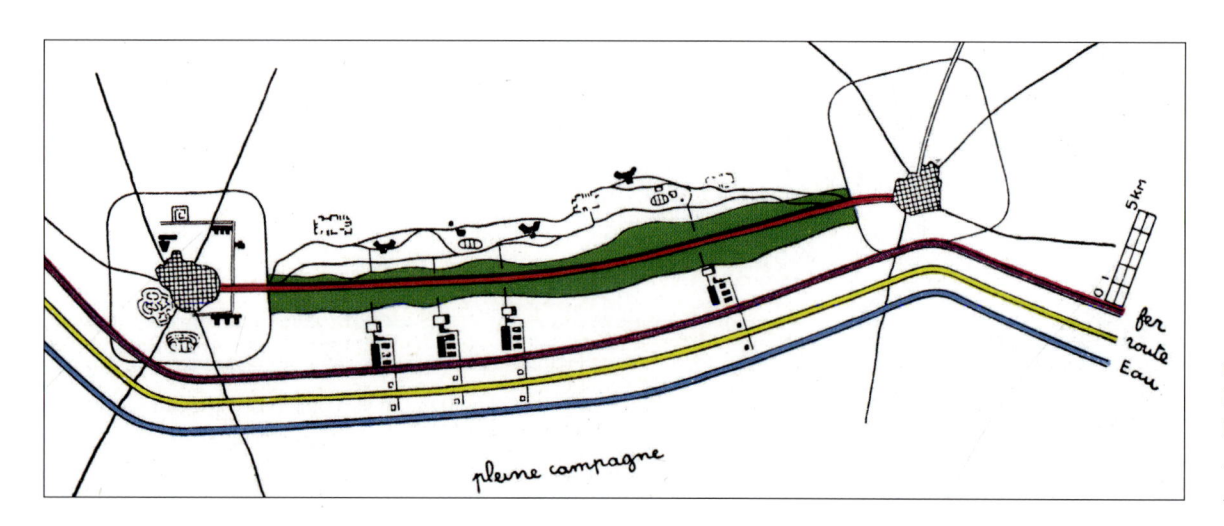

FIGURE 4.2 Le Corbusier's "industrial linear city." This linear city (green) runs between radio-concentric cities.
Source: © 2013 Artists Rights Society (ARS), New York/ADAGP, Paris/F.L.C.

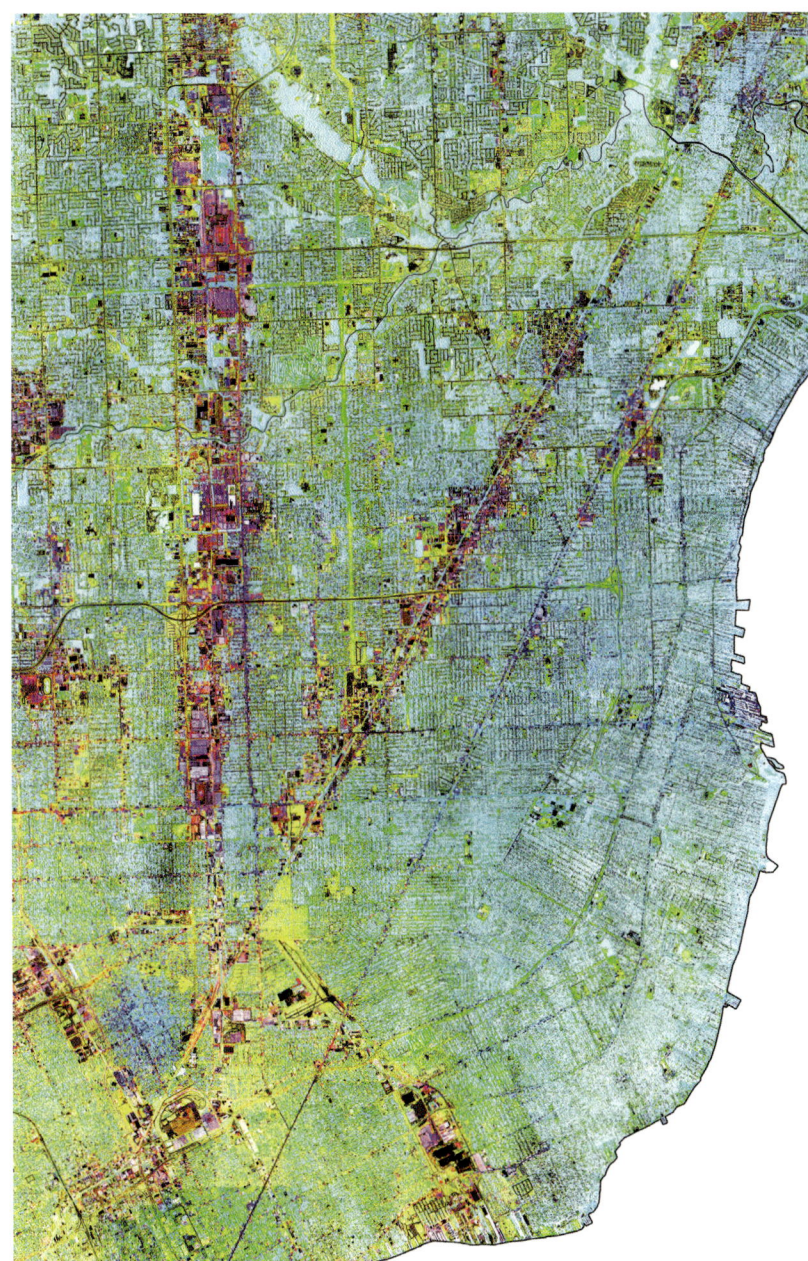

FIGURE 4.3 Mound Road and Groesbeck Highway linear cities. Linear cities as they emerge from the northeast Detroit and cross Eight Mile.
Source: Reza Amindabari, Map Creator

A second major linear city followed the northeast diagonal of the Grand Junction Railway as it runs parallel to Groesbeck Highway from Detroit into Macomb County. The third major linear city arose a decade later west of Detroit in the interstate era of the 1950s where an east-west Michigan Central line runs through suburban Livonia between Interstate 94 and Plymouth Road. Even the largest plants could locate easily on the half-mile-wide parcels that separated the railroad tracks from the arterials.

As Miliutin and Le Corbusier envisioned, the Detroit linear cities included an important housing component. During the 1940s, as we shall see, both Eero Saarinen and Frank Lloyd Wright put forward designs for "progressive communities" to house factory workers and their families in the green fields adjacent to the industrial corridors; at the same time, black activists such as Robert Weaver (later the first cabinet secretary of the U.S. Department of Housing and Urban Development) and Coleman Young (later the first black mayor of Detroit) organized to make this housing a model of integration as well as design. For a moment it appeared as if the Detroit linear cities would constitute a new progressive total environment, advanced both socially and technologically. But the housing that

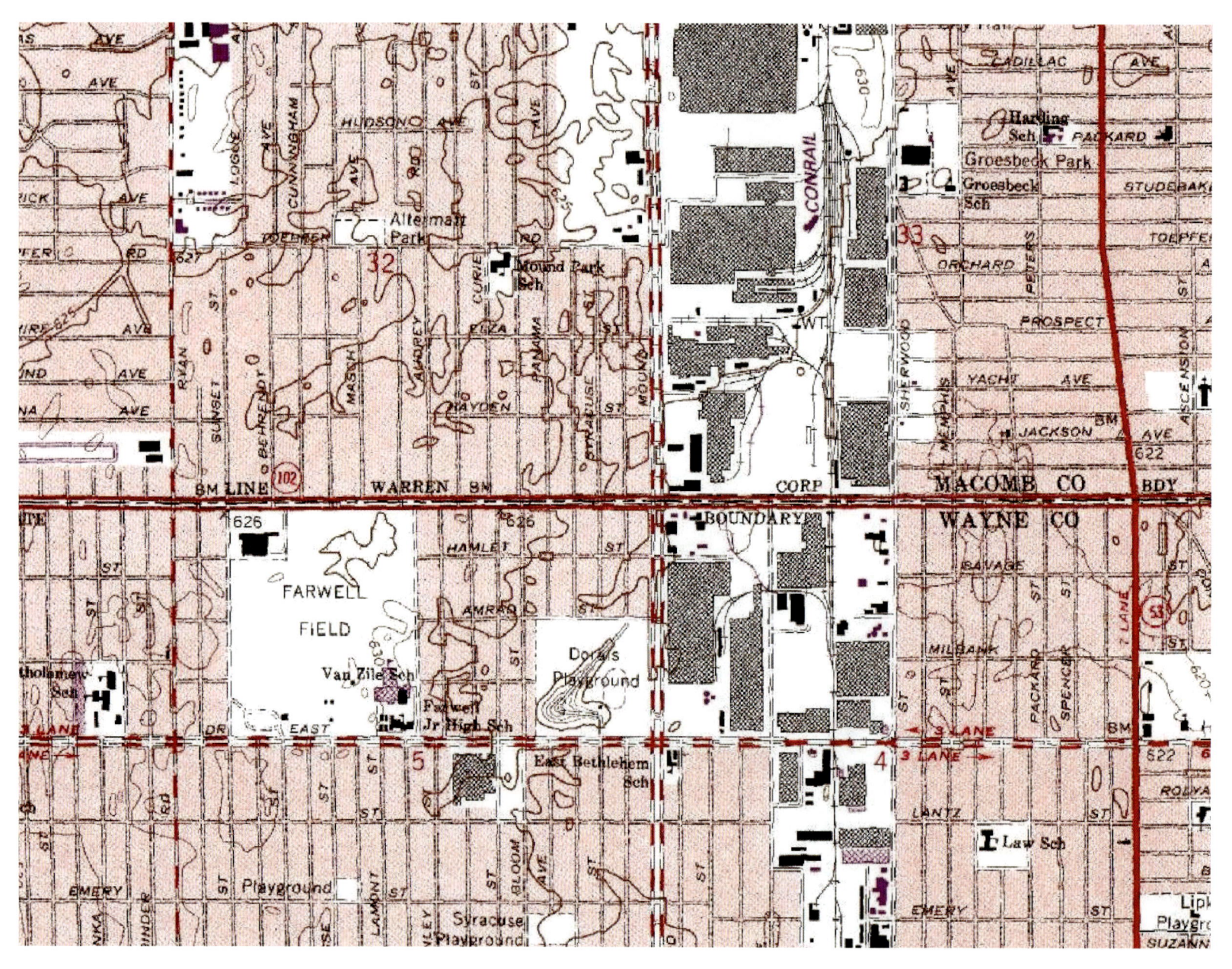

FIGURE 4.4 Mound Road linear city. This city crosses Eight Mile from Detroit to Warren, Michigan. Mound Road is the double line running north-south in the center of this U.S. Geological Survey Map circa 1980. The plant in Detroit is Chrysler/Briggs Body and that in Warren is Dodge Truck. The Conrail freight line is the former Michigan Central line.

Source: Map courtesy of the U.S. Geological Survey.

was actually built turned out to be conventional Federal Housing Administration (FHA) tract houses—and rigidly segregated to exclude blacks.

Nevertheless, the Detroit linear cities certainly succeeded as advanced sites for production. To grasp their tremendous power, we need only consider the Mound Road linear city in the early 1940s and its three major facilities, all designed by Albert Kahn: Dodge Truck at Mound Road and Eight Mile Road in 1938; the Hudson Naval Ordnance Plant at Mound and Nine Mile in 1941 (later the Chevrolet Warren Division and now the General Motors Powertrain Division); and the Detroit Tank Arsenal at Mound and Eleven Mile in 1941 (now the Army Tank-Automotive Command). Dodge Truck's original 1938 plant remains the model modernist factory, the American successor to Peter Behrens's AEG Turbine Factory in Berlin in 1910 and Walter Gropius's Fagus Shoe Factory in Alfeld, Germany, in 1911.[1]

During World War II, Dodge Truck had a more direct influence on the modern world; workers there assembled over 400,000 trucks, which provided essential mobility not only to the American Army but to the Soviet Army as well. Built to withstand the dirt roads of rural America, these trucks proved to be the only vehicles that could operate under even worse conditions in rural Russia. The Detroit Tank Arsenal had perhaps an even greater world impact. When the arsenal began production in 1941, Hitler's Wehrmacht was conquering Europe and the Soviet Union with an unprecedented blitzkrieg force of 4,000 tanks. From 1941 to 1945, the Detroit Tank Arsenal produced more than 22,000 tanks (Hyde 2003, pp. 113–28).

Such feats of production were possible only because the plants along the linear cities could gather raw materials and manufactures (especially steel, glass, and rubber) from around the Midwest and bring them, together with parts produced in the Detroit metropolitan area, into a single highly integrated production process located in assembly plants strung along the linear cities. Indeed, at its height as the wartime "Arsenal of Democracy," Detroit functioned almost as a single great plant, with the linear cities as its

FIGURE 4.5 Map of industrial uses, 1933.
Source: Sert, J. (1942). Can our cities survive? An ABC of urban problems, their analysis, their solution. Cambridge, MA: Harvard University Press, p. 113.

main "production lines." Yet the linear cities were hardly recognized as such during their height, and today we have to painstakingly reimagine them out of the neglected rail lines and many empty factories that now line them (see the Mound Road linear city in Figure 4.4). This chapter will attempt to revise and revision our basic concept of Detroit by mapping that vanished world of production from its origins to its astonishing heights.

Perhaps because the linear city does not match the standard image of either the crowded urban factory zone or the typical suburban industrial

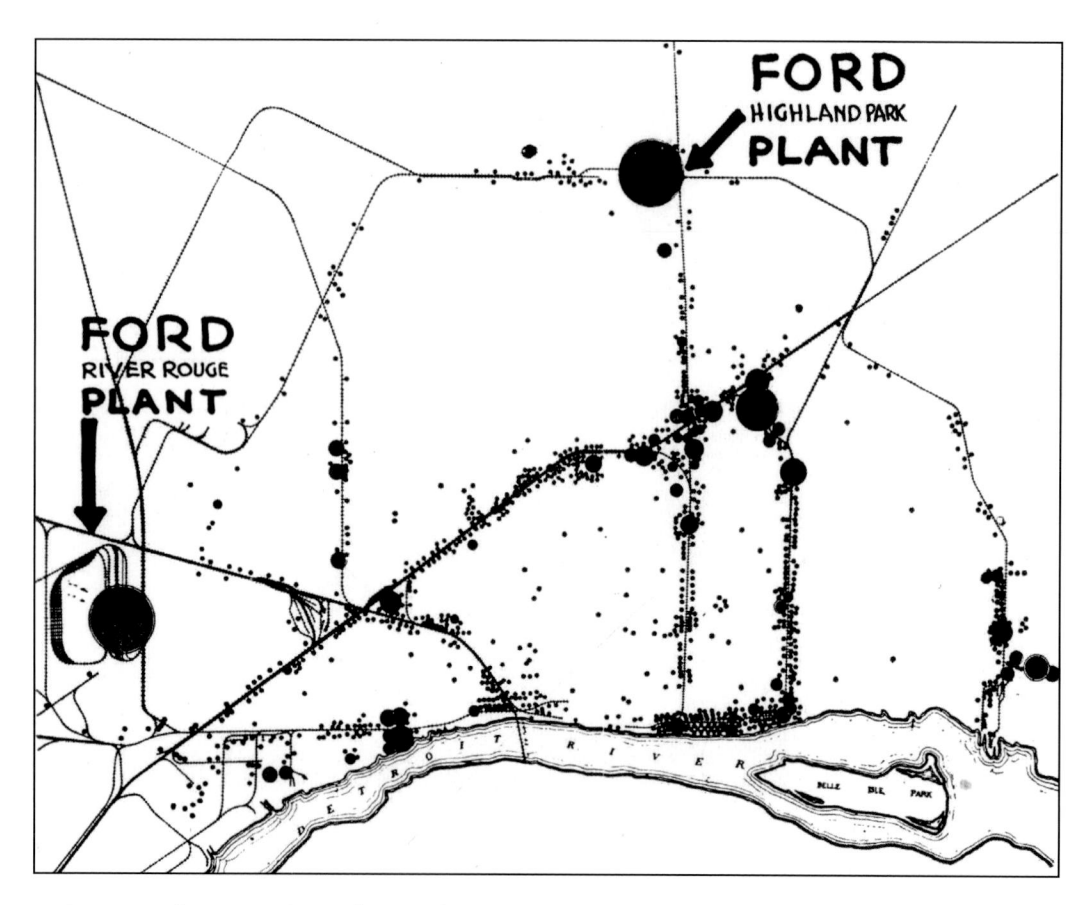

FIGURE 4.6 Location of Detroit's industries. *Source: Sert, J. (1942). Can our cities survive? An ABC of urban problems, their analysis, their solution. Cambridge, MA: Harvard University Press, p. 113.*

park, its significance in the evolution of the industrial metropolis has not been adequately discerned. Although observers as early as the 1930s recognized that Detroit no longer conformed to the older structure of an industrial city with well-defined clusters of manufacturing near its core, they remained uncertain how to characterize the new structure that was emerging. This difficulty is clearly evident in the remarkable map of Detroit produced by Richard Neutra and the American CIAM (International Congress of Modern Architecture) group for the 1933 meeting in Athens (see Figure 4.5).

Jose Luis Sert reproduced the map in his 1942 book, *Can Our Cities Survive?* (a compendium of CIAM urbanism) over this caption:

"This extraordinary metropolis [Detroit] is the largest purely industrial center in the United States. It has automobile plants scattered without any plan over a vast region, and it has grown so haphazardly that its residential sections are all mixed up." (Sert, 1942, p. 113). Indeed, the map does appear to depict a seemingly haphazard mixture of manufacturing and residential areas extending over the city of Detroit and its nearby suburbs.

Nevertheless, a much smaller map reproduced on the same page (see Figure 4.6) presents a vital clue to Detroit's industrial structure that Sert for some reason failed to grasp fully. The caption for the

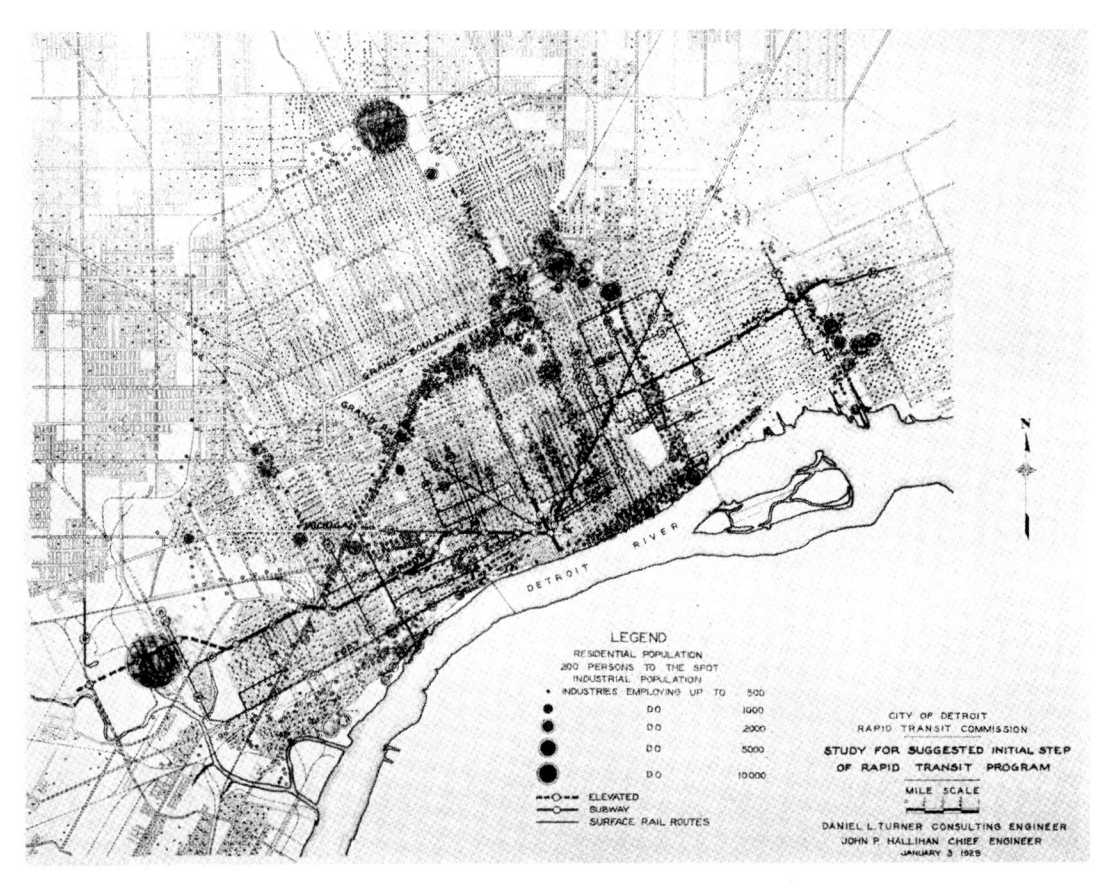

FIGURE 4.7 Study for projected rail system. *Source: Detroit Department of Street Railways. (1929). Report of the Street Railway Commission and the Rapid Transit Commission to Hon. John C. Lodge, Mayor and Hon. The Common Council on a rapid transit system for the city of Detroit. Detroit, MI: Street Railway Commission.*

smaller map reads, "The schematic map shown below (designed by the Rapid Transit Commission of Detroit) shows the location of industry along the main lines of communication." This map is in fact a redrawn version of a map in a 1929 report proposing a rapid transit system for Detroit (see Figure 4.7).

In the original map, it is obvious that the location of Detroit industry is anything but scattered or "haphazard" in its location. The "main lines of communication" are in fact the major rail lines coming into the city. Ironically, these rail lines are clearly the basic determinants of the location of Detroit's automobile production in 1929.

THE ROLE OF RAILWAYS

This rail-based principle of location was hardly unique to Detroit. Before motorized trucking, goods moved over city streets slowly and expensively on horse-drawn wagons; only if a factory were located along a rail line could manufacturers efficiently load and unload goods onto boxcars parked on sidings. Throughout industrial America, manufacturers therefore favored locations along the rail lines. Detroit, as it happens, was particularly well endowed with multiple rail lines built in the nineteenth century because of the city's role as a regional hub and river port for timber, agricultural, and manufactured products. No fewer than seven major rail lines converged on the city, including the Grand Trunk Railroad (a Canadian line with connections to Ontario at Port Huron); the Père Marquette and the Detroit, Grand Haven, and Milwaukee Railroad; and several lines of the Michigan Central Railroad, part of the New York Central system and the dominant line in southeast Michigan with connections to Canada through the Windsor Rail Tunnel (Zunz 1982, pp. 300–301). As Detroit emerged as an industrial power, factories began to spread from their original clustering along the Detroit River out along the rail lines, a movement very well shown in the 1920 map showing the location of the city's industries (see Figure 4.8). This moderate dispersion was a common pattern in the rapidly industrializing cities of late-nineteenth-century America, as factories sought cheap land that was located at the edge of the developed area of a city and that was also adjacent to one of the rail lines. In the nineteenth century and early twentieth century, however, this pattern did not produce a linear city as Miliutin or Le Corbusier conceived it, because cities grew so fast that once-peripheral factories were very quickly engulfed in solid blocks of mixed-use housing and workshops. As the sociologists of the Chicago School mapped that city in the 1920s in their famous concentric circles diagram, the archetypal twentieth-century industrial city was not linear in form but was centered around a major downtown surrounded by a circular "factory zone" of dense factories, workshops, and workers' housing, which was in turn surrounded by a peripheral zone of suburban middle class housing (Burgess 1925, p. 51).

In both the Chicago School model and in the real city of Chicago, factories could escape the congestion and high costs of the "factory zone" only by moving well beyond even the zone of suburban housing to build what Graham Taylor called "satellite cities." These were planned industrial villages with major factories and workers' housing, such as Pullman, Illinois (built in 1880, thirteen miles from the historic core of Chicago) and the "new town" of Gary, Indiana (built in 1906, twenty-five miles from Chicago's core, to accommodate United States Steel's massive plant) (Taylor 1915). As we shall see, the Detroit linear cities would furnish a third option that provided the space and efficiency of the satellite city without the need to build and plan a separate new community.

A close look at the 1929 Detroit Rapid Transit Commission map (Figure 4.7) shows both the rule—the Chicago-style absorption of factories located along the rail lines into the dense fabric of Detroit's rapidly-growing factory zone—and the very significant exception: a "proto linear city" based on Ford's Highland Park plant at what was then the far northern periphery of the metropolis. As to Chicago-style growth, an excellent example is the Packard Motors plant (now one of Detroit's most famous ruins), the earliest of the city's major assembly plants, begun in 1903 on open land along a Michigan Central line. By 1929 it was fully engulfed in the dense fabric of the city.

AUTOMOBILE PLANT LOCATIONS AND STRATEGIES

The location of one plant from the earlier era, however, stands out as different from the rest of Detroit: inconsistent with the Chicago School model, and pointing forward toward the linear city concept. This was Henry Ford's 1910 "Crystal Palace," designed by Albert Kahn and built for the Model T. Located in Highland Park, it stands on Woodward and Manchester Avenues at a location that Ford himself described as then "away out in the country from Detroit" and in any case well beyond the fashionable neighborhood of upper-middle-class housing called "Boston-Edison," where Ford himself lived at the time of its construction (Chandler 1964, p. 41). And yet it is not a satellite city such as Pullman or Gary, or Ford's later super-plant at River Rouge in Dearborn. Ford in 1910 grasped the revolutionary principle and power of the linear city, and that understanding was critical to his success at Highland Park. Ironically, by the late 1910s and 1920s he had retreated to an idiosyncratic version of the satellite

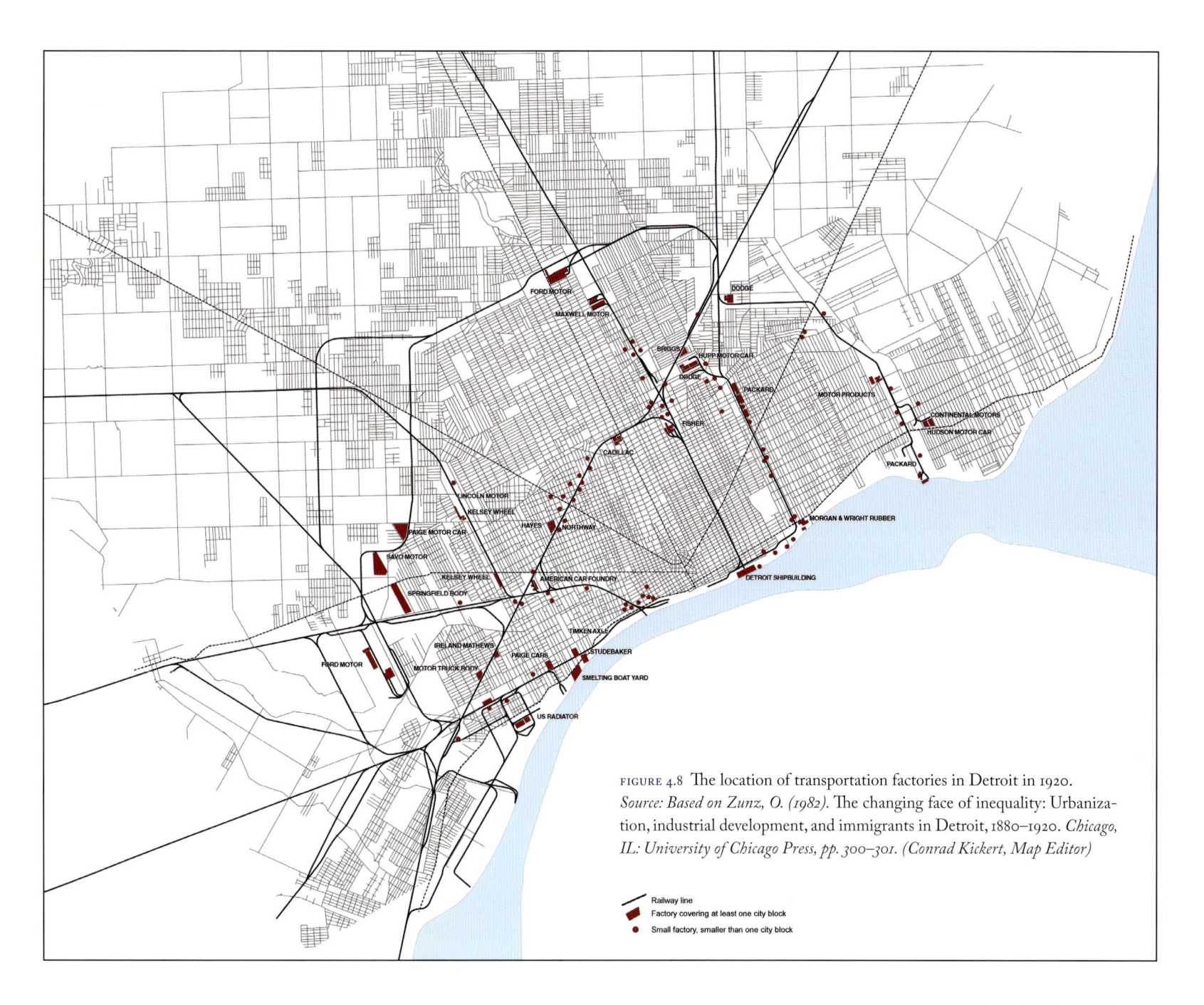

FIGURE 4.8 The location of transportation factories in Detroit in 1920. *Source: Based on Zunz, O. (1982). The changing face of inequality: Urbanization, industrial development, and immigrants in Detroit, 1880–1920. Chicago, IL: University of Chicago Press, pp. 300–301. (Conrad Kickert, Map Editor)*

― Railway line
▰ Factory covering at least one city block
• Small factory, smaller than one city block

DETROIT: Linear City 85

FIGURE 4.9 Aerial View, Ford Motor Company, Highland Park Plant, 1923.
Source: From the collections of The Henry Ford.

city whose deficiencies seriously undermined his supposedly super-efficient new mega-facility at River Rouge (Brinkley 2003).

In 1910, however, Ford's judgment was still unimpaired by an almost megalomaniacal quest for total control that later dominated his leadership (Brinkley 2003, pp. 81–97). With the initial success of the Model T (introduced in 1908), he was determined to radically "scale up" production at a new plant; in choosing a location, as in so much else, he ignored conventional wisdom and looked at the problem of industrial location (and the industrial city) with a fresh perspective. Ford understood that he needed both a large tract of cheap land *and* highly efficient transportation links to the rest of the city and the rest of the country. The links back to the city were especially important, because Ford very well understood that his hopes for "scaling up" could not be accomplished within the Ford company alone but would depend on parts from a multitude of suppliers located in the older Detroit factory zones and throughout southeast Michigan.

In that context, his choice of a sixty-acre tract "away out in the country" in Highland Park (Figure 4.9) made perfect sense, because it was located at the intersection of the Detroit, Grand Haven and Milwaukee Railroad trunk line and the Detroit Terminal Railroad, a "belt line" that circled the city (Figure 4.10). The "belt line" is a particularly interesting (but now forgotten) aspect of the early-twentieth-century industrial metropolis. One weakness of a factory zone where the major plants are strung out along the various lines coming into the city is that these plants need to receive supplies from all around the region and the country, not just from other plants that are located along their particular railroad line. Similarly, they need to ship throughout the region and the country, not just to the locations served by the rail line they border. To remedy this problem, the railroad companies in many cities, including Detroit, banded together to build a belt line that in effect intercepted all the major trunk lines coming into a city; the Detroit Terminal Railroad was completed in 1909. A box car coming into the city on one railroad could be reshuffled in the belt line's yards to reach a factory located along another railroad's line; similarly, a boxcar loaded at a factory along a given railroad line could be reshuffled at the yards to the line that best connected with its ultimate destination. Finally, locations along the belt line itself became very convenient locations for factories ("Detroit Terminal Relief Is in Sight" 1912).

In locating at Highland Park, Ford had discovered a new kind of strategic location for Detroit's industrialization. The Detroit, Grand Haven, and Milwaukee track connected him directly with his main outside supplier—the Dodge Main plant, located closer to the center of the metropolis in Hamtramck. Until 1919 when Ford bought them out, the Dodge brothers were not only Ford's largest suppliers, but also owned 10 percent of the Ford Motor Company (Brinkley 2003, p. 143). Other smaller suppliers dependent on Ford hastened to locate along this line, as well as assembly plants of other companies such as Maxwell Motors that benefited from the concentration of suppliers. Meanwhile, Ford also had direct access to the Detroit Terminal Railroad for deliveries from suppliers and for shipment of his cars and parts throughout the United States. By 1914 Ford was receiving some 100 boxcars of supplies over the Detroit Terminal Railroad daily, and shipping out 170 boxcars daily loaded with assembled automobiles. Ford recalls that

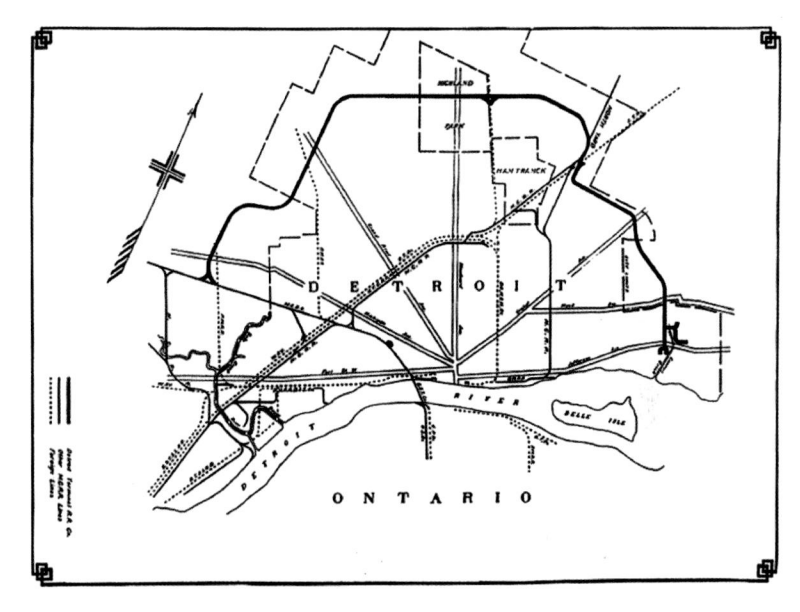

FIGURE 4.10 Detroit Terminal Railroad (belt line). The Ford plant is located at the top of the map in Highland Park between Woodward Avenue (double line) and the notch to the east where the beltline crosses the Detroit, Grand Haven line. The Chalmers Motors plants that would later become the Jefferson Avenue plants of the Chrysler Corporation are located at the eastern end of the line.
Source: Detroit Terminal Railroad. (1914, June 19). Railway Age Gazette, 56, p. 1523.

the Highland Park plant at its peak in the 1920s, now expanded to 180 acres, loaded a *thousand* boxcars a day on the Detroit Terminal Railroad with finished cars for dealers throughout the United States (Chandler 1964, p. 56).

Although scholars have focused on the assembly-line methods of production within the Highland Park plant, they understand less about how Ford's revolutionary methods of production were dependent on parts from suppliers from around the region and the country, parts that reached the plant over its rail connections. Alfred P. Sloan (then head of the Hyatt Roller Bearing Company) estimated that Ford in the mid-1910s was the ultimate purchaser of more than 50 percent of his production of ball bearings (Sloan 1964,

p. 71). But by the late 1910s Ford had turned against this complex but mutually beneficial system as he strove to detach himself from the rest of Detroit in his new "magic kingdom" of the River Rouge, where every aspect of the production process would be under his complete control. Every part for the Model T would be manufactured at the Rouge, and Ford also sought to own all the sources of raw materials (coal, iron ore, etc.) so that he could manufacture the parts from his own steel mills, glass works, and other facilities.

Although the Rouge became world famous as the symbol of advanced industrial production, it was in the *urban* context a giant step backwards: a vain attempt to mimic the complexity of the city within a massive multifunction plant completely owned and controlled by one man. Not surprisingly, Ford ultimately discovered that he could not produce steel and glass more efficiently than the manufacturers who specialized in those products, still less could he replace the skills and innovations of his suppliers. Only Ford's literally impregnable position as "first mover" enabled his company to survive his megalomania. Ford therefore never realized the full benefits of the proto linear city that he had pioneered at Highland Park; these went instead to his competitors at GM and Chrysler. Alfred P. Sloan, whose company was bought out by GM in 1916 and who became president of GM in 1923, responded to Ford's River Rouge initiative by going in the opposite direction, emphasizing GM's potential for flexibility. Whereas Ford was still offering a single unchanging brand, the Model T, General Motors opted for "a car for every purse" and annual model changes (Sloan 1964).

More importantly for our purposes, Sloan rejected Ford's industrial autarchy and sought to build GM by building on Detroit's and the Midwest's strengths in its networks of specialized suppliers. As he put it, "We try, wherever possible, to test our internal supplying divisions against external competition and to make a continuing judgment on whether it is better to make or buy . . . we purchase a large proportion of the items that go into our end products [which Sloan estimated at 55 to 60 percent] because there is no reason to believe that by producing them we could obtain better products, or service, or a lower price." (Sloan 1964, p. 187). To support this philosophy, Sloan pioneered an elaborate system of accounting that enabled management to accurately price a part, whether it was manufactured at the assembly plant, by another GM division, or by an outside supplier (Raff 1991).

This resulted in a transportation system and set of plant locations that tied GM efficiently and effectively into the city and the region. It was the emerging linear city that best satisfied these needs. As it happens, however, GM plants were inherited from separate car companies (Chevrolet, Pontiac, Buick, Oldsmobile and Cadillac) and were widely scattered throughout southeastern Michigan, with only Cadillac truly based in Detroit and a particular concentration of Chevrolet and Buick plants in Flint, a city that functioned as GM's "satellite city." So it was the third of the Detroit Big Three automobile corporations, Chrysler, that took the lead in bringing the true scale and power of the linear city to Detroit and the world.

Chrysler's long and painful decline after World War II has tended to hide that corporation's innovative role in Detroit from its founding in 1924 through the 1940s. Formed under the leadership of engineer Walter P. Chrysler out of a merger of two near-bankrupt car companies, Maxwell and Chalmers, Chrysler necessarily relied heavily on existing networks of suppliers to compete with the better-established Ford and GM. Chrysler himself was a former head of GM's Buick division, and a strong exponent of Alfred P. Sloan's management, accounting, and production techniques. Chrysler's acquisition of Dodge in 1928 gave Chrysler the engineering expertise and production capacity of the Dodge Main plant in Hamtramck that had previously helped to fuel Ford's expansion (Hyde 2003, p. 91).

Like Ford in 1910, Chrysler's strategy involved making maximum use of the Detroit Terminal Railroad to connect Chrysler plants and to draw on the resources of the Detroit area. The massive assembly plant that the Chrysler Corporation had inherited from Chalmers Motors was located at Jefferson Avenue at the end of the Detroit Terminal Railroad loop around the city, and Chrysler soon added a second plant nearby. (Today, the Jefferson North Assembly plant remains one of Chrysler's major production facilities.) In the late 1920s, after the initial success of the Chrysler automobile produced at the old Maxwell plant, Walter P. Chrysler pushed an ambitious plan to make his corporation a competitor with Ford and Chevrolet in the low-priced mass market. To manufacture the new Plymouths, he expanded an existing plant built by Dodge on Lynch Road into the largest automobile plant in the world under one roof.

The Lynch Road plant established a new industrial geography for Detroit. It occupies the site where the Detroit Terminal Railroad intersects the combined Michigan Central/Grand Trunk Railway tracks as they cut a diagonal across the city. The nearby Dodge Main was reoriented from its rail-based orientation to the Ford plant in Highland Park to the new Plymouth plant. Designed to produce more than 1,000 cars a day along the longest assembly lines in Detroit, the new Plymouth plant could thus draw effectively from the other Chrysler plants and from suppliers throughout the city and the region. By 1935 the success of the Plymouth brand, especially against a struggling Ford, had enabled Chrysler to displace Ford as the number two automaker in Detroit. Chrysler had in effect reoriented his company and Detroit itself around a new linear city for Detroit industrialization (Hyde 2003).

The scale and location of the Lynch Road Plymouth plant, moreover, pointed strongly toward a decentralized future for the Detroit region (see Figure 4.11). It definitively established the single-story plant as the most efficient form for automobile production. Although Chrysler was able to find a site for the plant within the built-up area of Detroit that was not only large enough but also had outstanding rail connections, it was clear that such inner-city sites would not be easily found in the future. Just north of the plant lay the North Yards of the Terminal Railroad, where the dual line of the Michigan Central and the Grand Trunk Railway that ran through the city separated into a Michigan Central line running north between Mound and Van Dyke Avenues, and a Grand Trunk line running northeast, parallel to Groesbeck Highway. Both rail lines quickly reached cheap, open land in the Macomb County suburbs. The North Yards thus became the starting point for both the Mound Avenue and Groesbeck Highway linear cities, the point where the linear cities connect with the older industrial areas of Detroit.

Again, Chrysler took the lead in 1938 by locating its first important plant since the Lynch Road Plymouth plant on the north (suburban) side of Eight Mile along the Mound Road/Michigan Central corridor. Designed by Albert Kahn, the Dodge Truck assembly plant in Warren, Michigan, has rightly become a symbol for Detroit modernism at its height. Less well known was Kahn's success in integrating the open plan of the factory with the rail lines that adjoin it. The advantages of the Mound Road linear city were so clear (especially for the largest plants) that, when the United States began to rearm in 1940–41, Mound Road became the favored site for some of the most massive war production plants anywhere in the world. In Detroit, as in the other great industrial cities, the war drove decentralization as massive plants sought correspondingly large sites, which were necessarily outside the developed factory zone. In Detroit, however, this meant the intensification of the already-existing outward movement to the linear cities, especially Mound Road. Not only did Dodge Truck radically expand, losing some of its earlier classic form (see Figure 4.12), but Hudson Motors built the Naval Ordinance Plant at Mound and Nine Mile, and Chrysler built and managed the Detroit Tank Arsenal at Mound and Eleven Mile—both well outside of the city of Detroit's borders. The Tank Arsenal gives perhaps the best idea of not only the scale of these wartime facilities but also their integration with

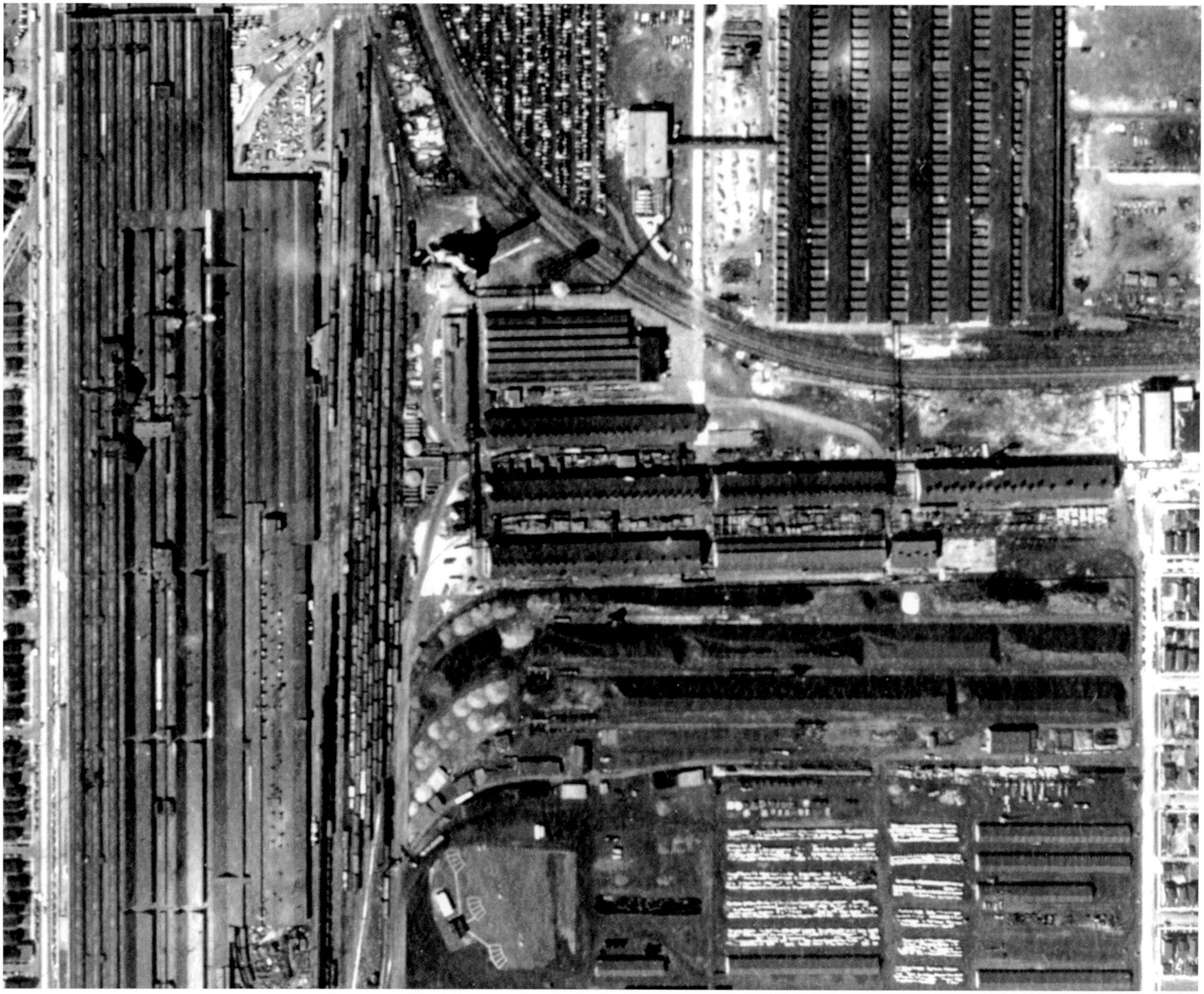

FIGURE 4.12 "Command Reconnaissance Cars" produced at the Dodge Truck Plant, 1943. The classic Kahn building is to the right.
Source: Courtesy of the Library of Congress, Prints & Photographs Division, FSA/OWI Collection (LC-USW3-007130-C). Photographer: Arthur S. Siegel.

FIGURE 4.13 The ultimate World War II assembly line. Tank Arsenal, Warren, Michigan, 1943.
Source: Courtesy of the Library of Congress, Prints & Photographs Division, FSA/OWI Collection (LC-USE6-D-001267). Photographer: Alfred T. Palmer.

the rest of Detroit through the linear city. Located on the one-square-mile site bordered by Mound Road on the west, Van Dyke Avenue on the east, Eleven Mile on the south and Twelve Mile on the north, the Tank Arsenal's main glass-and-steel structure was 500 by 1,380 feet, enclosing 690,000 square feet (64,000 m²) on a single level (Hyde 2003; see Figure 4.13). A side track from the Michigan Central line actually ran through the building. The site also included a test track and employed some 5,000 workers. Yet the workers and the 1.3 million square feet (120,000 m²) were only a fraction of the 14,000 workers and 3.2 million square feet (300,000 m²) of production space that Chrysler utilized throughout the Detroit area to manufacture parts for the tanks. Thus, one can say that the Mound Road linear city was indeed the "assembly line" for the Detroit region.

FIGURE 4.11 The Lynch Road Plymouth plant, left, running north south along Mt. Elliott Avenue, with subsidiary foundry and axle plants, 1949. The belt line is the curved line at the top of the picture.
Source: Courtesy of DTE Aerial Photo Collection.

HOUSING AND THE LINEAR CITY

World War II was the challenge that pushed Detroit's mastery of production to its limits. But, with the basic production structure of the linear city in place by the mid 1940s, the one element from Miliutin's and Le Corbusier's ideal type that remained unbuilt was *housing*. Both Miliutin and Le Corbusier understood that by placing factories along rail and highway lines between existing cities, one could then locate workers' housing on

FIGURE 4.14 Tract houses under construction near Mound Road linear city, July 1941. *Source: Courtesy of the Library of Congress, Prints & Photographs Division, FSA/OWI Collection (LC-USW3-009164-C). Photographer: Arthur S. Siegel.*

the abundant, cheap land on either side of the highway/rail corridors. The problem of industrial housing could thus be solved, with crowded urban factory districts relegated to the past. Their designs presumed, of course, a top-down planning structure (whether Soviet or technocratic) in which investment in workers' housing could be coordinated with industrial location. In Detroit, corporate capitalism was capable of implementing linear city planning concepts even more strongly than Miliutin or Le Corbusier could have imagined, but the automobile companies did not usually concern themselves with housing. The more anarchic capitalism of small-scale suburban developers proved highly capable of building linear city workers' housing—in their own fashion, of course.

In July 1941 the Office of War Information (OWI) sent veteran photographers from the team of Farm Security Administration photographers made famous during the Dust Bowl years to Detroit to record the rearmament efforts. Their photographs of the massive new factories along Mound Road are among the most important documents of that period. But many were also fascinated by (and quick to photograph) the small suburban tract houses that were under construction in the former farm land to the east and west of the industrial corridor (see Figure 4.14). The Federal Housing Administration (FHA) had in the 1930s created the template for what we now see as "Levittown style" postwar suburbia: the affordable, small tract house designed to be mass produced; standardized, automobile-oriented subdivision design; and a system for low-interest, low-down-payment long-term self-amortizing mortgages financed by local thrift institutions. Although the full impact of the FHA system would come only after World War II, the OWI shows us that all its elements were already present near Mound Road by 1941.

The outbreak of war in December 1941 put an end to all but the most necessary workers' housing, so it was not until 1947 or 1948 that the subdivisions shown in the 1941 OWI photographs were completed. But an almost inevitable linkage developed—in the United States, at least—between the linear city and the postwar suburban subdivision. Both were part of the new world of mass-produced prosperity that emerged after Depression and World War II. For the postwar workers of the Detroit linear city, the American dream was guaranteed in what became known as the "Treaty of Detroit." This was the name given to a series of labor agreements between the Big Three and the United Auto Workers (UAW), negotiated by labor leader Walter Reuther around 1950, that provided for long-term, multi-year contracts; guaranteed scheduled wage increases based on cost-of-living allowances and increased productivity; and generous fringe benefits such as health insurance, unemployment insurance, and pensions.

As sociologist Daniel Bell commented in 1950, "GM may have paid a billion for [labor] peace but it got a bargain. General Motors has re-

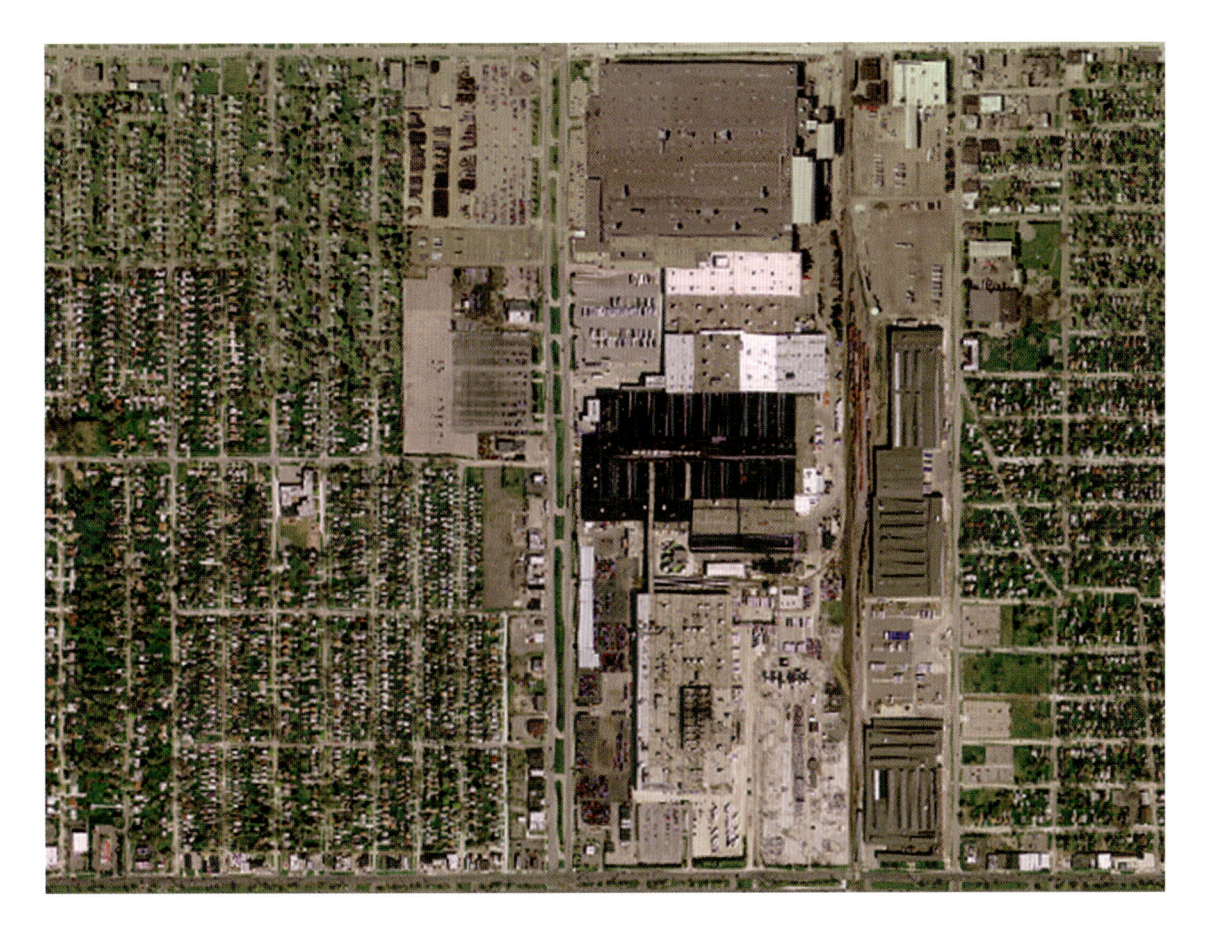

FIGURE 4.15 The postwar linear city in its mature stage. GM Powertrain on Mound Road (center of picture) and Nine Mile (the former Hudson Naval Ordnance Plant) surrounded by workers' tract housing.
Source: SEMCOG (Southeast Michigan Council of Governments). (2010). 2010 Southeast Michigan Regional Imagery Project.

gained control over one of the crucial management functions . . . long range scheduling of production, model changes, and tool and plant investment" (Bell 1950, p. 53). GM was now free to maximize the planned efficiencies of the linear city, while workers in return got stable, relatively high paying jobs. Moreover, the jobs were located in suburbs where the FHA system of house building and finance produced affordable single-family tract houses (see Figure 4.15) whose total mortgage, taxes, and other expenses were generally less than one-quarter of what a production-line worker earned. For working men, such wages bought the house, the car, and a wife who stayed at home to raise the kids. Here at last was workers' piece of the "American dream."

THE INTERSTATE ERA

One important issue for further research that is beyond the scope of this chapter is how the linear cities relate to the system of arterial and interstate highways that arose in the postwar era. The first Detroit-area limited-access highway, the Davison Expressway (constructed in 1942), runs east-west between Highland Park and Hamtramck, parallel to the

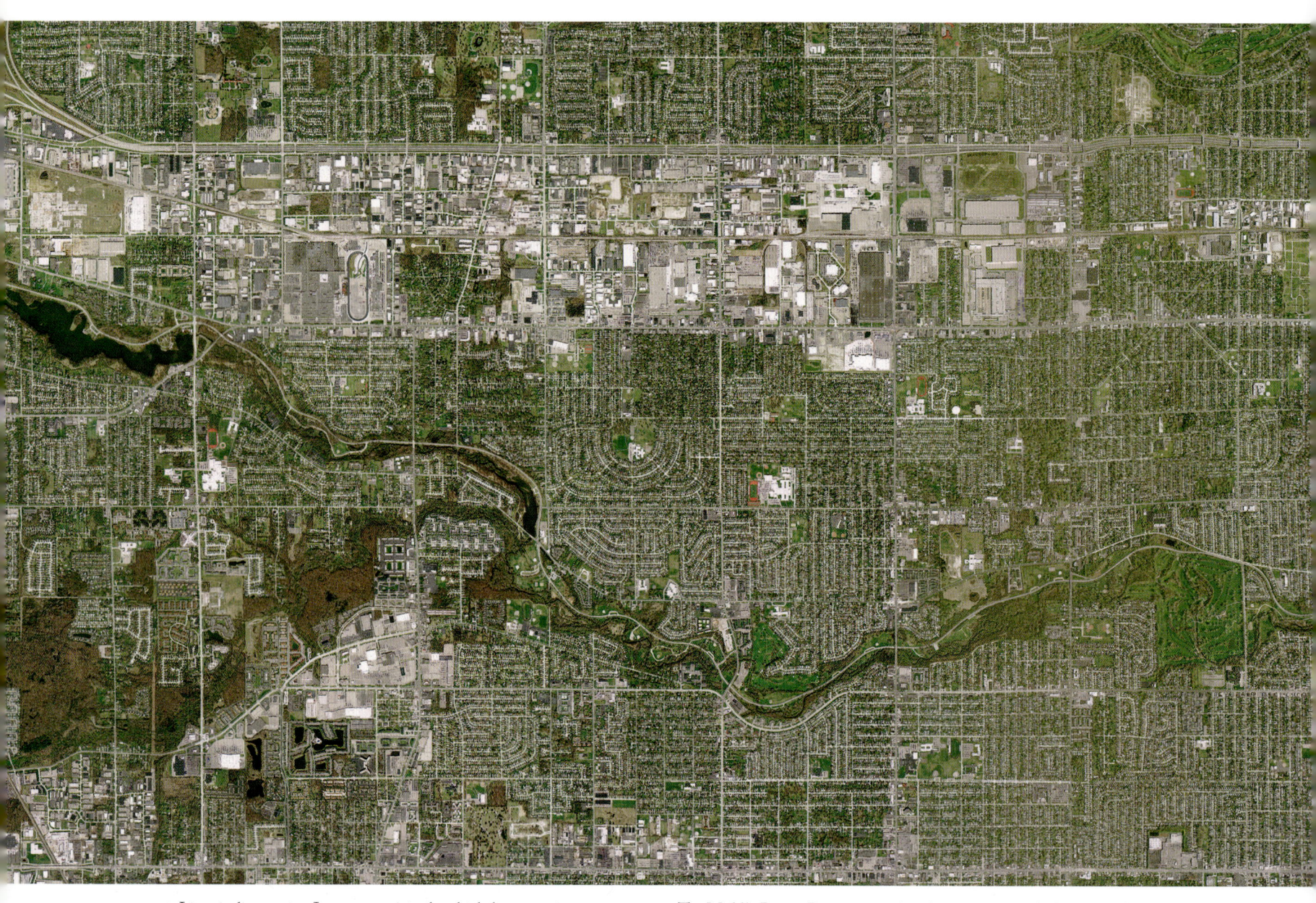

FIGURE 4.16 Livonia linear city. Interstate 96 is the thick line running east-west through the upper part of this image. Plymouth Road, a thinner line, marks its southern boundary. As in Mound Road and Groesbeck Highway, the immense scale of the industrial plants contrasts with the multitude of tract houses below. The Middle Rouge River regional parkway is seen at the bottom, a linear park very much in the spirit of Miliutin's and Le Corbusier's earlier plans.
Source: U.S. Geological Survey satellite image. SEMCOG (Southeast Michigan Council of Governments). (2010). 2010 Southeast Michigan Regional Imagery Project.

beltway railroad, and was built mainly to relieve truck congestion and provide a similar industrial connecting service between plants on the east and west sides of the city. Interstate 696 running east-west through Macomb County now performs a similar service for the northern suburbs. As previously mentioned, only the postwar Livonia linear city seems to belong to the interstate era (see Figure 4.16); perhaps it is more accurate to say that its rise reflects the Korean War boom in the same way that the Mound Road and Groesbeck Highway linear cities reflect World War II. Located some six miles from the western edge of the city of Detroit, the Livonia linear city is wholly suburban; its northern boundary, once Schoolcraft Road, is now Interstate 96; its southern boundary is Plymouth Road, and it is bisected by a branch of the Michigan Central Railroad that connects to Detroit rail yards and the Windsor rail tunnel.

LINEAR CITY PERSPECTIVE

From the perspective of Detroit's current troubles, it is hard to resist the temptation to celebrate the Detroit linear cities at their peak when they represented what was arguably the most powerful, efficient, and productive metropolitan industrial complex anywhere in the world. The linear cities elegantly solved the problem of reconciling the concentration of the city with the need for rapid and unobstructed movement of goods. In many ways they represented the ideal balance between the older, denser industrial city and the suburban dispersion that was to come. Moreover, the linear cities reconciled in their very form the changing balance between rail and road.

Yet one can also be critical of the Detroit linear city from today's perspective. If the linear city in the early 1940s represented a synthesis of concentration and decentralization, that synthesis was brief. The scale and efficiency of the linear city very quickly made the older multi-story Detroit plants obsolete, just as the wide lawns and automobile-friendly environment of the new Macomb County suburbs made the old bungalow neighborhoods seem cramped and old fashioned. The dense network of skills embodied in these old neighborhoods withered too.

In 1958 GM opened its massive Tech Center designed by Eero Saarinen on Mound Road in Warren just beyond the Tank Arsenal. Alfred P. Sloan envisioned this "crown jewel" of the Mound Road linear city as a way to give GM the technological and design dynamism to support the ever-increasing productivity envisioned in the wage settlements of the Treaty of Detroit (Sloan 1964, pp. 205–31). But GM built these shining new research laboratories on a magnificently landscaped campus setting surrounded by a high fence and strictly separated from what was left of Detroit's urban "creative milieu." As the subsequent sad history of GM's long decline in technology and automotive design attests, Saarinen's magnificent campus could not compensate for the knowledge base and creativity that were lost when GM and the rest of the Big Three fenced themselves off from the hundreds of innovative smaller companies that withered and died in the city of Detroit (Knowles and Leslie, 2001).

The linear city model, moreover, moved production strongly and quickly beyond the borders of the city of Detroit at Eight Mile Road. This would not have mattered if the city had been able to annex its suburbs (as Detroit had done through the 1920s) or if some form of regional governance had ensured that the wealth generated by the productivity of the linear cities was equitably distributed to the city of Detroit as well as to its suburbs. Of course, the opposite was the case. Decentralization of industry and workers' housing produced a bonanza for suburban municipalities while condemning the city of Detroit to a constantly decreasing tax base. Even worse, the new tract housing in these suburbs was very much "white only"; as late as 1970 (two years after the passage of the 1968 Fair Housing Act), Warren, Michigan—where most of the Mound Road linear city was located—had 179,000 people, of whom 132 were black; Livonia, site

FIGURE 4.17 Kramer Homes, now Kramer Homes Co-Operative, on Ten Mile Road in Center Line, Michigan, about a mile east of the Mound Road linear city. Row housing is built around a village green and community center/elementary school. Architect: Eero Saarinen, 1951
Source: SEMCOG (Southeast Michigan Council of Governments). (2010). 2010 Southeast Michigan Regional Imagery Project.

of the Livonia linear city, had 110,000 people, of whom 42 were black. By contrast, the city of Detroit in 1970 had 1,511,000 people, of whom 659,000 were black (Farley, Danziger, and Holzer 2000, p. 157.)

This result is especially disappointing, because for a brief moment it appeared that the Detroit linear cities would become model communities as progressive in their racial and social policies as they were advanced technologically. In July 1941, precisely when the OWI photographers were photographing the tract houses near the Mound Road linear city, the United States Housing Corporation, a federal agency for war workers' housing, began construction of the Kramer Homes on East Ten Mile in Center Line, a small city now surrounded by Warren. Designed by Eero Saarinen (with J. Robert F. Swanson), the Kramer Homes embodied the communitarian ideals coming out of the New Deal "greenbelt towns" and similar projects. Instead of single-family detached houses, the Kramer Homes were organized as row houses grouped around a shared "village green" dominated by a combined community center and elementary school (see Figure 4.17). With strong support from Walter Reuther, then head of the GM section of the UAW, Detroit-area progressives hoped to make the Kramer Homes the model for workers' housing in the suburbs and an antidote to the FHA's individualistic tract house mentality (Defense Houses at Center Line Michigan 1941).

Also in the summer of 1941, a small group of automobile workers deeply influenced by the cooperative movement turned to Frank Lloyd Wright to design a cooperative community based on his Broadacre City utopian ideals of factory workers living on large plots as part-time farmers. Wright obliged with an inspired design for "Usonian" houses set on generous farm/garden plots based on low-cost berm (packed-earth) construction (see Figure 4.18). The co-op purchased a 160-acre farm for the project in what is now Madison Heights, west of Mound Road. The first house for the co-op was begun in July 1941. Unfortunately, the coming of war cut short the project, and it was resumed in more conventional form after World War II (Riley 1994; Wright 1954).

Finally, 1941 also saw a strong push by black civil rights leaders in the Detroit area to fight the "color line" and the "job ceiling" that they saw was leading directly to an even more divided metropolis. Robert Weaver, later appointed the first U.S. Department of Housing and Urban Development Secretary in 1965, wrote a notable 1943 article in which he documented the struggle for equal employment on the Mound Road linear city (Weaver 1943). At Dodge Truck, the Hudson Naval Ordnance Plant, and the Detroit Tank Arsenal, white workers initially refused to work alongside

FIGURE 4.18 Frank Lloyd Wright's berm house for Cooperative Homesteads, 1941. *Source: Courtesy of The Frank Lloyd Wright Foundation Archives (The Museum of Modern Art, Avery Architectural & Fine Arts Library, Columbia University, New York).*

blacks, going so far as to stage wildcat strikes that shut down production at the height of the war effort. Nevertheless, the federal government in Washington and the leadership of the UAW strongly supported equal opportunity; the "color line" at the linear city plants was broken in 1942–43, and white resistance declined (see Figure 4.19). But wartime gains were generally lost as white GIs returned to claim their old jobs, and even the UAW cooled on integration as their majority-white rank-and-file strongly resisted initiatives to break the color line (Farley et al. 2000).

Among the young black activists working to promote equal job opportunity and equal housing was Coleman Young, later mayor of Detroit from 1974 to 1994 (Young, 1994). In fact, Coleman Young wound up presiding over a struggling black-majority city radically abandoned by its former white residents in one of the most racially divided metropolitan regions in the country. Moreover, the "Treaty of Detroit" was in effect rescinded as automobile production in the United States shifted from the Big Three to non-union plants along the so-called Southern Automotive Corridor whose foreign owners were highly subsidized by Southern Republican politicians. As Detroit-area plants closed, the once-proud Macomb County suburbs suffered, particularly with the effects of the post-2007 mortgage crisis and high unemployment. The Detroit linear cities have lost their pre-eminence in world manufacturing production.

FIGURE 4.19 Black war worker finishing part for tail section of an airplane at Briggs Manufacturing at the southern end of the Mound Road linear city, 1942. In addition to tanks and trucks, Detroit was a notable center for aircraft production in World War II.
Source: Courtesy of the Library of Congress, Prints & Photographs Division, FSA/OWI Collection (LC-USE6-D-002791). Photographer: Alfred T. Palmer.

But history has many strange and unexpected turns. As the rail system revives in the United States, we can again grasp the remarkable balance between auto and rail, and between dispersion and concentration, that was at the heart of the linear city. And, as the Detroit auto corporations begin to recover from their near-death experience in 2008 and turn not only to more energy-efficient vehicles but also to more energy-efficient and space-conserving production facilities than those now dispersed along the Southern Automotive Corridor, one can imagine a reopening of the facilities along the Detroit linear cities, now equipped as superbly efficient sites for the production of a more balanced transportation system. Moreover, as alternatives to conventional suburban tract housing emerge today, they might well adapt some of the features of Wright's and Saarinen's vision of cooperative housing. The "color line" that defined the Detroit suburbs as white only finally appears to be bending if not breaking, so the communities that surround the renovated linear cities might yet fulfill Weaver's and Young's hopes that they would become models of racial integration. If Miliutin's and Le Corbusier's earlier vision of a techno-utopia built around the linear city is dead, renewed technology and socially committed design might still have a chance of reviving the progressive possibilities that lie dormant in the Detroit linear cities.

NOTES

1. Hedrich Blessing, a famed architectural firm that specialized during this time period in industrial photography, photographed the Dodge Truck factory. Its inclusion in the Heidrich Blessing body of work signifies the factory's standing in the period's modern architecture. The archival photographs are housed at the Chicago History Museum.

REFERENCES

Albert Kahn Associates. (1937). *Industrial and commercial buildings.* Detroit, MI: Albert Kahn.

Bell, D. (1950, July). The treaty of Detroit. *Fortune, 42*(1), 53.

Boesiger, W., and Girsberger, H. (Eds.). (1967). *Le Corbusier: 1910–1965.* New York, NY: Praeger.

Brinkley, D. (2003). *Wheels for the world: Henry Ford, his company, and a century of progress, 1903–2003.* New York, NY: Viking.

Burgess, E. (1925). The growth of the city: An introduction to a research project. In R. Park and E. Burgess (Eds.), *The city: Suggestions for investigation of human behavior in the urban environment* (pp. 47–62). Chicago, IL: University of Chicago Press.

Chandler, A. (1964). *Giant enterprise: Ford, General Motors, and the automobile industry: Sources and readings.* New York, NY: Harcourt.

Collins, G. (1959a). Linear planning throughout the world. *Journal of the Society of Architectural Historians, 18*(3), 74–93.

Collins, G. (1959b). The ciudad lineal of Madrid. *Journal of the Society of Architectural Historians, 18*(9), 38–53.

Defense Houses at Center Line Michigan. (1941, October). *Architectural Forum, 75,* 211–42.

Detroit Department of Street Railways. (1929). *Report of the Street Railway Commission and the Rapid Transit Commission to Hon. John C. Lodge, Mayor and Hon. The Common Council on a Rapid Transit System for the City of Detroit.* Detroit, MI: Street Railway Commission.

Detroit Terminal Railroad. (1914, June 19). *Railway Age Gazette, 56,* 1522–23.

Detroit terminal relief is in sight. (1912, August 24). *Michigan Manufacturer and Financial Record, 9*(8), 6.

Farley, R., Danziger, S., and Holzer, H. (2000). *Detroit divided.* New York, NY: Russell Sage Foundation.

Hyde, C. (2003). *Riding the roller coaster: A history of the Chrysler Corporation.* Detroit, MI: Wayne State University Press.

Knowles, S. and Leslie, S. (2001). "Industrial Versailles:" Eero Saarinen's Corporate Campuses for GM, IBM, and AT&T, *Isis 92*(1), 1–33.

Marx, K., and Engels, F. (1988). *The communist manifesto* (Norton Critical Edition). New York, NY: Norton. Originally published in 1848.

Michigan Central Railroad Station in Detroit. (1914, January 9). *Railway Age Gazette, 9*(2), 73–81.

Miliutin, N. (1974). *Sotsgorod: The problem of building socialist cities.* A. Sprague (Trans.). Prepared for publication by G. Collins and W. Alex. Cambridge, MA: MIT Press. Originally published in 1930.

Raff, D. (1991). Making cars and making money in the interwar automobile industry: Economies of scale and scope in the manufacturing behind the marketing. *Business History Review, 65*(4), 721–53.

Riley, T. (Ed.). (1994). *Frank Lloyd Wright: Architect.* New York, NY: Museum of Modern Art.

Saarinen, E. (1962). *Eero Saarinen on his work.* New Haven, CT: Yale University Press.

Sert, J. (1942). *Can our cities survive? An ABC of urban problems, their analysis, their solution.* Cambridge, MA: Harvard University Press.

Sloan, A. (1964). *My years with General Motors.* Garden City, NY: Doubleday.

Taylor, G. (1915) *Satellite cities: A study of industrial suburbs.* New York, NY: Appleton.

Weaver, R. (1943). Detroit and Negro skill. *Phylon, 4*(2), 131–43.

Wright, F. (1954). *The natural house.* New York, NY: Horizon.

Young, C. (1994). *Hard stuff: The autobiography of Coleman Young.* New York, NY: Viking.

Zunz, O. (1982). *The changing face of inequality: Urbanization, industrial development, and immigrants in Detroit, 1880–1920.* Chicago, IL: University of Chicago Press.

5

COMPARING PEOPLE AND PLACES WITH TRANSPORTATION ACCESSIBILITY IN METROPOLITAN DETROIT

JOE GRENGS

The ability to reach opportunities is an important social goal, particularly in the metropolitan regions of the United States where urban form is characterized by sprawling land use patterns and high degrees of segregation by race and class. Yet transportation policy has long focused singularly on achieving fast mobility, not on reaching opportunities. Under mobility-based policy, the fundamental criterion for success is to move more vehicles more quickly from origin to destination. An accessibility-based perspective, by contrast, challenges this dominant view because movement is not what people ultimately want from their transportation system. Instead, what travelers want is interaction in the form of personal contact with the people and places with which they like to engage. Travelers are not interested in mere movement, but rather in what they get for the movement—the variety and quality of places they can reach for any given distance of travel. Transportation scholars define accessibility as the "potential of opportunities for interaction" (Hansen 1959, p. 79) or the "ease of reaching places" (Cervero 1996, p. 1), as opposed to mobility, which is the "ease of movement." A shift of attention away from mobility toward accessibility leads to new policy responses because it allows for a role for proximity in designing transportation solutions. Instead of an exclusive focus on building transportation infrastructure to achieve faster mobility, an accessibility-based transportation policy recognizes the importance of urban form in achieving transportation goals.

Mobility-based measures often hide injustices that arise from transportation policy. First, mobility-based measures—such as levels of congestion—describe infrastructure segments, not people. Measuring attributes of infrastructure segments offers little help in understanding equity among social groups. And such measures ignore people without cars, who are those most disadvantaged by the cities we build today.

Second, achieving success in providing congestion relief through added highway capacity has the effect of inducing "urban sprawl," whereby land developers respond to faster travel by building destinations farther and farther apart (Transportation Research Board 1995). Thus, mobility-based transportation policy contributes to the sprawl that, researchers have shown, particularly harms people of color and low-income people, who disproportionately live near the urban core because of discrimination in housing markets, and who have fewer resources to adapt to spreading land use patterns (Bullard, Torres, and Johnson 2000; Pendall 1999; Squires and Kubrin 2005). Accessibility is a more useful concept than mobility when it comes to evaluating social equity, because accessibility properly places emphasis on people and their relationships to places, and because it captures the effects of not only the infrastructure of transportation systems but also the spatial arrangement of the destinations that are important to people in their lives.

Through a series of maps, this chapter examines the geographic distribution of accessibility in the three-county region of Detroit, a place that has come to symbolize "spatial mismatch" conditions (Kain 1968), meaning a disconnect between some people and the jobs available to them. The maps reveal dramatic differences among residents of the region in the ability to reach important destinations such as jobs, child-care centers, and supermarkets. And the concept of accessibility underscores the importance of having a private car in a region where public officials and civic leaders built roads primarily to accommodate cars without offering a reasonable alternative in the form of public transit service.

TRANSPORTATION AND GEOGRAPHY IN THE DETROIT METROPOLITAN REGION

Although the counties included in the Detroit metropolitan area have changed over time, the three-county core consists of Macomb, Oakland, and Wayne Counties, illustrated in Figure 5.1, with a 2010 population of 3.9 million in the three counties and 714,000 in the city of Detroit (U.S. Bureau of the Census 2011a). The region is characterized by a depopulating urban core with high rates of poverty surrounded by a mixture of suburbs, many of which are more prosperous than the central city, others of which also suffer from population and job loss. Detroit is among just a

FIGURE 5.1 Detroit three-county region.
Source: U.S. Census Bureau, 2000.

few metropolitan regions that show extreme decentralization in employment, with at least four out of every five jobs located beyond ten miles of the central business district (CBD) (Glaeser, Kahn, and Chu 2001; Lang 2000). The Detroit region faces among the most severe levels of residential segregation between blacks and whites of any metropolitan region in the country (Iceland, Weinberg, and Steinmetz 2002; Lewis Mumford Center 2003). Taken together, job sprawl and racial segregation lead to a troubling distance between blacks and jobs (Stoll, 2005).

The region is well served by interstate freeways and state highways but underserved in public transit. Detroit is the largest urban area in the nation without regionally oriented heavy or light rail transit, so residents must rely exclusively on buses to meet their public transit needs.[1] Public transit funding and service are unusually low compared to peer regions of similar population and historical development (Grengs 2010). Aside from performance indicators, Detroit's public transit is also unusual for its institutional arrangement. Through 2013, transit service was not coordinated by a regional authority as it is in most places. Two transit agencies provided bus service to the region—one serving the suburbs and the other serving the central city.[2] The Suburban Mobility Authority for Regional Transit (SMART) primarily provided service among suburban jurisdictions, with commuter route services into downtown Detroit. The Detroit Department of Transportation (DDOT), part of the Detroit municipal government, provided service principally within the city boundary. As of this writing, the two agencies do not coordinate their routes, schedules, or fares, yet many riders transfer between the services of these separate agencies, taking it upon themselves to match up the schedules and stops.[3] In recognition of the high demand for integrated service, SMART has implemented an "open door policy" that allows SMART drivers to pick up passengers waiting at DDOT bus stops along SMART routes, but only on weekends and weeknights after 6 p.m., and only if the waiting passenger flags down the SMART bus. Drivers apply the policy unevenly, depending on the driver and time of day, contributing to confusion and frustration among transit riders (Gowland, Simoncelli, and Wilson 2010). DDOT is an agency within a municipality in fiscal crisis that struggles to provide basic services like streetlights, garbage pickup, snow plowing, and timely police and fire protection. People in the region perceive DDOT as highly inefficient, and it provides extremely unreliable bus service (Sandula 2011). Because of these unusually weak institutions and lack of regional coordination, the geography that separates many low-income central-city residents—the majority of whom are black—from jobs in the suburbs is made even more severe with a public transit system that impedes a reverse commute. Many efforts to integrate this system of separate transit services have been unsuccessful for decades because of an inability to cooperate across municipal borders; several extensive plans for rapid transit failed to gain the support of key politicians and the public between the 1920s and the 1970s (Batterman 2010; Gerritt 1998).

Despite poor public transit service, many Detroit residents must rely on buses for their travel needs because many households in the city do not have access to a car. About 24 percent of Detroit's households reported having no private vehicle available in 2010, compared to about 9 percent of households nationwide (U.S. Bureau of the Census 2011b). Although this suggests a high level of dependency on public transit, lack of a private vehicle is not as severe in Detroit as it is in some cities with similar historical development, including Philadelphia (35 percent of city residents without a car), Buffalo (31 percent), and Baltimore (31 percent) (U.S. Bureau of the 2011b).[4] Detroit's comparably lower share of 24 percent is likely due in part to the lower quality of public transit service in the region, forcing some low-income residents that might otherwise forgo an automobile to purchase and maintain a private vehicle for the household.

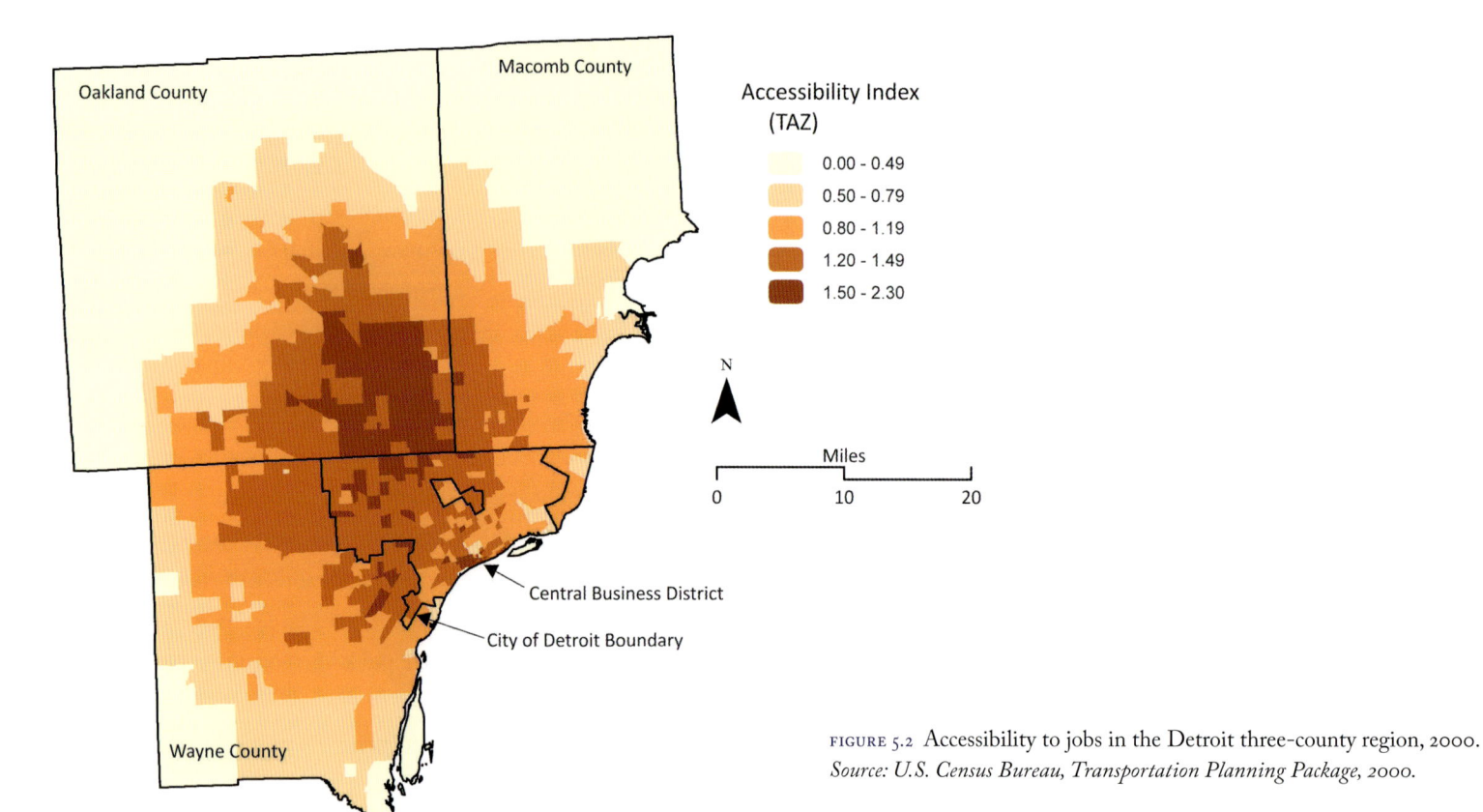

FIGURE 5.2 Accessibility to jobs in the Detroit three-county region, 2000.
Source: U.S. Census Bureau, Transportation Planning Package, 2000.

METHOD AND DATA FOR MEASURING ACCESSIBILITY

Accessibility is measured in this study with a technique commonly used by planning scholars to evaluate the relative ease of reaching destinations in a metropolitan region (Cervero, Rood, and Appleyard 1999; Isard 1960; Shen 2000). The accessibility index can be thought of as a summation of the number of destinations reachable from a zone or neighborhood, adjusted according to the relative difficulty of travel. To interpret the index, higher scores mean a greater advantage in reaching destinations.[5]

Data come from a variety of sources including the 2000 Census Transportation Planning Package (CTPP) (U.S. Bureau of the Census 2004a, 2004b); 2000 Census of Population and Housing, Summary File 3 (U.S. Bureau of the Census 2002); a household travel survey conducted for the state of Michigan in 2005 (Michigan Department of Transportation 2005); and travel demand modeling data provided by the Southeast Michigan Council of Governments (SEMCOG) for travel times. Data for destinations come from the private vendor InfoUSA, Inc., a provider of proprietary business data and a source of data commonly used for small-scale employment analysis. The zones that appear in maps are transportation analysis zones (TAZs), delineated by local transportation officials for tabulating traffic-related census data. A TAZ typically consists of one or more census blocks, block groups, or census tracts.

DESCRIBING PATTERNS OF ACCESSIBILITY WITH MAPS

Accessibility to jobs in the Detroit region is illustrated in Figure 5.2. Unlike many other metropolitan regions, Detroit's central business district does not lie in the highest-accessibility zones. Instead, most of the highest-accessibility zones occur several miles from the CBD, most outside the central city, with some extending beyond twenty miles from the CBD. The geographic distribution of accessibility is unusual: the territories with the highest accessibility to jobs are more decentralized and dispersed in Detroit than in other metropolitan regions. Studies that use a technique similar to the one used here show that accessibility is highest at or near the CBD in other metropolitan regions, with zones of highest accessibility more centralized, more concentrated, and more clustered than in Detroit.[6]

Accessibility in the Central City and Its Neighborhoods

Even though the zones of highest accessibility occur at a great distance from the CBD, the central city of Detroit remains comparatively high in job accessibility relative to many other places in the three-county region. To quantify the visual observations in the map, I categorize the region into three territories to compare population-weighted average accessibility scores: central city, inner-ring suburbs (arbitrarily defined as TAZs within five miles of the central city boundary), and outer-ring suburbs (TAZs beyond five miles of the central city boundary). Using the weighted average accessibility scores for all workers, analyzing the city of Detroit results in an average score of 1.25, compared to the inner-ring suburbs score of 1.25 and the outer-ring suburbs score of 0.85. Although these territory categories hide considerable variation within them, the results indicate that the city of Detroit and the inner-ring suburbs experience comparably high degrees of job accessibility among these three territory categories.

Even though the average job accessibility is relatively high for the city as whole, accessibility varies substantially among places within the city of Detroit. Figure 5.3 shows three inner-city zones, the boundaries of which have been drawn to capture particularly high rates of poverty and unemployment, representing the kinds of places where spatial barriers are likely to harm job prospects. The map shows that zone A (in the southwest of Detroit) and zone B (in the north of Detroit and partially covering the city of Highland Park) are relatively accessibility rich, with average scores of 1.24 and 1.23 respectively. This means that, on average, people living in these two zones are experiencing a level of job accessibility at least as high as about 65 percent of all people living in the metropolitan region.

But inner-city places also experience considerably different levels of accessibility. Residents of zone C (east of the CBD), with an average score of 1.06, are substantially worse off than their counterparts in the other two zones. Figure 5.3 also makes clear that people experience varying degrees of job accessibility even within a single zone. For instance, accessibility within zone C ranges from 0.98 to 1.52. These findings are consistent with other studies such as Shen's (1998) in Boston that concluded that the inner city remains relatively accessibility rich despite the sprawl of suburban jobs, but that neighborhoods of the inner city experience considerable variation in accessibility. Transportation planners might use such mapping analysis at a fine-grained geographic scale to help them prioritize scarce resources when targeting services to neighborhoods.

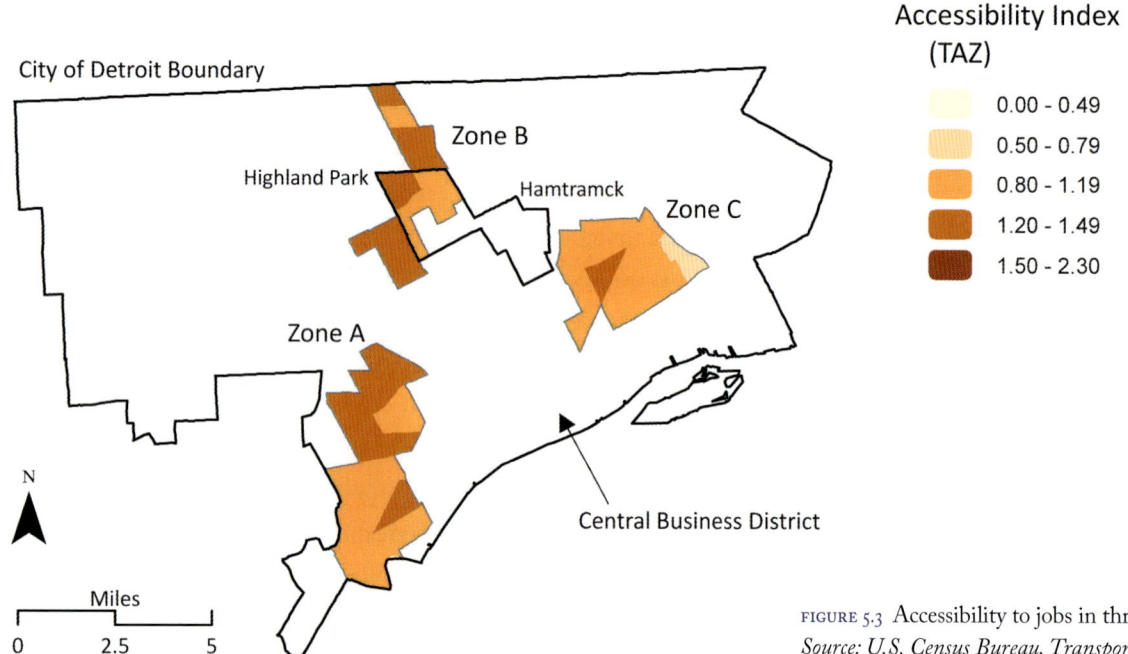

FIGURE 5.3 Accessibility to jobs in three neighborhoods in the city of Detroit, 2000. Source: U.S. Census Bureau, Transportation Planning Package, 2000.

Comparing Social Groups

Mapping accessibility allows for comparing differences between social groups in the region. Figure 5.4 presents data in three dimensions, with a focus on how accessibility is experienced by the white population in the region. (Note that the map's north arrow points left because the three-dimensional scene is most revealing at this angle.) The shading shows accessibility, with the darkest shades indicating the highest levels of accessibility occurring in the inner-ring suburbs, just to the northwest of Detroit. To make a visual comparison between accessibility and population, the height in the maps represents residential density at each zone, depicting in this case where white populations reside relative to accessibility. The map shows that the white population is distinctly absent from the central city and that it is fairly evenly spread throughout much of the rest of the region. By simultaneously comparing the shading with the height of the zones, the map suggests that the white population tends to experience the full range of accessibility, from the highest to the lowest.

By comparison, Figure 5.5 shows accessibility relative to the black population in the region. The black population is highly concentrated in and near the central city, depicted by the very high bars tightly clustered at the core of the region. The shading of these bars indicates that a large share of the black population lives where accessibility is moderately high. To contrast the two maps, whites are more evenly spread among the accessibility categories than blacks, reflecting the wider variation in neighborhoods occupied by whites throughout the region.

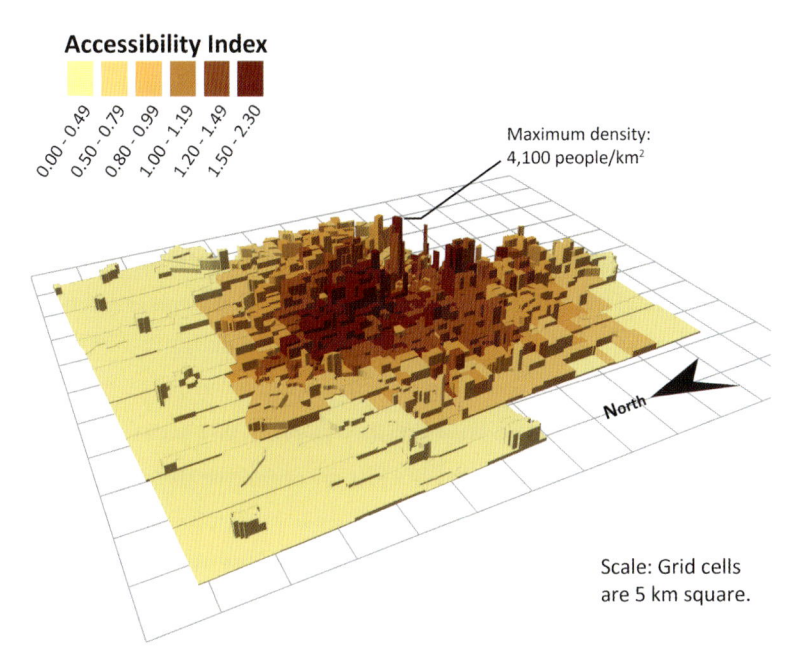

FIGURE 5.4 Accessibility to work, with white population density (people/square mile) for the Detroit three-county region, 2000.
Source: U.S. Census Bureau, Transportation Planning Package, 2000.

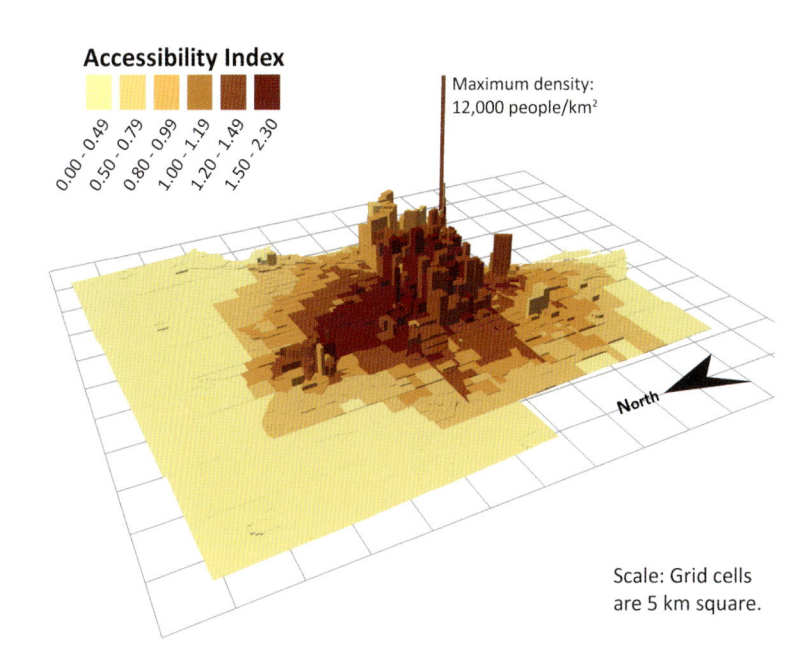

FIGURE 5.5 Accessibility to work, with black population density (people/square mile) for the Detroit three-county region, 2000.
Source: U.S. Census Bureau, Transportation Planning Package, 2000.

Social Equity and the Importance of Automobiles in Accessibility

The analysis so far has investigated job accessibility by location alone, simply comparing one zone to the next across the region. This analysis, however, tells only part of the story because it does not take proper account of the differences between social groups in regard to travel mode. Having an automobile makes a big difference in how a person experiences accessibility, and the availability of a vehicle differs considerably between social groups (Pucher and Renne 2003). The following analysis accounts for differences in the availability of a vehicle by analyzing accessibility at the level of the household, rather than the zone.

Figure 5.6 accounts for differences in the availability of a vehicle by analyzing accessibility at the level of the household rather than the zone. It compares accessibility to jobs in the three-county region for the two populations of blacks and whites, and it illustrates three points. First, notice the difference between the shapes of the two lines. For white households, the line proceeds in a straight rise, at virtually a diagonal from the origin. This means that accessibility is evenly spread among whites: about half of whites enjoy high accessibility, and about half of whites experience low accessibility. The line for black households, by contrast, is roughly in the shape of an S. Blacks tend to experience either high or low accessibility, with little middle ground in between. Second, in comparing the groups in the aggregate, blacks are better off than whites: About 80 percent of blacks experience higher accessibility to jobs than whites. Indeed, over half of black households reside in

COMPARING PEOPLE AND PLACES WITH TRANSPORTATION ACCESSIBILITY 107

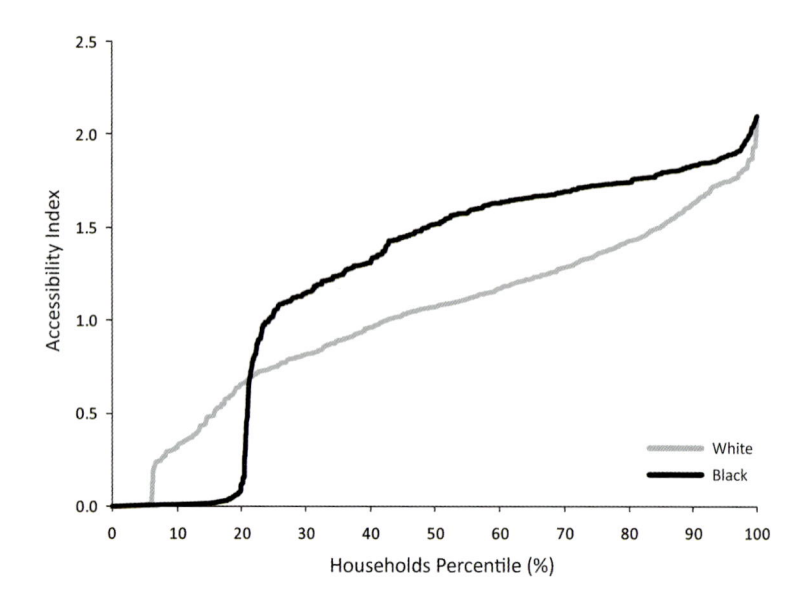

FIGURE 5.6 Accessibility to work as households percentiles, by race, in the Detroit three-county region, 2000.
Source: U.S. Census Bureau, Transportation Planning Package, 2000.

places where the accessibility indicator is very high (higher than 1.5), compared to only about 15 percent of white households experiencing this degree of accessibility. This high level of accessibility among blacks can be explained by their central location. Third, even though about 80 percent of black households are better off than white households in terms of accessibility, the remaining 20 percent of black households experience extreme disadvantage in accessibility. It is here that we see the strong effect of mode of travel on accessibility outcomes.

Workers without a car must rely on public transit, but accessibility by transit in Detroit is highly inferior to accessibility by car. Although not shown by maps here, transit accessibility is very low even in the central city, where transit service is most prevalent, and it varies little throughout the region. Not only is transit accessibility universally poor, but the best locations for transit fall short of even the worst locations for auto accessibility. Public transit is such a severely inferior substitute for owning a car in Detroit that even if carless persons relying on public transit live where transit service is best, they can do little better in reaching jobs than the worst off among their counterparts who live in the farthest reaches of the metropolitan periphery and travel by car (Grengs 2010).

Beyond Getting to Jobs: Accessibility to Non-Work Places

It is possible to map accessibility not just for evaluating the ease of reaching jobs but also for examining how accessibility varies for non-work trips such as shopping, recreation, and visiting friends. Non-work trips make up the vast majority of travel. In 2009, travelers in the United States made 78 percent of their trips and 73 percent of their vehicular travel distance for non-work purposes (U.S. Department of Transportation 2011). To visually assess non-work accessibility, I investigate maps for thirteen purposes of trips by automobile and transit travel.[7]

Most trip purposes indicate a high degree of centralization in the accessibility pattern, meaning that the highest-accessibility zones occur near the CBD, with a gradual tapering off in all directions. Although not shown here, maps reveal a centralized pattern for the following kinds of trips: convenience stores, child-care facilities, schools, religious meetings, social visits, and hospitals. Finding that many types of trips conform to a centralized pattern is not surprising, because accessibility is highly influenced by the density of destinations, and these kinds of destinations tend to follow residential density patterns.

Despite the strong tendency toward centralization for some kinds of trips, other trips exhibit a spreading-out effect in which the highest-accessibility zones stretch over an expansive territory that extends

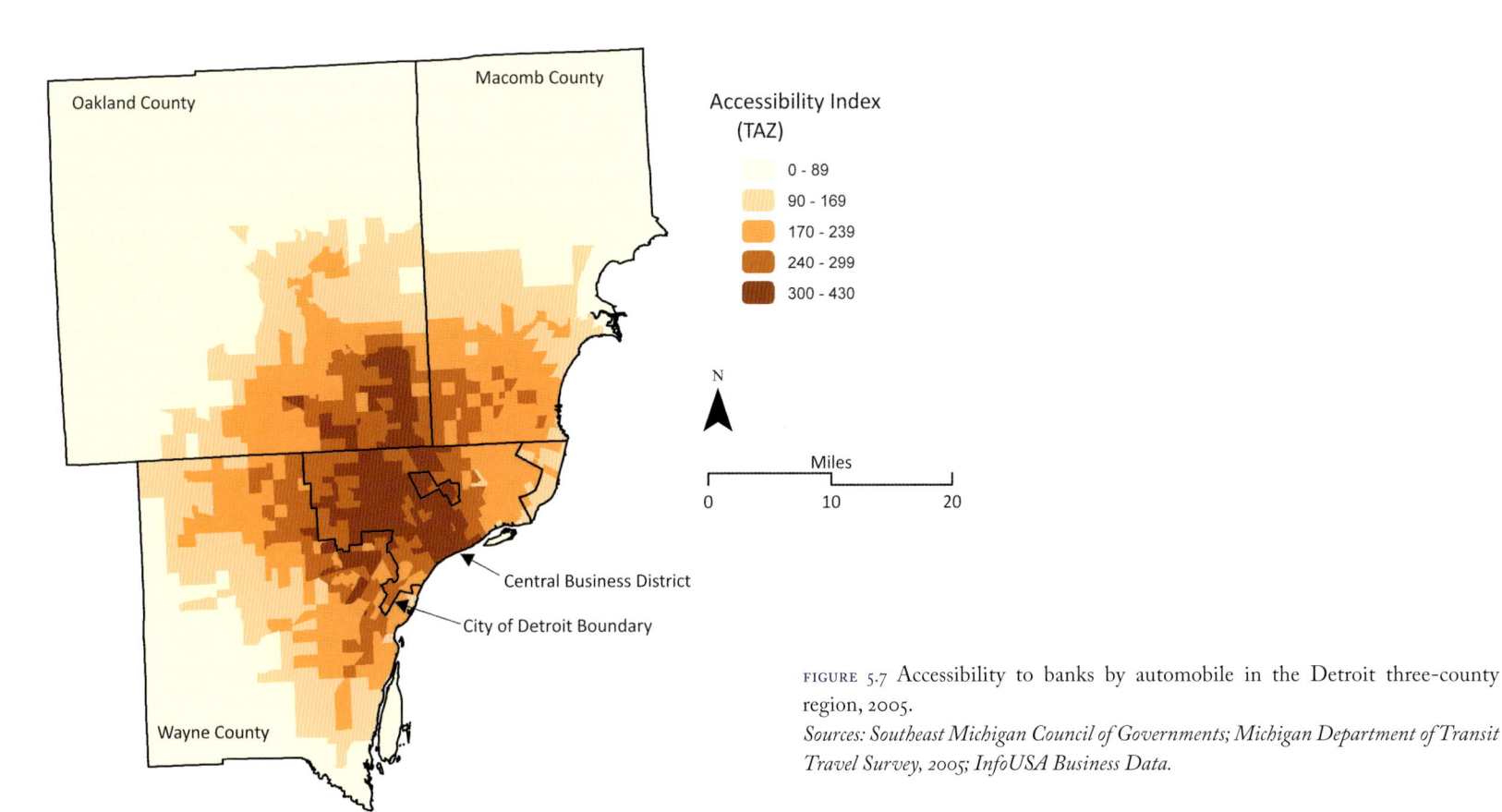

FIGURE 5.7 Accessibility to banks by automobile in the Detroit three-county region, 2005.
Sources: *Southeast Michigan Council of Governments; Michigan Department of Transit Travel Survey, 2005; InfoUSA Business Data.*

beyond the central city. Figure 5.7 provides an example of this spatial patterning in accessibility, for the case of banks by automobile travel. (Others with a similar pattern include services, libraries, medical clinics, and restaurants.) One explanation for the spreading-out effect of these trips is that a larger share of the regional destinations is situated outside of the urban core. But this land use effect—the physical location of the destinations—is not the only explanation. These are also trip purposes for which travelers are more willing to travel long distances, and the measures used here account for this with the effect of spreading out high values of accessibility.

The most unusual spatial pattern is where the highest-accessibility zones occur only beyond the central city; this pattern occurs in the cases of shopping and supermarkets. Figure 5.8 illustrates the pattern for travel to supermarkets by automobile. The pattern is striking in the degree of low accessibility throughout the central city and is explained by an absence of major supermarket chains in the urban core. By 2007, some observers noted that no major-chain supermarket was left in Detroit (Smith and Hurst 2007), a situation that only began to change several years after that (as with the Midtown opening of Whole Foods in 2013). The pattern is also striking in the degree of localization of places of high accessibility:

COMPARING PEOPLE AND PLACES WITH TRANSPORTATION ACCESSIBILITY 109

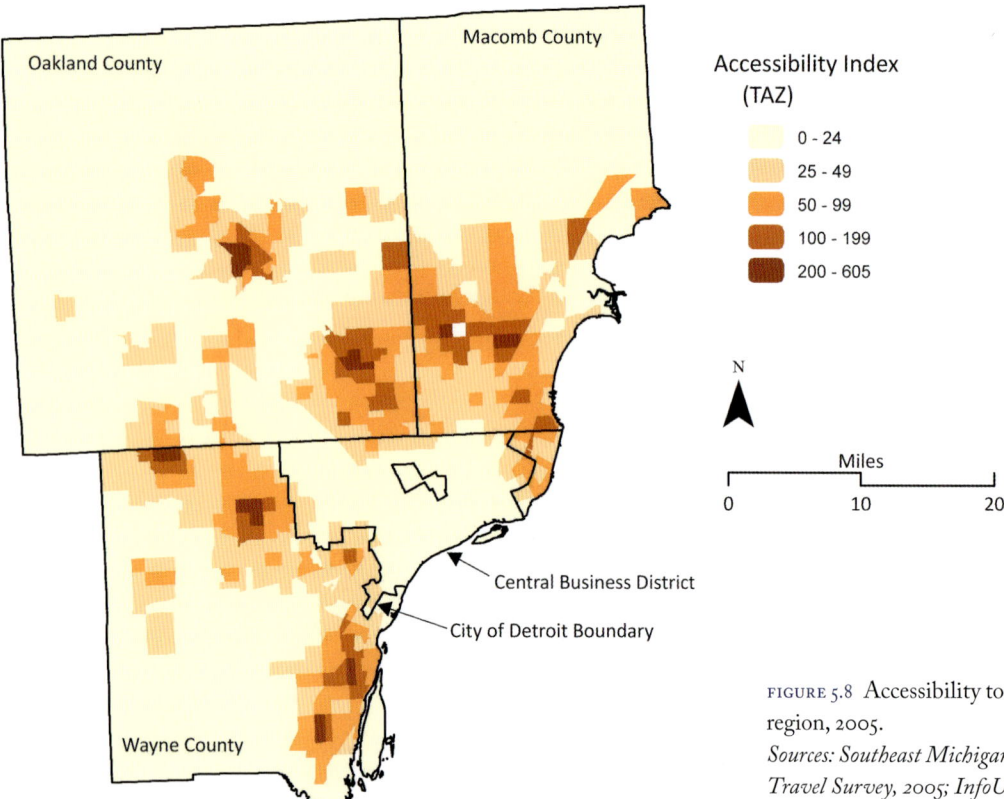

FIGURE 5.8 Accessibility to supermarkets by automobile in the Detroit three-county region, 2005.
Sources: Southeast Michigan Council of Governments; Michigan Department of Transit Travel Survey, 2005; InfoUSA Business Data.

accessibility tapers off quickly with distance from a supermarket because travelers tend to place high value on nearby destinations in their selection of supermarkets. Vulnerable social groups—African Americans, people of Hispanic origin, and people in poverty—experience substantial disadvantage in accessibility to shopping and supermarkets (Grengs 2009). This finding is consistent with other accessibility-based studies by Grengs (2001) in Syracuse and by Helling and Sawicki (2003) in Atlanta, suggesting that supermarkets may represent a universal concern with respect to accessibility disadvantages (Moore and Diez Roux 2006; Raja, Ma, and Yadav 2008; Zenk, Schulz, Israel, James, Bao, and Wilson 2005).

The results presented here offer only partial insights into the differences between social groups in the ability to reach opportunities. "Accessibility" is defined in this study in a very narrow sense, focusing strictly on the potential for travel in terms of the cost of time. It does not address differences between destinations that also affect accessibility, such as product selection, product quality, parking availability, store hours, perception of safety and crime, service friendliness, prices, and payment options. A more complete analysis of accessibility among social groups would include these important dimensions of accessibility. Another dimension that is likely to be particularly relevant in the context of a racially segregated region like

Detroit is the degree of comfort that travelers experience when visiting places outside of familiar surroundings. The fear of racial hostility has a long history in Detroit (Farley, Danziger, and Holzer 2000; Sugrue 1996; Thomas 2013; Zunz 1982) and likely has a strong influence on travel patterns. Unfortunately, these other dimensions of accessibility are difficult to measure, especially at the metropolitan scale of study; so far, transportation scholars have not studied them in detail. The definition of accessibility in this study allows for a better understanding of the physical constraints on travel, but it is not sufficient for appreciating the full range of the relative ease of reaching opportunities among social groups.

CONCLUSION

Mapping accessibility helps us to see differences between people in the ability to reach opportunities, and the maps call attention to the importance of having a car in achieving this. The inner city is not disadvantaged by its geographic position in regional space. On the contrary, the inner city actually offers substantial advantages in reaching jobs, with one major qualification: residents need a car. Inner-city residents in Detroit are not disadvantaged by their location, but rather are disadvantaged by a lack of cars and poor transit service. People without cars are deprived of good accessibility even if they live in the central city. Municipal governments—especially those like Detroit that are fiscally strained—are not by themselves capable of providing adequate public transit services to a metropolitan region, suggesting the need for regional cooperation and additional investments from higher levels of government. Improving public transit service in Detroit to achieve levels of accessibility approaching merely the median for the region would take many years and likely decades. In the meantime, proposals to use public funds to help poor people gain access to cars are appropriate in Detroit, as a complement to other approaches like expanding public transit services,

and policy makers ought to consider them (O'Regan and Quigley 1998; Waller 2006). Providing cars to low-income people would, however, face a number of challenges: the need to mitigate the accompanying worsened air pollution, energy consumption, and traffic congestion, and the need to compensate poor households for the substantial burdens they would face from the costs of car ownership, including fuel, license, registration, insurance, loan interest, maintenance, and parking (Blumenberg and Manville 2004; Grengs 2010).[8]

The maps of accessibility offer insights into policy aimed at social equity. African Americans as a group are not disadvantaged in a way that the conventional understanding of the spatial mismatch hypothesis would suggest.[9] Instead, blacks experience two extremes. Most blacks are actually advantaged by virtue of their central location, but a substantial share of blacks are extremely disadvantaged because of disproportionately low rates of car ownership coupled with unusually inferior transit service. People without cars lack good accessibility even if they live in the central city, where auto accessibility is among the highest in the region. Vulnerable social groups in Detroit are disproportionately without cars in a metropolis deliberately designed for cars (Grengs 2008).

The accessibility maps are consistent with one of the suggestions by Porter (1995) in an influential article that argued that central cities have competitive advantages. Porter argued that underserved markets in central cities justify commercial redevelopment based solely on economic grounds. To the extent that policy makers and private developers overlook accessibility as a vital ingredient in determining the value of land, the finding that central locations continue to provide high levels of accessibility to many destinations, even in a place as distressed as Detroit, suggests promise for much-needed investment. However, accessibility is but one of multiple influences on such decisions, and transportation planners ought to find how accessibility influences revitalization efforts.

NOTES

1. Construction began in 2014 on a short streetcar system extending from the CBD to New Center. Please note as well that much of the commentary in this chapter is based on data that predates a post-2012 influx of young white professionals into the CBD, changing their level of accessibility.
2. Other transit agencies provide service to the Detroit region but are not included in this analysis because they have a minor effect on accessibility to the study region. The Detroit People Mover is an automated guideway that circulates around downtown Detroit, and Transit Windsor provides bus service between downtown Detroit and Windsor in Ontario, Canada.
3. Transfers can be purchased on buses for $0.25 and can be used between the two agencies but cost an additional $0.50 when transferring from DDOT to SMART.
4. American Community Survey data are subject to sampling error. Figures reported here have margins of error reasonable enough to make comparisons across cities.
5. The method is described in more detail in Grengs (2010) and Grengs, Levine, Shen, and Shen (2010).
6. Other studies include Shen (1998) for Boston; Sanchez, Shen, and Peng (2004) for the six cases of Atlanta, Baltimore, Dallas, Denver, Milwaukee, and Portland; and Grengs et al. (2010) for San Francisco and Washington, D.C.
7. The thirteen trip destinations/purposes used in this study are supermarkets, convenience stores, banks, child-care facilities, schools, services, libraries, religious meetings, medical clinics, shopping, social visits, hospitals, and restaurants. The method is outlined in Grengs (2009).
8. Vehicle insurance rates are notoriously high in the Detroit metropolitan region and throughout Michigan (Galster and Booza 2008), a cost that would undoubtedly be burdensome for low-income households in maintaining a private vehicle.
9. See Grengs (2008) for an exploration of how this pertains to other groups as well, including people of Hispanic origin and people living below the federally defined poverty line.

REFERENCES

Batterman, J. M. (2010). *Color lines: Race and rapid transit in metropolitan Detroit, 1969–1980* [Bachelor of Arts Thesis]. Portland, OR: Reed College.

Blumenberg, E., and Manville, M. (2004). Beyond the spatial mismatch: Welfare recipients and transportation policy. *Journal of Planning Literature,* 19(2), 182–205.

Bullard, R. D., Torres, A. O., and Johnson, G. S. (Eds.). (2000). *Sprawl city: Race, politics, and planning in Atlanta.* Washington, DC: Island Press.

Cervero, R. (1996). Paradigm shift: From automobility to accessibility planning. Working Paper 677, Institute of Urban and Regional Development. Berkeley: University of California.

Cervero, R., Rood, T., and Appleyard, B. (1999). Tracking accessibility: Employment and housing opportunities in the San Francisco bay area. *Environment and Planning A, 31,* 1259–78.

Farley, R., Danziger, S., and Holzer, H. J. (2000). *Detroit divided.* New York, NY: Russell Sage Foundation.

Galster, G., and Booza, J. (2008). Are home and auto insurance policies excessively priced in cities? Recent evidence from Michigan. *Journal of Urban Affairs,* 30(5), 507–27.

Gerritt, J. (1998, July 14). Metro transit system needs city, suburb collaboration. Detroit Free Press, p. A1.

Glaeser, E. L., Kahn, M., and Chu, C. (2001). *Job sprawl: Employment locations in U.S. metropolitan areas.* Washington, DC: Brookings Institution.

Gowland, L., Simoncelli, J., and Wilson, E. (2010). *No one gets where they want to go: Analysis of SMART's Michigan 200 local.* Unpublished manuscript prepared for the Urban and Regional Planning program, University of Michigan, Ann Arbor, MI.

Grengs, J. (2001). Does public transit counteract the segregation of carless households? Measuring spatial patterns of accessibility with GIS. *Transportation Research Record: Journal of the Transportation Research Board,* 1753, 3–10.

Grengs, J. (2008). *Social equity and the spatial distribution of job accessibility in Detroit.* Washington, DC: U.S. Department of Transportation, Federal Transit Administration.

Grengs, J. (2009). *Nonwork travel and accessibility: A social equity analysis of Detroit.* Washington, DC: U.S. Department of Transportation, Federal Transit Administration.

Grengs, J. (2010). Job accessibility and the modal mismatch in Detroit. *Journal of Transport Geography,* 18, 42–54.

Grengs, J., Levine, J., Shen, Q., and Shen, Q. (2010). Intermetropolitan comparison of transportation accessibility: Sorting out mobility and proximity in San Francisco and Washington, DC. *Journal of Planning Education and Research,* 29(4), 427–43.

Hansen, W. G. (1959). How accessibility shapes land use. *Journal of the American Institute of Planners,* XXV(2), 73–76.

Helling, A., and Sawicki, D. S. (2003). Race and residential accessibility to shopping and services. *Housing Policy Debate, 14*(1), 2.

Iceland, J., Weinberg, D. H., and Steinmetz, E. (2002). Racial and ethnic residential segregation in the United States: 1980–2000, Census 2000 Special Reports, CENSR-3. Retrieved November 11, 2005, from www.census.gov/hhes/www/housing/housing_patterns/front_toc.html

Isard, W. (1960). *Methods of regional analysis: An introduction to regional science.* Cambridge, MA: MIT Press.

Kain, J. F. (1968). Housing segregation, Negro employment, and metropolitan decentralization. *Quarterly Journal of Economics, 82*(2), 175–97.

Lang, R. (2000). *Office sprawl: The evolving geography of business.* Washington, DC: Brookings Institution.

Lewis Mumford Center. (2003). Metropolitan racial and ethnic change—Census 2000. Retrieved November 11, 2005, from http://mumford.albany.edu/census/WholePop/WPsort.html

Michigan Department of Transportation. (2005). 2004–2005 comprehensive household travel data collection program: Michigan travel counts, final report. Lansing, MI: Michigan Department of Transportation.

Moore, L. V., and Diez Roux, A. V. (2006). Associations of neighborhood characteristics with the location and type of food stores. *American Journal of Public Health, 96*(2), 325–31.

O'Regan, K. M., and Quigley, J. M. (1998). Cars for the poor. *Access, 12,* 20–25.

Pendall, R. (1999). Local land use regulation and the chain of exclusion. *Journal of the American Planning Association, 66*(2), 125–42.

Porter, M. (1995). The competitive advantage of the inner city. *Harvard Business Review, 73*(3), 55–71.

Pucher, J., and Renne, J. L. (2003). Socioeconomics of urban travel: Evidence from the 2001 NHTS. *Transportation Quarterly, 57*(3), 49–77.

Raja, S., Ma, C., and Yadav, P. (2008). Beyond food deserts: Measuring and mapping racial disparities in neighborhood food environments. *Journal of Planning Education and Research, 27*(4), 469.

Sanchez, T. W., Shen, Q., and Peng, Z.-R. (2004). Transit mobility, jobs access and low-income labour participation in U.S. metropolitan areas. *Urban Studies, 41*(7), 1313–31.

Sandula, M. (2011, November 20). DDOT fails. Michigan Citizen. Retrieved from http://michigancitizen.com/ddot-fails-p10494-1.htm

Shen, Q. (1998). Location characteristics of inner-city neighborhoods and employment accessibility of low-wage workers. *Environment and Planning B, 25,* 345–65.

Shen, Q. (2000). Spatial and social dimensions of commuting. *Journal of the American Planning Association, 66*(1), 68–82.

Smith, J. J., and Hurst, N. (2007, July 5). Grocery closings hit Detroit hard: City shoppers' choices dwindle as last big chain leaves. *Detroit News,* p. 1.

Squires, G. D., and Kubrin, C. E. (2005). Privileged places: Race, uneven development and the geography of opportunity in urban America. *Urban Studies, 42*(1), 47–68.

Stoll, M. (2005). *Job sprawl and the spatial mismatch between blacks and jobs.* Washington, DC: Brookings Institution.

Sugrue, T. J. (1996). *The origins of the urban crisis: Race and inequality in postwar Detroit.* Princeton, NJ: Princeton University Press.

Thomas, J. M. (2013). *Redevelopment and race: Planning a finer city in postwar Detroit.* (2nd ed.). Detroit, MI: Wayne State University Press.

Transportation Research Board. (1995). *Expanding metropolitan highways: Implications for air quality and energy use (Special Report 245).* Washington, DC: National Academy Press.

U.S. Bureau of the Census. (2002). 2000 census of population and housing, Summary Files 1 and 3, generated through American FactFinder. Retrieved from www.census.gov/main/www/cen2000.html

U.S. Bureau of the Census. (2004a). 2000 census transportation planning package [CD-ROM]. CTPP-Part 1-Final-IN, MI: Data by place of residence. Washington, DC: U.S. Department of Transportation, Bureau of Transportation Statistics.

U.S. Bureau of the Census. (2004b). 2000 census transportation planning package [CD-ROM]. CTPP-Part 2-Final-IL, IN, IA, MI: Data by place of work. Washington, DC: U.S. Department of Transportation, Bureau of Transportation Statistics.

U.S. Bureau of the Census. (2011a). 2010 census of population and housing. Summary File 1, United States, Technical Documentation. Washington, DC: U.S. Government Printing Office.

U.S. Bureau of the Census. (2011b). 2010 American community survey 1-year estimates, generated through American FactFinder. Retrieved from http://factfinder2.census.gov

U.S. Department of Transportation. (2011). 2009 national household travel survey. Retrieved from http://nhts.ornl.gov/index.shtml.

Waller, M. (2006, January/February). Opportunity and the automobile. *Poverty and Race*, 15, 3–7.

Zenk, S. N., Schulz, A. J., Israel, B. A., James, S. A., Bao, S., and Wilson, M. L. (2005). Neighborhood racial composition, neighborhood poverty, and the spatial accessibility of supermarkets in metropolitan Detroit. *American Journal of Public Health*, 95(4), 660–67.

Zunz, O. (1982). *The changing face of inequality: Urbanization, industrial development, and immigrants in Detroit, 1880–1920*. Chicago, IL: University of Chicago Press.

6

MAPPING DELRAY

Understanding Changes in a Southwest Detroit Community

MARÍA ARQUERO DE ALARCÓN AND LARISSA LARSEN

Although the North American economy is considered post-industrial in character, pockets of heavy industry remain. Located at the confluence of the Detroit River and River Rouge, southwest Detroit is an amalgam of residential housing, ongoing industrial activity, and expanding transportation infrastructure. Some of the most deteriorated pockets of residential housing exist within the neighborhood of Delray. Historical accounts of this neighborhood in the early 1900s provide a glimpse of an active, mixed-use Hungarian enclave whose residents were attracted by the employment opportunities of the nearby industrial manufacturing facilities. Gone is the promise once present for neighborhood residents of economic advancement through industrial labor, and much economic activity has left. However, a proposal to locate the American side of a second international bridge in Delray returned public attention to this area. This urban landscape is a striking example of how global economic advancements can occur simultaneously amidst local decline.

Georgakas and Surkin (1998, p. 209) write that "Detroit has served as a metaphor for much that is wrong in America during the second half of the twentieth century, just as it once served as a metaphor for much that was positive in America. But Detroit is much more than a metaphor. Detroit is a real place where real people live." Inspired by this quotation, we wanted to understand how Delray as a "real place" changed over time (Figure 6.1). Although Delray's people and products contributed directly to Detroit's place as the Arsenal of Democracy in World War II, its postwar history is one of economic decline. A once-active place has shifted into a neglected space in which the majority of residents are united by their poverty and tangential relationships to the mainstream labor market. This chapter is a

FIGURE 6.1 Delray and the industrial geography of Detroit. This map of Detroit illustrates the industrial areas in the city along the railway corridors. Delray is the shaded area of the extracted map (bottom right). Adjacent to Delray are (1) Boynton, (2) Oakwood Heights, (3) Carbon Works, (4) Springwells, (5) Southwest Detroit Mexican Town, and (6) Hubbard Richard.
Source: GIS Layers, SEMCOG 2011. Final map composite elaborated by the authors.

short account of Delray's establishment, productive and social zenith, slow decline, and current state of desperation. We tell this account of Delray's history in a chronological sequence in order to highlight how economic, social, political, and environmental changes are entangled and cumulative in their impact. We obtained information from historical maps and city directories, scholarly literature, newspaper articles, city plans and documents, as well as observations gained by one author's five-year involvement with a Delray community group and a local environmental justice organization.

We argue that Delray's current conditions are not just the result of economic decline but also the result of intentional and unintentional actions on the part of elected officials and city departments. Delray serves regional needs by accepting unwanted wastes, absorbing the pollution from industrial processing, and now potentially hosting another major piece of transportation infrastructure, a second international bridge. We conclude that the "aspatial" character of the global economy that drives this international transportation project makes it difficult for neighborhood residents to find responsible parties from whom they can seek spatially based compensation, and we argue that a portion of the bridge's financial earnings should be returned to improve southwest Detroit.

DELRAY'S EARLY ESTABLISHMENT

Delray is located on the Detroit riverfront approximately 2.5 miles southwest of downtown Detroit. We are defining contemporary Delray as an area that measures approximately 700 acres in size and is physically bounded by the Detroit River on the south, the River Rouge on the west, the Fisher Freeway (I-75) on the north, and Clark Street on the east.

The area's natural springs and good-quality well water earned it the name "Belle-Fontaine" (Beautiful Fountain) from early French settlers (Campbell 1922; Eckert 1993). The first division of land by the French prioritized access to the Detroit River by using long narrow parcels perpendicular to the river's edge at the center of the settlement in downtown Detroit, as noted in chapter 1. The tilted northwest-southeast orientation of today's street grid still contains a few French street names such as Livernois, Campau, and Hubbard; the earliest Catholic parishes recall the settlement's French origins (Burton, Stocking, and Miller 1922). Fort Wayne is a remnant of American and British conflict that dates to the 1840s, and this gated and largely unoccupied 83-acre riverfront property is located along the riverfront in Delray.[1] Augustus Burdeno, a large area landowner, gave the area the name "Delray" in 1851 after he returned from the Mexican War's Battle of Molino del Rey.

In a 1920 economic summary of the region, Thomas Munger wrote that in Detroit, "transportation governs production" (1920, p. 9 and 116). This statement was also true for early Delray. Advancements in water transportation and infrastructure—such as the first steam vessel in 1818, the steam barge in 1848, and the opening of the Erie Canal in 1825, the Soo Locks in 1855, and the initial phase of the Welland Canal in 1829—significantly increased activity on the Great Lakes and established Detroit's importance as a regional center. Originally forty feet wide and four feet deep, the canal connected Lake Erie, at Buffalo, to the Hudson River (Eckert 1993).

This canal and lock improvements linked the Great Lakes with New York City and the Atlantic Ocean and circumvented the need to cross the Appalachian Mountains. Erie Canal's opening and successive improvements directly affected Delray by increasing the demand for docks and port facilities along the shoreline. Before the 1880s, Delray's waterfront still contained significant open space and wetlands interspersed with dock facilities and other uses. In 1888, the construction of the Short Cut Canal improved navigability along the River Rouge. After draining some of the marshy lands between Fort Wayne to the northeast and the River Rouge mouth to the southeast, Delray's riverfront hosted the Michigan State Fair in the 1880s and the Detroit International Exposition between 1889 and 1894 (Figure 6.2).

By 1821, a system of territorial roads was initiated. One of the earliest roads connected Detroit and Toledo, permitting the movement of food and military supplies. In 1827, a road linked Detroit with Indiana; by 1835, roads connected Detroit with both Flint and Chicago (Base 1970; Munger 1920). Railroad development followed in 1836. By 1850, 779 miles of rail radiated from Detroit; by 1870, ten different railroad companies oversaw 1,638 rail miles. During this time, the railroad network expanded quickly within Delray and helped the area emerge as an industrial node of regional significance. Delray's railroad network followed the shoreline in an effort to ensure the efficient exchange of goods between water and land transportation modes. From the optimistic perspective of early entrepreneurs, Delray was destined to be a great manufacturing center (Farmer 1890).

FIGURE 6.2 The 1889 Detroit International Exposition in Delray. Detroit's Great Fair and Exposition was "ten days of the world's greatest and most unique attractions." A space of twenty acres was devoted to "Art, Industry, Invention and Amusement."

Sources: Illustration (top left) from Calvert Lithography Co. (1889). Accessed from the Library of the Congress. Other images courtesy of the Burton Historical Collection, Detroit Public Library.

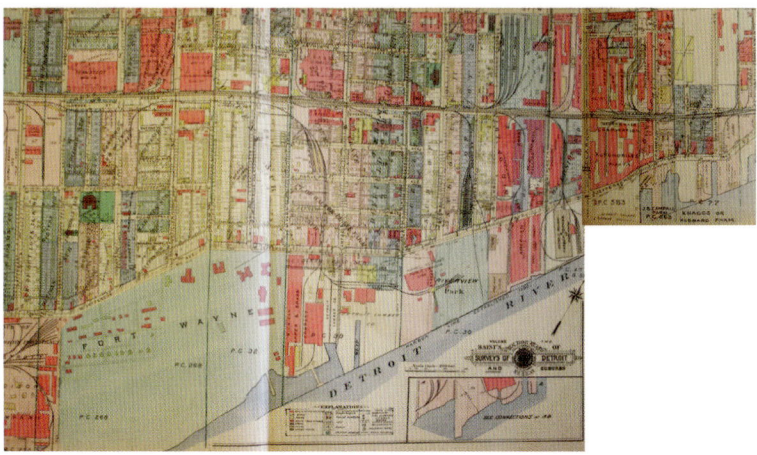

FIGURE 6.3 Historical evolution of the area surrounding Fort Wayne. The two maps illustrate the dramatic industrialization over four decades. The area was transformed from residential subdivisions to a dense mixture of rail network, industrial structures, and residential pockets.
Sources: Top: *Baist, G. (1885)*. Baist Real Estate atlas of surveys of Detroit and suburbs, Michigan. *Courtesy of the Bentley Historical Library, University of Michigan.* Bottom: *Baist, G. (1926)*. Baist Real Estate atlas of surveys of Detroit and suburbs, Michigan. *Courtesy of the Bentley Historical Library, University of Michigan.*

DELRAY'S INDUSTRIAL LANDSCAPE

Consistent with the manufacturing history of Detroit, many of Delray's early waterfront industries relied on access to regional sources of coal, timber, limestone, and iron ore, as well as local sources of water, salt, and sand. One of the earliest factories in Delray was the Michigan Malleable Iron Works plant. Built under the supervision of T. H. Simpson and James McMillan, later elected as U.S. Senator, and his brother, William C McMillan, the plant started operations in 1882. Employing 350 men, the plant attracted residents from throughout the Midwest, particularly Hungarians from Cleveland; Toledo; and South Bend, Indiana (Beynon 1935; Burton, Stocking, and Miller 1922). James McMillan continued to contribute to Delray's establishment as a manufacturing center with his entrepreneurial investments between 1865 and 1890. McMillian founded the Michigan Car Company and was financially connected with the Detroit Car Wheel Company, the Baugh Steam Forge [axles], and the Detroit Iron Furnace Company. McMillan later diversified his investments into shipbuilding and a passenger steamship operation (Official Paper of the Michigan Manufacturers Association 1910, p. 21). Delray's focus on heavy industry was furthered with the establishment of a second iron works, Detroit Iron Works & Steel Company on Zug Island in 1901 (Klug 1999).

The Detroit City Glass Works was another significant early employer in Delray. The company, founded by Louis Blitz, produced artistic and commercial glass. Leake (1912) wrote that, "Blitz owned additional properties in Delray, including many houses for his employees. Blitz's importance as an early actor in both Delray and Detroit is conveyed in his 1905 *Detroit Evening News* death notice. The obituary stated, "Through the sudden death of Louis Blitz there has been taken from the business community of Detroit . . . a far-sighted manager whose initiative was responsible for the founding and expansion of large and important industrial plants, the village of Delray being, in large part, a monument to his genius for productive undertakings" (Leake 1912, p. 956).

Opening in 1888, the Detroit Copper and Brass Rolling Mills was another early Delray manufacturer. Located on an eight-acre site on the Wabash railroad at McKinstry Street, this plant employed 200 men. The Detroit Copper and Brass Rolling Mills buildings were just downstream from The Michigan Copper and Brass Company, which began operations in 1907 on River Street, east of Fort Wayne. This plant employed 650 people (Burton, Stocking, and Miller 1922). Other industries were American Agricultural Chemical, Detroit Chemical Works, Detroit Lumber Company, Peerless Portland Cement Company, Detroit Edison Power, and Scotten & Company Tobacco Works (Klug 1999) (Figure 6.3).

Just as Detroit would emerge as a center of the new automobile industry in the early twentieth century, early automotive start-up companies also came to Delray. In 1901, automobile production started in Delray with the C.H. Blomstrom Motor Company. As the industry matured, Delray hosted manufacturing sites for Studebaker, Timken Detroit Axle, Fisher Body, Fleetwood Body, Star Conumdrum Wheel, and Stuart Commercial Car (Official Paper of the Michigan Manufacturers Association 1910).

The discovery of underground salt deposits attracted several other long-time Delray Industries. The Solvay Process Company of Syracuse, New York, established a manufacturing center in Delray in 1895 (Figure 6.4). The Solvay Company became one of the major employers in the district when it purchased the 67-acre waterfront Detroit Exposition grounds and an additional 300 acres south of the River Rouge and Zug Island (Burton, Stocking, and Miller 1922, p. 543). Solvay produced soda ash, caustic soda, ammonia, tar, and other alkaline products. Within a few years, the factory had expanded into an industrial complex with a "main building, a boiler house, a gas producer plant, a paper filler plant, coke ovens and by-product building, lime kilns, a machine shop, a copper shop, stables, and houses" (Klug 1999). By 1900, Solvay employed a total of 1,000 workers and produced during three eight-hour shifts a day. Solvay established a veritable village within Delray.

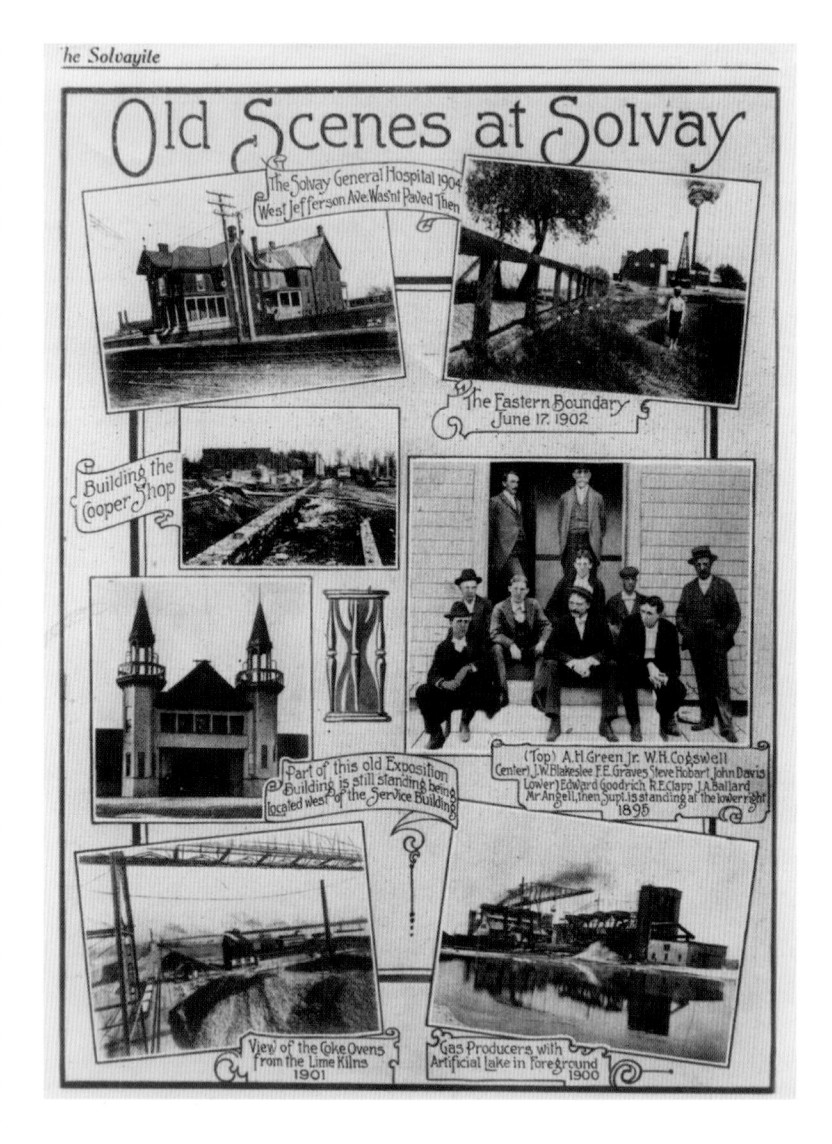

FIGURE 6.4 Scenes at Solvay. This collection of images illustrates some of the facilities in and around the Solvay Company in Delray. These include the General Hospital (1904), Solvay's eastern boundary (1902), the copper shop, the remains of the old Exposition building, the coke ovens (1901), and the gas facilities with an artificial lake behind. *Source: Courtesy of the Burton Historical Collection, Detroit Public Library.*

and a hospital (Figure 6.5); the company also hosted the district's water pumping station. The Solvay Process Company would be renamed Allied Chemical and operated in Delray until the late 1960s (Ilka 1979).

Also in response to the discovery of salt, the Detroit Salt Company opened in 1906 (MacDonald 2010). In its early days of operation, the salt was used for food processing and leather treatment. Although the mineshaft opening was located south of River Rouge, just outside of Delray's boundaries, its expansive network of tunnels extended underneath the community and the Detroit River.[2]

THE ORGANIC EMERGENCE OF DELRAY'S RESIDENTIAL AREAS

Pre-industrial Delray, with a village-like residential character, contained modest frame houses occupied by early French and German settlers (Figure 6.6). With the arrival of the new industries, the need to provide housing and services for workers altered the original residential pattern. In 1885, annexation by Detroit extended the city into a part of what is now known as the Delray neighborhood by establishing Detroit's southwestern boundary at Livernois Avenue (at that time, Livernois was called Artillery in reference to Fort Wayne). The 3,600 residents of Delray incorporated as a village in 1898. In 1906, Detroit annexed the village of Delray and thus extended its southwestern boundary to the River Rouge. The city added one more area southwest of the River Rouge in its final wave of annexation in the 1920s (Jackson 1985). This segment, plus a large area annexed west and north of the existing city, created an expansive Detroit of 139 square miles in the expectation that continued population growth would fill out its low-rise, low-density building pattern.

Near the end of the nineteenth century, new inhabitants moved to Delray because of new industries. The Detroit Board of Commerce reported in 1906 that a total of 6,627 residents lived in the newly annexed

FIGURE 6.5 Delray/Solvay General Hospital located on West Jefferson Avenue, at Green Street. *Top:* Image of the 105-bed hospital in 1967. *Bottom:* Image of the hospital in the 1940s. The hospital changed hands from Solvay to Harper Hospital in 1914. It was closed in 1991.
Source: Courtesy of Walter P. Reuther Library, Wayne State University

The Solvay Lodge provided living quarters for staff without families, and the company offered employees subsidized lunches at its dining hall, a mutual benefit association, and athletic and recreational activities (Burton, Stocking, and Miller 1922, p. 543). Solvay took a leading role in the modernization of the community, providing the village with paved streets, sewers, fire service,

Delray. A continuous flow of population arrived to participate in automobile manufacturing. The quick development of low-cost housing took place in close proximity to the factories so that employees could easily walk to work. Although the area also contained residents of Polish and Armenian background, Hungarian immigrants' predominance in Delray earned the community the title of Little Hungary or the more pejorative label Hunkytown (Figure 6.7). Using the city of Detroit's Board of Education census and the Polk's Detroit directory, Beynon (1936) concluded that approximately 45 percent (10,040 individuals) of the city's Hungarian residents lived in Delray by 1925. This was reportedly the third largest Hungarian community in the United States (Kenyon 1951).

River Road (today called West Jefferson Avenue) and Fort Street were the primary commercial streets of Delray. In 1901, the first Hungarian multi-purpose saloon opened on River Road, near West End Ave. Furniture stores, bakeries, barber shops, banks, auto dealerships, insurance agencies, real estate offices, print shops, movie theaters, many churches, and a library served the new residents (Klug 1999). Other establishments of the time included "candy stores." Named for the candies exhibited in the store windows, these Prohibition-era stores reportedly sold and served liquor to predominantly white, native-born Detroiters (Beynon 1934, p. 606).

The district, developed without official planning intervention, approached its social highpoint in the late 1920s to the early 1930s. The first proposed building zone ordinance dating from that time defined three main uses in Delray: industrial, residential and unrestricted (Figure 6.8). However, it did not establish clear restrictions for physical separation

FIGURE 6.6 Typical homes in Delray. *Top:* Typical home in the district (undated). *Center:* Typical home located in Peter Cooper Avenue, now Solvay Street. *Bottom:* Backyard of home on River Road, with Zug Island in background, 1903.
Source: Courtesy of the Burton Historical Collection, Detroit Public Library.

according to use. In most of Delray's neighborhoods, the ordinance delineated a height restriction of fifty feet in lieu of Detroit's typical thirty-five feet for residential properties, thus allowing bigger building footprints and taller structures to coexist. The lack of policies to regulate the coexistence of residential building and industrial facilities would later challenge the ability to update both sets of land uses.

Delray's population peaked in the 1930s, with roughly 30,000 residents. According to the 1930 census, 94 percent of Delray residents were white and 4 percent were black. The Depression severely affected many of the working-class residents of Delray and adjacent neighborhoods. High unemployment levels led to homelessness and the need for soup kitchens and shelters (Vargas 1989). As the Depression lifted, many of Delray's industries shifted toward wartime production, but Delray residents increasingly found work at manufacturing facilities outside of their neighborhood. This outside employment included the city of Dearborn's mammoth Ford River Rouge Complex, which was only two miles west of Delray's approximate center and employed 85,000 workers at its peak (Bak 2003).

THE INCREASING PRESENCE OF PUBLIC INFRASTRUCTURE IN DELRAY

The consolidation of international water transportation routes and the rise of the automobile empire affected the physical landscape of Delray. The tunnels for train and automobile connections to Windsor, Ontario as well as the Ambassador Bridge were all located just north of the neighborhood and developed between 1910 and 1929. Collectively, these three pieces of infrastructure dramatically reduced the importance of the Detroit River ferries (Eckert 1993). In 1933, the Detroit Wayne County Port District was established with jurisdiction over the waters and entire shoreline of Wayne County.

FIGURE 6.7 Images portraying the "Hungarian Streetscapes" of Delray. Delray was a vibrant community with a cluster of shops and other business run largely by Hungarian families.
Source: Courtesy of the Burton Historical Collection, Detroit Public Library.

After the initial flurry of industrial siting within Delray, the city began adding significantly to the area's utilities. In an effort to serve the area's industry, Detroit Edison added two coal-burning power plants to the district in the 1920s. The City of Detroit Wastewater Treatment Plant, located in the confluence of the Detroit and Rouge Rivers (Figure 6.9), opened in 1940 after 600 housing units were demolished. The city government added a full secondary treatment system to the primary treatment system in the 1970s to comply with the Clean Water Act requirements. This addition

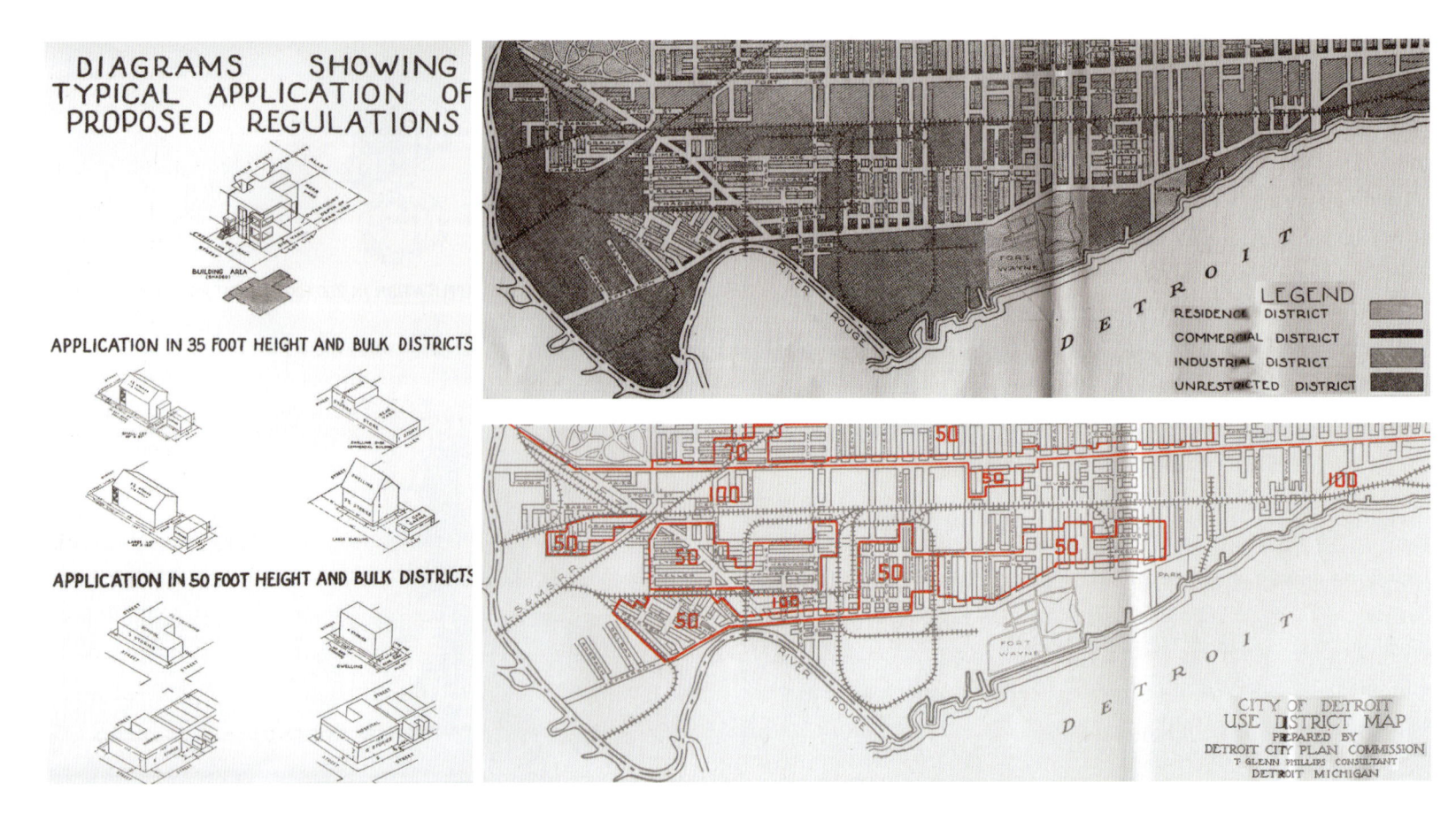

FIGURE 6.8 Images from the 1922 building zone ordinance. The diagrams show the application of the ordinance in Delray, where the lack of transition between residential and industrial areas was already problematic.
Source: City of Detroit. (1922). Proposed building zone ordinance. *Detroit, MI: City Plan Commission.*

required the demolition of an additional 300 housing units (Ilka 1979). Today, this wastewater treatment plant remains North America's largest in terms of processing volume and it continues to use an incinerator from the 1950s to burn off solid waste.³

Even before World War II ended, industrial firms had starting moving out of Detroit and Delray, going to nearby suburban and exurban locations. In the early 1940s, city planners were aware that industrial relocation was occurring, and they were cognizant of its potential negative impact on the city's economic well-being. In addition, studies developed during the 1940s ranked the industrial fabric of Delray as deficient due to aging structures, an inadequate city block system, the lack of available land for extended industrial use, and the need for improved access and parking. At that time, "fifty percent of the city's labor force was employed in manufacturing," making the location of industrial facilities important in the city's spatial pattern (Thomas 2013, p. 16). As a result, in addition to protecting the central business district from the encroaching "blight" of lower-income neighborhoods with substandard housing and rebuilding public facilities, the city government prioritized the protection of industrial areas in its planning efforts. "Protection" in this context meant recognizing that industrial facilities required larger sites and increased access to transportation infrastructure. Detroit, like many other cities in the United States, emerged from World War II with areas of deteriorating community facilities, middle-class flight to the suburbs, downtown decline, industrial exodus, inadequate affordable housing, and racial conflict. Some of the problems were due to deferred capital investments because of the Depression and military spending. Other problems were the result of city's unplanned development pattern coupled with rapid population growth. This conscious emphasis on protecting industrial areas at the expense of interspersed residential areas was illustrated in the city of Detroit's 1951 Master Plan's vision for Delray.

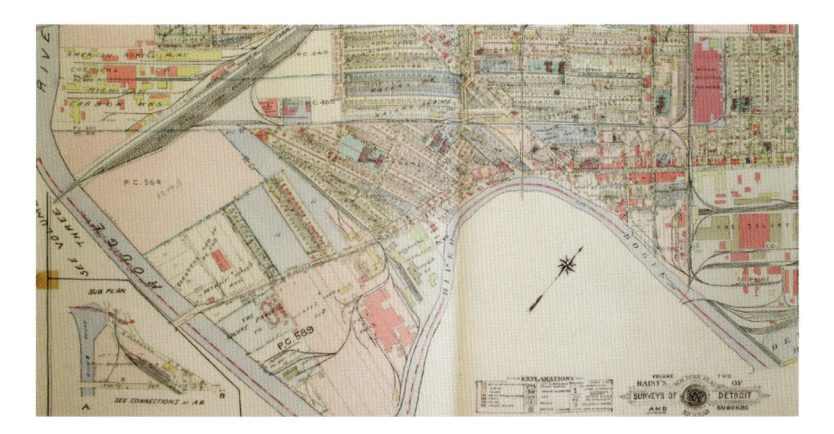

Detroit's 1951 Master Plan applied two major concepts. One concept was the development of large industrial and commercial corridors. The second concept was the use of Perry's "neighborhood unit" to identify approximately 150 neighborhood units and organize these into 16 community clusters (City of Detroit 1951; Thomas 2013). The area south of West Vernor Highway, where Delray is located, was zoned as industrial despite the presence of a significant residential community, and no neighborhood units were proposed in this location. Neighborhood units were envisioned for six Southwest Detroit neighborhoods to the north of Vernor Highway, but the plan neglected the 24,000 residents of Delray and targeted the area as industrial in the future land use maps (Figure 6.10). As a result of the industrial vision for Delray, the plan

FIGURE 6.9 Evolution of the area surrounding the present Detroit Waste Water Treatment Plant on West Jefferson Avenue. The images render three periods: (*top*) the carbon works area before the construction of the facility in 1926, (*center*) aerial image of the area in 1949, and (*bottom*) image of the expanded facility in 2010.
Sources: Top: *Baist, G. (1926). Baist Real Estate atlas of surveys of Detroit and suburbs, Michigan. Courtesy of the Bentley Historical Library, University of Michigan.* Center: *Aerial Image, 1949, courtesy of DTE Energy.* Bottom: *Aerial image, 2010, Google Earth.*

1943 Existing Land Use Map

■ Residential ■ Commercial ■ Industrial ■ Institutional, Recreational

1951 Proposed Land Use Map

■ Industrial ■ Institutional, Recreational

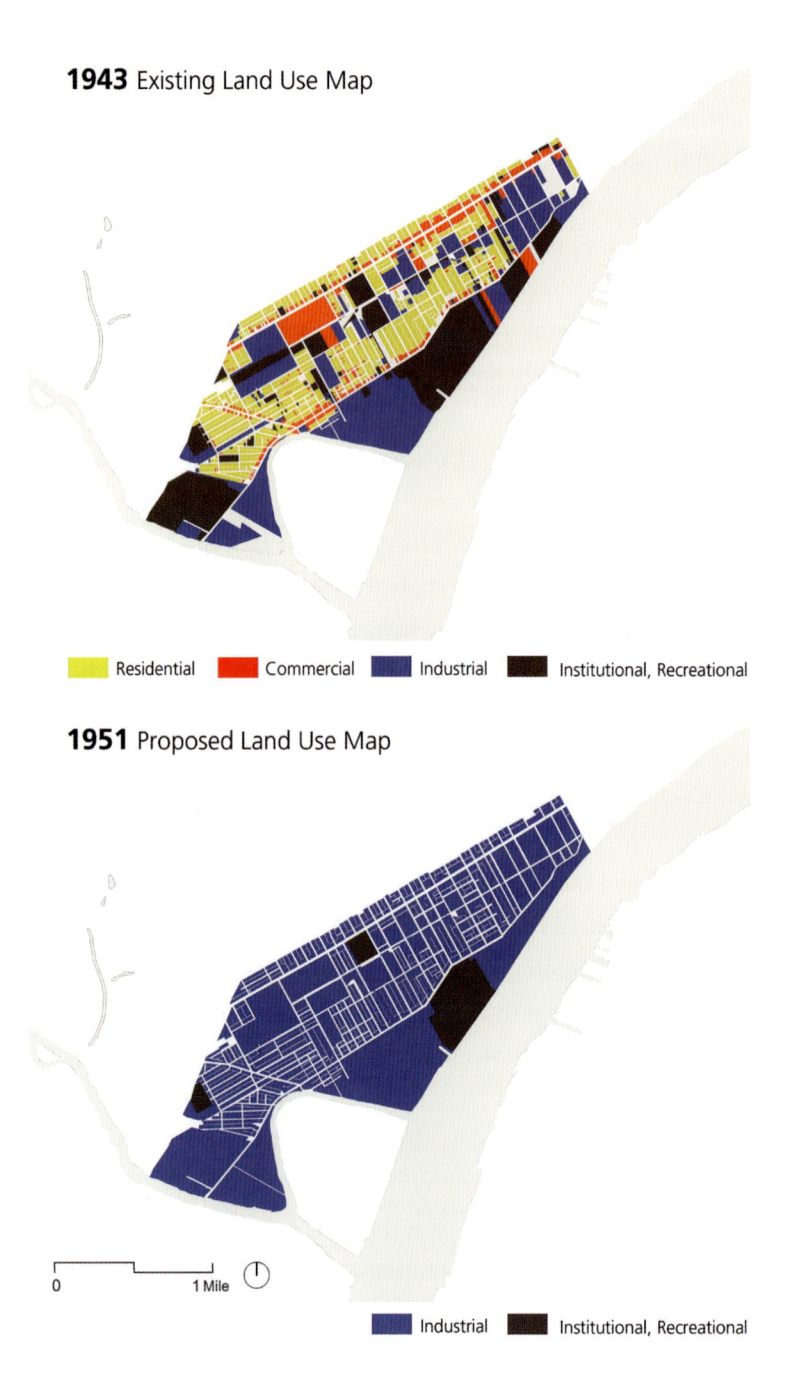

recommended closing key community facilities such as elementary, intermediate, and high schools (Figure 6.11).

The City Plan Commission's "Industrial Renewal," a 1956 citywide technical report of industrial land use, categorized one-third of the industrial corridors as deteriorated; this included Delray, identified as corridor number 19. The inventory stated that within the industrial/residential mix, Delray contained 289 acres of blighted housing; 57 acres of housing worthy of conservation; 113 acres of class 4 industrial land, the worst ranking, requiring clearance and redevelopment; and 332 of class 3 industrial land, requiring redevelopment and conservation (City of Detroit 1956b, Table I, 26A) (Figure 6.12). The tight urban pattern in Delray's residential areas inhibited industries from building the new prototype of industrial plant, which would have been a single-story plant with plenty of ground space for future expansion and for employee parking (City of Detroit 1951, 1956a).

THE DIVISIVE FISHER FREEWAY

In the 1960s, several incidents occurred that contributed to Delray's decline. Interestingly, Detroit's urban riots of 1967 had little direct impact on the area. Maidenberg (1969, p. 4B) notes that, "during the riots, blacks and whites patrolled the streets [of Delray] asking for quiet. There were no incidents." Delray's defining moments of this period involved the construction of a freeway and the city's interest in creating a new industrial park in Delray.

Detroit's enthusiasm for creating an expressway system preceded World War II and predated the 1956 Federal Highway Act that would reshape hundreds of U.S. cities and towns within a decade. This enthusiasm for high-speed automobiles is not surprising, considering the city's

FIGURE 6.10 Comparison of the Existing Land Use Map and the Proposed Land Use Map from the 1951 Master Plan. The plan designated most of Delray as industrial based on studies of the existing industrial clusters developed in the previous decade. At the time, there were 31,373 residents in Delray.
Sources: Elaborated by the authors.

FIGURE 6.11 Images of the first McMillan School, the later McMillian School in the 1960s, and the school's centennial celebration in 1989. The school was named after U.S. Senator James McMillan. The building served as a primary and secondary school. It was demolished in 2008.
Source: Photographs by J. Klein. Courtesy of the Burton Historical Collection, Detroit Public Library.

historical and economic attachment to the car industry. Highway engineers demolished hundreds of houses in Detroit, primarily in lower-income neighborhoods and in neighborhoods of people of color, to make way for the highways (Thomas 2013). Most relevant for Delray was the development of the Fisher Freeway (I-75) in 1964. This interstate ran parallel to Fort Street, effectively disconnecting Delray from the surrounding neighborhoods to the north (Figure 6.13). The purpose of I-75 was to connect the Ambassador Bridge and the vehicular tunnel beneath the river to other major roads. A 1979 *Detroit News* article on Delray's deterioration states, "Its modern-day problems are traced by natives to the construction in 1964 of the Fisher Freeway. The freeway cemented the area's boundary on the north, completing its encirclement, or worse, making it an island easily bypassed" (Ilka 1979, p. 1B and 6B).

Compounding the physical and psychological damage to residents of Delray from the construction of I-75, many large Delray employers left the area in the 1960s. Reflecting larger economic changes and America's loss of dominance in global industry, the Solvay Process Company (Allied Chemical), the Michigan Malleable Iron Works, Studebaker Corporation Automobiles, and Graham-Paige Mfg. Co., all closed (Maidenberg 1969).

Despite these industrial closings, the city government continued to identify heavy industry and manufacturing as the core of Detroit's economic development strategy, and official documents suggested that providing larger sites would stem the loss of industry to the outlying communities. In 1963, Delray contained 5,018 dwelling units. That year, the Detroit City Plan Commission released its riverfront study and restated the city's vision for an industrial Delray. The study included an inventory that noted that 34 percent of the river frontage in Delray was private property, 12 percent was occupied by the railroads, and 6 percent was claimed by utility use. This meant that only 25 percent of the river frontage was under public ownership. This study identified the Delray area for future port development sites as well as industrial redevelopment. Proposed redevelopment areas targeted heavy industrial uses. In a 1969 newspaper article, Charles Blessing, then director of the Detroit City Plan Commission, stated that his office had felt the "lash" of the Delray community's displeasure with the city's vision for Delray. He restated the findings of the 1963 study and the city council's subsequent

MAPPING DELRAY 127

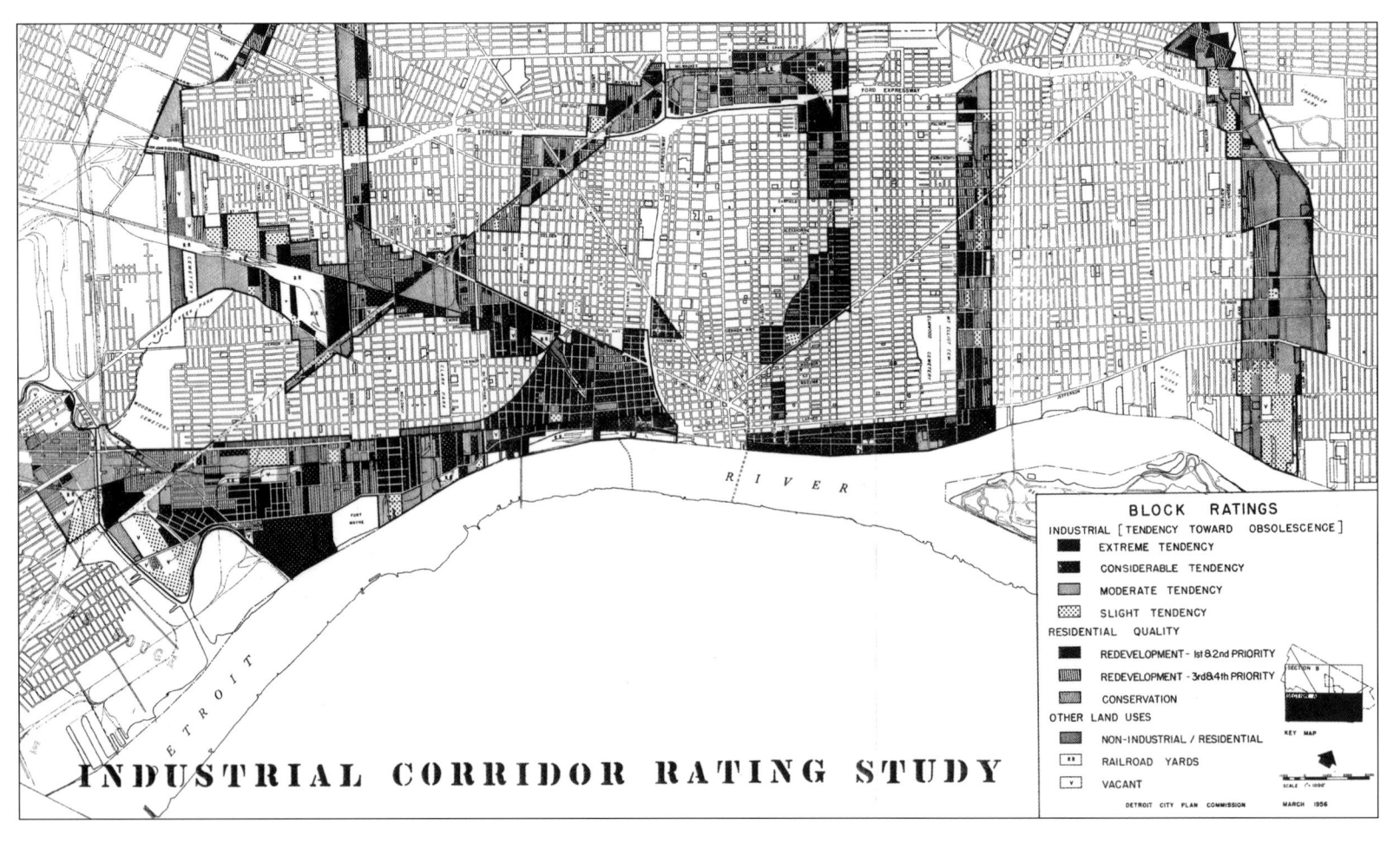

FIGURE 6.12 Assessment of Detroit's industrial corridors. This graphic illustrated the existing conditions and attitudes of Detroit's existing industries in 1956. Delray was categorized as "deficient."

Source: City of Detroit. (1956b). Industrial renewal: A comparative study of the tendency towards obsolescence and deterioration in major industrial areas in the city of Detroit. *Master Plan Technical Report Second Series, March 1956. Detroit, MI: City Plan Commission, Fig. 2.*

approval of $7.7 million dollars in 1965 to remove the remaining residential structures and realize an industrial park in Delray. However, after the 1967 riots, this earmarked money was redirected to improve housing elsewhere in the city. Blessing stated that the industrialization of Delray was an effort "to enhance the city's tax base" but that the neighborhood "may remain residential for quite some time" (Maidenberg 1969, p. 1B).

Between 1950 and 1970, Delray lost 11,000 residents while the proportion of black residents increased from 13.5 to 27 percent. Many of Delray's white residents left for the nearby suburbs of Allen Park, Melvindale, and Wyandotte. Local residents recount how these new suburbs became the promised land for residents financially able to leave. Consistent with the outward migration of many white working-class and middle-class families, the exodus exacerbated the city's economic stress and significantly

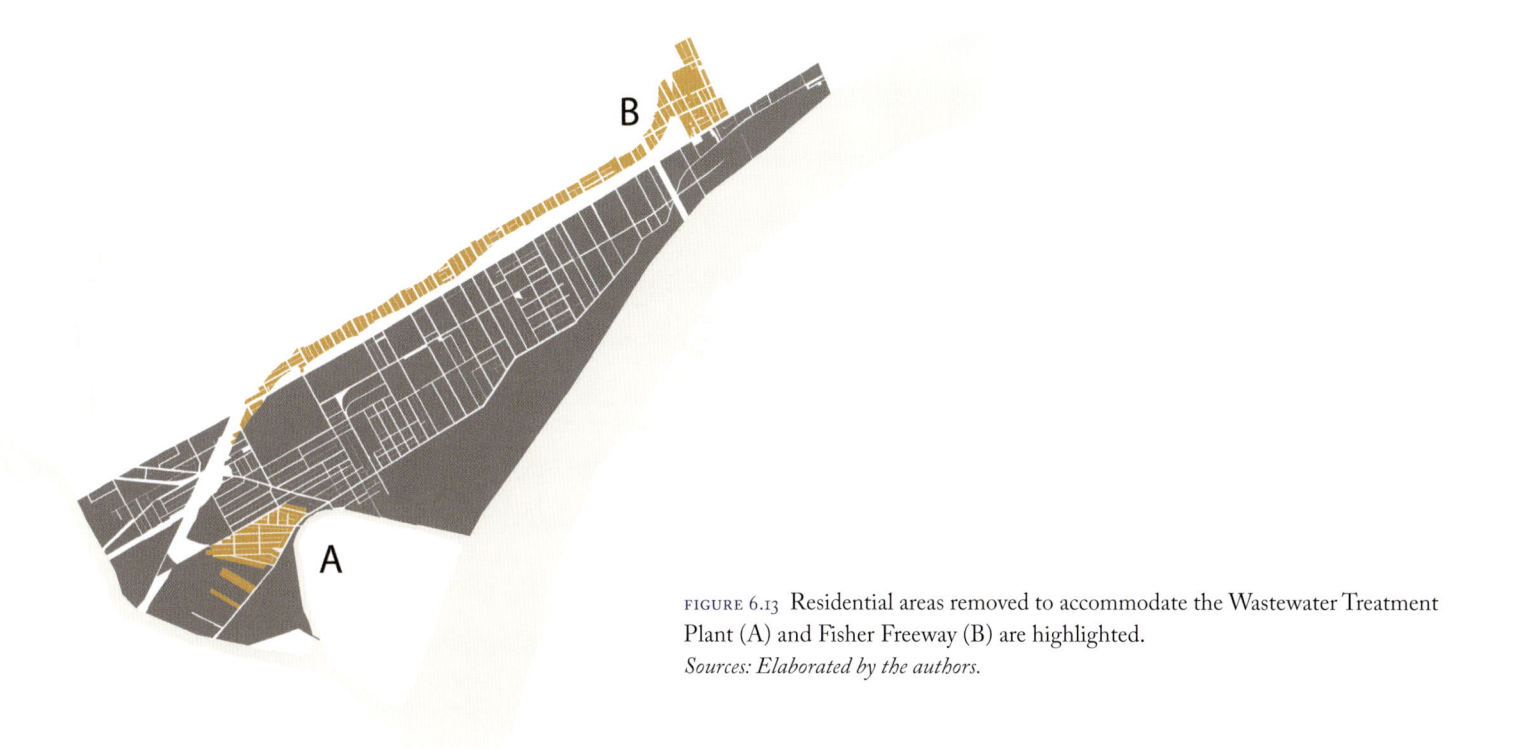

FIGURE 6.13 Residential areas removed to accommodate the Wastewater Treatment Plant (A) and Fisher Freeway (B) are highlighted.
Sources: Elaborated by the authors.

reduced the stability of many neighborhoods, including Delray (Farley, Danizer, and Holzer 2000).

Although the official plans openly prioritized industry, efforts to assist the remaining residents of Delray transition out of the area were not forthcoming. The industrial designation of the 1951 Master Plan did effectively guide the development of infrastructure to support the industrial facilities in the postwar years and indirectly signaled the decrease of public services and investments within Delray. The 1973 Master Plan acknowledged the remaining residents (Figure 6.14). While the plan's strategy recognized that remaining residents needed "just compensation" and that planners needed to employ "imaginative and creative use of zoning tools" (City of Detroit 1973, Art. 203.0104, II-17), the document also stated that a slow "natural" transition from residential to industrial was expected:

> [T]he area south of West Fort Street illustrates the ways in which existing structures serve to limit the Master Plan. That area has such an interdependent structure of rail lines and heavy industry that the removal of either or both does not appear to be a possibility within the time period of this plan. Noise, traffic and airborne effects of these industries so blight the balance of the district that it is not, and cannot be made, a good living area. Consequently, the future general land use map shows the whole area south of West Fort as best suited to industrial use. Despite these liabilities,

1976 Existing Land Use Map

■ Residential ■ Commercial ■ Industrial ■ Institutional, Recreational

1976 Proposed Land Use Map

■ Industrial ■ Institutional, Recreational

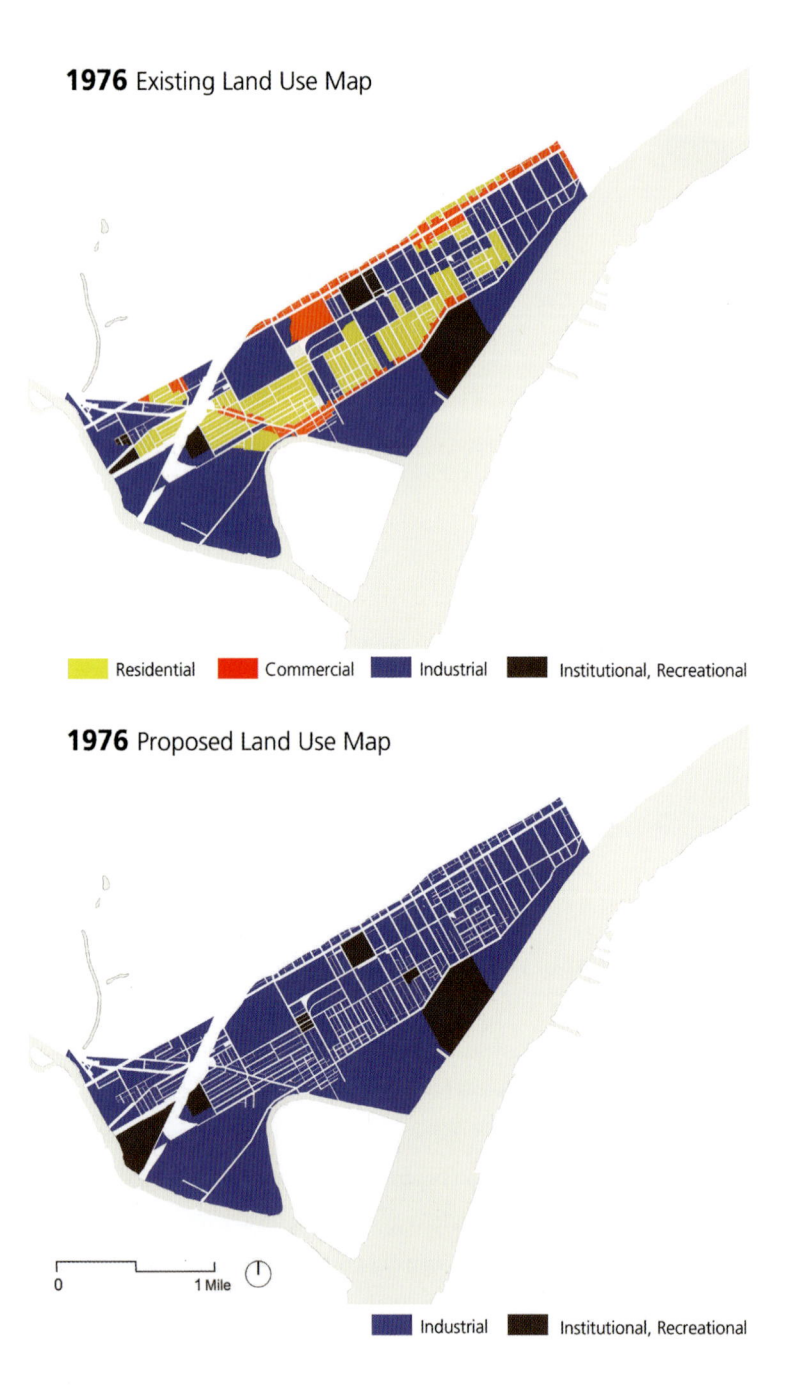

many homes in that area are sound structures, and have some years of useful life. Where such conditions exist it is the object of the land use plan to encourage industrial development in the area when it is ready for change rather than to cause an immediate changeover. (City of Detroit 1973, Art. 203.0104, II-17)

In 1979, the city's economic development office resurrected the industrial park concept for Delray. This time, the idea was to create a 375-acre area for a single tenant. But the closing of the Dodge Main plant in January 1980, in another part of the city, diverted the mayor's attention away from Delray. The Dodge Main plant was an industrial manufacturing complex that had employed 35,000 workers at its peak. In the wake of this loss, Detroit undertook one of the largest industrial redevelopment projects in the nation, but the city government and General Motors (GM) chose a site other than Delray. The project, the GM Detroit-Hamtramck Assembly Plant, popularly known as the Poletown plant, spanned both Detroit and Hamtramck, and site clearance required the removal of a mixture of 1,176 commercial, residential, and industrial structures within GM's demanding one-year time line. Public attention to the conversion of Delray into an industrial park faded in light of this massive undertaking (Darden, Hill, Thomas, and Thomas 1987).

LANDSCAPE OF DECLINE

At the time of the 1985 Master Plan, roughly 8,000 residents lived in Delray. The West Waterfront section of the master plan recognized the "great complexity in land use issues" (City of Detroit 1985, 411.0508) (Figure 6.15). In its summary of West Riverfront subsector issues, the plan proposed a

FIGURE 6.14 Comparison of the Existing Land Use Map and the Proposed Land Use Map from the 1976 Master Plan. The loss of residential fabric since the 1940s (see Map 6.2) is already visible in the Existing Land Use Map. The plans for the future industrial land use remain consistent with the previous master plan. *Sources: Elaborated by the authors.*

1985 Existing Land Use Map

■ Residential ■ Commercial ■ Industrial ■ Institutional, Recreational

1985 Proposed Land Use Map

0 — 1 Mile

■ Residential ■ Commercial ■ Industrial ■ Institutional, Recreational

major change in direction. It declared support for the viability of the residential community's coexistence within the industrial uses:

> It is recommended that the City give encouragement to all needed community support systems: shopping, schools, recreation, etc. Housing will need to be rehabilitated or replaced. Air quality should be improved. Housing should be protected against industry by changing the zoning of the edges of industrial corridors near residences from M4, intensive industrial, to M2, restricted industrial. (City of Detroit 1985, Art. 411, 411.0508-4).

This section of the Master Plan also mentioned the potential conflict if the wastewater treatment facilities were to expand. Regarding the port facilities, and the potential to benefit from the Free Trade Zone, the plan encouraged the consolidation of (1) freight transportation facilities, (2) industries related to the port or the use of water for transportation, and (3) food processing and distribution facilities.

Another economic blow to Delray came in 1986 when GM announced that it would be closing the Fleetwood and Clark Street plants. The Fleetwood plant was a forty-eight-acre site on the northwest side of Delray (on the southwest corner of Fort and West End Street). The plant operated in conjunction with the Clark Street plant that was approximately 1.5 miles to the north on the southwest corner of Michigan Avenue and Clark Street. The two plants employed a combined 6,600 workers at that time, and the factories produced large rear-wheel drive vehicles with V8 engines. These vehicles included the Cadillac

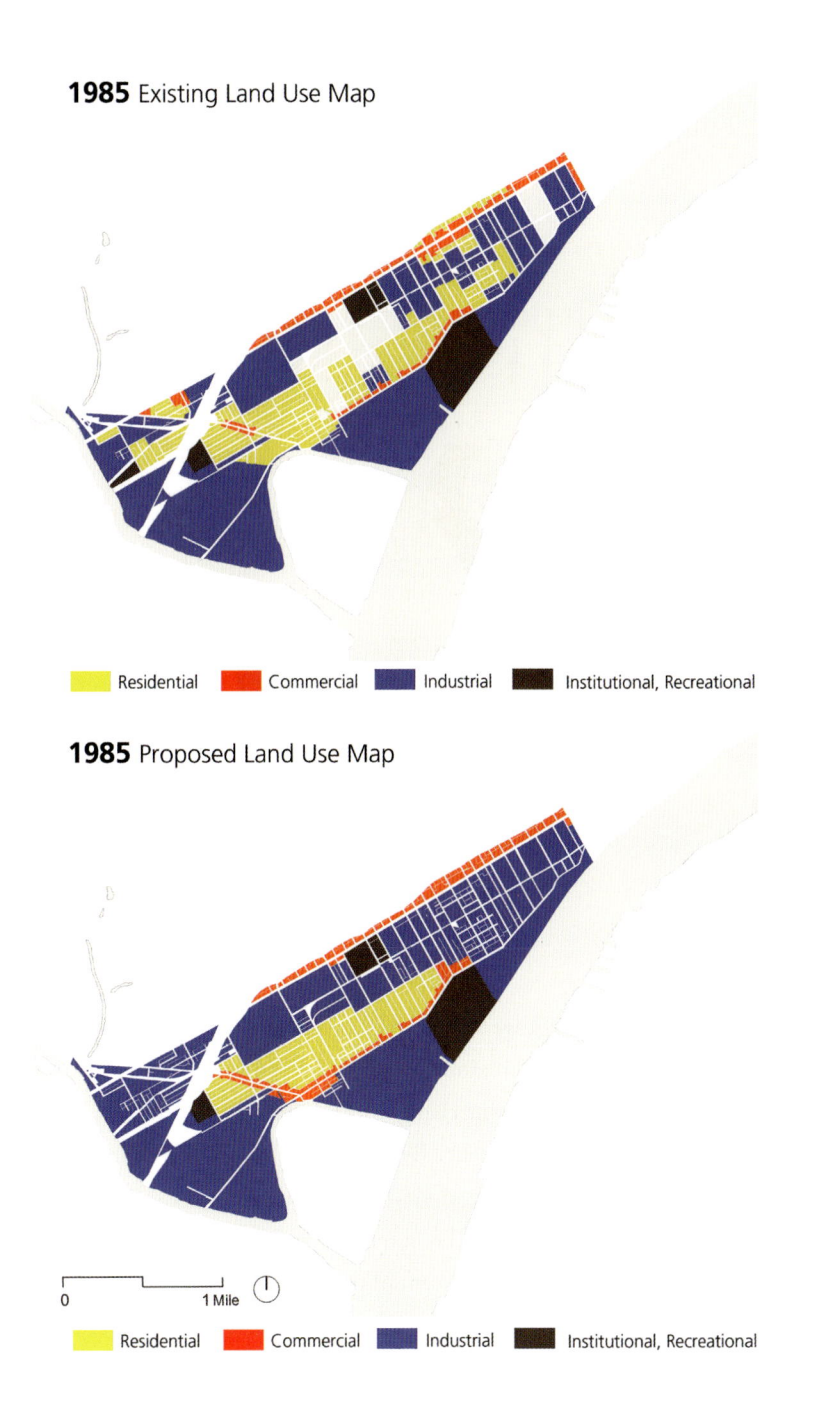

FIGURE 6.15 Comparison of the Existing Land Use Map and the Proposed Land Use Map from the 1985 Master Plan. This master plan acknowledged the shrinking residential stock and suggested different measures to sustain the existing residential fabric.
Sources: Elaborated by the authors.

MAPPING DELRAY 131

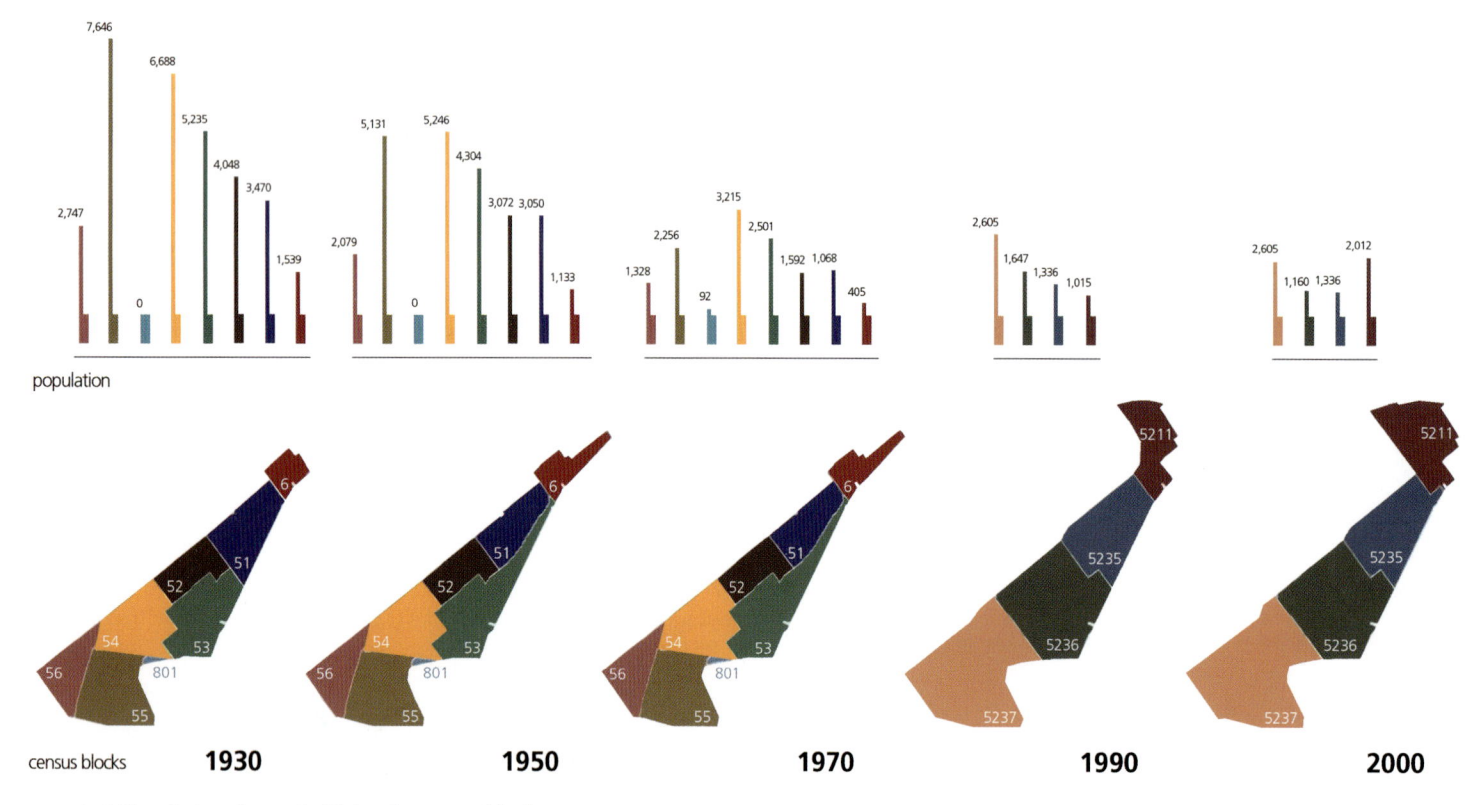

FIGURE 6.16 Population change in Delray by census blocks.
Sources: Tigerline 2000 and National Historic Information System, 1930–2000.

Fleetwood, Buick Roadmaster, and Oldsmobile 88. In the 1986 press release, GM stated that by closing the Fleetwood/Clark Street plants at the end of 1987, they were responding to decreased market demand for these large V8 engine cars and the need for reorganization. "Reorganization" in this context meant enlarging the capacity at the manufacturing plant in Arlington, Texas, where labor costs were lower (Wilkerson 1986, p. D10). Although the majority of the GM employees who had worked at the Fleetwood plant no longer lived in the Delray neighborhood, the loss of the daily influx of well-paid workers into the area was a blow for Delray's stability and its remaining retail and restaurants.

One of the most important changes in this period concerns the composition of the remaining residents. By 1990, 6,603 residents lived in Delray. This meant that between 1970 and 1990, Delray had lost almost 60 percent of its inhabitants (Figure 6.16). The number of residents identified as Hispanic or Latino increased to 41 percent of the population and poverty levels increased. Delray had become a place of last resort for low-cost housing.

LANDSCAPE OF DESPERATION

The revised Master Plan of Policies adopted by the City Council in 1992 offered only minor changes in the vision for Delray. As with previous plans, the city's statements lacked defined implementation programs. The plan stated that

> The challenge here [in Southwest Detroit] is to allow the operation and expansion of industry while retaining a viable residential community. The future should see this area with sound, comfortable neighborhoods built upon the existing residential base, served with adequate shopping, entertainment, and community facilities but structured so as to coordinate with the healthy growth of Detroit's reviving and evolving industrial base. (City of Detroit 1992, p. III-146)

In this public statement of future intent, the neighborhoods of Southwest Detroit, including Delray, are recognized as viable entities requiring "support." During Coleman Young's twenty-year mayoral administration (from 1974 to 1994), efforts to improve the city primarily involved discrete development projects. These projects, including the GM Poletown plant as well as the downtown Joe Louis Arena, were scattered throughout the city, thus diminishing their ability to represent a substantive cluster of change amidst the city's expansive area. The election of Mayor Dennis Archer elevated the value of comprehensive urban planning as an important method by which to strategically direct public and private development and investment (Thomas 2013).

Detroit's application for the Empowerment Zone program, however, showed how deeply marginalized Delray was by the 1990s. President Bill Clinton's administration had tapped the U.S. Department of Agriculture and the U.S. Department of Housing and Urban Development to create the Empowerment Zones/Enterprise Communities program. Successful urban applicants for the first round received $100 million in social service grants over ten years as well as tax incentives, regulation waivers, and preferential opportunities for additional federal funds for a ten-year period. The highly competitive application process required input from city residents, community organizations, and members of the Detroit business community as the basis for a detailed strategic plan for economic development, housing, and other social programs. This public planning process initiated long-overdue and often difficult conversations about how to improve life in Detroit. The business community committed to investing 1.9 billion dollars in conjunction with the federal funds. The application was successful: in 1994 Detroit became one of six central cities in the country chosen for designation. What is most significant about the Empowerment Zone in relation to Delray is the absence of much of Delray's territory, as we have defined it, within the zone's defined boundaries. The omission suggests either that the community lacked a strong, united voice and/or that city planners and community leaders doubted the possibility of regeneration in this area.

The 2009 Master Plan of Policies, the city's official statement of expected future land use at the time of this writing, identifies future residential areas in Delray as a part of the city's West Riverfront area (Figure 6.17). The plan notes that the area lost more than a quarter of its dwelling stock and population in the previous decade, and the remaining community suffered from "among the highest proportions of low-income households and low-value dwelling units in the City" (City of Detroit 2009, p. 162). Although environmental issues, vacant lots, and declining housing characterize the area according to the 2009 Master Plan's text, the document declares support for the redevelopment and reinforcement of Delray. It identifies Jefferson Avenue as the commercial thoroughfare for the community. The plan states that Fort Street's intense traffic justifies the development of intensive commercial uses to capitalize on the high density of truck traffic in the surroundings of the customs facility. For the first time,

2009 Existing Land Use Map

Residential ▇ Commercial ▇ Industrial ▇ Institutional, Recreational

2009 Proposed Land Use Map

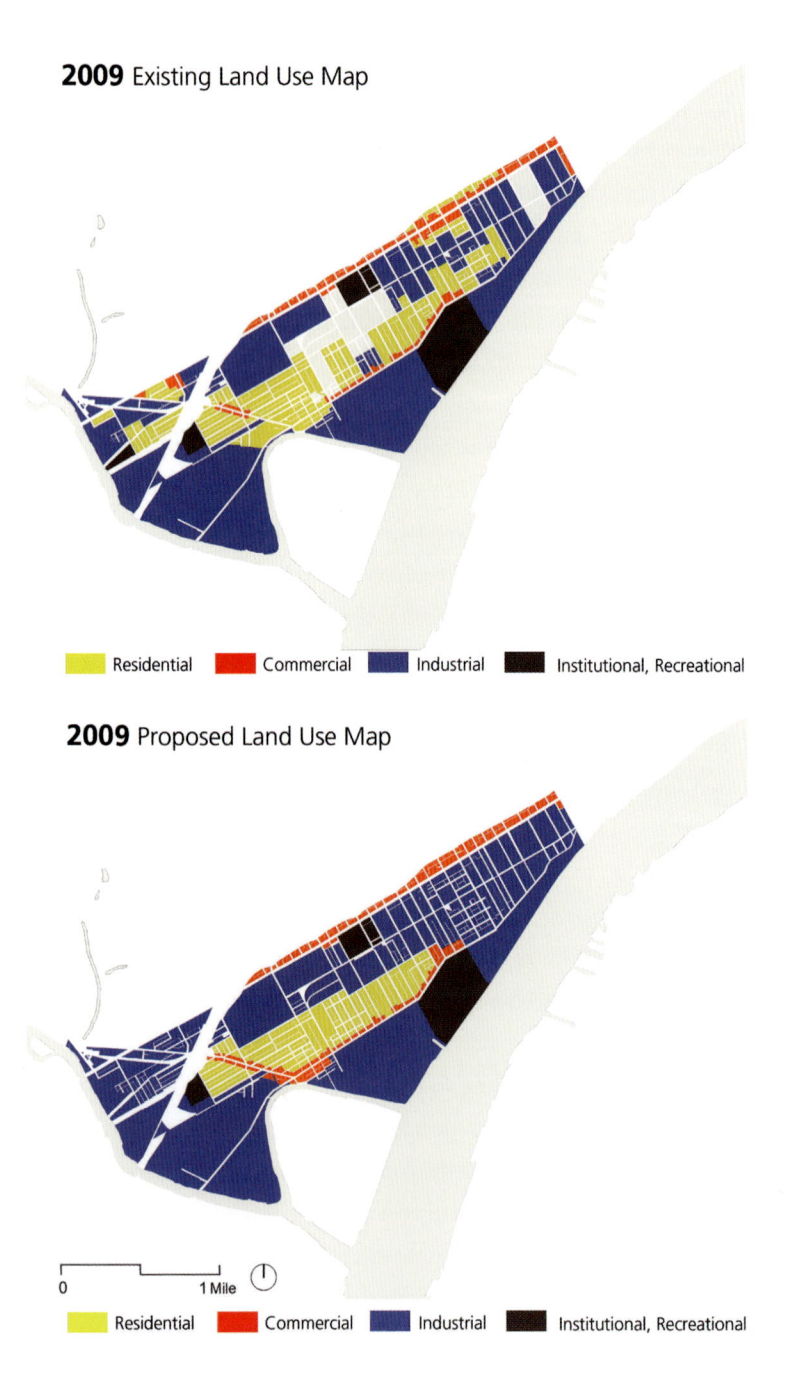

0 — 1 Mile

Residential ▇ Commercial ▇ Industrial ▇ Institutional, Recreational

this master plan recognizes the need to prioritize environmental remediation north of West Jefferson to facilitate future residential development in the Delray neighborhood, and insists on the need to buffer the industrial land uses from the residential areas. In the policies aiming to improve environmental quality, the riverfront appears as a priority. The plan also mentions the need to address the ongoing problem of illegal dumping.[4]

The residents of Delray are now a diverse collection of races and ethnicities, but this strength pales in comparison to the area's challenges. Issues of air pollution, unsafe residential streets (due to the thousands of trucks that traverse the neighborhood), poor bus service, illegal dumping, and unreliable emergency services are top residents' concerns. Some residents live here because of poverty and have few opportunities to find housing elsewhere. Many of the houses are worth less than $10,000 each, rentals are common, and at least two-thirds of the residential parcels are now empty. Other residents—primarily elderly women—live here because this is the only home they know. These elderly residents have decreasing mobility; though their family members worry about the poor living conditions of Delray, they are more fearful of the trauma that moving would induce.

At the time of urban renewal efforts in the 1960s, planning was often rightly criticized for its aggressive actions that destroyed communities. These urban renewal mistakes were made in postwar Detroit in general, but a different error was committed with respect to Delray. The city failed to assist Delray's poorest residents to move to healthier neighborhoods with more services and better amenities before the neighborhood disintegrated into its current condition (Figures 6.18 and 6.19). Planning efforts in Delray committed the error of omission. Although this type of error may appear less egregious, clearly public inaction is partially responsible

FIGURE 6.17 Comparison of the Existing Land Use Map and the Proposed Land Use Map in the Master Plan of 2009.
Sources: Elaborated by the authors.

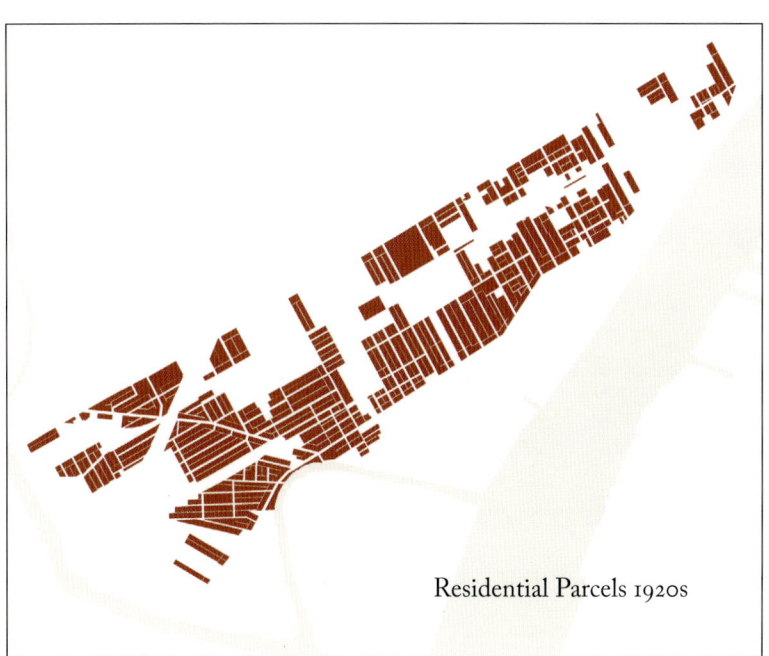

FIGURE 6.18 Decreasing presence of residential parcels over time: 1880s, 1920s, 1960s, and 2000s.

Sources: Elaborated by the authors.

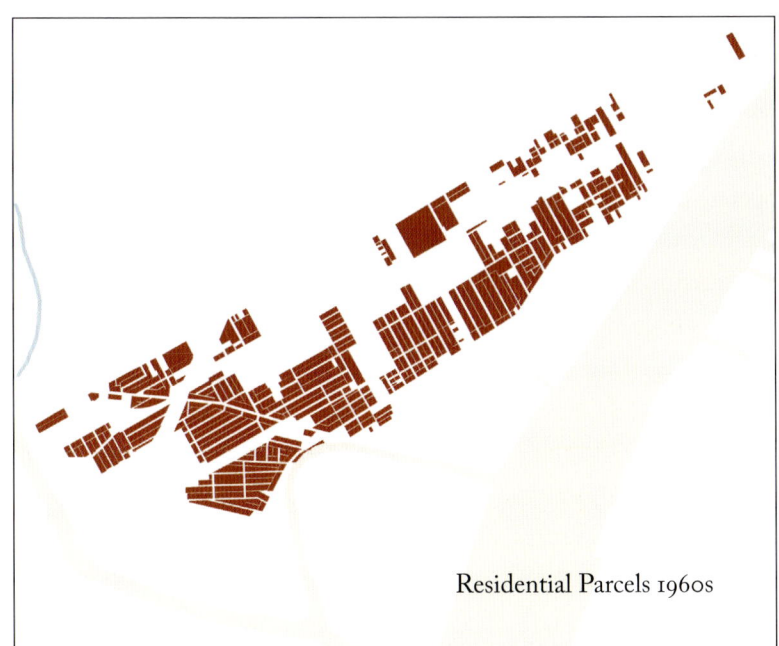

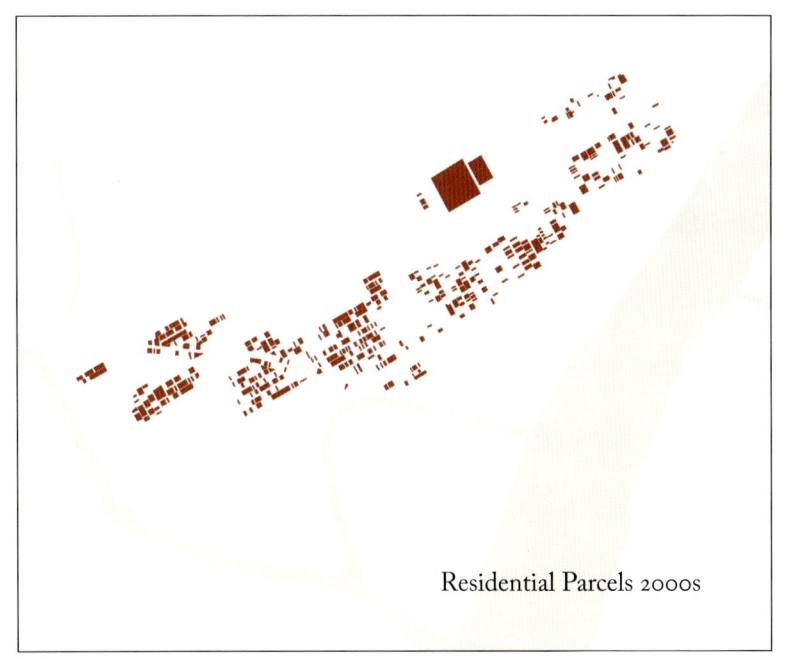

MAPPING DELRAY 135

FIGURE 6.19 Typical residential street in Delray, 2010.
Source: Photograph by Arquero de Alarcon & Larsen.

for the difficult conditions that exist today in Delray's remaining fragments of residential neighborhoods.

DELRAY'S RENEWED IMPORTANCE TO DETROIT AND THE REGION IN THE AGE OF GLOBAL TRADE

It is ironic that Delray's most fundamental characteristic—its location on the waterfront—has returned it to the public conversation as an appropriate place for a second international bridge. The proposed New International Trade Crossing (NITC) would connect the Delray neighborhood in southwest Detroit and an area in Windsor, Ontario, allowing for optimal connection to Canadian highways for truck traffic. The NITC planning process began in 2000. At that time, thirteen potential sites were identified; the Delray crossing was selected as the preferred site, and the Environmental Impact Statement was completed in December 2009. Unlike the existing Ambassador Bridge located less than a mile east of Delray's boundary, the NITC would be a publicly owned and operated bridge. The Michigan Department of Transportation (MDOT), which will direct the U.S. side of the bridge, plans to demolish approximately 300 Detroit homes in order to build the bridge plaza. Considering the relocation packages that will be offered, and the short-term and long-term financial implications of the moves, then this project could be an opportunity for many Delray residents to start over in locations less burdened by industrial wastes, diesel emissions, and neighborhood abandonment. However, residents living just beyond the proposed plaza's footprint would not be relocated, and they would shoulder even more environmental burdens.

Complicating the potential impact of a second bridge on the environmental conditions and traffic patterns of southwest Detroit is the alternative proposal by the Ambassador Bridge's owner, Manuel "Matty" Moroun. Moroun proposed constructing a twin span adjacent to his existing bridge, which he would pay for if he were allowed to own and operate it. In response to the NITC process, community residents formed the Community Benefits Coalition in 2008 in an effort to request that specific benefits for the local community (such as local hiring requirements, air quality assessment, and landscape buffers) be a contractual requirement of their agreement in exchange for the community's support for the NITC project.

Although the construction of an international bridge requires the coordination of multiple agencies at the state, federal, international, and local level, MDOT was charged with conducting the NITC planning process on the American side. When MDOT initially assumed lead responsibility on the U.S. side, they were quick to derail residents' questions or concerns by transferring responsibility to numerous public others and private entities. The implicit message of these conversations was that the city of Detroit is responsible for the problems in Delray, and these new infrastructure projects that serve larger systems and the region have no obligation to the people and institutions remaining. Dissatisfied with the initial public offerings to the host community, community residents have continued to request a Community Benefits Agreement. Just as it has become difficult to determine who controls decision making in the global economy, it has become difficult to determine responsibility in this infrastructure project because of such obfuscation. Resolving which bridge will be constructed and whether a Community Benefits Agreement will accompany it are an important pair of decisions with strong equity/inequity implications.

CONCLUSION

In this chapter, we have described how Delray's evolution partially paralleled that of Detroit's, changing from a small riverside settlement to a diversified regional manufacturing hub at the end of the nineteenth century, to the pinnacle of industrial production after World War II, to a declining Rust Belt area in the 1980s, and finally, in its latest rendition, as a physical link in a global economy (Figure 6.20). Location—the reason for Detroit's and Delray's establishment and successful early development—has returned as a twenty-first century economic development opportunity.

By mapping the dense network of waterways, roads, and rail connections developed in Delray during the 1800s, we discussed the establishment and consolidation of industry within the area from the turn of the century until its peak. These industries reflected Detroit's diversity of manufacturing processes and suppliers and attracted numerous immigrants who formed self-contained ethnic communities around the plants. However, beginning in the 1920s, bigger industrial complexes began to attract Delray residents outside the neighborhood to the River Rouge Complex and other outlying manufacturing facilities. If in the late 1800s ethnicity was the major factor shaping the spatial distribution of the urban populations in American cities, in the early 1900s class and race took the lead. "Cross-class neighborhoods, typical of nineteenth-century ethnic patterns, disappeared to be replaced by more cohesive socioethnic neighborhoods" (Zunz 1982, p. 6). Therefore, Delray's status as a Hungarian enclave changed. More recently, the unifying characteristic of the residents has been their extreme poverty and peripheral relationships to the formal economy. If, as Sugrue writes, "The fate of the city is the consequence of the unequal distribution of power and resources" (Sugrue 1996, p. 14), then Delray represents the city's inability to balance the shifting economic powers controlling the area's development with the remaining residents' needs for safety, services, amenities, and economic opportunities. From the 1920s until the 1980s, despite the presence of a significant number of residents, the city's plan for Delray was industrial. By the 1980s, when the official plan acknowledged the remaining residential neighborhoods of Delray, the long-term effects of environmental pollution, population decline, housing abandonment, loss of commercial services, and neglected public amenities had transformed Delray into an isolated wasteland in which some of the city's poorest residents lived in the most difficult conditions. In the last ten years, waste and composting facilities have opened within Delray, and a number of adjacent industrial facilities, such as the Marathon Oil Refinery and Severstol Steel, have expanded. Oddly, the current landscape is increasingly green as landscape succession follows abandonment. However, the welcome greenery masks numerous contaminated sites and encourages illegal dumping.

In Delray, many of Detroit's problems are not only present, but also amplified. The industrial character of the early landscape has continued relatively unplanned and unopposed. Although some industrial operations within the area have been lost, infrastructure elements have increasingly

1880s

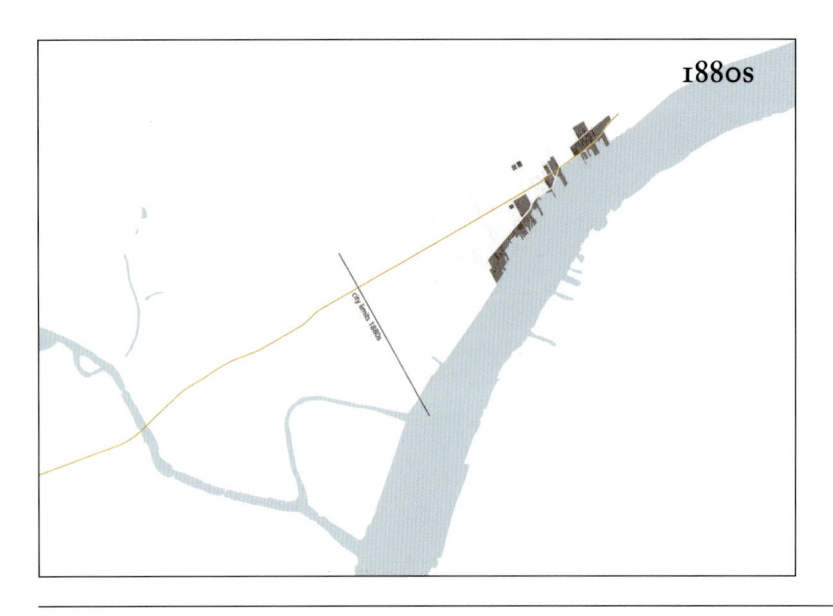

Sill Cooperage Co.
Bangk Steam Engine Co.
Brown Bros. & Co. Lumber Yard
Clark & Granger Mfg. Co.
Detroit & Lake Superior Copper Works
Detroit Gas Light Co.
Detroit Leather Co.
Ft. Wayne Soap Works
George H. Parker Tannery
Henry Heames & Son Stone & Lime Yard
John Beyster Planing Mill & Sash Factory
John Bigly & Co. Pork Packing House
Morton & Backus Lumber Dock
Scotten Lovett & Co. Tobacco Mfg.

1920s

American Agricultural Chemical Co. Michigan Carbon Works
American Brass Co.
Atlas Foundry
Bassett Mfg. Co.
Brass Goods
Cadillac Motor Car Plant
City Gas Works
Columbia Castings Co.
Detroit Chemical Co.
Detroit Edison Co.
Detroit Edison Coal Yard
Detroit Lumber Co.
Detroit Railway Harbor Terminal Co.
Detroit Street Railways
Detroit Sulphite Pulp & Paper Co.
Electric Refrigeration Co.
General Motors - Fisher Body Plant
Graham-Paige Mfg. Co.
Great Lakes Transit Corp.
Lumber Yard
LXL Glass Co.
Maple and Oak Flooring Works
Michigan Copper & Brass Co.
Michigan Malleable Iron Works
Morrell Street Plant Public Lighting Commission
Peerless Portland Cement Co.
Schultz Soap Works
Scotten Tobacco Works
Studebaker Corporation Automobiles
Ternstedt Mfg. Co.
The Barrett Co. Tar Works
The Solvay Process Co.
The Solvay Process Co.
US Radiator Corp.
Wayne Soap Co.

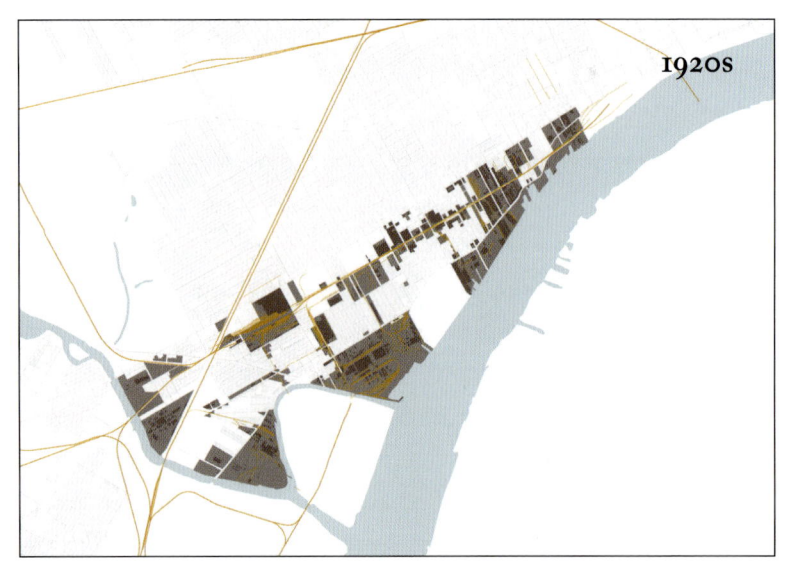

Figure 6.20 Delray major industries, evolution over time. *Top left to bottom right*: 1880s, 1920s, 1960s, and 2000s.
Sources: Maps elaborated by the authors with information from Baist Atlas, Sanborn Maps, and recent industrial business inventories.

1960s

Allied Chemical Corp.
American Charcoal Co.
Anderson Brass Co.
City of Detroit Public Lighting Commission, Mistersky Power Station
City of Detroit Sewage Treatment Plant
Department of Public Works
Detroit Chemical Works
Detroit Chemicals Specialties Inc.
Detroit Edison Co.
Detroit Harbor Terminals, Inc.
Detroit Marine Terminal Forwarders & Shippers
Detroit Union Produce Terminal Co.
General Mill Supply Co.
General Motors - Fisher Body Fleetwood Plant
Great Lakes Steel Corp.
Guardian Glass Co.
Hupp Corp.
McLouth Steel Corp.
Michigan Consolidated Gas Co.
Michigan Copper & Brass Co.
Michigan Malleable Iron Co.
Modern Materials Corp.
Peerless Cement Corp.
Rail & Waterways Coal Co.
Republic Carloading & Distributing Co.
Rockwell Standard Corp.
Scott Paper Co.
Scotten Dillon Co. Tobacco Works
Stuart Foundry Co.
Ternstedt Mfg. Co. Fisher Body Plant
The American Agricultural Chemical Co.
The American Brass Co.
The Great Atlantic & Pacific Tea Co.
Wayne Chemical Products Co.
Wrigley's Store's Inc. Produce Warehouse

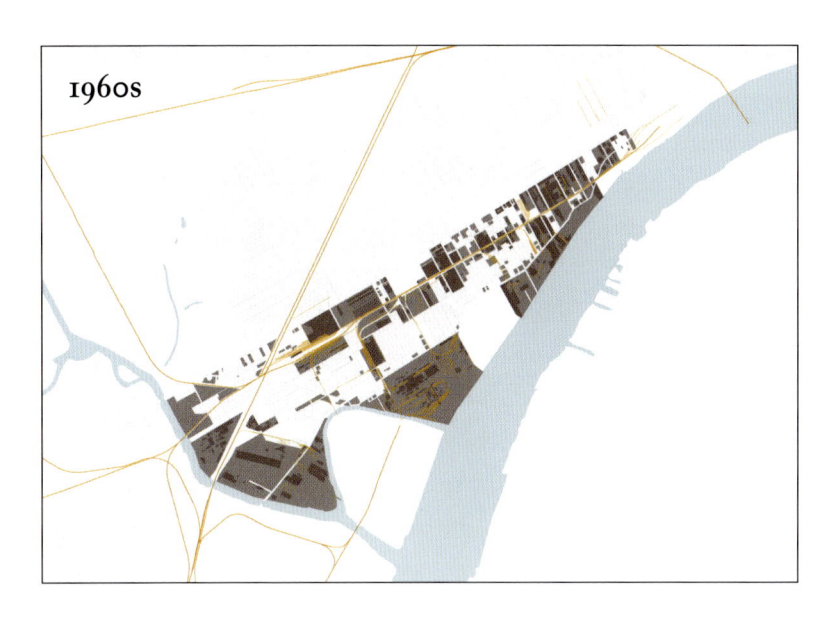

2000s

Anayas Pallets
Arvin Meritor, Inc.
Bridgewater Interiors
Causley Trucking Inc.
Clawson Concrete Company
Container Port
Detroit Engine & Kit Co.
Detroit Logistics Co.
Detroit Marine Terminals
Detroit Produce Terminals
Detroit Water & Sewage
East Michigan Trailer Sales
Flor-Dri Supply
Former Sybill
Fort Street Warehouse
Hascall Steel Castor
Jeford Industries
Metal Prep Technology
Motor City Intermodal
Motor City Intermodal Distribution
Motor Rail Delivery
Nicholson Terminal & Dock
Peerless Metal Powders Inc
Waterfront Petroleum Terminal

MAPPING DELRAY

dominated Delray, beginning with the two coal-powered electricity plants in the early 1920s, the waste water treatment plant in the 1940s, the more recent location of a recycling facility, and, finally, the pending location of the plaza for the second international bridge entry point. The physical location of the area and its generous waterfront, important in its establishment, assumed a renewed importance due to trade patterns between the United States and Canada. While the area's connections via transportation infrastructure have increased, the remaining residents live amidst the industrial landscape, exposed to increasingly elevated levels of air pollution. The possible placement of the NITC bridge footing within the Delray neighborhood recast the spatial issues of equity and highlighted changes in economic transactions. As Soja (2010) notes, the "rights to the city everywhere are becoming rights to the city region as a whole, to all the resources generated by the network of urban agglomerations forming the metropolitan regional economy and extending its reach to a global scale" (p. 100). Within this context of a-spatial global flows, we need to find avenues to return investment to the places like Delray whose residents, largely trapped by poverty, endure the many costs of these infrastructure projects of regional and global significance.

NOTES

The authors wish to acknowledge the excellent assistance of urban planning graduate students Pete Robie and Andrew Milne, for assisting in the meticulous compilation of historical information and contributing to the maps and figures, and Peter McGrath for his assistance in the edition process. We also wish to thank Karl Longstreth at the University of Michigan's Map Library for his advice and assistance.

1. In the mid-1840s, a brick star-shaped fort was built in response to territorial disputes with British Canada. The fort, with its forty buildings, has served multiple purposes over time. Beginning in the U.S. Civil War and lasting until the Vietnam War, Fort Wayne was a military induction site for Michigan soldiers. During both World War I and World War II, Fort Wayne served as a warehouse for locally produced munitions and supplies. In 1971, the Detroit Historical Department took control of the eighty-three-acre property. In 1996, Wayne County voters approved a millage to fund restoration of the fort as a recreational and historical site. However, today, Fort Wayne is largely unused and most observers would assume the chain-link fenced property is abandoned except for the deer and other wildlife that enjoy its grounds (Puls, 2000).

2. The mineshaft opening for the Detroit Salt Company is located at 12841 Saunders Street. The Detroit Salt Company closed in 1987 but was purchased by a new owner and reopened in 1998. The land is leased from the city to the company. Underground roads extend over 100 miles, and the mines cover an area over 1,000 acres in size. The area extends beneath Delray and the Detroit River (MacDonald, 2010).

3. Delray's role in hosting utilities and waste facilities continues to increase. The Waste Water Treatment Plant serves 35 percent of Michigan's population (approximately three million people) with service to Detroit and 76 surrounding communities in a 946-square-mile area with 3,400 miles of sewer line. The plant treats 2,600 million liters (700 million gallons) of wastewater per day. The plant uses combined sewer outflows: when rain causes water levels to exceed the plant's treatment capacity, raw sewage is released with stormwater runoff directly into the Detroit River (37.2 billion gallons in 2008 and 2009). Although the Michigan Chapter of Civil Engineers identified this wastewater treatment plant as one of the state's ten most important projects, the wastewater treatment plant has also been a problematic source of air pollution in Delray as its 1950s-era incinerator burns off the plant's solid waste.

4. *Detroit Future City* (2012), a highly publicized strategic plan not formally adopted by the city but heavily supported by local government and foundations, portrays Delray as industrial.

MAPS AND AERIAL IMAGERY SOURCES

The original maps and diagrams have been generated in ArcMap with the cartographic base of SEMCOG 2009/2011, and the Detroit Residential Parcel Survey from 2010.

Baist, G. (1885/1926). *Baist Real Estate atlas of surveys of Detroit and suburbs, Michigan.* Courtesy of the Bentley Library, University of Michigan.

Sanborn Map Company. (1983–1990). *Sanborn fire insurance maps, Michigan.* Teaneck, NJ: Chadwyck-Healey.

Historical Aerial Image Collection of Detroit from 1949 to 1997, Wayne University, courtesy of DTE.

Aerial image, 2010. Google Earth.

City of Detroit (1922, 1947, 1951, 1956a, 1956b, 1973, 1985, 1992, 2009).

REFERENCES

Bak, R. (2003). *Henry and Edsel: The creation of the Ford empire*. Hoboken, NJ: John Wiley Press.

Base, M. (1970). *The development of Detroit 1701–1920, a planning history* [research report]. Detroit, MI: Wayne State University, Division of International Studies.

Beynon, E. D. (1934). Occupational succession of Hungarians in Detroit. *The American Journal of Sociology, 39*(5), 600–610.

Beynon, E. D. (1935). Crime and custom of the Hungarians of Detroit. *Journal of Criminal Law and Criminology (1931–1951), 25*(5), 755.

Beynon, E. D. (1936). Social mobility and social distance among Hungarian immigrants in Detroit. *The American Journal of Sociology, 41*(4), 423–34.

Burton, C. M., Stocking, W., and Miller, G. (1922). *The city of Detroit, Michigan, 1701–1922*. Detroit, MI: Clarke Publishing Company.

Campbell, H. J. V. (1922, April). The departed waters of Detroit. Burton Historical Collection leaflet, *1*(4), 39.

City of Detroit. (1922). *Proposed building zone ordinance*. Detroit, MI: City Plan Commission.

City of Detroit. (1947). *The Detroit plan for blight elimination*. Detroit, MI: City Plan Commission.

City of Detroit. (1951). *The Detroit master plan: The official comprehensive plan for the development and improvement of Detroit as approved by the Mayor and the Common Council*. Detroit, MI: City Plan Commission.

City of Detroit. (1956a). *Industrial study: A survey of existing conditions and attitudes of Detroit's industry*. Detroit, MI: City Plan Commission.

City of Detroit. (1956b). *Industrial renewal: A comparative study of the tendency towards obsolescence and deterioration in major industrial areas in the city of Detroit*. Master Plan Technical Report Second Series, March 1956. Detroit, MI: City Plan Commission.

City of Detroit. (1973). *The Detroit master plan as amended October 1973*. Detroit, MI: City Plan Commission.

City of Detroit. (1985). *Detroit master plan of policies*. Detroit, MI: Planning Department.

City of Detroit. (1992). *Revised master plan of policies*. Detroit, MI: City Plan Commission.

City of Detroit. (2009). *Current master plan, adopted by City Council in July of 2009. City of Detroit master plan of policies*. Detroit, MI: City Plan Commission.

Darden, J. T., Hill, R. C., Thomas, J. M, and Thomas, R. (1987). *Detroit: Race and uneven development*. Philadelphia, PA: Temple University Press.

Detroit future city: 2012 Detroit strategic framework plan. (2012). Detroit, MI.

Eckert, K. B. (1993). *Buildings of Michigan*. New York, NY: Oxford University Press.

Farley, R., Danziger, S., and Holzer, H. J. (2000). *Detroit divided*. New York, NY: Russell Sage Foundation.

Farmer, S. (1890). *History of Detroit and Wayne County and early Michigan: A chronological encyclopedia of the past and present* (3rd ed.). New York, NY: Munsel & Co.

Georgakas, D., and Surkin, M. (1998). *Detroit: I do mind dying* (2nd ed.). Cambridge, MA: South End Press Classics.

Ilka, D. (1979, February 18). Delray fights to halt an outgoing tide. *Detroit News*, p. 1B and 6B

Jackson, K. (1985). *Crabgrass frontier: The suburbanization of the United States*. Oxford, UK: Oxford University Press.

Kenyon, N. (1951, June 3). City within a City: Delray, once beautiful, glories now in its wealth. *Detroit Free Press*, p. 1B and 6B

Klug, T. (1999). *Railway cars, bricks, and salt: The industrial history of southwest Detroit before auto*. Unpublished manuscript. Retrieved from www.old-delray.com/documents/Southwest_Detroit.pdf.

Leake, P. (1912). *History of Detroit: Chronicle of its progress, its industries, its institutions, and the people of the fair city of the Straits* (Vol. 3). Chicago, IL: Lewis Publishing Company.

MacDonald, C. (2010, April 19). Residents wary of Detroit's salt mine's neighborhood plan. *The Detroit News*, p. 1A. Record number ID: det-66075521.

Maidenberg, M. (1969, May 11). Delray: The determined struggle of a village condemned to die. *Detroit Free Press*, p. 4B.

Munger, T. L. (1920). *Detroit and World-trade: A Survey of the City's Present and Potential Foreign Trade and Seaboard Traffic, and the Facilities Therefor, with Special Reference to the Proposed St. Lawrence Deep Waterway to the Sea*. The Detroit Board of Commerce.

Official Paper of the Michigan Manufacturers Association. (1910, June 18). *Michigan Manufacturer, 2*(33).

Puls, M. (2000, September 25). Despite $4 million repair tax, Fort Wayne in shambles—City won't give up control; county wants a say in spending. *Detroit News*, p. 1A.

Soja, E. (2010). *Seeking spatial justice*. Minneapolis: University of Minnesota Press.

Sugrue, T. J. (1996). *The origins of the urban crisis: Race and inequality in postwar Detroit*. Princeton, NJ: Princeton University Press.

Thomas, J. M. (2013). *Race and redevelopment: Planning a finer city in postwar Detroit* (2nd ed.). Detroit, MI: Wayne State University Press.

Vargas, Z. (1989). Life and community in the "wonderful city of the magic motor": Mexican immigrants in the 1920s Detroit. *Michigan Historical Review, 15*, 45–68.

Wilkerson, I. (1986, November 7). Company's news; Blow to Michigan's recovery. *New York Times*, p. D10.

Zunz, O. (1982). *The changing face of inequality: Urbanization, industrial development, and immigrants in Detroit, 1880–1920*. Chicago, IL: The University of Chicago Press.

7

REMAKING BRIGHTMOOR

MARGARET DEWAR AND ROBERT LINN

By 2010, Detroit had lost more than 60 percent of its popuation since 1950 and 37 percent of its housing since 1960 (U.S. Bureau of the Census 1950, 1960, 2010). This loss transformed the character of the built city. By 2009, some neighborhoods remained much as they had been built, but others had lost more than half their structures and contained large amounts of vacant land. As Figure 7.1 shows, the density of vacant residential lots varied across the city. Large portions of the east side of the city had high densities of vacant lots, and many parts of the southwest and west sections also had considerable vacancy. In contrast, the northwest and west areas and the far eastern and northeastern edges of the city contained few residential vacant lots. Overall, as of fall 2009, about 26.6 percent of the city's residential lots were vacant, and another one percent of residential properties had structures awaiting demolition (Data Driven Detroit, 2009).

The emptiest areas of the city have attracted ruins voyeurism and vacancy tourism (for example, Chanan and Steinmetz 2005; Griffoen 2010-2011; Hemmerle 2009; Marchand and Meffre 2010; Moore and Levine 2010; Vergara 1999). With their focus on views of destruction and emptiness, observers often understate—and indeed may miss—the ways that residents and other property owners transform the city.

The perception of vacancy and ruins inspires ideas about how to remake the city. Much of this work assumes that agents (often not specified) can manipulate vacant areas of the city in interesting ways (for example, Rybczynski and Linneman 1999; Taubman College of Architecture and Urban Planning 1999–2005; Waldheim and Santos-Munné 2001). Ideas about future possibilities rarely attend to the invisible complexity of land ownership that may constrain anyone's decisions about reuse of property.

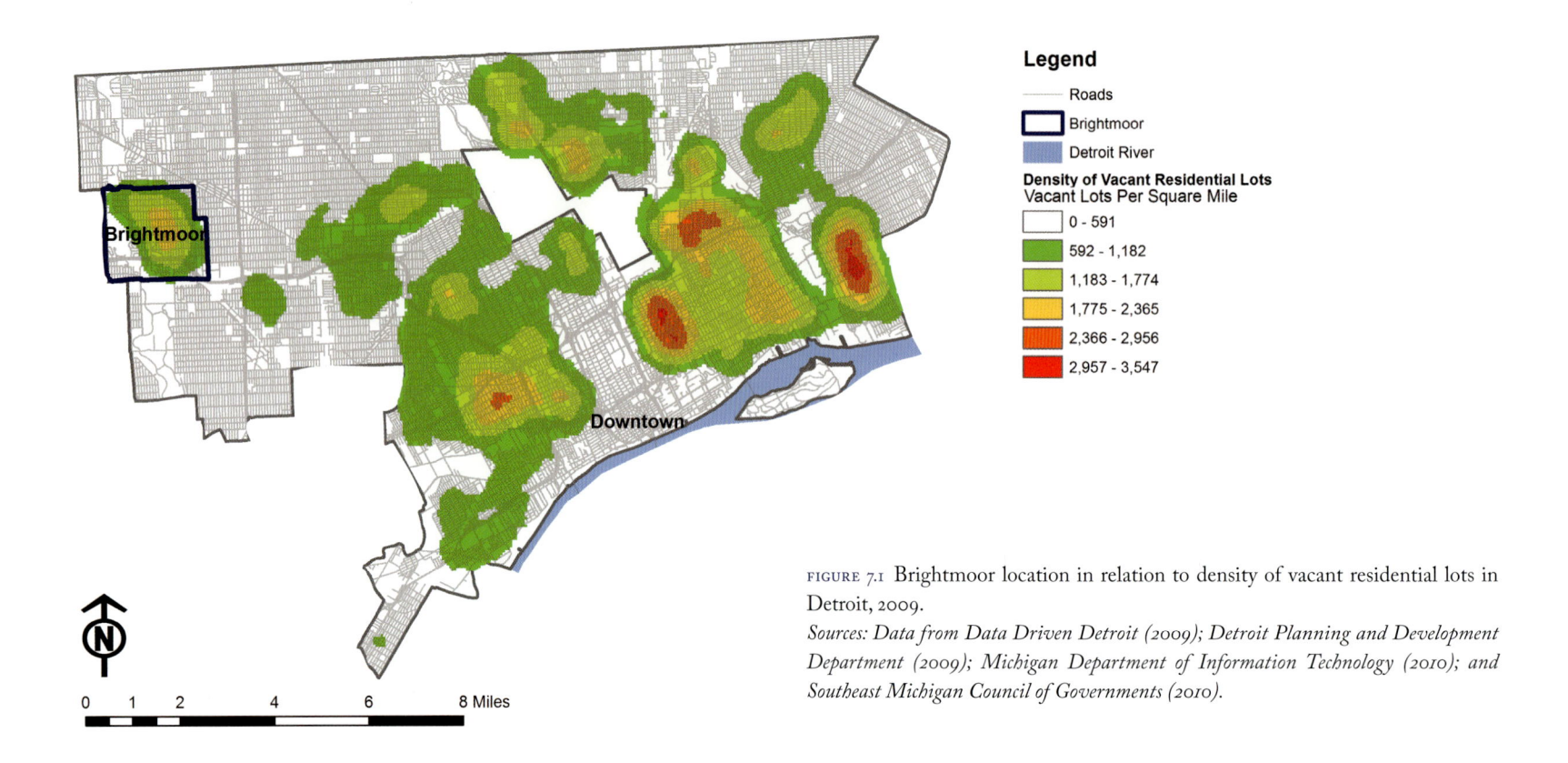

FIGURE 7.1 Brightmoor location in relation to density of vacant residential lots in Detroit, 2009.
Sources: Data from Data Driven Detroit (2009); Detroit Planning and Development Department (2009); Michigan Department of Information Technology (2010); and Southeast Michigan Council of Governments (2010).

But what changes do occur in areas of Detroit that have experienced extreme abandonment, and what prospects of future change may be possible? These questions remain largely unanswered even as scholars investigate change in cities with extensive disinvestment. Urban designers' interest has tended to focus on downtown and nearby areas, and they have not examined what happens in neighborhoods. Studies show extensive losses of structures and increasing size of blocks as redevelopment projects eliminate numerous downtown streets (for example, Plunz 1996; Ryan 2008; Smets 1996). One study of areas outside the downtown illustrated the transformation of urban fabric due to major residential redevelopment projects, several of them in urban renewal areas (Ryan 2006). The morphology of these areas became less dense and more car-oriented.

Urban design scholars investigating everyday uses of open space and gradual changes in neighborhoods, however, point to the ways that the users of space remake it. Chase, Crawford, and Kaliski (2008) emphasize local traditions and uses in forming public space, especially in urban neighborhoods. Moudon (1986, p. 133) argues, "Part of everyday life, [the gradual transformations of the buildings and spaces over time] are small, often inconspicuous interventions in the immediate environment." Their research suggests that neighborhoods with extensive abandonment will also show the evidence of "necessary interactions between people and their surroundings" (Moudon 1986, p. 133).

This chapter looks at a residential area far from downtown that has experienced extensive abandonment but has not become the site of city-government-initiated projects or urban renewal, a section of northwest Detroit that stands out as an isolated area of extensive vacancy and abandonment—Brightmoor (see Figure 7.1). The aim is to discover what the land use and physical fabric of the city are becoming as a result of many individuals' decisions every day. We argue that, in contrast to ruins voyeurism, which inaccurately suggests that empty fields and ruined buildings are without people, the way people make use of "disinvested spaces" ends up remaking those places, perhaps with more opportunities for varied ways of transforming space than in places that do not experience disinvestment. These changes result in part from city policies (such as a zoning regulation that new housing must sit on lots at least forty-five feet wide) and city programs (such as one that allows homeowners to buy an adjacent city-owned vacant lot). However, the transformation principally results from many actors' decisions in the everyday remaking of the city, carried out without a planner's or a policy maker's intervention or a major developer's investment. City leaders, urban planners, and urban designers should look closely at how residents and nonprofits remake quite vacant areas, for this reflects what they want these places to be. They should work with these parties in imagining and creating the future of the city.

Brightmoor is a useful case for examining the abandonment and remaking of the city. The area has a high level of vacancy but also areas that remain nearly intact, with all or almost all houses still occupied and only occasional vacant lots. Brightmoor has not received public attention for rebuilding, so change has occurred almost entirely because of individuals' and nonprofits' decisions to invest or disinvest. The next sections look first at Brightmoor's history and the reasons that it became an outpost of extreme abandonment, and then examines what Brightmoor has become. The research is based on field observation of physical conditions in 2010, on analysis of city administrative data, and on data from a 2009 city field census of residential property conditions. The chapter also draws on University of Michigan students' work in planning the future of Brightmoor with the participation of community leaders and numerous residents (Bradford et al. 2007; Doherty, Morris, Parham, Powers, Schumacher, and Wessler 2008).

THE ABANDONMENT OF BRIGHTMOOR

We define Brightmoor as the four-square-mile area within the boundaries of Puritan Street on the north, Fullerton Street on the south, Telegraph Road on the west, and Evergreen Road and Westwood Street on the east (see Figure 7.2).[1] B. E. Taylor purchased tracts of land in the early 1920s, subdivided them into properties 30- to 34-feet wide by 100- to 125-feet deep, and sold these lots. He also mass-built houses and sold these, requiring any purchaser to buy one or two additional lots with the one where the new house sat. Taylor built small wooden houses on timber foundations and used standard floor plans without bathrooms, furnaces, or basements. Some of these houses still stand, as shown in Figure 7.3. He sold his properties to the large number of white workers coming to Detroit, predominately from Appalachia, for jobs in the auto factories. Brightmoor's population grew quickly, from 8 in 1922 to more than 11,000 in 1925 (Carey 1940, p. 1). At the same time, many of the lots that Taylor sold remained undeveloped. As of 1938, only 25 percent of the more than 15,500 Taylor lots (about 3,500 of these outside the Brightmoor boundaries) had buildings (Loeb 2001, p. 57). In 1925 the city of Detroit annexed Brightmoor and eventually paved the

FIGURE 7.2 Brightmoor area.
Sources: Data from Michigan Department of Information Technology (2010); and Southeast Michigan Council of Governments (2010).

FIGURE 7.3 Example of a Taylor home in Brightmoor.
Source: Photograph courtesy Kimiko Doherty. From Doherty, K., Morris, L., Parham, T., Powers, S., Schumacher, E., and Wessler, B. (2008). A land use plan for Brightmoor. Ann Arbor: Urban and Regional Planning Program, University of Michigan, p. 3. Retrieved from www.tcaup.umich.edu/planning/students/student_work/project_galleries/brightmoor

streets and extended water and sewer lines (Carey 1940; Loeb 2001). Brightmoor's settlers had known similar poor housing conditions in Appalachia, but they had not lived so close to neighbors. As several of Brightmoor's leaders stated recently, Taylor built a slum. Taylor's subdivisions quickly deteriorated due to poor construction and inadequate sanitation. By 1943, many homes were run down (Bell 1994).

At its peak development in the 1970s, houses lined Brightmoor's streets, and garages lined the alleys. Some vacant lots existed, but most properties had structures, despite the initial poor construction. Figure 7.4 shows a figure-ground diagram of Brightmoor in 1978. The "figure" of structures shows up in black against the white "ground" of open space. Brightmoor's housing density was enough at that time for the structures

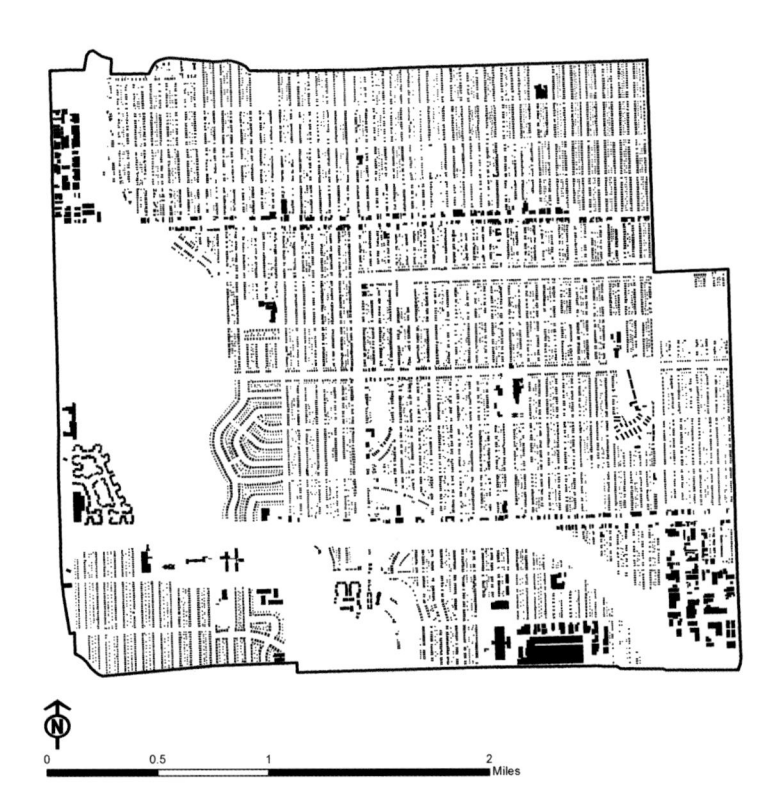

FIGURE 7.4 Figure-ground diagram of Brightmoor, 1978.
Sources: Data from Sanborn Map Company (1978); Detroit Planning and Development Department (2009); Michigan Department of Information Technology (2010); and Southeast Michigan Council of Governments (2010).

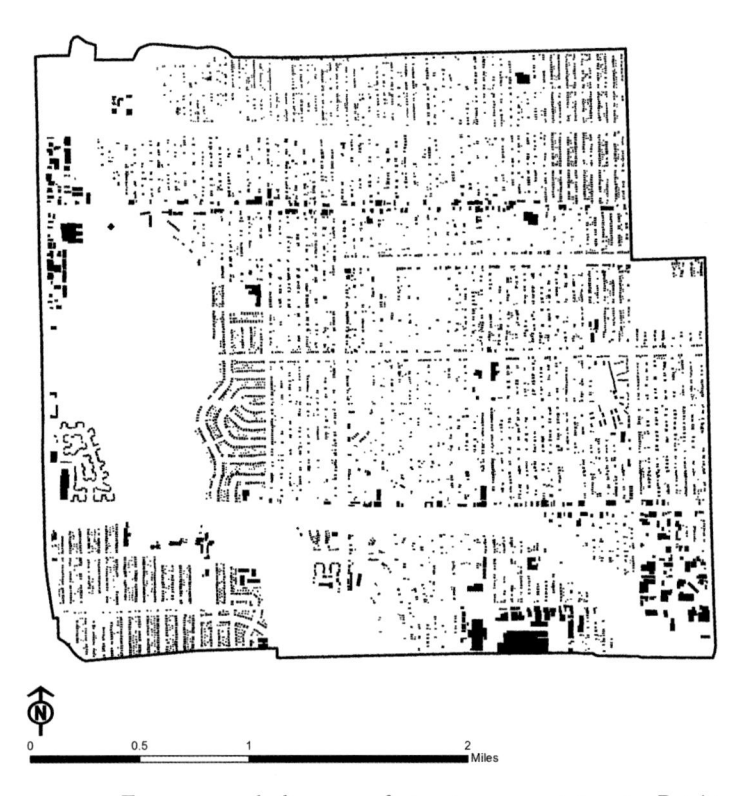

FIGURE 7.5 Figure-ground diagram of structures remaining in Brightmoor around 2009.
Sources: Data from Data Driven Detroit (2009); and Doherty, K., Morris, L., Parham, T., Powers, S., Schumacher, E., and Wessler, B. (2008). A land use plan for Brightmoor. Ann Arbor: Urban and Regional Planning Program, University of Michigan. Retrieved from www.tcaup.umich.edu/planning/students/student_work/project_galleries/brightmoor

to outline the street grid clearly. By 2009, the southwest corner of the area, the streets immediately east of Eliza Howell Park, and the blocks in the northwest corner of the area remained occupied and nearly intact. However, throughout the rest of Brightmoor, especially in the area that extended from Midland on the north to Fullerton on the south and from Lamphere on the west to Kentfield on the east, the majority of structures had disappeared. Figure 7.5 shows a figure-ground diagram of Brightmoor as of 2009. So few structures lined Brightmoor's streets that most streets became indistinguishable from vacant land in the image.[2]

The forces causing the city's loss of population and employment influenced changes in Brightmoor, although population decline began later than the rest of Detroit's, despite the poor housing conditions. As people gained choices about where to live and as Detroit's population declined, demand weakened for Brightmoor's Taylor-built housing.

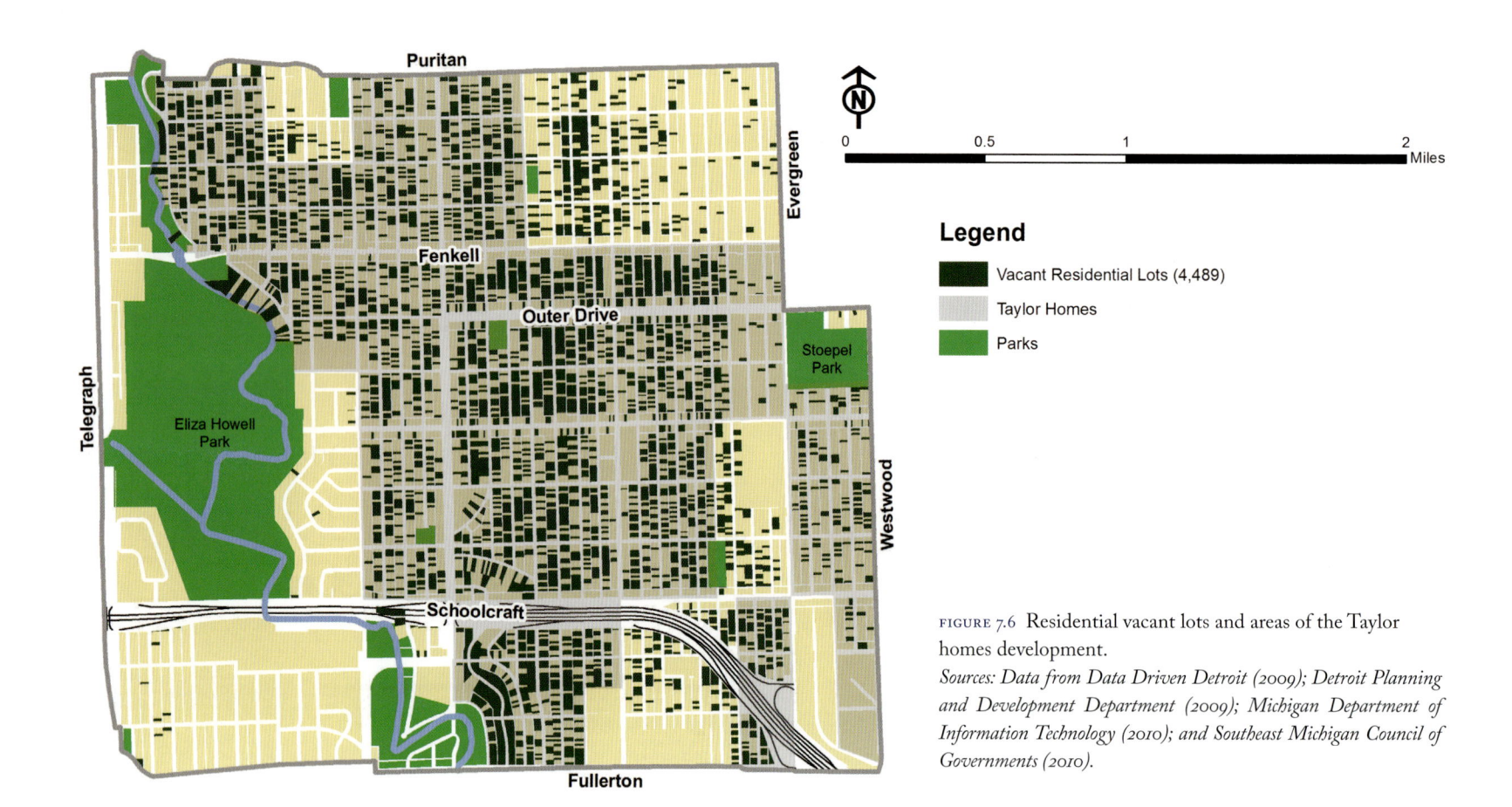

FIGURE 7.6 Residential vacant lots and areas of the Taylor homes development.
Sources: Data from Data Driven Detroit (2009); Detroit Planning and Development Department (2009); Michigan Department of Information Technology (2010); and Southeast Michigan Council of Governments (2010).

In 2009 vacant land was most concentrated where Taylor had built houses (see Figure 7.6), and vacant lots made up 40 percent of residential properties in Brightmoor (Data Driven Detroit 2009). Population in Brightmoor fell from a peak of about 35,000 in 1970 to about 15,400 in 2010, a loss of approximately 56 percent (Social Explorer 1970; U.S. Bureau of the Census 2010). The proportion of renters rose from 34 percent in 1980 to 54 percent of households in 2010; citywide, renters occupied 48.9 percent of housing units. This transformation from heavily owner-occupied to predominately investor-owned housing reflected loss of demand and helped speed disinvestment. As whites left, African Americans increased in share of the population, without the blockbusting real estate tactics that had afflicted other parts of the city in previous decades. Although Brightmoor residents had earlier fought incursions of African Americans, by the 1970s whites were apparently choosing to leave, not to fight (Farley, Danziger, and Holzer 2000; Sugrue 1996, pp. 222–24). By 2010, the percentage of residents classified as "white only" was 9.8 percent, slightly less than for the city as a whole (U.S. Bureau of the Census 2010). Crime and unscrupulous landlords took a toll. Crime associated with crack cocaine hurt the area in the 1980s and 1990s. By the late 1990s, Brightmoor had one of the highest concentrations of drug activity in the city (Hunter 1999). In the late 1990s, the largest securities fraud case in the state's history involved the bankruptcy of RIMCO, a company that owned thousands of homes in Detroit, with about 500 of these in Brightmoor. Most of these homes became vacant and dilapidated (Hulett 2011; King 2001; McWhirter 1999). In 2010, 28.5 percent of the housing units that remained were vacant, while the city's vacancy rate stood at 22.8 percent (U.S. Bureau of the Census 2010).

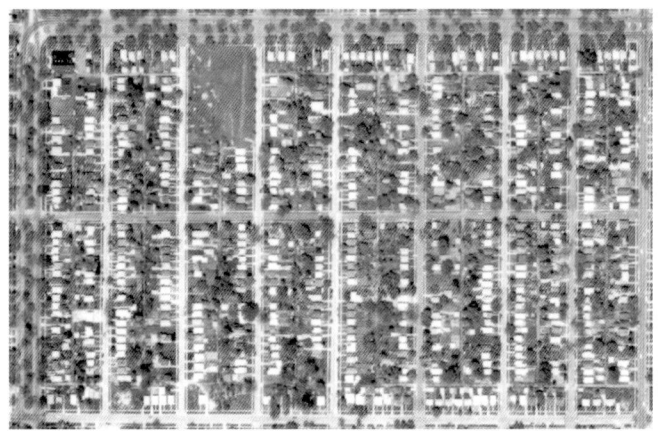

The series of aerial photos in Figure 7.7 shows the changes over time in a section of the now emptiest area of Brightmoor, with the boulevard of Outer Drive on the left and top of each photo. In 1949, the area still had many empty lots, but new housing construction was ongoing. In 1967, the area was more built out, although some vacant lots remained. As of 2009, a large share of the lots were vacant.

A look at a section of Brightmoor that includes the blocks shown in Figure 7.7 reveals some characteristics of residents who lived in the heavily abandoned area bounded by Fenkell (north), Lamphere (west), Lyndon (south), and Kentfield (east) in the late 2000s. About 1,676 people lived there in 2010 in 582 single-family houses, a density of fewer than five people and between one and two houses per acre. Children under eighteen years made up slightly more than 30 percent of the residents, about the same as for the city; persons sixty-five years and older constituted 7 percent, compared to 11 percent for the city. About 70 percent of residents lived in poverty in the period 2005–09, nearly double the rate for the city, which had the highest big-city poverty rate in the nation in 2009. About 14 percent of residents were

FIGURE 7.7 Aerial photos of a section of central Brightmoor showing increasing vacancy in (*top to bottom*) 1949, 1967, and 2010.
Sources: 1949 and 1967: Detroit Edison Energy; 2010: Southeast Michigan Council of Governments (2005–10).

REMAKING BRIGHTMOOR 149

unemployed in this period, a smaller percentage than the city's 22 percent rate of unemployment. Of residents over twenty-five years old, one-fifth had not completed high school or a GED (a smaller percentage than for the city); about one-third had completed high school but no further education (U.S. Bureau of the Census 2005–09a, 2005–09b, 2010, 2011).

THE REMAKING OF BRIGHTMOOR

As disinvestment, abandonment, and demolition destroyed structures and increased the amount of vacant land, residents, nonprofit organizations, and others reused some of the land. City, county, and state governments became the owners of large amounts of property. The following sections look at reuse and at property ownership.

Remaking the Property Pattern

As homeowners and nonprofit developers reused vacant properties, they gradually remade the property pattern of the more vacant areas of Brightmoor—they essentially replatted the area. De facto replatting, even if property lines were not officially changed in the city's maps and assessors' records, had the effect of reducing density and creating a "new suburbanism," in the words of Armborst, D'Oca, and Theodore (2008), in a riff on "new urbanism," the view in physical planning and urban design that advocates the style and density of historic urban neighborhoods. De facto replatting often means that residents have taken over properties for reuse even though they do not officially own these. The consolidated properties often exceed suburban lots in size.

Property owners purchased next-door properties. Beginning in the late 1970s, determined homeowners could make their way through city procedures to purchase an adjacent lot from the city government's inventory of tax-reverted properties. Brightmoor's houses occupied small lots, and little space separated houses. Acquiring an adjacent vacant lot meant a homeowner could have more open area between her house and the neighbor's. As the city government stopped maintaining alleys and garages deteriorated, a homeowner could build a driveway so she would not have to park in the street. Figure 7.8 shows the incidence of adjacent lot ownership and adjacent lot use (regardless of whether the city assessor shows the same people as the taxpayer of both properties) in Brightmoor.[3] Except in the most intact areas where few vacant lots existed, numerous property owners used an adjacent lot. Nearly 60 percent of these did not show up in the assessor's records.

Numerous homeowners owned three or more adjacent properties by 2009.[4] Figure 7.9 shows the prevalence of these in Brightmoor; a homeowner had opportunities to acquire many properties in the most vacant areas. These homeowners purchased lots from the city, but they also acquired properties from departing neighbors over many years (Armborst et al. 2008). Owners often fenced these "blots" (a term coined by Armborst et al. 2008 to mean a unit between a block and a lot) or "homesteads" (Doherty et al. 2008) and used the property for gardens, garages, driveways, additions to homes, play equipment, and storage. When a reporter asked two homeowners why they had taken over properties, they talked about improving their living environment. "'Cause we live next door to it," one said. "If you go up the next block from here, you'll see what it would look like. Just overgrown brush piles. Trash. Car parts." The family had planted an orchard, berry bushes, grape vines, and vegetable and flower gardens, all behind a six-foot-high chain-link fence (Davidson 2011b). Another homeowner, who had acquired four adjacent lots, said "If I want to go to the park, I just go out here to the back yard. . . . I can pretty much enjoy everything that I can there, without the travel time" (Davidson 2011a). Their purchases and improvements of property at a time when most property owners disinvested showed a commitment to the place. They stayed and made improvements despite the increasing blight around them.

FIGURE 7.8 Homeowners who use adjacent lots.
Sources: Data from Detroit Assessor (2009); Detroit Planning and Development Department (2009); Data Driven Detroit (2009); Michigan Department of Information Technology (2010); Southeast Michigan Council of Governments (2010); and Google Maps (2010).

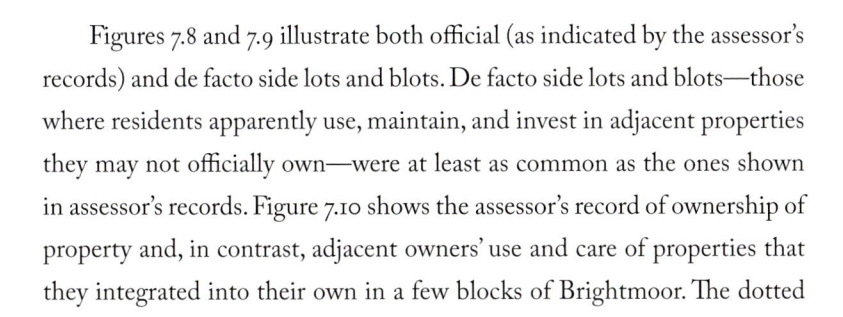

FIGURE 7.9 Homeowners who control three or more adjacent properties.
Sources: Data from Detroit Assessor (2009); Detroit Planning and Development Department (2009); Data Driven Detroit (2009); Michigan Department of Information Technology (2010); Southeast Michigan Council of Governments (2010); and Google Maps (2010).

Figures 7.8 and 7.9 illustrate both official (as indicated by the assessor's records) and de facto side lots and blots. De facto side lots and blots—those where residents apparently use, maintain, and invest in adjacent properties they may not officially own—were at least as common as the ones shown in assessor's records. Figure 7.10 shows the assessor's record of ownership of property and, in contrast, adjacent owners' use and care of properties that they integrated into their own in a few blocks of Brightmoor. The dotted red lines in the second part of the figure show where adjacent owners were using property that they did not necessarily own officially. Throughout Brightmoor, the state, city, or county owned 43 percent of the lots that homeowners had taken over without owning them; a nonprofit organization, Northwest Detroit Neighborhood Development, owned 15 percent; and a large number of individuals owned the remaining lots (Detroit Assessor 2009). Such use of property played an important role in enabling

REMAKING BRIGHTMOOR 151

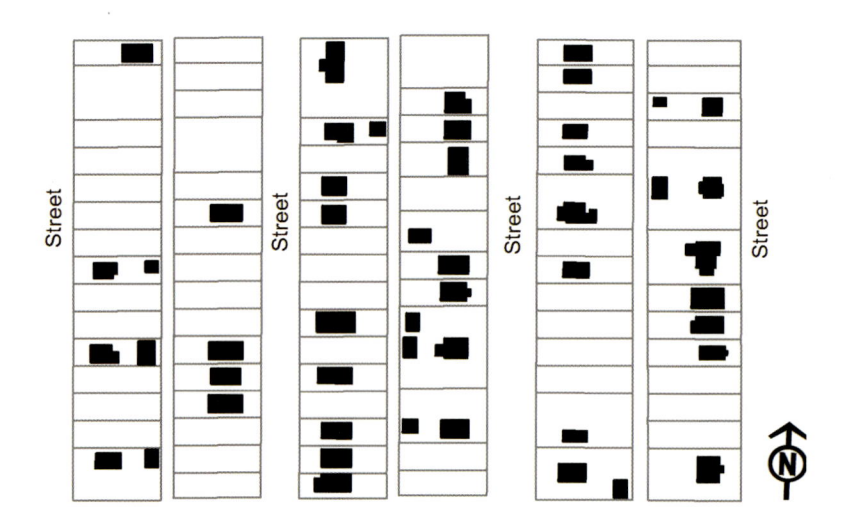

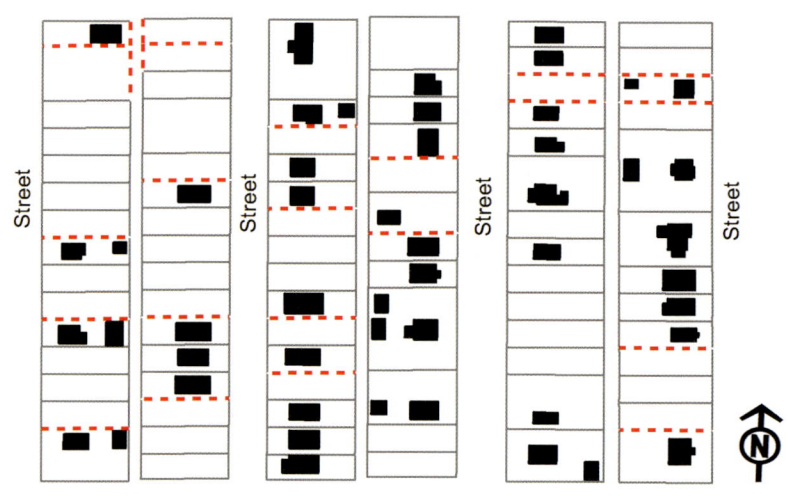

FIGURE 7.10 Official and de facto side lots and blots. Street names have been deleted to disguise the location of the property owners. *Left*: Assessor's recorded ownership. Larger lots show where adjacent owners have made purchases. *Right:* De facto use of and care for adjacent properties. Dotted lines show where owners have integrated adjacent properties into their own.
Sources: Data from Detroit Planning and Development Department (2009); Detroit Assessor (2009); and Google Maps (2010).

homeowners to create the environment they wanted around their homes and to control nearby activities in areas with insufficient police presence.

Figure 7.11 shows aerial photos of several Brightmoor blots. Some homeowners built additions to their homes and constructed patios and outbuildings elsewhere on their property. They had space for swimming pools and play equipment. In the left image of Figure 7.11, the owners had built several additions both on the side and at the rear of the original house. They had fenced the property and created a driveway. (Brightmoor homes did not originally have driveways; they had small garages accessed from alleys.) The owners appeared to have a swimming pool and a patio in the back of the house. In the middle image of Figure 7.11, the owners added to the original small house and built what may be a garage at the rear of the lot. They fenced the property; a few vehicles sat near the house at the edge of a large grassy area. The right image of Figure 7.11 shows a house on a fenced property with several additional small structures and a driveway. On the other hand, some properties showed no evidence of special uses and occasionally did not even have a fence.

Nonprofit developers built new affordable housing in Brightmoor beginning in the mid 1990s (Habitat for Humanity Detroit 2010; Northwest Detroit Neighborhood Development 2006). City of Detroit regulations required a lot at least forty-five feet wide, so developers needed two of the original Taylor lots in order to build a new house or three adjacent lots in order to build two new houses. Northwest Detroit Neighborhood Development (NDND) and Habitat for Humanity had built several hundred new houses in Brightmoor by 2009. Figure 7.12 shows figure-ground diagrams of several blocks south of Stoepel Park, in the Westwood Park neighborhood. These illustrate the change in morphology

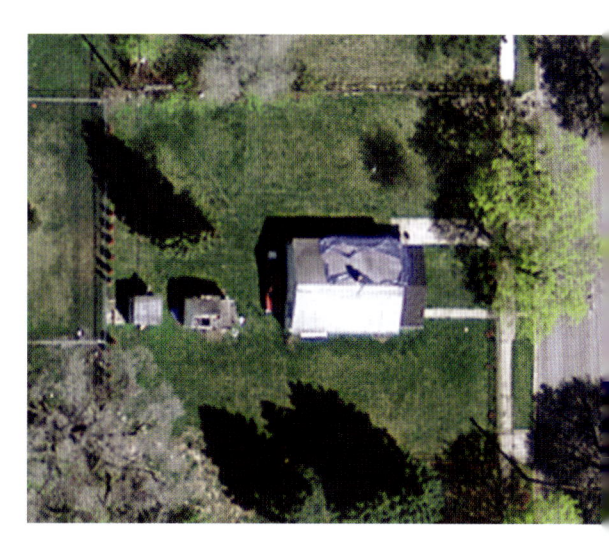

FIGURE 7.11 Three examples of blots or homesteads.
Source: *Southeast Michigan Council of Governments (2005–10)*.

where Habitat for Humanity and NDND built ninety new homes in the 1990s (Detroit Local Initiatives Support Corporation 2007). The 1978 figure-ground diagram shows small houses on uniformly small lots. Some of the lots had garages on the alley at the rear. Thirty years later, many of the small lots had been consolidated into larger properties. A few of the small houses remained, but most of the larger properties now had larger structures. The new homes for low- and moderate-income households on these blocks were considerably larger than the original Brightmoor houses. New development helped make Brightmoor less dense than its original platting.

What made possible the everyday replatting of Brightmoor, both in official consolidation of small lots into larger properties and through homeowners' use of adjacent properties, whether owned or not? These changes occurred gradually over several decades through many individuals' actions. First, many remaining residents' commitment to the place, reinforced by difficulties low-income households faced in finding better housing elsewhere, led to the purchase of side lots and the creation of blots. Instead of leaving, they worked to make better places to live, finding ways to make the property abandonment around them into an opportunity. They became stewards of land that might otherwise have become overgrown and a dumping area. Second, several nonprofit developers working in Brightmoor focused for many years on rebuilding sections of the area. Although abandonment and demolition removed structures more rapidly than new construction added to housing stock, these nonprofit developers used city-owned property to assemble lots for new construction (Thomas 2013). Third, the availability of city-owned land helped make possible side-lot and blot ownership as well as affordable housing development. Although the city government usually lacked clear procedures for selling property, the city owned so much land that residents and nonprofit developers could buy from the city without negotiating purchases from

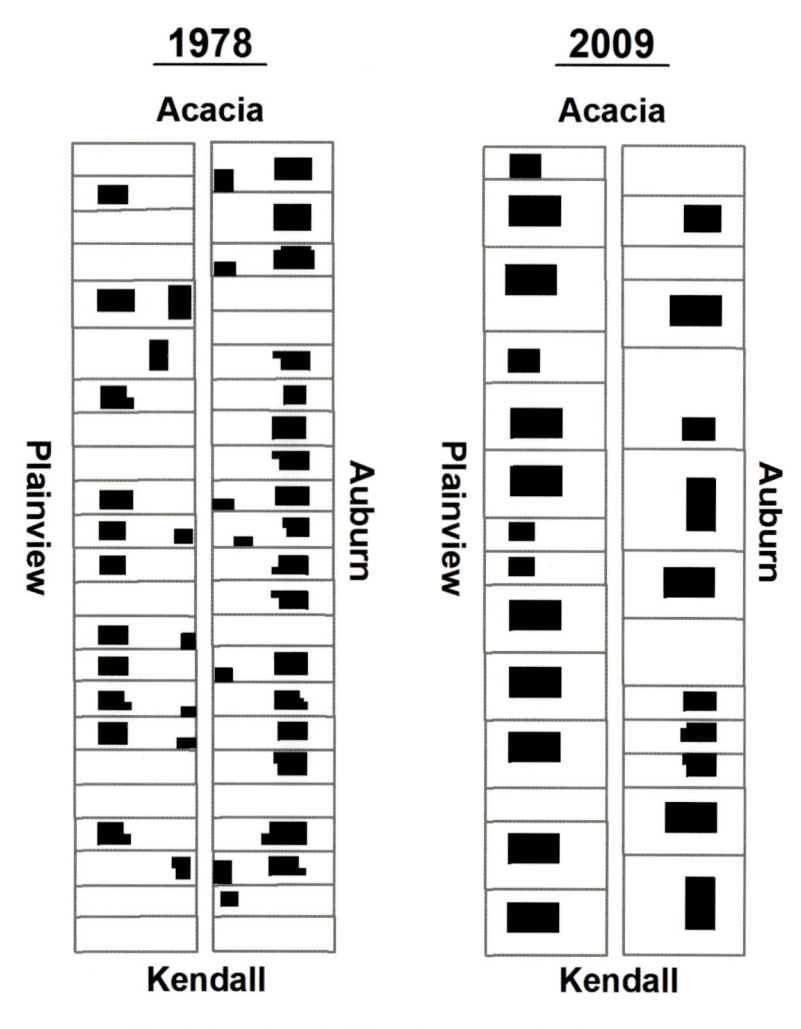

FIGURE 7.12 Morphology of new infill housing compared to housing in 1978. Sources: Data from Detroit Assessor (2009); Sanborn Map Company (1978); Google Maps (2010); Detroit Planning and Development Department (2009); and Southeast Michigan Council of Governments (2005–10).

numerous other owners (Dewar 2006; Rao and Dewar 2004). When selling to a nonprofit developer, city officials approved site plans and enforced regulations about the size of the lot required for a house. Finally, although nonprofit developers needed to follow city regulations and their properties underwent inspections during construction, little or no enforcement of city regulations and laws occurred elsewhere. As a Detroit resident from another part of the city stated at a citywide planning meeting in fall 2010, "You can do whatever you want with your property. No one from the city is going to tell you not to." This meant that residents could build additions on their homes, take over property they had not purchased, erect fencing that did not meet code, and use their land in ways not officially permitted in residential areas. They could make their own places with few neighbors around them; they made the best of the bad situation of widespread property abandonment.

Use of Vacant Land

Individuals and organizations reused land in ways that would not have been possible when Brightmoor was fully built. Figure 7.13 highlights flower and vegetable gardens. Residents and nonprofit organizations gardened more than 100 vacant lots in 2010. The number of gardens increased during the first decade of the 2000s. Starting in 2006, Riet Schumack, a Brightmoor resident, worked with neighbors to create gardens with the aim of bringing neighbors together to improve Brightmoor and to offer children healthy outdoor activities. This group, Neighbors Building Brightmoor, worked many of the gardens clustered in the area south of Fenkell, east of Eliza Howell Park, and west of Outer Drive (Neighbors Building Brightmoor 2012). Despite much public discussion about the potential for gardens and agriculture in the city, gardens occupied only a small fraction of the vacant lots in Brightmoor as of fall 2010. Vacant uncared-for residential lots made up about 84 percent of the nearly 4,500 vacant residential lots in 2009 (Data Driven Detroit 2009).

The vacant areas of Brightmoor often become de facto sidewalks, streets, alleys, and greenways. Although Brightmoor had been laid out with streets, alleys, and sidewalks, the routes across vacant lots created a different pattern of paths for moving through the area. Many streets and sidewalks remained useful, but the paths superseded impassable alleys, overgrown and broken sidewalks, and deteriorated or flooded streets that fallen trees or dumped trash sometimes blocked. The location of these trails, paths, and vehicle tracks suggests their purposes (see Figure 7.14).[5] Pedestrian trails, or "desire paths" (Griffoen 2009), are generally either public or private in nature, as their destinations and widths indicate. The widest paths cut across corners or blocks and served as shortcuts to commercial establishments or parks. Some of these large paths paralleled sidewalks and stretched for several blocks, creating unofficial greenways. Narrower, less travelled paths typically led to single homes or backyards. These "tributary" paths approached homes from the side or rear, suggesting that children and youth used Brightmoor's patchwork of trails. Both the larger and smaller paths avoided maintained vacant lots and homes as well as illegal dumping sites. In many cases, the paths abruptly changed direction to avoid crossing a well-maintained lot.

The area's vehicle tracks varied in type and purpose. Brightmoor's drivers employed the area's vacant lots for uses that ranged from utilitarian—such as off-street parking and construction detours—to amenities such as circular driveways, private drives, and alleys where none existed in the past.

Not all new uses improved Brightmoor. Illegal dumping was pervasive. Illegal dump sites would make the disinvested areas into a de facto landfill if nonprofit organizations did not put great effort into cleanups and prevention each spring. Despite this ongoing work, well over 500 dump sites existed in Brightmoor by early fall 2010 (see Figure 7.15).

What facilitated these uses of vacant land? The strong community organizing effort of Neighbors Building Brightmoor showed the changes that

FIGURE 7.13 Gardens in Brightmoor.
Sources: Data from Detroit Assessor (2009); Detroit Planning and Development Department (2009); Data Driven Detroit (2009); Michigan Department of Information Technology (2010); Southeast Michigan Council of Governments (2010); and field investigation by authors, September 2010.

neighbors working together, with the inspiration of Riet Schumack, could bring about in reusing vacant land for gardens and making a more pleasant environment. Members of the Brightmoor Alliance, a coalition of the organizations working in Brightmoor, envisioned using vacant land for growing more food. One pastor, indicating an almost empty block, said, "We could block off both ends of that street … and plant an orchard" (Yeoman 2012, p. 28).

FIGURE 7.14 Vehicle tracks and foot trails.
Sources: Data from Detroit Assessor (2009); Detroit Planning and Development Department (2009); Data Driven Detroit (2009); Michigan Department of Information Technology (2010); Southeast Michigan Council of Governments (2010); Google Maps (2010), Southeast Michigan Council of Governments (2005–2010); and field investigation by authors, September 2010.

FIGURE 7.15 Illegal dumping in Brightmoor.
Sources: Data from Detroit Planning and Development Department (2009); Michigan Department of Information Technology (2010); Southeast Michigan Council of Governments (2010); and field investigation by authors, September 2010.

At the same time, few households remained in the area of Brightmoor with the most plentiful vacant land. Gardens depended on neighbors to work, but too few neighbors may have remained to support gardens in a large share of the vacant lots. Reuse of a much larger share of property for growing produce would need to rely on a larger-scale, less labor-intensive agricultural operation. Further, the few residents could not exert the social control to prevent the vehicle trails that dumpers used and the widespread dumping that Brightmoor experienced except in some blocks. Neighbors Building Brightmoor organized boarding of vacant houses and painting of murals on the boards, communicating that neighbors cared about the property; these actions deterred dumping. As Figure 7.16 shows, residents tried to prevent dumping in other ways as well, but their efforts could not stop dumping over an area as large as Brightmoor and needed greater support from organizations and from city enforcement officials, which rarely came.

FIGURE 7.16 Resident effort to prevent dumping.
Source: Photograph courtesy Kimiko Doherty. From Doherty, K., Morris, L., Parham, T., Powers, S., Schumacher, E., and Wessler, B. (2008). A land use plan for Brightmoor. Ann Arbor: Urban and Regional Planning Program, University of Michigan, p. 3. Retrieved from www.tcaup.umich.edu/planning/students/student_work/project_galleries/brightmoor

Ownership as Evidence of Ideas for the Future

Many individuals and organizations have ideas about how they can transform Brightmoor in the future. Their acquisition of property offered an indication of their intentions. The leaders of several religious institutions hoped to build in the blocks near their principal locations, in part to improve the conditions for people living in the area and in part to provide housing and jobs for parishioners or followers, perhaps through an elderly housing development (for example, Brightmoor Pastors Alliance 2011). Religious leaders also became interested in encouraging gardens. Figure 7.17 shows the locations of religious institutions and the properties they owned as of 2009. This map likely understates the interest of these institutions because they may have sold property after they developed it.

NDND, Motor City Blight Busters, and Habitat for Humanity owned hundreds of properties (see Figure 7.18). NDND, by far the largest landowner, acquired property to make development of new housing possible in the future (Beebe & Associates 2001). From 1999 through 2006, NDND built about 230 new houses using Low Income Housing Tax Credits (Thomas 2013). These structures, scattered in several areas of Brightmoor, were highly visible houses in good condition. Because the organization needed two adjacent lots in order to build a new house, the leaders took advantage of many opportunities to accumulate lots they might use in the future, though they had no immediate plans for building on these (Doherty et al. 2008). When mortgage foreclosures increased enormously and the economy entered a severe recession in 2007, NDND could not continue building houses and struggled to maintain their lots and to pay property taxes on them.

Investors from outside Brightmoor also owned many properties as of 2009. Figure 7.19 shows properties owned by outside investors who had more than three properties in Brightmoor (that is, individuals who merely inherited a house from a family member are not included). Outside investors owned more than 1,200 properties, about 10 percent of all Brightmoor properties.

FIGURE 7.17 Property owned by religious institutions.
Sources: Data from Detroit Assessor (2009); Detroit Planning and Development Department (2009); Michigan Department of Information Technology (2010); and Southeast Michigan Council of Governments (2010).

FIGURE 7.18 Property owned by nonprofit developers.
Sources: Data from Detroit Assessor (2009); Detroit Planning and Development Department (2009); Michigan Department of Information Technology (2010); and Southeast Michigan Council of Governments (2010).

(Brightmoor has 12,059 parcels of property.) About 100 of these properties had commercial use. Of the remaining residential properties, three-fourths had rental housing; the rest were vacant lots. Nearly all the investor-owned properties were concentrated in the emptiest area of Brightmoor in 2009.

Investors had at least two motivations in owning Brightmoor property. They profited by collecting rent but providing little maintenance as housing became increasingly run down. As of fall 2009, between 10 and 15 percent of investors' structures required demolition (Data Driven Detroit 2009; Detroit Assessor 2009). One landlord had hundreds of blight citations (Detroit Department of Administrative Hearings 2010).

Some investors aimed to sell property for much higher prices than they had paid by acquiring tracts that others would need for their development plans. Investors owned numerous vacant lots where NDND had talked about

FIGURE 7.19 Property owned by investors from outside Brightmoor who own at least three properties in Brightmoor.
Sources: Data from Detroit Assessor (2009); Detroit Planning and Development Department (2009); Michigan Department of Information Technology (2010); Southeast Michigan Council of Governments (2010); and Michigan Department of Labor and Economic Growth (2010).

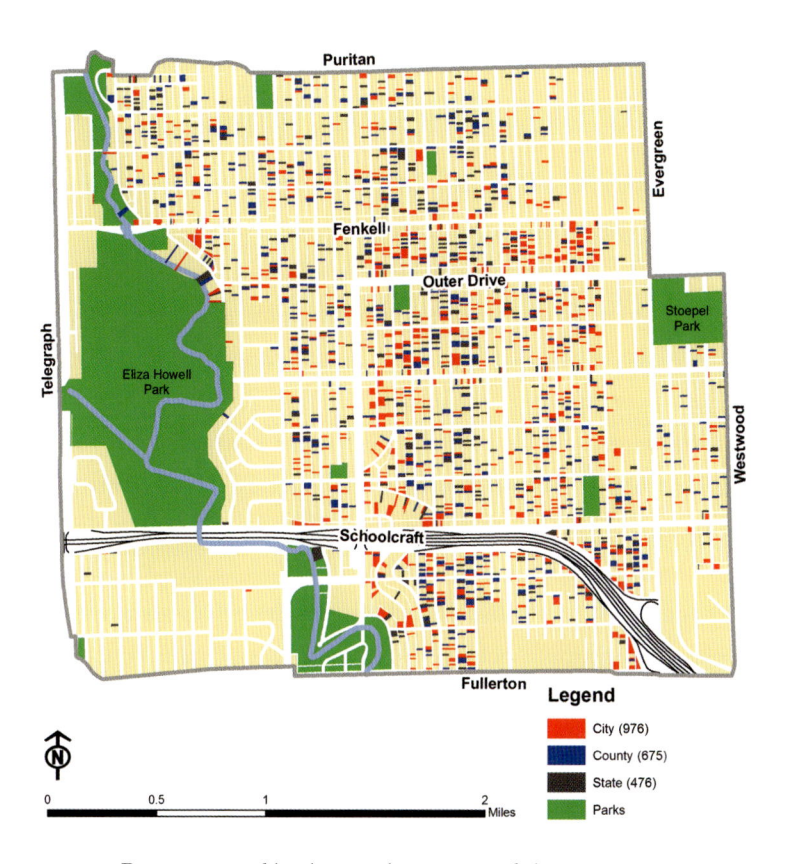

FIGURE 7.20 Property owned by the city, the county, and the state.
Sources: Data from Detroit Assessor (2009); Detroit Planning and Development Department (2009); Michigan Department of Information Technology (2010); Southeast Michigan Council of Governments (2010); Michigan Land Bank Fast Track Authority (2010a, 2010b); and Wayne County Treasurer (2010).

undertaking a major townhouse development; they owned many properties in areas where religious institutions had considered redevelopment.

Unintended Ownership

When owners abandon property, they stop paying property taxes. Over the last forty years, the city, county, or state eventually received much of this property; which entity took possession depended on the terms of state law at the time of the tax foreclosure and the nature of agreements between the governmental units. The city, county, and state owned more than 2,000 properties in Brightmoor in 2009, one-sixth of all properties in the area (see Figure 7.20). Officials often lacked the resources to demolish derelict structures promptly, to mow lots, or

REMAKING BRIGHTMOOR 159

to clear dumping. The city of Detroit established a land bank in 2009 in order to meet requirements of the second federal Neighborhood Stabilization Program, whose purpose was to reduce the damage to neighborhoods from mortgage foreclosures (Detroit Land Bank 2012). Although county land banks elsewhere in the state took ownership of tax-foreclosed property and acted as steward, the Detroit Land Bank remained uninvolved in areas such as Brightmoor where demand for land was very weak. The land bank lacked funding that might have enabled the organization to do more.

City, county, and state officials had no planned reuse for their property; in combination with nonprofit and federally owned property, this land amounted to about 27 percent of Brightmoor properties (McKenna Associates and AAB Development Strategies 2009, p. 2.27). City residents and government officials could define clearer approaches to reuse of areas where so much publicly owned land exists. *Detroit Future City*, a framework to guide the direction of change in the city, appeared in early 2013; this plan projected much of Brightmoor within the next fifty years as "innovation productive" land use with some areas that would be "traditional low density" residential and "green residential." The "innovation productive" land use would include agriculture, forestry, and remediation of contamination, for example (*Detroit Future City* 2012). This plan offered a generalized overview, "from 35,000 feet up," as one of the authors said. Community Development Advocates of Detroit, the trade association for community development organizations, launched a process in late 2012 with the Brightmoor Alliance to envision a more detailed, block-by-block, community-based plan for future land use in Brightmoor.

During the 1990s and first few years of the 2000s, many homeowners took out subprime mortgages and mortgages with "exotic" terms such as balloon payments (Immergluck 2009) as they purchased homes or refinanced. By 2010, tens of thousands of properties had

FIGURE 7.21 Property owned by financial institutions or by the federal government. *Sources: Data from Detroit Assessor (2009); Detroit Planning and Development Department (2009); Michigan Department of Information Technology (2010); and Southeast Michigan Council of Governments (2010).*

gone through mortgage foreclosure in Detroit. When owners stopped making mortgage payments, foreclosure processes led to sheriff sales in which the properties were sold to other parties or transferred to the mortgage lenders. The insurer of the mortgage became the owner when the lender did not receive the value of the outstanding mortgage in the sale (Detroit Office of Foreclosure Prevention and Response 2012). Figure 7.21 shows the properties owned by a mortgage holder (collectively called "real estate owned" or "REO" properties) or by the Department of Housing and Urban Development, the Department of Veterans Affairs, or the Federal Housing Administration—all mortgage insurers. Such houses often sat empty for a long time with little attention from their owners. Vandals and scrappers often destroyed them and increased blight before the financial institutions or federal agencies transferred the properties to new owners. The pattern in Figure 7.21 shows that REO properties existed across Brightmoor, in the emptiest areas where landlords owned many of the remaining structures, but also in the most intact areas with high rates of home ownership.

The prevalence of REO property in the intact areas indicated that even in those areas with the highest housing values, numerous mortgage-foreclosed homes had failed to sell at a sheriff's auction. REO property at a point in time does not show the extent of the harm of mortgage foreclosures in the most intact residential areas of Brightmoor. For instance, in the neighborhood east of Eliza Howell Park and immediately north of the freeway, 18 percent of homes went into mortgage foreclosure from 2008 through 2011 (Wayne County Register of Deeds 2011). Many of these homes do not appear in Figure 7.21 because new owners, often investors, purchased them. The increase in investor-owned properties and incursions of blight due to periods of vacancy after mortgage foreclosure threatened to cause future disinvestment in areas where housing had remained strong and homeowners had maintained their homes over the last few decades, even while other parts of Brightmoor had suffered high rates of population and housing loss.

IMPLICATIONS FOR URBAN DESIGNERS AND URBAN PLANNERS

People's interaction with the environment in a heavily abandoned area of a city gradually transforms that place. Residents achieve changes in neighborhoods by the way they use the space. Through communal control of property, groups of residents have improved living conditions in some sections of Brightmoor. At the same time, Brightmoor residents cannot yet control the large amount of vacant land, either through encouragement of positive uses such as gardening or through prevention of negative uses such as dumping.[6]

The ownership of Brightmoor land in 2009 revealed that institutions such as religious organizations and nonprofit developers hoped to reuse property. Investors from outside the area also had intentions, such as extraction of the last value from rental housing and interference with others' plans for development. The complexity of private and public ownership shows both the potential to implement decisions about use of considerable amounts of land and the difficulty of assembling large, contiguous properties for new approaches, such as those that observers (for example, Waldheim and Santos-Munné 2001) have imagined.

What do these observations of the everyday remaking of Brightmoor and of patterns of property ownership suggest about directions for planning and policy in heavily abandoned areas of the city? They point to building upon the ways that people are already remaking their environments into better places for them to live, to reinforcing their commitment to stay, and to supporting them in turning vacancy into an asset. Those committed residents often seem almost invisible in discussions about how to plan for the future of such areas (for example, McKenna Associates and AAB Development Strategies 2009). "We understand that changes have to happen," said Kirk Mayes, executive director of the Brightmoor Alliance. "Don't make it turn into something that happens *to* us. Allow us to do it together" (Yeoman 2012, p. 29).

Efforts should encourage owner investment. The large number of properties that adjacent owners control and care for suggests considerable demand for these properties. City officials could deed property to homeowners to expand their properties or offer long-term leases at minimal cost for city-owned land. City officials should continue to ignore code violations that do not cause harm. For instance, officials can continue to overlook violations of regulations about fence height and placement.

Public officials can facilitate the communal use of land through the work of neighborhood groups and nonprofit organizations by being generous with land. State, county, and city officials could provide permits with few, if any, restrictions for positive uses and long-term, low-rent or no-rent leases to enable groups to make investments, such as putting in the labor to turn a vacant lot into a garden.

City officials and local nonprofit organizations could encourage new kinds of positive uses in very vacant areas on public or nonprofit-owned land. These uses could include forests, small farms, composting sites, hoop greenhouses for growing crops in a longer season, a warehouse for collecting materials from deconstruction, and others (Doherty et al. 2008; Geisler, Greenstein, Hu, Minthorn, and Munsell 2009). This effort could increase the use of land in the emptiest areas in ways that make those areas better places to live and decrease the amount of untended property vulnerable to dumping.

More resources need to go into preventing dumping to complement nonprofits' continuing work on cleanup. Efforts in other parts of the city have shown that physical barriers can prevent trucks from driving onto a vacant lot, and no-dumping signage helps decrease dumping as long as enforcement officials also respond to calls about violators.

Code enforcement should focus on pressing investors to maintain their buildings so that renters have safe, decent living conditions. Local leaders also could work with renters who have shown they do not damage property to help them move into the less-empty areas of Brightmoor (moving to responsible landlords' well maintained structures) to make those areas better populated and deter further spread of blight. Such efforts would benefit from creation of federal and state programs to help pay the costs. Demolition of abandoned and derelict buildings should take place quickly.

In Brightmoor, as in other areas of extensive abandonment, some blocks remain nearly intact. Nonprofit organizations, resident associations, and city officials need to work to prevent the spread of blight into those areas that mortgage foreclosures threaten. They could draw on the resources and advice of the Detroit Vacant Property Campaign, part of Michigan Community Resources (a nonprofit that provided assistance to community-based groups in addressing issues of vacancy and blight), and others (Bober, Bratt, Burt, Naqvi, Rothman, and VanderZee 2007; Detroit Vacant Property Campaign 2010).[7]

CONCLUSION

The findings of this chapter reinforce notions of what a "just city" (Fainstein 2010) should be in the context of extensive abandonment (see also Fainstein 2000; Krumholz, Cogger, and Linner 1975). Remaining residents of heavily abandoned areas and the residents of areas experiencing disinvestment should have choices about their futures. In the nearly empty areas, residents should be able to stay if they wish and receive adequate services, or they should be able to choose to leave. Residents should also have a strong role in deciding the future of the places where they live. Finally, any policies should aim to ensure that people living in areas with extensive abandonment remain at least as well off as before (Dewar and Weber 2012). At the same time, living up to such principles would prove difficult because residents' low incomes narrow their choices, because many homeowners lost their greatest financial asset when their housing's value collapsed, and because recreating a neighborhood social network elsewhere requires substantial support services at least initially.

This chapter examined whether and how people remake a heavily abandoned residential area through everyday changes and suggested intentions revealed in investments in property in a place where most disinvest. A purpose was to uncover greater complexity than pictures of ruins and vacancy reveal.

The findings show the importance for urban designers and urban planners of looking more deeply into how committed residents and nonprofits might want to change a place and the importance of working with them, rather than overlooking them, in remaking the city after abandonment.

NOTES

1. The Brightmoor Alliance, a coalition of scores of organizations working in Brightmoor, designates these boundaries. The Skillman Foundation, the Next Detroit Neighborhood Initiative, and Detroit Local Initiatives Support Corporation define Brightmoor's boundary in varied ways.
2. Figure 7.5 overstates vacancy in the northwest corner of Brightmoor, east of the river. This area has few remaining structures, but dense tree cover makes distinguishing these in aerial photos difficult.
3. We defined "adjacent lot owners" as those who owned a house and one adjoining vacant lot. We used city assessor data (Detroit Assessor 2009) to determine the name and address of the taxpayer of record and found all pairs of adjacent properties with the same taxpayer (the taxpayer is not necessarily the owner, but we assumed this was usually the owner). The Detroit Residential Parcel Survey (Data Driven Detroit 2009) showed which adjacent properties included an occupied home. Figure 7.8 does not include pairs of adjacent vacant lots with the same owner. In addition, we overlaid the parcel map on recent aerial photos from Google Maps (2010) and assembled data on homeowners who were using sidelots even if these were not recorded in the assessor's data.
4. Using city assessor data to document ownership and Detroit Residential Parcel Survey data (Data Driven Detroit 2009) to determine whether each parcel was an occupied home or a vacant lot, we identified properties where owners of houses owned two or more adjoining vacant lots. Using Google Maps (2010), we added properties where neighbors were using multiple adjacent properties even though the city assessor record did not document them as the taxpayers. Field research would likely identify additional lot use not evident from aerial photos.
5. We traced the paths and tracks visible from aerial photos (Google Maps 2010). We assumed single tracks were footpaths and double tracks were vehicle tracks. We looked at paths' origins and destinations to derive ideas about their purposes.
6. Other uses, squatting in structures, for instance, also affect the character of the physical space but are more difficult to observe so are not discussed in this chapter.
7. Others' plans for heavily abandoned areas of Brightmoor, other parts of Detroit, and other cities recommend many more measures (Cleveland Urban Design Collaborative 2006; *Detroit Future City* 2012; Doherty et al. 2008; McKenna Associates and AAB Development Strategies 2009); such detail goes beyond the scope of this chapter. A city government faced with major budget challenges can also face considerable barriers to increasing activities in such areas.

REFERENCES

Armborst, T., D'Oca, D., and Theodore, G. (2008). Improve your lot! In S. Rugare and T. Schwarz (Eds.), *Cities growing smaller*. Cleveland, OH: Kent State University.

Beebe, K., & Associates (2001, October). *Brightmoor revitalization strategy*. Detroit, MI.

Bell, Z. (1994, February 8). Block by block: The challenged Brightmoor fights for a bright future. *Detroit Free Press*, p. 1B.

Bober, D., Bratt, P., Burt, K., Naqvi, S., Rothman, B., and VanderZee, D. (2007). *Putting back the welcome mat: A neighborhood guide for turning vacant houses into homes*. Ann Arbor: Urban and Regional Planning Program, University of Michigan. Retrieved May 2013 from http://sitemaker.umich.edu/urpoutreachreports/housing___community_development__h_/da.data/2408150/ReportFile/a_neighborhood_guide_for_turning_vacant_houses_into_homesopt.pdf

Bradford, T., Butler, S., Dancik, G., Davidoff, K., Goski, A., Gray, N., et al. (2007, April). *Towards a brighter future: A plan for southeast Brightmoor*. Ann Arbor: Urban and Regional Planning Program, University of Michigan. Retrieved May 2013 from http://sitemaker.umich.edu/urpoutreachreports/housing_community_development_h_/da.data/1900030/ReportFile/towards_a_brighter_future_-_a_plan_for_southeast_brightmoor.pdf

Brightmoor Pastors Alliance. (2011, February). A better Brightmoor. Statement distributed at a meeting of the Detroit Works Project.

Carey, J. W. (1940, May 1–2). *The growth of Brightmoor. Brightmoor: A community in action*. Detroit, MI: Brightmoor Community Center.

Chanan, M., and Steinmetz, G. (2005, March 15). *Detroit: Ruin of a city* [film].

Chase, J., Crawford, M., and Kaliski, J. (Eds.). (2008). *Everyday urbanism* (Expanded Edition). New York, NY: Monacelli Press.

Cleveland Urban Design Collaborative. (2006). *Oak Hill community design charette, Youngstown, Ohio*. Cleveland, OH: Kent State University.

Data Driven Detroit. (2009). Detroit residential parcel survey [data file].

Davidson, K. (2011a, December 5). Blotting—not squatting—in Detroit neighborhoods [audio recording]. National Public Radio.

Davidson, K. (2011b, November 9). Empty places: It's not squatting . . . It's blotting [audio recording]. Michigan Public Radio.

Detroit Assessor. (2009). Parcel data [data file].

Detroit Department of Administrative Hearings. (2010). Online blight violation information screen. Retrieved from www.detroitmi.gov/Default.aspx?tabid=2615

Detroit Edison Energy. (1949 and 1967). *Wayne State University DTE aerial photograph archives*. Retrieved September 2010 from www.clas.wayne.edu/photos/ap_index.htm

Detroit future city: 2012 Detroit strategic framework plan. (2012). Detroit, MI.

Detroit Land Bank. (2012). Our history. www.detroitlandbank.org/history.htm.

Detroit Local Initiatives Support Corporation. (2007). *Northwest strategic investment area: Investment strategy.* Detroit, MI.

Detroit Planning and Development Department. (2009). Parcel map [data file].

Detroit Office of Foreclosure Prevention and Response. (2012). *Community stabilization and the impact of the foreclosure crisis in Detroit: Progress toward recovery June 2008–December 2011.*

Detroit Vacant Property Campaign. (2010). *Vacant property toolbox* (2nd ed.). Detroit, MI. Retrieved from http://detroitvacantproperty.org/technical/vacant_property_toolbox_2nd_ed.pdf

Dewar, M. (2006). Selling tax-reverted land: Lessons from Cleveland and Detroit. *Journal of the American Planning Association, 72*(1), 167–80.

Dewar, M., and Weber, M. (2012). City abandonment. In R. Weber and R. Crane (Eds.), *The Oxford Handbook of Urban Planning*. New York, NY: Oxford University Press.

Doherty, K., Morris, L., Parham, T., Powers, S., Schumacher, E., and Wessler, B. (2008). *A land use plan for Brightmoor*. Ann Arbor: Urban and Regional Planning Program, University of Michigan. Retrieved from www.tcaup.umich.edu/planning/students/student_work/project_galleries/brightmoor

Fainstein, S. S. (2000). New directions in planning theory. *Urban Affairs Review, 35*(4), 451–78.

Fainstein, S. S. (2010). *The just city.* Ithaca, NY: Cornell University Press.

Farley, R., Danziger, S., and Holzer, H. J. (2000). *Detroit divided.* New York, NY: Russell Sage Foundation.

Geisler, N., Greenstein, S., Hu, C., Minthorn, C., and Munsell, M. (2009, August). *Adversity to advantage: New vacant land uses in Flint.* Ann Arbor: Urban and Regional Planning Program, University of Michigan. Retrieved May 2013 from http://sitemaker.umich.edu/urpoutreachreports/environment___land_use__e_/da.data/3158560/ReportFile/adversity_to_advantage.pdf

Google Maps. (2010). Northwest Detroit aerial photographs. Retrieved from http://maps.google.com

Griffoen, J. (2009). Streets with no name. Sweet Juniper blog. June 23. www.sweet-juniper.com/2009/06/streets-with-no-name.html

Griffoen, J. (2010–2011). Sweet Juniper blog. Retrieved August 28, 2010, from www.sweet-juniper.com

Habitat for Humanity Detroit. (2010). *History and mission.* Retrieved September 18, 2010, from www.habitatdetroit.org/about_us/history

Hemmerle, S. (2009). The remains of Detroit. *TIME*. Retrieved August 28, 2010, from www.time.com/time/photogallery/0,29307,1864272,00.html

Hulett, S. (2011). Rethinking what—and where—"the good life" is. Michigan Public Radio. Retrieved December 2, 2011 from www.michiganradio.org/post/rethinking-what-and-where-good-life

Hunter, G. (1999, December 19). Dealers crowd out long-time residents. *Detroit News*, p. 15A.

Immergluck, D. (2009). *Foreclosed: High-risk lending, deregulation, and the undermining of America's mortgage market.* Ithaca, NY: Cornell University Press.

King, R. J. (2001, August 29). MCA exec pleads guilty to fraud: Former controller of bankrupt mortgage lender faces prison. *Detroit News*, p. 1B.

Krumholz, N., Cogger, J., and Linner, J. (1975). The Cleveland policy planning report. *Journal of the American Institute of Planners, 41*, 298–304.

Loeb, C. S. (2001). *Entrepreneurial vernacular: Developers' subdivisions in the 1920s.* Baltimore, MD: Johns Hopkins University Press.

Marchand, Y., and Meffre, R. (2010). *The ruins of Detroit.* Göttingen, Germany: Steidl.

McKenna Associates and AAB Development Strategies. (2009, July 21). *Brightmoor neighborhood plan, Detroit, Michigan.*

McWhirter, C. (1999, September 28). Homes can't hide blight: Vandalism, abandoned buildings plague Brightmoor, obscuring signs of rebirth. *Detroit News*, p. 1D.

Michigan Department of Information Technology. (2010). Political jurisdictions and roads [data file]. Retrieved from www.mcgi.state.mi.us/mgdl/?rel=ext&action=sext

Michigan Department of Labor and Economic Growth. (2010). Corporation division business entity search. Retrieved from www.dleg.state.mi.us/bcs_corp/sr_corp.asp

Michigan Land Bank Fast Track Authority. (2010a). Property owned by the City of Detroit [data file].

Michigan Land Bank Fast Track Authority. (2010b). Detroit property owned by the MLBFTA [data file].

Moore, A., and Levine, P. (2010). *Detroit disassembled.* Bologna, Italy: Damiani Editore.

Moudon, A. (1986). *Built for change: Neighborhood architecture in San Francisco.* Cambridge, MA: MIT Press.

Neighbors Building Brightmoor. (2012). Map of Brightmoor Farmway. Retrieved May 29, 2014, from http://neighborsbuildingbrightmoor.org/blog/page/2/

Northwest Detroit Neighborhood Development. (2006). Northwest Detroit Neighborhood Development. Information sheet.

Plunz, R. (1996, April). Detroit is everywhere. *Architecture, 85*(4), 55–61.

Rao, N. B., and Dewar, M. (2004). *Streamlining acquisition of city-owned land for affordable housing development: A case study from Detroit.* Urban and Regional Research Collaborative Working Paper 04-07. Ann Arbor: Urban and Regional Planning Program, University of Michigan. Retrieved May 2013 from http://sitemaker.umich.edu/urrcworkingpapers/all_urrc_working_papers&mode=single&recordID=539848&nextMode=list

Ryan, B. D. (2006). Morphological change through residential development: Detroit, 1951–2000. *Urban Morphology, 10*(1), 5–22.

Ryan, B. D. (2008). The restructuring of Detroit: City block form change in a shrinking city, 1900–2000. *Urban Design International, 13,* 156–68.

Rybczynski, W., and Linneman, P. (1999). How to save our shrinking cities. *The Public Interest, 135,* 30–44.

Sanborn Map Company. (1978). *Sanborn fire insurance maps, 2541–2923.* Detroit: Bentley Historical Library, University of Michigan.

Smets, M. (1996). Detroit als wegwerpstad. Beeld van een company town / Detroit—A disposable town, picture of a company town. *Archis, 3,* 66–80.

Social Explorer. (1970). *Essential demographic profile.* Retrieved September 14, 2010, from www.socialexplorer.com

Southeast Michigan Council of Governments. (2005–10). 2010 Southeast Michigan Regional Imagery Project [data file]. Retrieved September 2010 from www.semcog.org/Aerials.aspx

Southeast Michigan Council of Governments. (2010). Park and river data [data file]. Retrieved September 2010 from www.semcog.org/data.aspx?id=246

Sugrue, T. J. (1996). *The origins of the urban crisis: Race and inequality in postwar Detroit.* Princeton, NJ: Princeton University Press.

Taubman College of Architecture and Urban Planning. (1999–2005). *Detroit urban design charrette.* Retrieved September 2010 from http://taubmancollege.umich.edu/charrette/past.html

Thomas, J. M. (2013). Targeting strategies of three Detroit CDCs. In M. Dewar and J. M. Thomas (Eds.), *The city after abandonment* (pp. 197–225). Philadelphia: University of Pennsylvania Press.

U.S. Bureau of the Census. (1950). Census of population and housing—1950. Retrieved September 18, 2010, from www2.census.gov/prod2/decennial/documents/41557421v3p2ch02.pdfm

U.S. Bureau of the Census. (1960). Census of population and housing: 1960 (vol. III). American FactFinder. Retrieved September 13, 2010, from http://factfinder2.census.gov.

U.S. Bureau of the Census. (2005–09a). Poverty status in the past 12 months by sex by age, by employment status for the population 16 years and over, sex by educational attainment. American Community Survey 2005–2009 5-Year Estimates. Tables B17001, B23001, B15002. Washington, DC.

U.S. Bureau of the Census. (2005–09b). Fact sheet for Detroit, Michigan. American Community Survey 2005–2009 5-Year Estimates. Washington, DC.

U.S. Bureau of the Census. (2010). Summary file 1. Census 2010. Washington, DC.

U.S. Bureau of the Census. (2011). 2012 statistical abstract. Table 708. Washington, DC.

Vergara, C. (1999). *American ruins.* New York, NY: Monacelli Press.

Waldheim, C., and Santos-Munné, M. (2001). Decamping Detroit. In G. Daskalakis, C. Waldheim, and J. Young (Eds.), *Stalking Detroit.* Barcelona, Spain: Actar.

Wayne County Register of Deeds. (2011). Sheriff's deeds 2008–2011 [data file].

Wayne County Treasurer. (2010). Detroit properties owned by the treasurer [data file].

Yeoman, B. (2012). The death and life of Detroit. *The American Prospect, 23*(4), 25–31.

PART III

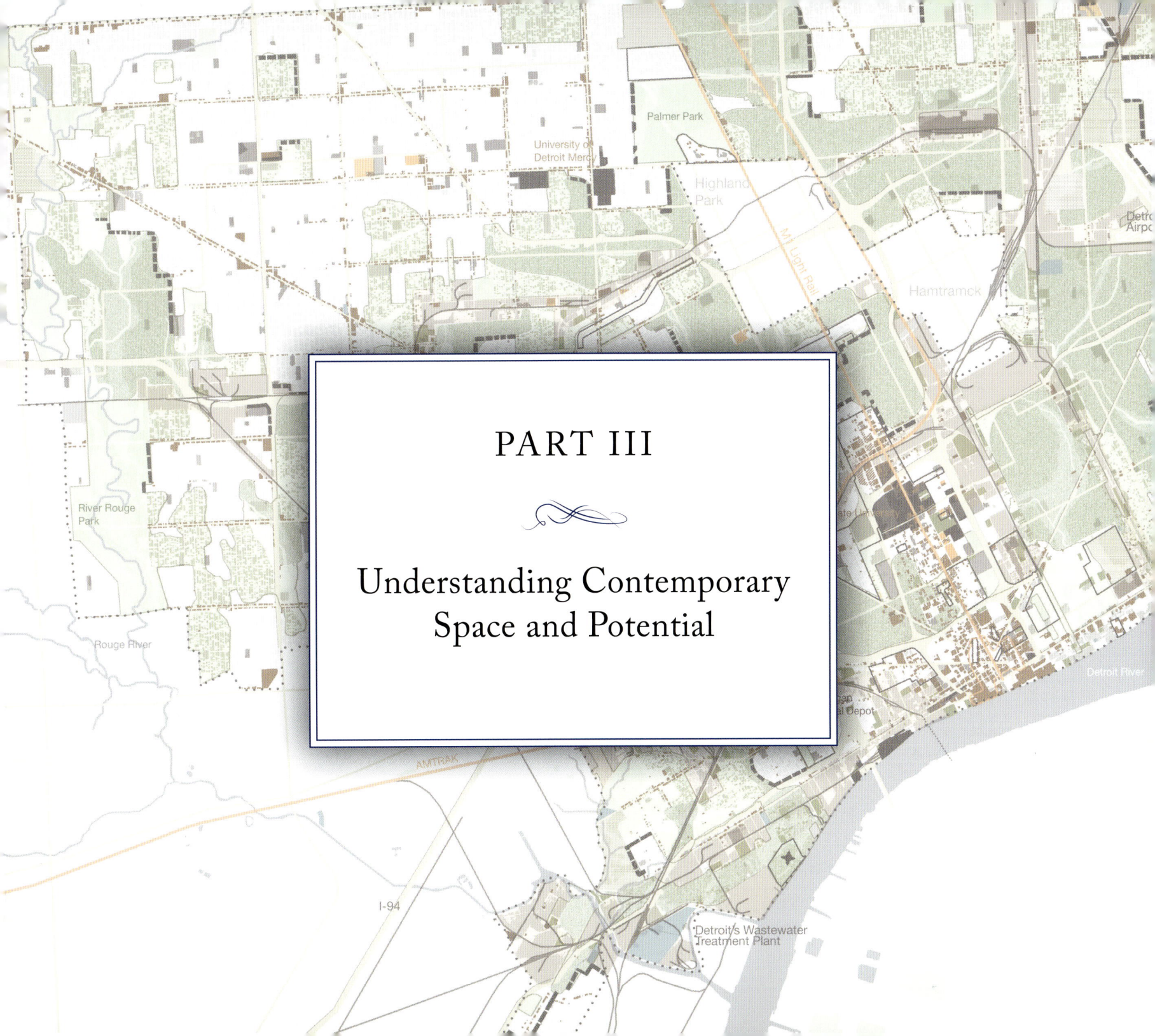

Understanding Contemporary Space and Potential

8

MAPPING THE URBAN LANDSCAPE
Revealing the Archipelago

LARS GRÄBNER

All indicators suggest a need to rethink the urban landscape of Detroit. Population shrinkage and industry dislocation have led to an increase of fallow land, meaning vacant land with no buildings or visible usage. Perforation of the physical urban fabric has progressed to a stage that it challenges the city's capacity to provide adequate living quality and productive efficiency. Economic challenges and demographic shifts, especially the process of shrinkage and outward migration, have rendered traditional planning tools ineffective, and new tools are only slowly emerging. Yet, at the same time, the situation presents the chance for future-oriented approaches that lead to new urban interventions and spatial interpretations.

In the search for adequate approaches to find new urban potential, this chapter's investigation uses a sequence of mappings to take stock of the current situation. The maps in this chapter are created from survey maps and data, and they systematically superimpose selected data in various combinations. The purpose of this strategy was to render visible several potential reconfigurations which otherwise are difficult to imagine.

A main goal for this chapter is to use mapped data to construct optimistic approaches concerning how to reinterpret the urban landscape, and to suggest a series of new possibilities for urban intervention. Current and past landscape features, especially historic hydrological systems, offer ecologic guidance for the framework. The nature of discovery through mapping allows a multitude of interpretations, and thus can become an enabling process, stimulating collective, interactive dialogue. Consequently, this project aims to help create a bridge between technology, innovation, and sociocultural discourse. This chapter intentionally downplays the realities of current political agendas and conflicting interests of major local landowners and other stakeholders, which would come into play in any actual implementation. It nevertheless builds an argument for a potential redesign of the city's land use, envisioning a possible ecologically based future that leaders and stakeholders might consider when they are able to pursue options for action.[1]

Because other post-industrial cities and regions face similar circumstances, to different degrees, this chapter also summarizes ecological and environmental approaches taken in other countries, such as in the Ruhr Valley in Germany, as well as in the United States. Although the reductive nature of maps suggests that they embody a spatial and compositional truth, this mapping project about Detroit was not meant to reflect objective reality. Rather, the project provides a liberating tool for seeing what it might be like to orchestrate creative solutions, such as prospects for urban vacant land, transitional areas, and denser residential contexts. Detroit, when viewed through the analytical lens of sequential topic-based mapping, has astonishing potential in its landscape.

This chapter suggests that articulating the attributes of a landscape may help create a model for urbanism. The concept of landscape urbanism (Waldheim 2006), in which large-scale landscape based on ecological principles becomes one element of urban infrastructure, seems to offer possible solutions for Detroit's high levels of land vacancy. If the landscape were to become the ordering mechanism of urban development and spatial planning, it would inevitably need to become an integral component of the economic, political, and social future of the city. This chapter attempts to reveal the significant contribution to the ecology and economy of the city that landscape components could offer, while supporting the idea of the need for flexibility in order to accommodate future programs, activities and developments. The project reveals possible locations for an archipelago of inhabited "islands," determined by the strategic medium of a productive landscape, and proposes these as the main framework for a sustainable and future-oriented organization of the city. This approach is open ended, flexible, and visionary in nature.

A NEED FOR ACTION

Contemporary culture tends to associate success with growth. Traditional urban planning aided the organization and administration of land-use aspects of growth. Functional separation of land uses and the control of development within each geographic sector aimed mainly to enable optimal new land uses. In cities that have lost high proportions of people and jobs, such measures have been proven ineffective. Urban shrinkage is a widespread phenomenon, primarily in countries in Western and Eastern Europe, in Russia, and in the United States. It occurs because of the post-industrial shift from manufacturing to service industries, suburbanization, or dissolution of socialist systems (in Eastern Europe and Russia). German examples include the city of Dresden and the Ruhr industrial region; U.S. cities include Youngstown, Ohio; Buffalo, New York; Cleveland, Ohio; St. Louis, Missouri; and Flint, Michigan. The notion of "shrinking cities," an emerging research agenda in the field of urban and regional planning, might offer a paradigm shift from growth-centered planning to a more careful and place-based approach toward more livable cities, with unprecedented opportunities to improve green space networks and natural systems. Planners are in a unique position to reframe decline as an opportunity: they have a chance to reenvision cities and to explore nontraditional approaches to their growth at a time when cities desperately need them (Hollander, Pallagst, Schwartz, and Popper 2009).

After tumultuous years of battling the loss of population and attempting to maintain the original infrastructure, services, and administration, the city of Detroit and its citizens have come to the realization that the situation will need a different approach. For the first time, city government leaders have used the term "right sizing," also referred to as "shrinking" (Oswalt 2005). In 2010

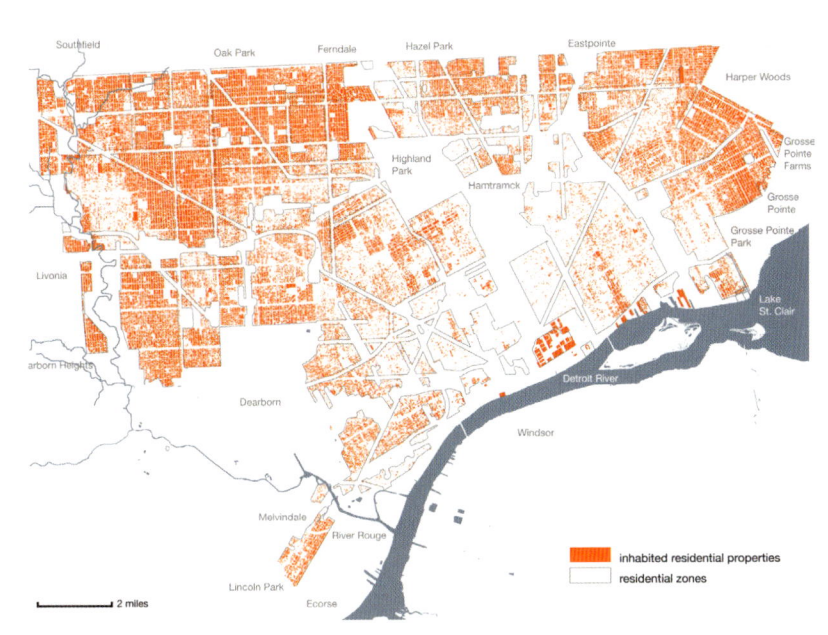

FIGURE 8.1 Inhabited residential parcels within residential land use pattern. The identification of both stable residential neighborhoods and areas of perforation allows a first approach toward evaluating intensity and typology of future interventions.
Sources: Data from City of Detroit, Planning and Development Dept.; Detroit Data Collaborative (2010); and Data Driven Detroit (2010).

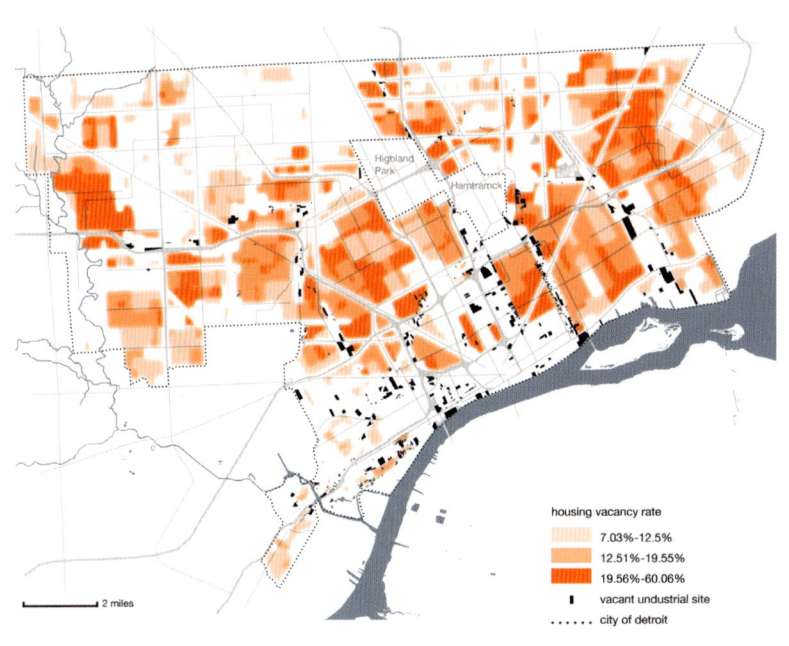

FIGURE 8.2 Housing vacancy rates and vacant industrial sites.
Sources: Data from City of Detroit, Planning and Development Dept.; Detroit Data Collaborative (2010); and Data Driven Detroit (2010).

Mayor David Bing launched a planning initiative, Detroit Works, designed to address the need to reenvision land use in the city (Davey 2011).[2] With the awareness that the population will not grow, the city has entered a new era of realism. Numerous organizations are already working on ideas and concepts to acknowledge the situation and find ways to tackle the new direction.

The excess supply of fragmented vacant land allows no clear prediction of how the city might develop and in which way the built and spatial environment will adapt to the situation (see Figures 8.1 and 8.2). Based on the traditional means of planning, the new city is hardly amenable to planning. An unconventional and creative strategic framework is inevitably necessary. But then questions will arise: Which patterns of change in land use will occur? What kind of reoccurring planning and urban design patterns will emerge? What kind of new social and economic opportunities might reveal themselves?

SUPPLY AND DEMAND

The development of urban structures stems from a direct relationship between demand and supply. The question is whether a large-scale urban restructuring process can meet the demand for safety, public transportation, public green space, free choice of housing, stable social networks, and a healthy environment, as well as quality educational and cultural institutions. With the current state of Detroit's dwindling tax base, supplies are not adequate to meet these demands or to invest in larger endeavors.

In creating a new urban strategy, it would be necessary to reveal and then stimulate untapped opportunities for supply in order to support demand effectively. Traditional means of planning would have to be suspended; in order to reconstruct a coherent urban space, it would be necessary to choose more agile and flexible approaches. In order to stimulate local economies, strategies of conversion and "unbuilding" of large parts of the infrastructure would have to be part of any efforts to adapt to local circumstances.

Coincidental advantages of its location allowed Detroit to emerge from a trading post to an automobile-manufacturing site. Detroit's location on the Great Lakes presented ideal supply opportunities for raw materials and for the automobile industry to develop. Today, the city can profit not only from its manufacturing base and its ability to adapt to new technological advances in related industries, but also from a growing number of innovators. Small manufacturers and independent groups are reacting to the current state of the economy with their own contributions. It is possible that the large and small businesses located in or near Detroit today are capable of manufacturing new products for a new city.

Examples of opportunities for products that could be produced in Detroit include wind generators, solar cells, high-tech building materials, compact co-generation plant units, and biogas. It is with this prospect in mind that Wayne State University, General Motors, and the Henry Ford Health System created Tech Town, a large research and technology park that hosts Next Energy, an alternative energy incubator (Vachon 2011). In the meantime, however, other cities have taken a lead in sustainable practices. A number of different indices measure city performance in environmentalism, but Detroit has not emerged high in these rankings. In 2008, the U.S. Census Bureau and the National Geographic Society's Green Guide ranked all U.S. cities over 100,000 in size by thirty categories, including producing electricity from renewable resources, transportation habits, low

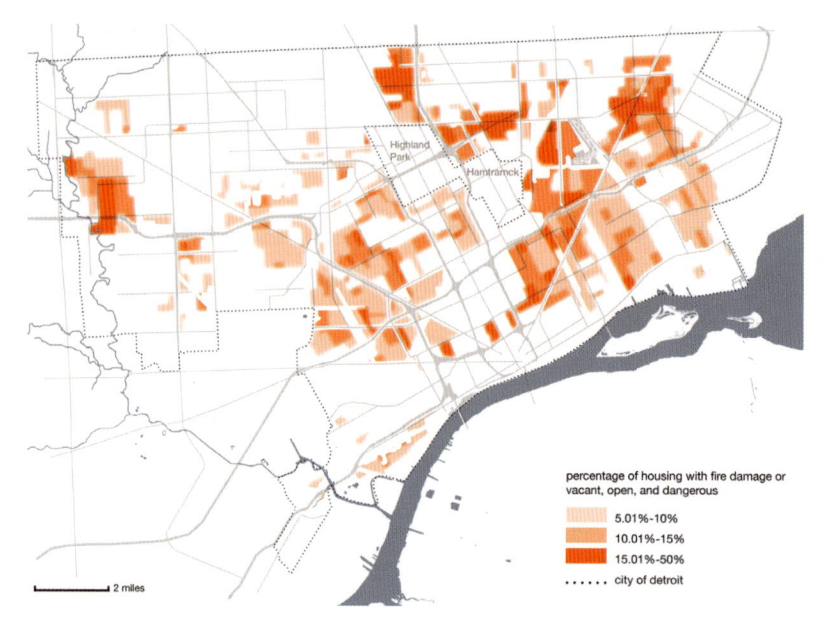

FIGURE 8.3 Percentages of structures within a census block group that are fire damaged or are vacant, open, and dangerous.
Sources: Data from City of Detroit, Planning and Development Dept.; Detroit Data Collaborative (2010); and Data Driven Detroit (2010).

energy and green living, and recycling. In a ranking of the fifty greenest cities in the United States, Portland, Oregon; San Francisco, California; Boston, Massachusetts; and Oakland, California, ranked highest (Svoboda 2008). Detroit did not make the top fifty. Another index of the world's cities, the Green City Index, looked at twenty-seven major U.S. cities by a different set of criteria, which included land use, water, waste, air, and environmental governance. Of the twenty-seven large cities studied, San Francisco and Vancouver ranked highest on the 100-point scale, with a score in the 80s. Detroit ranked last, with a score of 28 (Economist Intelligence 2010).

Yet Detroit's industrial history suggests that it has been the city's nature to constantly reinvent itself, adapt to technological changes, and develop new markets. Detroit's citizens would need to tap their history of

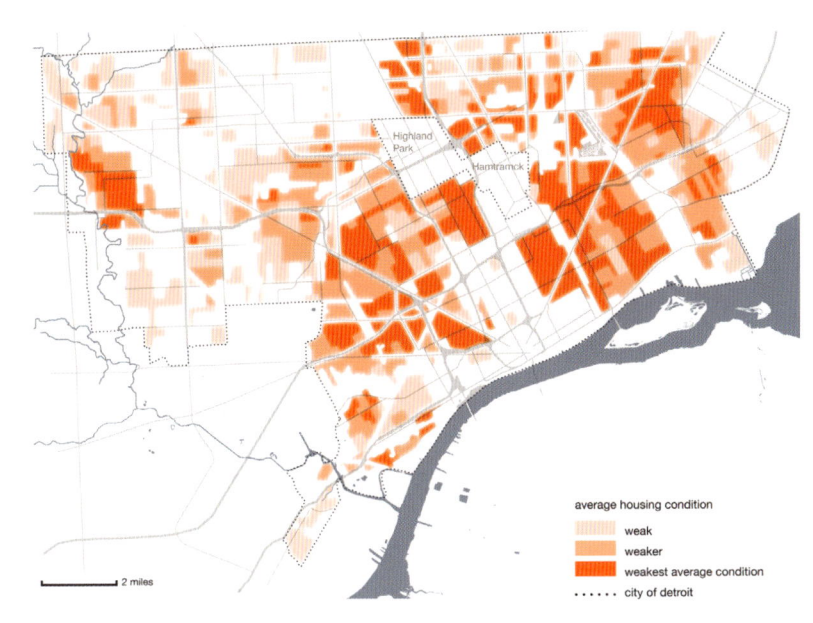

FIGURE 8.4 Average housing conditions by census block group.
Sources: Data from City of Detroit, Planning and Development Dept., Detroit Data Collaborative (2010); and Data Driven Detroit (2010).

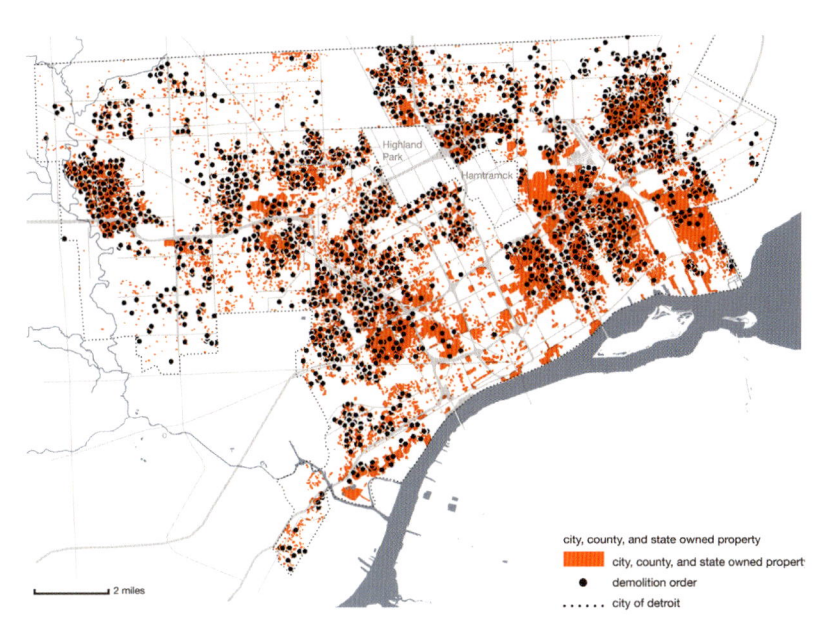

FIGURE 8.5 Combined city-, county-, and state-owned property. Demolition orders are superimposed.
Sources: Data from City of Detroit, Planning and Development Dept.; Office of the Wayne County Treasurer Foreclosure Data, Residential Demolition Program, City of Detroit, Associated Press 04-01-2010, SOC Map 03-23-2010.

agility in order to solve conditions of shrinkage. Detroit could help meet current environmental needs to reduce carbon emissions, create employment opportunities, restore hydrological systems, and improve economic status through reducing the maintenance of excess infrastructure, intensifying economic use of fallow land, and reducing the increased economic burden of stormwater overflow occurrences.

The efforts of various grass-roots initiatives, nonprofit organizations, and advocate groups in Detroit have incrementally enhanced living quality as well as social and economic conditions. Due to increased awareness and public participation in recent years, even during periods of relative governmental inactivity, these incremental changes have gained in strength, and could help turn around the entire structure of the city.

Architects, artists, community groups, and nonprofit organizations in Detroit have put forward a great number of concepts—evidence of an increase in interest, creativity, and innovation. See, for example, the framework proposed by the Community Development Advocates of Detroit (2010). This push of innovation, however, has not yet changed the nature or evolution of the restructuring process. Neighborhood stabilization initiatives and economic growth zones have been largely dependent on outside resources that may not continue—namely foundation grants and federal and state subsidies. The city government leaders, aware of the risk of losing political popularity if they target resources to some areas but not to others, have often applied these funds without a larger contextual vision for the city (Thomson 2012). At the same time, frustrated by the lack of adequate city initiatives, numerous neighborhood organizations, environmental groups, churches and nonprofit organizations started their own initiatives. A commonly agreed-upon comprehensive plan, and set of strategies based on a participatory structure, would possibly have made those investments and actions more successful and sustainable. Alternative concepts for the city need to be created and implemented in a way that encourages interactive collaboration among the city government, the citizens, and community-based organizations.

LAND OF OPPORTUNITY

A gradual loss of population, unevenly spread across the urban landscape, has fragmented Detroit into a rhizome-like fabric of undeveloped lands. Field surveys in 2009 revealed 91,488 vacant residential lots and at least 30,806 vacant residential buildings with another 2,721 possibly vacant. Of the vacant lots, one-fourth were "improved" in some way, such as by paving, or construction of an accessory structure, fence, or park (Detroit Data Collaborative 2010).

As city government demolished vacant structures for the sake of public safety, a variety of natural changes followed for many of these vacant lands, as once-urban residential lots turned into un-built landscape and even wilderness. The city became a habitat for deer, foxes, coyotes, wild geese, bats, rabbits, snakes, and birds, including pheasants and herons.

Many have labelled Detroit's preponderance of unpopulated spaces as urban decay, following the traditional mindset that population and growth is desirable. However, the fallow land should be viewed in terms of its potential. The city has gained space—it has become a land of opportunity (Figure 8.6).

Fallow land may be transformed by informal uses, as described in chapter 7. Vacancies due to demolition and abandonment transform into opportunities for activity. Highly acceptable options include communal

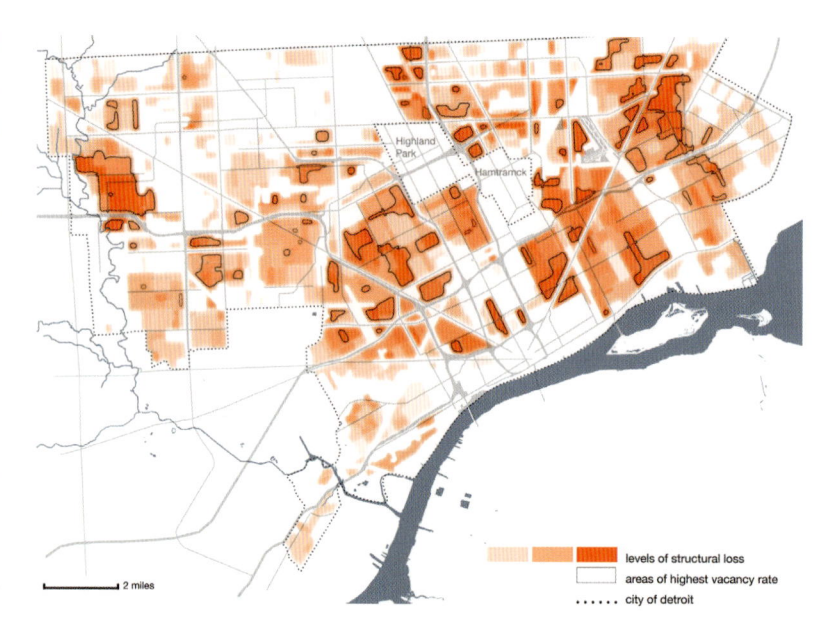

FIGURE 8.6 Analysis of figures 8.1 through 8.5 showing the structural loss and vacancy that create opportunities. This information is partially a base for future intervention strategies, and allows the establishment of the "land of opportunity."

grounds and a variety gardening possibilities (Spiegel 2007). Detroit itself has hosted several urban gardening initiatives dating back to the early 1900s. Citizens have created a number of community gardens as they put the land to good use, maintain it, and therefore unburden the city government from some of its maintenance responsibilities. The Detroit Agriculture Network (DAN), an umbrella organization, supported 875 gardens according to a 2011 source, and undocumented estimates suggest that over 1,300 community gardens exist altogether (Bittman 2011). These temporary uses are low cost and inspire local entrepreneurs to envision new uses for the vacant land. They can provide a temporary use that does not inhibit long-term, profitable use (Hollander et al. 2009). Studies show that the maintenance of vacant land, such as through gardening, can stabilize or even increase the market value of area properties. However, these gardens raise troublesome problems of property rights and tenure when the gardening is done by citizens who do not own the land (Hollander et al. 2009; Lawson and Miller 2013). Future development might be hindered if gardening on city-owned property is not regulated, especially if the economic, social and cultural impact of the activities led to apparent improvements in the community. Another important concern is contamination. Because of the previous industrial uses of the land, gardeners must test the soil and, if necessary, remediate it so that edible produce does not absorb toxins from the soil. This decontamination process, known as bioremediation, can be accomplished by constructing planting beds with clean imported soil or growing particular crops that remove toxins (Gallagher 2010, p. 55).

Although the city has gained space, the fragmentation of vacant parcels limits the possibilities in some ways. Urban farming is a solution that addresses vacancy on a larger scale than small vegetable gardens and parks. In 2013 the city government adopted a long-awaited urban agriculture ordinance that made such land use legal. But larger land parcels are needed for such farms to be profitable and efficient to maintain; this requires consolidation.

Another possible large-scale intervention would be to form an urban landscape park to create a variety of cultural and economic opportunities through the integration of existing abandoned and active industrial sites, infrastructure, agriculture and housing in a coordinated landscape as a cultural attraction. Thus the transformation process could be partially aesthetic as well as functional and economic.

POTENT FORMER INDUSTRIAL SITES

In addition to abandoned or demolished homes, former industrial and commercial areas are also becoming vacant. The appropriate response to such vacancies would depend on the type and condition of the structures or the social fabric of the immediate area. In the past, the unpredictability of the economic development, its environmental status as well as legal issues of a location have not always allowed for stabilization or for replanning for a different use.

The vacated industrial areas mainly housed automotive manufacturing and related industries. The relocation of these facilities was largely affected by the companies' changing requirements, availability of workers, increased taxation of businesses within the City of Detroit or attractive tax incentives offered by other municipalities. To a large extent, and with little exception, companies have not been held accountable for their deserted structures and lands, and are not required to redevelop or to remediate their former locations. Thus, Detroit has a vast number of abandoned factories and contaminated properties. Financially incapable of restoring and redeveloping all of the sites for other future uses, the city now has a catalogue of historic structures that vividly tell a story of the heyday of innovation and productivity. Some famous examples are the Packard Plant, built between 1903 and 1911 and abandoned in 1956; The Fisher Body Plant 21, built in 1919 and vacated in the 90s; and the Michigan Central Depot rail station, built in 1913 and abandoned in 1988.

In addition to industrial sites that have been abandoned by the owners, some areas lay unused due to planned development projects never brought to fruition. Initial plans by the city government to develop part of the east riverfront's former industrial area with three casinos failed, but the casinos moved elsewhere, into the CBD. The land near the riverfront that had been purchased by the city for this project sat vacant for years due to bureaucratic difficulties, although it has recently been partially developed for a walkway and linked-park development sponsored by the Detroit Riverfront Conservancy (Detroit Riverfront Conservancy 2014).

The Detroit Dry Dock Company Building, a historic structure also known as the Globe Trading Company Building, still awaits the adaptive

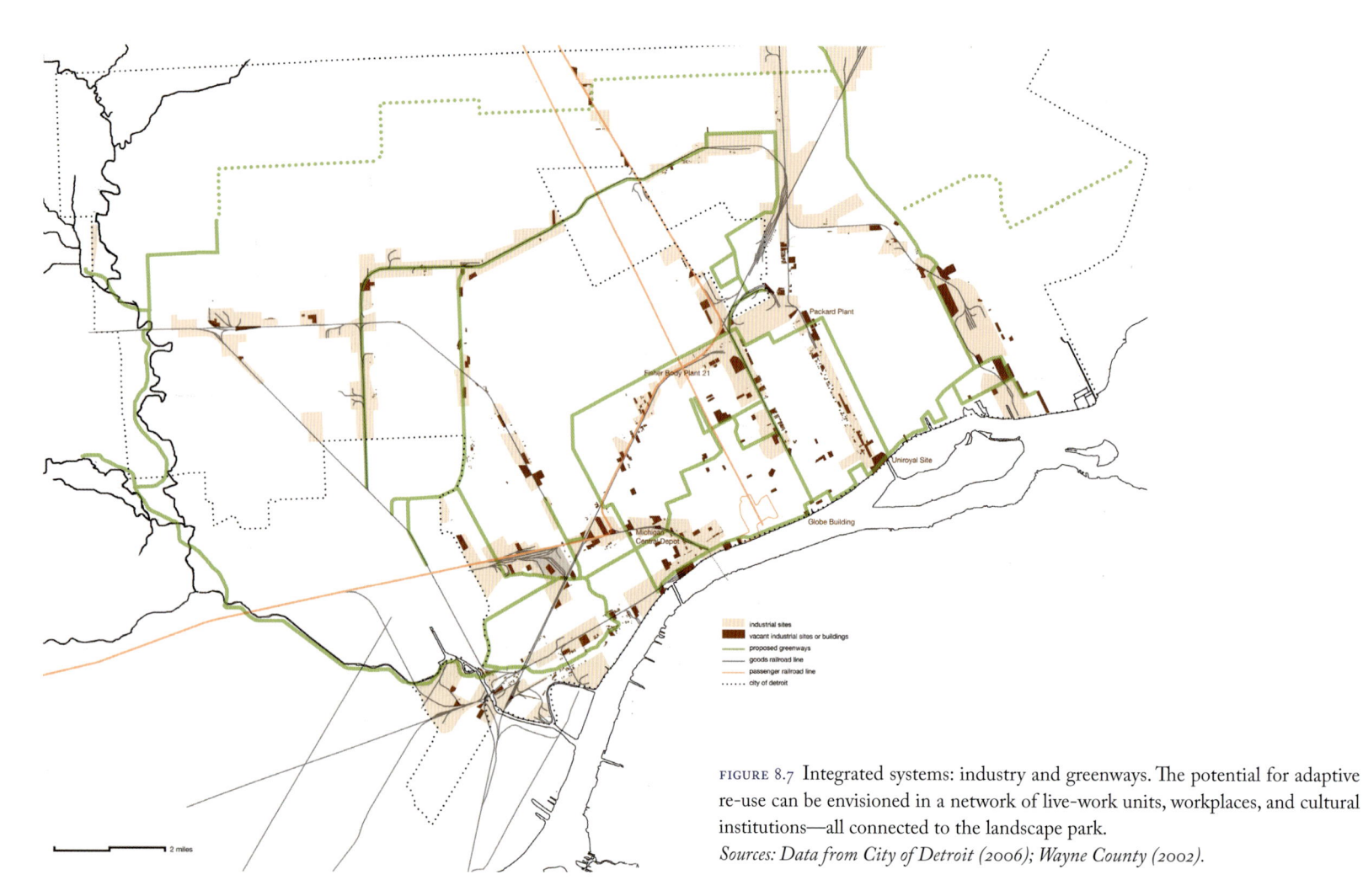

FIGURE 8.7 Integrated systems: industry and greenways. The potential for adaptive re-use can be envisioned in a network of live-work units, workplaces, and cultural institutions—all connected to the landscape park.
Sources: Data from City of Detroit (2006); Wayne County (2002).

reuse that has been planned since 2006. Adjacent to the recently inaugurated Dequindre Cut Greenway, which will connect the Eastern Market with the riverfront by converting the old rail line into a combination bike and pedestrian pathway, the Globe Building, if redeveloped, could represent an ideal relationship between the cultural uses of the land and possible integration of historic former industrial sites.

A strategy of creating highly flexible corridors (Figure 8.7) could stimulate functioning industry as well as adaptive reuse of land and existing buildings. Following the model of existing greenways in other cities, these corridors would create a citywide network of interconnected live-work units, offices, industrial sites, and cultural institutions; such greenways have been proposed in at least two area land use plans (City of Detroit

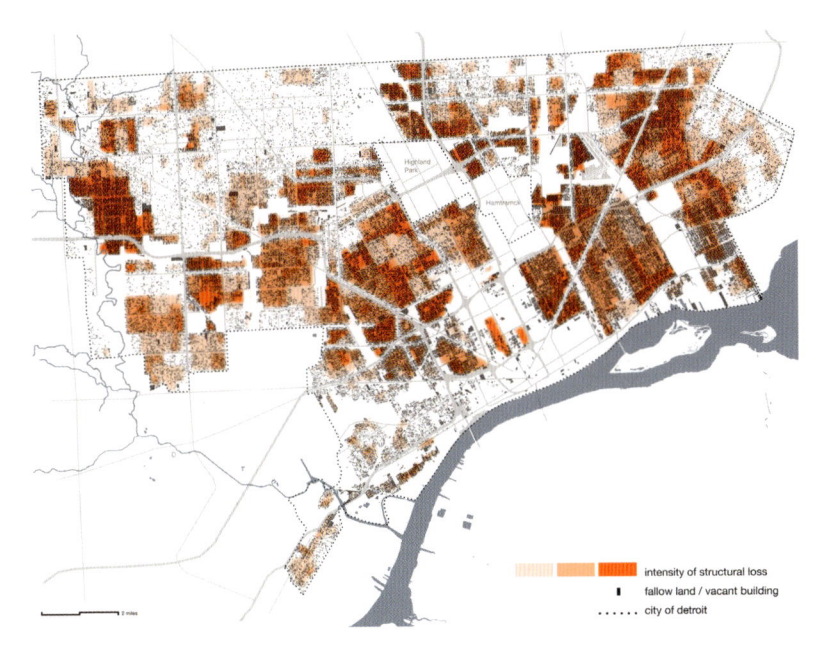

FIGURE 8.8 The superimposition of data of actual vacant parcels and residential buildings onto the analytical map of structural loss (Figure 8.6) allows the evaluation of intervening actions with higher precision and intention.
Sources: Data from City of Detroit, Planning and Development Dept., Detroit Residential Parcel Survey, Data Driven Detroit (2010).

2006; Wayne County 2002). Cultural events and prestigious office locations would therefore not be limited to downtown, but rather would be supported by a network of efficient infrastructure.

MAPPING THE POTENTIAL

In the process of mapping the potential of the urban landscape, I have conducted several steps in this analysis, which focuses on residential areas, rather than commercial areas and the CBD. Also, this analysis does not include Hamtramck, Highland Park, or other communities outside the city limits of Detroit; in future reiterations, this would be necessary to gain a true picture of the extent and opportunities of an integrated regional effort.

Mapping densities, building and property vacancies, and the rate of fire damage and condition of existing homes led to a combined map of the intensity of structural loss and the amount of vacancies throughout the city, thus revealing potential areas for intervention (Figure 8.8). Location matters; vacancy rises in proximity to industrial zones, whereas proximity to public urban green spaces is often an indicator of higher quality housing stock. Also, relatively stable neighborhoods tend to be located closer to the fringes of the city and closer to communities outside the city of Detroit. Most vacancies occur in areas closer to downtown, although exceptions do exist. (See also chapters 2 and 7 for more information.)

In order to start the urban and spatial restructuring process, I attempted to find a sensible initial intervention strategy. The Detroit Water and Sewerage Department has stated that the environmental damage imposed on the city by a lack of capacity to deal with stormwater, which creates sewage overflows, could be offset by uncovering or "day-lighting" buried streams and creeks and restoring wetlands in the city. Day-lighting streams can positively affect the ecology, economy, and culture of cities. A number of U.S. cities have successfully improved their urban conditions in this way since the uncovering of Strawberry Creek in Berkeley, California. A report of the Rocky Mountain Institute discusses at least twenty-three realized projects and mentions the same number as considered projects in the United States (Pinkham 2000). One of the most significant aquatic habitat restorations in the country to date is the Saw Mill River in Yonkers, New York. The day-lighting and ecological restoration promises to spur economic growth. According to the Sam Mill River Coalition, the effort will benefit thousands of residents, commuters, and shoppers (Daylight in Yonkers 2011). Municipalities have carried out day-lighting projects for various reasons, but the foremost benefit seems to be the mitigation of flooding problems and diversion of rainwater before it mixes with sewage in the combined sewer systems, thus reducing overflows and the burden

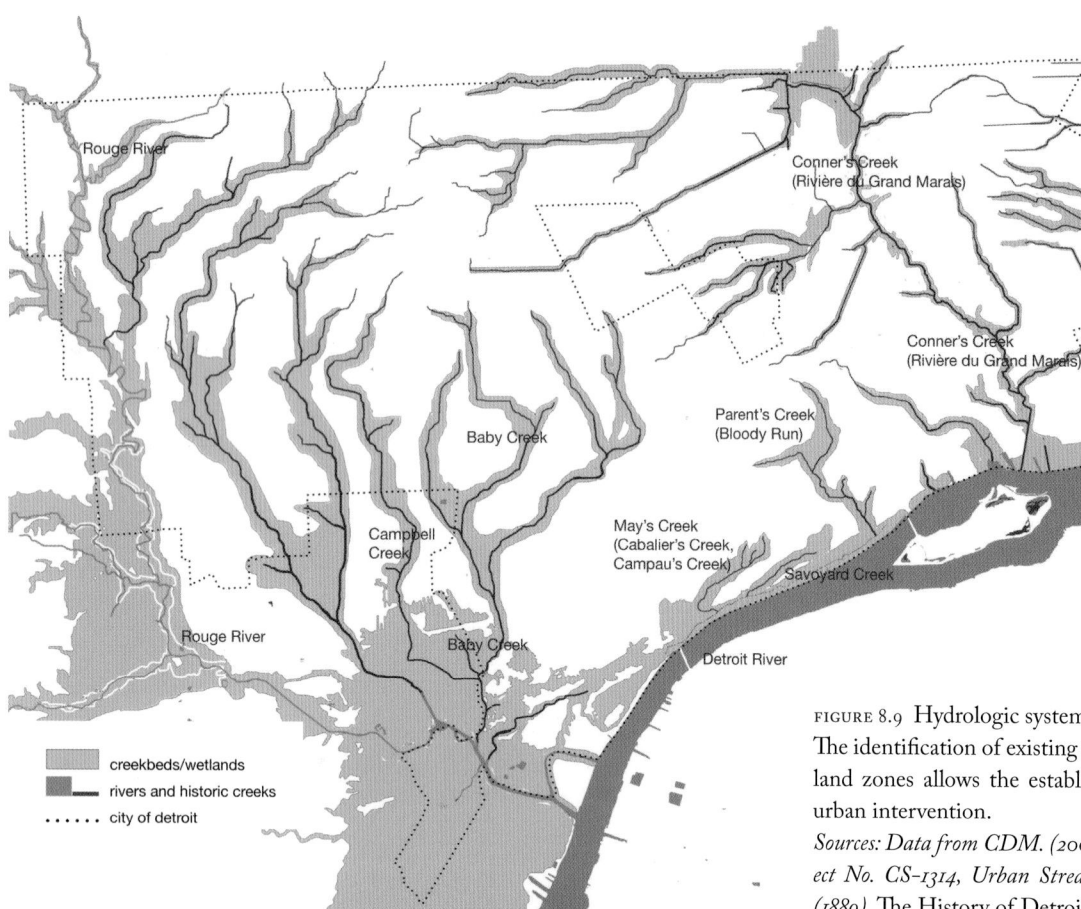

FIGURE 8.9 Hydrologic system of existing and former rivers and streams in Detroit. The identification of existing and former rivers, streams, and creeks with their wetland zones allows the establishment of a new structural base for the ecological urban intervention.
Sources: Data from CDM. (2003, September). Wastewater master plan, *DWSD Project No. CS-1314, Urban Streams Restoration (Technical Memorandum); Farmer, S. (1889). The History of Detroit and Michigan.*

on treatment plants. Other benefits are recreational amenities, educational values, an increase in property values, and the creation of job opportunities (Pinkham 2000).

Others have already pointed out potential application of such ideas to Detroit (Gallagher 2010). Most of the streams and rivers were buried under sewers, but these bodies of water do still exist. For a sustainable yet feasible approach, one approach would be to consolidate land in conjunction with uncovering historic streams, in an effort to restore the natural hydrological systems. See Figure 8.9 for a map of historic streams and rivers, generated from various sources and overlaid on the areas previously suggested and mapped as places of highest potential for intervention (CDM 2003; Farmer 1886).

Most realized projects elsewhere in the United States are relatively limited in scale, ranging in area between 0.5 and 4 square miles. Two cities are encouraging examples of aquatic restoration that could serve as role models for Detroit. Kalamazoo, Michigan, realized a 7.4-square-mile project in 1995

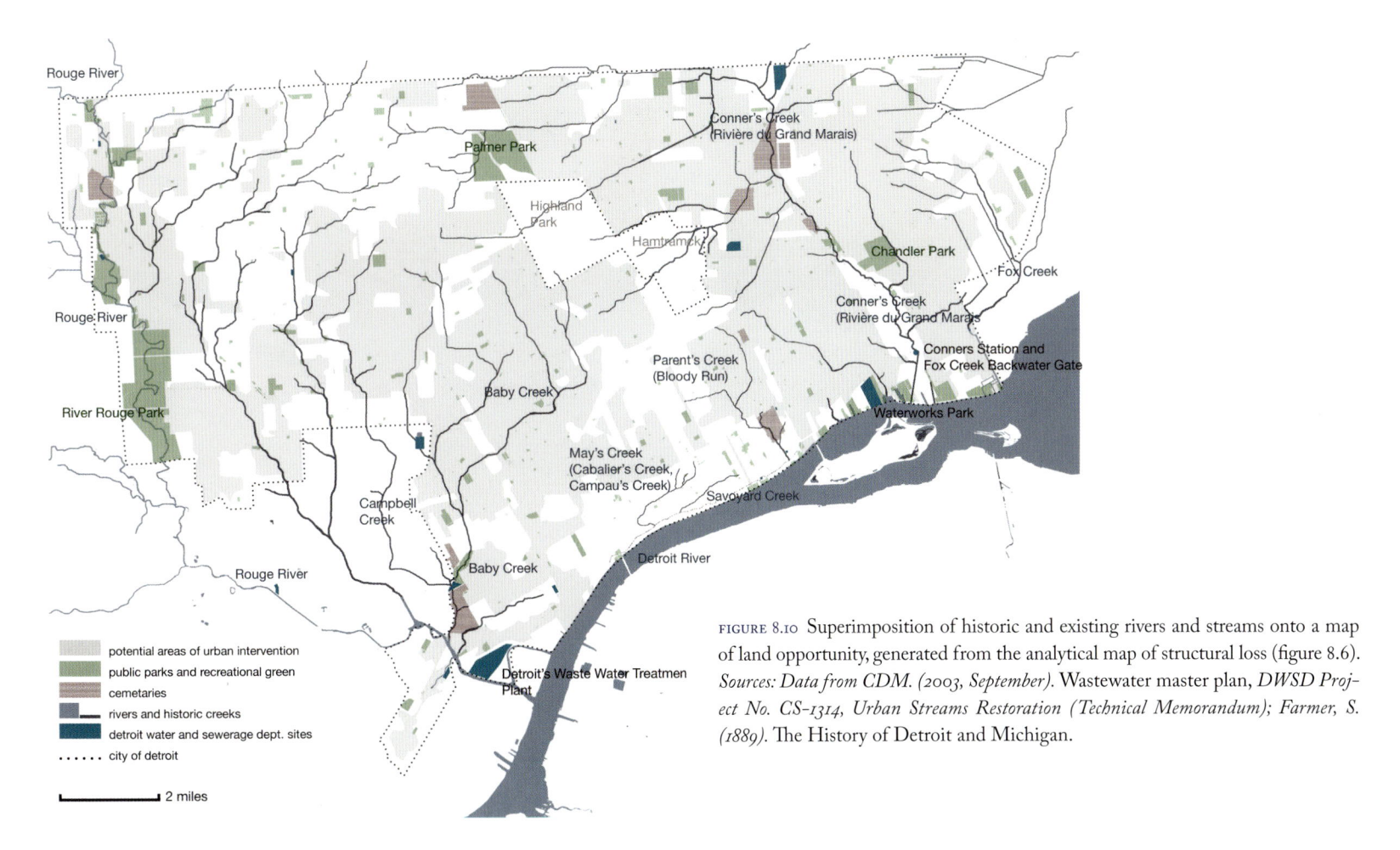

FIGURE 8.10 Superimposition of historic and existing rivers and streams onto a map of land opportunity, generated from the analytical map of structural loss (figure 8.6). *Sources: Data from CDM. (2003, September). Wastewater master plan, DWSD Project No. CS-1314, Urban Streams Restoration (Technical Memorandum); Farmer, S. (1889). The History of Detroit and Michigan.*

by creating a 1,550 foot long stream in the CBD. In Omak, Washington, the Omak Creek project, located in a 140-square-mile watershed, encompassed 1,500 feet of culvert. Here, the restoration focused on stream function, fish passage, and revitalization of the lumber industry (Pinkham 2000).

In such cases, day-lighting efforts are limited to inner-city redevelopment projects in which local ecological improvements are initiated with a maximum of public exposure. These projects require high public investment in supportive infrastructure. In the case of Detroit, any day-lighting of streams would perhaps occur in areas of low density outside of downtown and densely populated areas, limiting the investment while benefitting the city at large.

For vacant areas located close to the watersheds, ecological restoration could become the first step of a restructuring process, as in Figures 8.10, 8.11, and 8.12. Such areas could become part of a continuous landscape park. According to this proposal, areas with low residential density may qualify as transitional zones, where low-density housing is

MAPPING THE URBAN LANDSCAPE 179

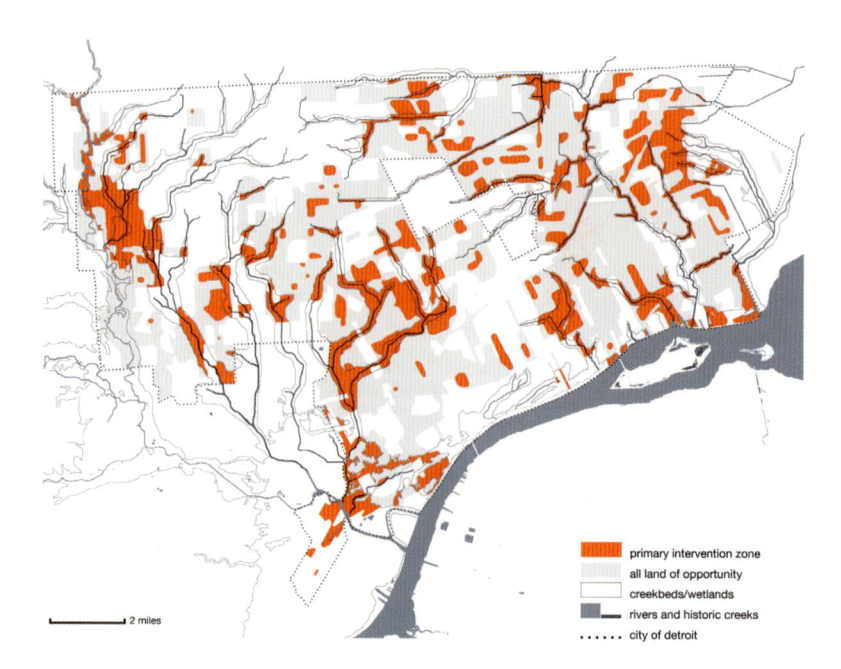

FIGURE 8.11 Restoration of wetlands in areas of highest potential for urban intervention. The restoration of the hydrologic system is guided by the levels of opportunity, generated in figure 8.10.

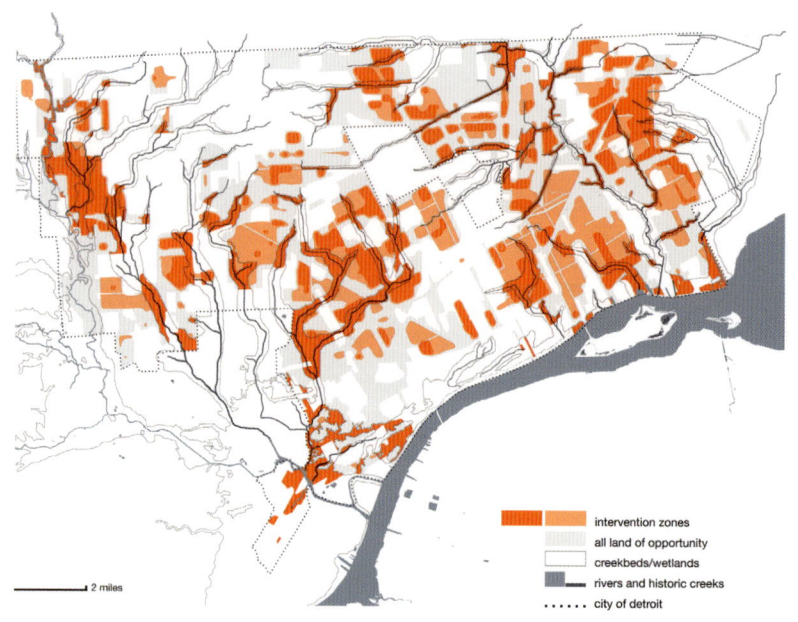

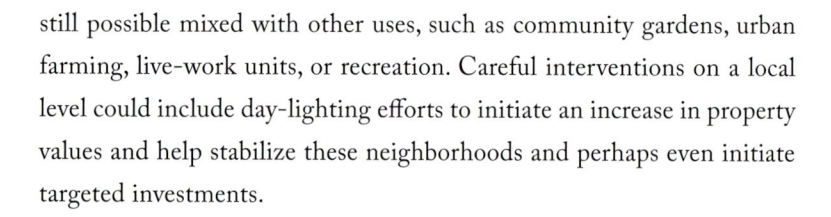

FIGURE 8.12 Gradual expansion of the landscape in areas of high levels of opportunity.

still possible mixed with other uses, such as community gardens, urban farming, live-work units, or recreation. Careful interventions on a local level could include day-lighting efforts to initiate an increase in property values and help stabilize these neighborhoods and perhaps even initiate targeted investments.

REVEALING THE ARCHIPELAGO

Due to political opposition and fiscal limitations, city leaders have thus far rejected any plan to shut down areas and relocate residents. Sparsely populated areas still retain a substantial number of people who object to the idea of their neighborhoods being decommissioned (*Detroit Future City* 2012; Hollander et al. 2009).

The city lost 25 percent of its population between 2000 and 2010, and consequently the situation of many neighborhoods has changed. Increased distress, combined with public awareness and demand for positive change and basic services, has produced a possible acceptance of positive and visionary programs.

We now focus on a possible strategy for creating the archipelago, with the landscape and the islands forming a sustainable relationship in mutual support. This strategy is in keeping with the natural tendency to close ranks, in order to create neighborhoods and districts that are vital and socially and economically sustainable. Each of these districts would, over time, develop a specific identity (if this does not already exist), better allowing the inhabitants to relate to and care for their nearby urban context. The city would

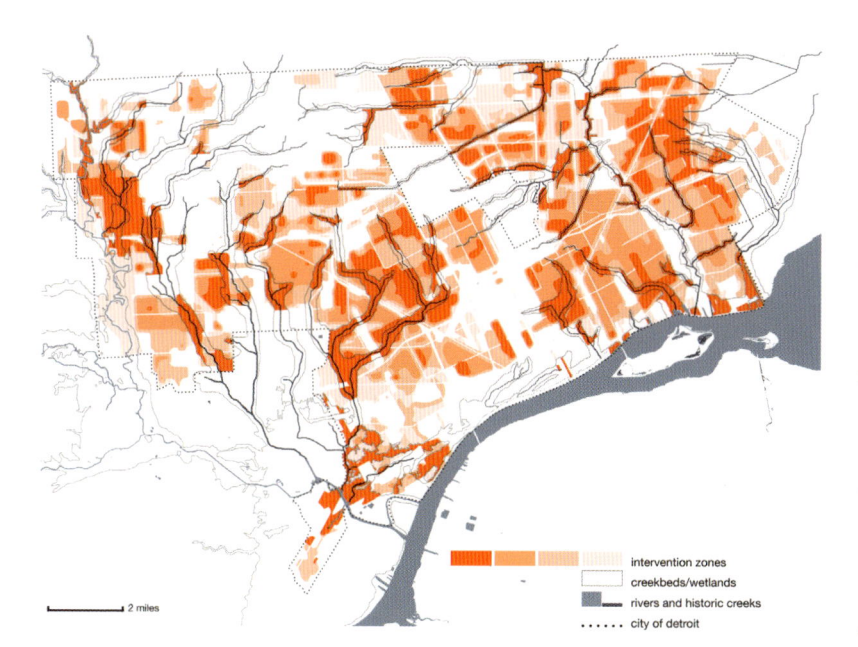

FIGURE 8.13 Levels of categories for urban intervention. The levels of urban intervention range from the opportunity for entire restructuring processes and clearance from structures (darkest) to reinterpreting low-density neighborhoods (lightest).

FIGURE 8.14 The productive landscape park. The establishment of the urban landscape park allows for a range of land uses and activities (ranked by intensity of intervention). In park areas, uses include wetland restoration, energy crop production, solar fields, recreational opportunities, and cultural amenities. In transition areas, uses include low-density residential areas, urban farming and neighborhood gardens, recreational amenities close to residents, and energy crop production.

become an archipelago of individually developing islands, each having a special character. Consequently, clear limits of expansion for each of these islands would be necessary in order to encourage densification.

A specific scheme for denser islands emerges out of the inventory of viable neighborhoods revealed through the mapping process. It parallels an earlier study undertaken by Detroit's Planning Commission in 1990 concerning vacant land in the city (Hollander et al. 2009), updated with the 2009 study of vacant land (Detroit Data Collaborative 2010).

By creating awareness of the landscape's essential role, an appreciation for the vacated land can be fostered. Restoring the city's hydrological system would help develop a healthy and sustainable ecological environment.

Figure 8.12 shows that corridors of green spaces, uncovered streams, and wetlands can connect most areas of highest vacancies. Uncovering historic streams and restoring wetlands could help develop the productive future potential of the land, such as relieve flooding problems, divert urban runoff from combined sewer systems, improve water quality, recreate the aquatic habitat, and serve as recreational areas or even as initiator for neighborhood revitalization projects, as consultants have proposed to the city's water and sewage department (CDM 2003, p. 20).

One challenge would be to create a workable agenda that would enhance the attractiveness of the landscape within the greater region and, at the same time, create a coherent and future-oriented urban order. An inherent goal would be to initiate a healthy relationship between the ecology and the economy by increasing the soil quality and biodiversity, improving the hydrology, and reducing atmospheric emissions such as carbon dioxide. Reducing carbon dioxide is a central concern of urban settlements today. This could be achieved in large part by reducing energy use in general. One opportunity is the construction of highly energy-efficient new homes. The single-family home, currently the prevailing residential typology, could be replaced by alternatives, especially in denser urban areas. Efficient heating methods—e.g., district heating provided by co-generation plants or, as suggested by Gallagher (2010), geothermal wells—would add to the overall efficiency and provide economical alternatives to current models.

The concept of urban islands could also allow Detroit residents to directly benefit from the offerings of the landscape surrounding them. The economic interdependency of the open land and the urban settlement is an old concept, which dates back to the medieval town, when surrounding adjacent agricultural land supported the city. (Today, urban residents do not depend on food produced at close range, because of both climate and concerns about soil, but also because of the benefits of highly efficient logistical networks. However, greater agricultural production may be possible.)

The productive landscape would no longer be seen as vacant spots in the fragmented urban fabric, but as a support system bounding the inhabited islands as part of an interrelated, but continuous system. This system would inherently provide opportunities for a variety of functions, necessary for the support of the islands. The land would be taken out of its standby condition and turned effectively into a contributor to the economic and ecologic development of the city.

Energy Landscape

The land can also help produce energy for heat and electricity, which may lead to a higher appreciation for the landscape. Transformation into larger, continuous free spaces would be necessary to grow a source for energy through creating a productive landscape, as we will explain later, but also could become the essential instrument of urban design. We can characterize such land as a new type of post-industrial urban landscape park. Based on the sequence of mapping used to identify land of potential interventions in various intensities, Figures 8.13 and 8.14 suggest that an area of almost 58 square miles could become such an urban landscape park, of which the greater portion (38.6 square miles) could be entirely devoted to various kinds of energy production and soil remediation as well as wetland restoration. In these areas, we find the highest possibilities for the productive landscape (e.g., biofuel production), due to the highest levels of vacant land and abandonment. Biofuel initiatives could possibly secure federal funds from the U.S. Department of Agriculture or the U.S. Department of Energy, both of which support projects in clean energy research and production in various categories (U.S. Office of Management and Budget 2012). If the vacated land would directly provide its benefits of energy production to the new efficient housing areas in the boundaries of the intensified residential and mixed-use areas, a publicly acceptable and desirable scenario could be developed and marketed, one that improved living conditions and lowered energy costs.

The landscape park would need economic productivity, such as agricultural production. If the agricultural product were biocrops, the energy for residents could be produced locally. Biocrops are a variety of perennial grasses and short rotation woody crops that crop managers turn into methane with the assistance of anaerobic digesters (Castleman 2001; Keoleian and Volk 2005). Methane could feed into the existing gas grid, or, more efficiently even, become fuel in small co-generation plants within the neighborhoods that provide heat and electricity. Local farmers could form cooperatives to contract with residents of the area, providing district heating and power supply through efficient, neighborhood-sized co-generation plants.

Heat distribution would incur the least amount of losses via short distance district heating pipes serving homes on the perimeter of the landscape.

A multitude of different crops could be selected to produce an aesthetic and enjoyable landscape, making the park area suitable for recreational use. Low crops like switch grass, giant miscanthus grass, and willow shrubs could alternate with spatially defining poplar trees. Larger areas could be planted with rotating crops such as rye or corn. The landscape would inherently be dynamic and would change with the seasons and over the years. The landscape would undergo constant changes and adjustments: switch grass would be harvested twice a year; willow has a rotation cycle of five years; and poplar will be cut every seven years; and so on, thus allowing shifts, modifications and even replacements. As the basis for this concept, local farmers could form cooperatives to contract with residents of the area, providing district heating and power supply through efficient, neighborhood sized co-generation plants.

In addition to the energy efficiency created by local production, the productive landscape could also reduce the energy required to create energy for the area households and schools. Long-term studies in Denmark show that giant miscanthus grass, for example, can achieve an annually net energy gain between 22 to 40 MWh/ha (85–154 kW/h per square mile), depending on pretreatment, such as wet oxidation, with a maximum achievable efficiency of an output/input ratio of 6.9 to 10.6 and for willow 7.3 to 12.3 (Uellendahl et al. 2008).

The efficiency of localized co-generation plants for individual blocks or small neighborhoods would allow a maximum use of the generated biogas (Methane). From 11,000 to 16,500 households could receive heat in this way, and electricity could be produced for an equivalent of 22,000 to 33,000 households per year,[3] if all of the available 10,000 hectares (38.6 square miles) of landscape were put to production. If additionally a minimum of 50 percent of the transitional areas (19.4 square miles/5,025 hectares) could contribute also to energy production, between 13,700 and 20,600 homes could be heated and 27,800 to 41,700 homes could be supplied with electricity in total. Between 5.3 and 8 percent of the 259,000 households in Detroit (per 2008–2012 census data) could be supplied with heat, and 10.7 to 16.1 percent of the households could be supplied with electricity from renewable energy sources in this way. This tremendous contribution to the economy of Detroit would have a positive impact on the employment market and new-home construction, particularly energy-efficient dwellings, which can be directly associated with the energy landscape park.

Anaerobic digestion is also suitable for producing energy from used wooden building material. Suitable wood, separated from superfluous housing stock, could supplement bio-crop material and offset the investment cost of farming. This use of material that would otherwise be refuse would reduce the amount of garbage as well as the cost for landfills. The system is versatile on many fronts. Other cities have already created ideas for utilizing their accumulated biodegradable material—like fall leaves,[4] wood, and collected yard waste—to generate energy, instead of composting this organic matter (Svoboda 2008).

Some plant materials might be slightly less efficient in their energy production, but have the advantage of being able to absorb toxins from the soil. Bioremediation is a process whereby plants accumulate toxins in soils and render them harmless. Unlike costly soil exchanges and excavations and other mechanical cleaning processes, this cost-effective procedure is not environmentally disruptive. Using bioremediation, arsenic, lead, cadmium, zinc and many other heavy metals can be extracted from contaminated brownfield sites. Most plant types that are suitable for this purpose, such as willow, poplar, hemp, sunflowers, and Indian mustard, can then become harvestable crops or be discarded safely (Gallagher 2010; Greger and Landberg 1999). As some writers have already suggested, the slow process of bioremediation over a longer period of time could be advantageous in the case of former industrial sites in Detroit (Gallagher 2010). In addition, the new landscape could also provide areas for new solar farms, producing additional electricity. Like any other energy-providing installation (e.g., coal and nuclear plants), solar plants would need subsidies, but they may be especially suitable as pilot projects to secure federal and state funding. This investment would resemble a stable and long-term commitment for about twenty to thirty years, ultimately reducing additional carbon dioxide emissions in the process.

Case Studies in Landscape Strategies

As a recent example of a successful solar energy project, the Waldpolenz Solar Park near Leipzig, Germany, an area that is just two square kilometers (0.8 square miles), generates forty megawatts. This is enough to provide 40,000 households with electricity. The solar plant displaces twenty-five tons of carbon dioxide annually (Green Planet 2011).

Another successful case study for the implementation of a large-scale landscape strategy in a situation comparable to that of Detroit is Emscher Park, Germany. "Germany's 1989–99 International Building Exhibition (IBA) in the Northern Ruhr—once the heartland of Europe's steel and coal industry—confronted regional challenges by simultaneously repairing environmental damage and projecting economical renewal" (Shannon 2006, p. 148). A program of integrated urban regeneration involved approximately 120 projects. Project planners did not restore the natural landscape, but rather ecologically stabilized it. They also reused many enormous relics of their industrial era as centers for cultural activities. Most impressive, however, was the coordinated planning and implementation done on the regional scale: the result was Emscher Landscape Park, a green corridor connecting the seventeen cities between Duisburg and Kamen along the ecologically recovered Emscher River and its 350 kilometers of tributaries.

The success of Emscher Park is the result of a unique implementation strategy. By initiative of the state, a privately organized IBA-Planning Association has been created for the duration of ten years. Its primary function is to be a motivating engine for projects and a moderator of planning processes. The association did not implement any projects on its own, but took the responsibility to stimulate and support local initiatives, communities and municipalities, companies, and infrastructure authorities to improve the quality of urban and landscape developments, architecture, and the handling of former industrial sites. In 1989 the association asked the public for proposals for projects. It received over 400 submittals in six guiding categories. The projects relied on differentiated and creative implementation strategies for realization. International planning and design competitions created a basis for each of the projects. Existing economic development programs by the state, federal government, and the European Union (total 60 percent) supported the IBA projects. The private sector invested the remaining 40 percent.

The IBA has created a number of initiatives: exhibitions, symposia, and workshops with experts and the general public. The German contribution to the Venice Biennale exhibition in 1996 was Emscher Park, in a submission titled "Change without Growth," which resulted in international recognition. The Department of Urban and Regional Planning of the TU Dortmund University has conducted a long-term research project concerning the effects and results of the IBA in order to extrapolate various ideas for projects, processes, and procedures for future national and international regional restructuring processes (Uttke 2008).

Urban Boundaries

Using landscape parks for urban development would help ensure the quality of the transition between urbanized and non-urbanized areas. In order to foster distinct qualities and atmospheres for islands of neighborhoods, and to initiate development and investment within each island, boundary conditions are important. An abrupt division between densely populated

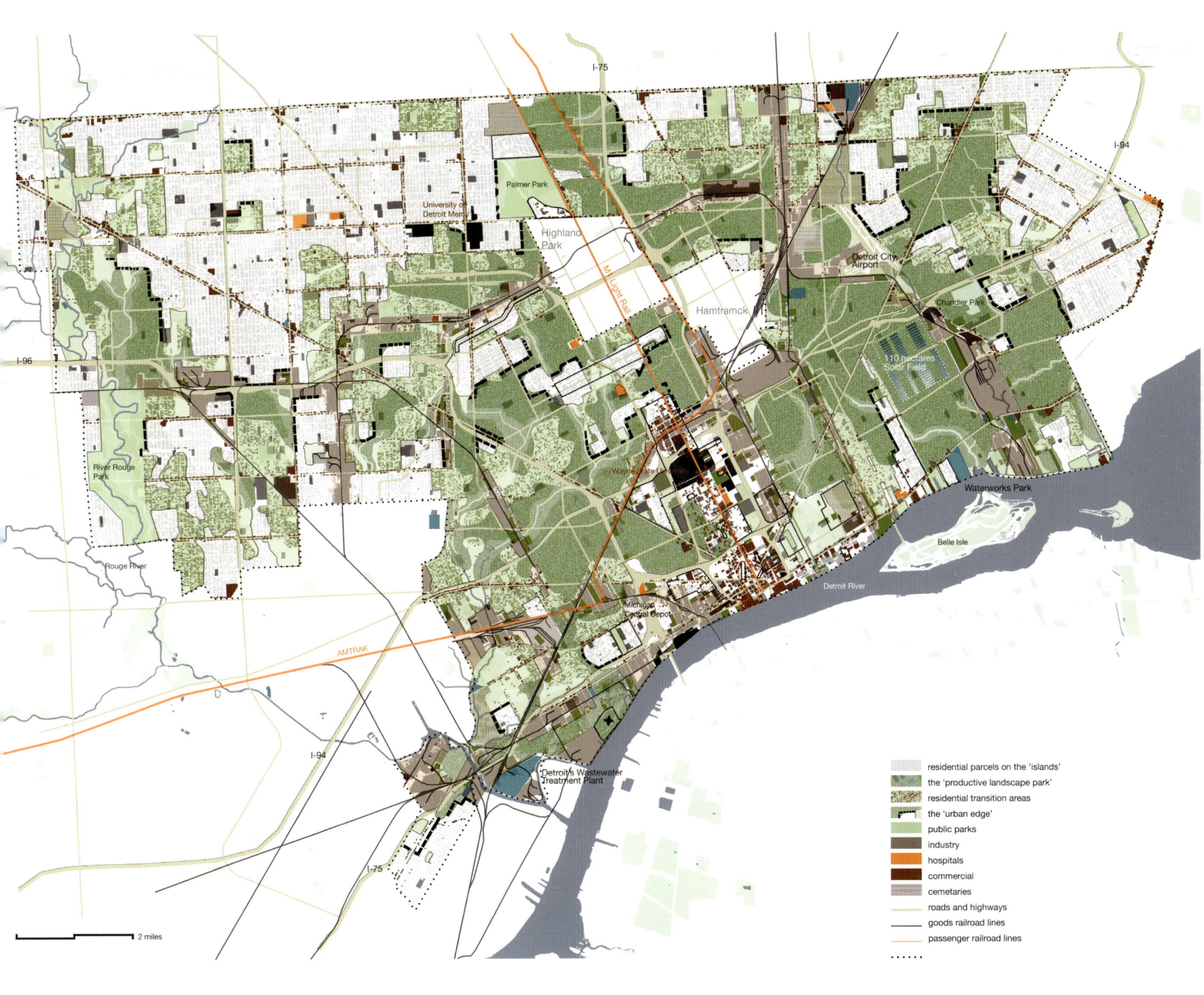

FIGURE 8.15 Synoptic representation of the project.

urban areas and the open landscape offers a development boundary to foster redensification toward the inner neighborhood. The intervention can be described as the "sea wall." The sea wall would be an urban typology with compact building types, comprised of a mix of housing, live-work units, and small businesses and services, for a long-term attractive, robust, and flexible part of the city. A main goal of the dense boundary area would be to attract a wide variety of different residents in order to accommodate a mix of younger and older people, from lower to upper middle class.

By concentrating the commercial land use at the islands' boundaries, one might initiate a revitalization of the fragmented commercial corridors along major roads in Detroit. Clear public space elements with a mix of housing, cultural, social and public functions, such as adjacent municipal facilities, could allow visual and physical access to the open landscape and also strengthen existing businesses by creating prime urban locations and a mixed-use characteristic.

Transitional Areas

Finally, transitional areas, where housing is generally in good condition, but where the density is currently low (and may stay low in the future) would be possible, as community-based organizations themselves have indicated for Detroit's future (Community Development Advocates of Detroit 2010). In order to protect these areas from economic or social deterioration, and to create an incentive for homeowners to support these areas, a rural mixed-use character should be accepted and enhanced. In these areas, characterized here as "the shoreline," a variety of activities would be possible on larger lot sizes. Medium- to low-density housing types, such as courtyard houses, row houses, and detached single family homes, could allow for community gardens, small- to medium-size urban farming, and a variety of recreational activities. Here, the access to the open landscape park would also be possible, generating a diverse and dynamic quality of life (Figure 8.15).

CONCLUSION

The terms "urban restructuring" and "conversion" stand in direct opposition to the terms "urban renewal" and "restoring." Urban restructuring is not winding back the clock and imitating some time in history (unless we look at the conditions of the late 1910s, when the city had roughly as many citizens as today). The expectations for a new kind of dynamic city need creative thinking; the city needs "to reflect a true expression of the best endeavors of contemporary life" (Saarinen 1943, p. 79). This suggests the need for restructuring.

The contemporary situation of Detroit is a challenge because of the process of shrinkage, but it is important to explore options. With so little experience with the planning and design of a shrinking city on this scale, this chapter focused on conditions and relationships in order to determine the potential for a coherent—but, at the same time, highly malleable and adaptable—space based on ecological principles.

The investigation showed that the excess of fallow land offers a high potential for positively contributing to the local economy and thus might play a primary role in the future planning process. The ecologically responsible production of heat and electricity creates a potent possibility as incentive for the development of new efficient housing stock for relocating citizens, while contributing to the social sustainability of neighborhoods. Decentralized energy production could be economically beneficial, and the production of biocrops could mitigate environmental damage by reducing the use of fossil fuels.

A variety of possibilities emerge when planning the productive landscape. Because the productive landscape needs to be maintained and harvested, and energy needs to be produced, new green industry could generate much-needed employment opportunities while reducing the high cost of unsustainable practices. The planning and maintenance of a productive landscape has the potential to become a primary tool for the urban development in a fragmented city. Potential uses of fallow land are varied and could directly benefit the economy and social structure of the urban context. However, it is vital that the landscape remain, as a whole, in public ownership or be held in trust for the community in order to gain the support of the population and to ensure a long-term social, cultural, and economical benefit to them.

As they proceed to establish concrete ways to guide the city's development, the stakeholders will have to develop a catalogue of clear guidelines to secure planning reliability and sound legal protection. These instruments will create relative predictability in the planning process of interdependent urban designs, programs, actions, and outcomes, thus providing a higher probability for the invested parties to foresee the success and stability of their contributions.

NOTES

1. Editor's Note: This chapter was drafted two years before the issuance of *Detroit Future City* (2012).
2. This culminated in *Detroit Future City* (2012), described in the epilogue.
3. According to experience with over 3,500 biogas facilities, the German Federal Agency for Food, Agriculture and Consumer Protection has issued rules of thumb for biogas production through anaerobic digestion. Using average efficiency and taking regional differences into account, one hectare (2.47 acres) of agricultural land of grassy crops can provide 10,000 to 15,000 kWh electricity annually.

    Assumed for this calculation is a Combined Heat and Power Plant (CHP) with efficiency rates of 38% electric and 50% thermal. Therefore, one acre can provide electric energy for 1 to 1.5 households of four persons (assumed annual usage of 4,500 kWh), and 1.5 to 2.3 acres are necessary to heat one household of four persons (assumed average annual heating energy use of 12,000 kWh).

    Calculated based on charts provided by the Fachagentur Nachwachsende Rohstoffe e. V. (FNR) (Society for Renewable Resources), an institute supported by the German Federal Agency for Food, Agriculture and Consumer Protection. *Sources:* Biomass Regulation (2012), Rule of thumb numbers biogas (KTBL, 2013), Biogas Guide (FNR, 2013), biogas production and supply guide (FNR, 2014), electricity generation from biomass (DBFZ, 2013) and author's own calculations.
4. Svoboda, E., Mika, E., Berhie, S., (2008, August 02) "CASE STUDY: Grass Power. Boston has preliminary plans for a plant that would turn 50,000 tons of fall color into power and fertilizer. The facility would first separate yard clippings into grass and leaves. Anaerobic bacteria feeding on the grass would make enough methane to power at least 1.5 megawatts worth of generators, while heat and agitation would hasten the breakdown of the leaves and twigs into compost." From *Popular Science* 2008, www.popsci.com/environment/article/2008-02/americas-50-greenest-cities?page=1%2C1.

REFERENCES

Bittman, M. (2011, May 17). Imagining Detroit. *New York Times.* Retrieved from http://opinionator.blogs.nytimes.com/2011/05/17/imagining-detroit/?hp

Castleman, T. (2001). *Hemp biomass for energy.* Retrieved from http://fuelandfiber.com/Hemp4NRG/Hemp4NRGRV3.htm

CDM. (2003, September). *Wastewater master plan,* DWSD Project No. CS-1314, Urban Streams Restoration [technical memorandum]. Detroit, MI: City of Detroit Water and Sewerage Department. Retrieved from www.dwsd.org/downloads_n/about_dwsd/masterplan_wastewater/volume3/Urban_Streams_Restoration,_City_of_Detroit.pdf

City of Detroit. (2006, June). *Non-motorized urban transportation master plan.* Prepared for The City of Detroit, Traffic Engineering Division, Department of Public Works. Authors: Giffels-Webster Engineers, Carter-Burgess, Archive DS, Brogan and Partners. Detroit, MI. Retrieved from www.detroitmi.gov/Portals/0/docs/planning/planning/nonmotor/Nonmotorized_Urban_Transportation_Master_Plan.pdf

Community Development Advocates of Detroit. (2010, February). *Community development futures task force: Neighborhood revitalization strategic framework.* Retrieved from http://datadrivendetroit.org/wp-content/uploads/2010/09/CDAD_Revitalization_Framework_2010.pdf

Davey, M. (2011, April 5). The odd challenge for Detroit planners. *New York Times.* Retrieved from www.nytimes.com/2011/04/06/us/06detroit.html?pagewanted=all

Daylight in Yonkers [editorial]. (2011, August 21). *New York Times.* Retrieved from www.nytimes.com/2011/08/22/opinion/daylight-in-yonkers.html

Detroit Data Collaborative. (2010). *Detroit residential parcel survey.* Retrieved from www.detroitparcelsurvey.org

Detroit future city: 2012 Detroit strategic framework plan. (2012). Detroit, MI.

Detroit Riverfront Conservancy. (2014). Retrieved from www.detroitriverfront.org/riverfront#east

Economist Intelligence Unit. (2010). *U.S. and Canada green city index.* Siemens Corporation. Retrieved from www.siemens.com/entry/cc/features/greencityindex_international/all/en/pdf/report_northamerica_en.pdf

Farmer, S. (1886). *The history of Detroit and Michigan: Or, the metropolis illustrated; A full record of territorial days in Michigan, and the annals of Wayne County.* Detroit, MI: Silas Farmer & Co.

Gallagher, J. (2010). *Reimagining Detroit.* Detroit, MI: Wayne State University Press.

Green Planet. (2011). *Waldpolenz Solarpark in Germany.* Retrieved from www.green-planet-solar-energy.com/index.html

Greger, M., and Landberg, T. (1999). Use of willow in phytoextraction. *International Journal of Phytoremediation, 1*(2), 115–23.

Hollander, J. B., Pallagst, K., Schwartz, T., and Popper, F. J. (2009). Planning shrinking cities. *Progress in Planning* (special issue: Emerging Research Areas), *72*(4), 223–32.

Keoleian, G., and Volk, T. (2005). Renewable energy from willow biomass crops. *Critical Reviews in Plant Sciences, 24*(5–6), 385–406.

Lawson, L., and Miller, A. (2013). Community gardens and urban agriculture as antithesis to abandonment. In M. Dewar and J. Thomas (Eds.), *The city after abandonment.* Philadelphia: University of Pennsylvania Press.

Oswalt, P. (2005). *Shrinking cities.* Ostfildern-Ruit, Germany: Hatje Cantz.

Pinkham, R. (2000). *Daylighting: New life for buried streams* [report]. Snowmass, CO: Rocky Mountain Institute. Retrieved from www.rmi.org/Knowledge-Center/Library/W00–32_DaylightingNewLifeBuriedStreams

Saarinen, E. (1943). *The city: Its growth, its decay, its future.* Cambridge, MA: MIT Press.

Shannon, K. (2006). From theory to resistance: Landscape urbanism in Europe. In C. Waldheim (Ed.), *The landscape urbanism reader* (pp. 141–61). New York, NY: Princeton Architectural Press.

Spiegel, E. (2007). Wohnen und Wohnungen als Sturkturelemente der Stadt. Hat jede Vergangenheit eine Zukunft? In U. Giseke and E. Spiegel (Eds.), *Stadtlichtungen, Irritationen, Perspektiven, Strategien* (pp. 63–84). Guetersloh, Germany: Bauverlag BV.

Svobada, E. (2008, February). America's 50 greenest cities. *Popular Science.* Retrieved from www.popsci.com/environment/article/2008–02/americas-50-greenest-cities?page=1

Thomson, D. (2012). Targeting neighborhoods, stimulating markets. In M. Dewar and J. Thomas (Eds.), *The city after abandonment.* Philadelphia: University of Pennsylvania Press.

Uellendahl, H., et al. (2008). Energy balance and cost-benefit analysis of biogas production from perennial energy crops pretreated by wet oxidation. *Water Science and Technology, 58*(9), 1841–47.

U.S. Office of Management and Budget. (2012). *Fiscal year 2012: Budget of the U.S. government.* Retrieved from www.gpo.gov/fdsys/browse/collection.action?collectionCode=BUDGET&browsePath=Fiscal+Year+2012&searchPath=Fiscal+Year+2012&leafLevelBrowse=false&isCollapsed=false&isOpen=true&packageid=BUDGET-2012-BUD&ycord=390

Uttke, A. (Ed.). (2008). *International building exhibition Emscher Park: The projects 10 years later.* Essen, Germany: Klartext Verlag.

Vachon, P. (2011, November 25). Detroit's Tech Town: An incubator of creativity. *Miller-McCune.* Retrieved from www.miller-mccune.com/business-economics/detroits-tech-town-an-incubator-of-creativity-37975

Waldheim, C. (2006). Landscape as urbanism. In C. Waldheim (Ed.), *The landscape urbanism reader* (pp. 35–53). New York, NY: Princeton Architectural Press.

Wayne County. (2002). *Rouge River gateway master plan.* Detroit, MI: Hamilton Anderson Associates.

9

REDESIGNING COMMUNITY WITH PROPINQUITY

Fragments of Detroit's Region

JUNE MANNING THOMAS

It is not possible to understand fully a central city without understanding as well its region, defined here as its metropolitan area. In this era of high mobility and interconnected social and economic structures, political boundaries function less as barriers than as permeable borders, and Detroit's region has rightfully become a focus of analysis and study for those interested in cities and their regions. In this chapter, we will consider some aspects of the region and its relationship to the city of Detroit, in part by describing small portions of the region, some of which have fared well and some of which have not in the modern battle for survival. This wider view will help provide context for understanding the possibilities for Detroit's city and region.

This book's introduction offered some such regional context, as did occasional chapters. Chapter 2 by Bekkering and Liu showed that several factors influenced the physical evolution of the historical city and, to some extent, of the region. In chapter 4, Fishman described the linear city: a particular urban factory-rail-housing configuration that for a while reshaped Detroit, and then straddled municipal boundaries, but finally dissolved into largely suburban industrial enclaves. In chapter 8, Gräbner assumed regional context but focused on reimaginations of Detroit's landscape. It was Grengs's chapter, chapter 5, that forced us to remember that the city of Detroit exists within a regional context. He demonstrated, using the lenses of transportation and accessibility, that metropolitan Detroit looks very different depending on where a person lives and that person's race, income, and access to a car. Decades of redevelopment efforts, industrial strategies, land use plans and initiatives, street and transit reconfigurations, and other civic improvement efforts have thus far failed to counteract the hard facts of regional fragmentation and exodus from the central city by people and capital, and little evidence suggests that these trends will reverse anytime soon.

The conditions that exist now are in part the result of decades of federal and state policies and programs that worked too well in their particular aims. What were these aims? The federal government intended to encourage single-family housing construction after World War II, but it did so in racially exclusionary subdivisions, many of which lay outside of central cities. It attempted to facilitate automobile and truck mobility, but, in doing so, it created a federal highway program that tore through central-city neighborhoods and, at least during critically important years following the Highway Act of 1956, discouraged commuter rail transit. It encouraged regional cooperation in some ways, but it brought into being weak regional planning agencies with no clout to enforce concerted action in land use, rail transit, and other critical aspects of metropolitan decision making. These federal actions had a particularly strong negative impact on the central city of Detroit (Freund 2007; Sugrue 1996; Thomas 2013). State actions in Michigan were likewise problematic: they supported home-rule legislation that helped multiply the number of municipalities and discouraged annexation (Jacobs 2009), and they watered down annexation opportunities for increasingly distressed, boundary-bound central cities. In striking contrast to efforts in more innovative states, Michigan's state-level policies enabled only weak regional planning and growth management (Boyle and Mohamed 2007).

Added to such governmental actions were massive changes in the economy. As described in chapter 4, the city of Detroit held preeminence in the region's automobile industry for only a short time. In some areas, industrial suburbanization actually preceded residential suburbanization. Between 1950 and 1980, all of the twenty automobile plants built in metropolitan Detroit were located in the suburbs (Darden, Hill, Thomas, and Thomas 1987). Only with expensive public incentives did General Motors and Chrysler build two urban assembly plants during Coleman Young's administration, which ended in 1994 (Thomas 2013). Jobs and commerce continued to leave the central core, particularly as Detroit's automobile makers lost market share to competitive global manufacturers; metropolitan Detroit's automobile manufacturing declined in economic clout and decentralized to other regions of the United States and then to other countries.

Reversing such trends and policies, however, is not necessarily the best goal for the present. Even if such reversal could be done, it would probably not erase the very real fiscal, social, and economic constraints now facing Detroit. In many ways large and small, the state and the region have practically abandoned the city and its people. This is an issue of both inadequate spatial justice (Soja 2010) and of economic survival. According to many scholars, strong metropolitan economies, with vibrant central cities, are necessary in order for metropolitan areas to survive in the global economy, based increasingly on advanced services and technology (Florida 2004; Glaeser 2011; Sassen 1991). Given this context, it is important to overcome historic difficulties and set a new course of action for metropolitan Detroit.

This chapter will discuss the disparate state of the Detroit metropolis largely in terms of its social context. We will first explore the concepts of *Gemeinshaft* and *Gessellshaft* as ways of understanding the concept of "community," and then examine two key questions. The first question relates to regional context: what are the current realities of fragmentation in metropolitan Detroit, as a whole and for selected cities and suburbs? The second: what are the prospects for creating a greater sense of community in subsectors of the region, if not at the metropolitan level? The first question is easier to answer, because so much source material exists about metropolitan Detroit's lines of division. The second question, more intimidating, we will try to answer only partly. Small geographic communities characterized by diversity of race and ethnicity can, under certain circumstances, survive, and we will describe one such locality. But only a few regional initiatives have the potential to make substantive changes. It is not yet clear whether metropolitan Detroit can become a diverse, mutually supportive community.

COMMUNITY AND PROPINQUITY

The German scholar Tonnies characterized community as the association, based on "positive mutual affirmation" between human beings (Tonnies 2001, p. 17), a definition that still rings true. But he distinguished between two types of association, *Gemeinschaft,* and *Gesellschaft*. Although he first published his treatise in 1887, and sociologists and other scholars have since advanced this subject through exploration of phenomena such as social capital (Putnam 2000), Tonnies's terminology is still in use, and these concepts offer a way to start thinking about this subject. By *Gemeinschaft,* he meant community in the sense of close ties that would be expected among family members and residents of small villages, and in which the individual valued the interests of the association higher than personal interests. Tonnies characterized *Gemeinschaft* as the bond one might find between biological units, such as a mother and child, a married couple, or other kinship groups. Associated with such relationships would be clear ideas about authority, obligation, obedience, respect, and mutual amity, which he saw as a form of morality and connected with religious sensibilities as well as humanistic values.

Tonnies recognized that community could also develop from a sense of place, as in a village, when people live in close proximity to one another. "This in turn becomes community of *spirit,* working together for the same end and purpose. Community of place is what holds life together on a physical level, just as community of spirit is the binding link on the level of conscious thought" (Tonnies 2001, p. 27). A neighborhood could have the same characteristics as a village; proximity could "cause the people to meet and get used to each other and to develop intimate acquaintance" (Tonnies 2001, p. 28). He saw friendship as a part of *Gemeinschaft,* but noted that friendship "grows most easily where people share the same or a similar calling or craft. But such a tie must be formed and fostered through easy and frequent meeting, which is most likely to happen within the *town*" (Tonnies 2001, p. 29, emphasis in the original translation).

Tonnies's concept of *Gesellschaft,* on the other hand, was associations based largely on mechanical forms of contact, summarized in the word "society". Lacking the close, transcending loyalties and bonds one might find in *Gemeinschaft, Gesellschaft* refers to a group of people living in proximity but "without being essentially united—indeed, on the contrary, they are . . . essentially detached" (Tonnies 2001, p. 52). In such a context, "everyone is out for himself alone and living in a state of tension against everyone else" (p. 52). Although his examples referred to economic relationships, he implied that atomized relationships characterize the larger social order as well. Legal systems try to keep the peace in a situation that is largely disunited, but "the core of social existence and social purpose consists of concord, custom and religion" (p. 248). Although Tonnies based his ideas of *Gemeinschaft* on the small-scale realities of families, villages, and towns, he made a plea for cultivating these values at a higher geographic level: "*national character* and its *culture* are far better preserved by the order and way of life of *Gemeinschaft*" (p. 249). This leap in scale allows us to think about this concept at the level of the metropolitan region, as well.

The shift of these concepts to modern times has not been smooth. In the early to middle twentieth century, some speculated that urbanization associated with industrialization destroyed place-based *Gemeinschaft* because increasing concentrations of people jeopardized human bonding. Chicago sociologist Louis Wirth (1939) argued that urbanization in industrial cities led to atomization, creating a system of social disorganization and psychological stress. Even champions of cities such as Lewis Mumford, and most certainly proponents of modified decentralization such as Ebenezer Howard and Frank Lloyd Wright, assumed that large industrial cities were antithetical to optimal social organization (Fishman 2012). The work of sociologists such as Herb Gans, who uncovered viable *Gemeinschaft* communities in Boston neighborhoods that were slated for slum clearance (Gans 1962), and of urbanologists such as Jane Jacobs, who championed community life in city neighborhoods with diverse street life such as Greenwich Village, New York City (Jacobs 1961), showed that life in central cities was not necessarily at variance with the idea of social community. Yet even as they wrote, many such communities were already disintegrating because of suburbanization. Clearance-based redevelopment and highway construction further obliterated many neighborhood-based communities resembling those described by these authors.

In addition, technology helped change urban community life. Although decentralization dated back to the streetcar era, and federal subsidies further spurred suburbanization, twentieth-century communications technology raised the level of disaggregation to new heights. In 1963 Melvin Webber published an influential book chapter, "Order in Diversity: Community without Propinquity," a title that we have adapted for the purposes of this chapter. Webber argued that people no longer needed to live close to one another in order to develop community. In fact, he suggested that the traditional city was becoming outdated because transportation and communication systems were obliterating the constraints of space, allowing people, geographically distant, to connect with each other without needing central cities (Webber 1963).

Since Webber published that chapter, enhanced communication technology has made propinquity even less necessary for social connections. Telephones, postal mail, and fax machines morphed into e-mail, cell phones, online chat rooms and blogs, computer-based social networks, and other means of instant contact. As noted by communication specialist Calhoun, however, many "virtual communities" are pale reflections of true community (Calhoun 1998). In terms of social complexity, they fall far short of the myriad functions of support, identity, and bonding that space-based communities can serve. Calhoun was particularly concerned about the loss of the urban public sphere, which he saw as historically necessary for public life and functional societies, a concern expressed by other authors as well (Sennett 1977). Calhoun suggested that exposure to different people, in person—through association in informal settings such as public festivals, churches, markets, and coffeehouses—is necessary for a functional society. He argued as well that "democracy must depend also on the kind of public life which historically has flourished in cities . . . as the outgrowth of social practices which continually brought different sorts of people into contact with each other and which gave them adequate bases for understanding each other and managing boundary-crossing relations" (Calhoun 1998, p. 391.) Electronic tools, in this view, can foster connections in ways never before imagined, but could never be a substitute for the richer interactions described by Calhoun.

FRAGMENTED DETROIT

Tonnies's description of *Gesellschaft* sounds remarkably similar to the current Detroit region: decentralized and atomized. Islands of space-based or space-reinforced community—strong neighborhoods and tightly knit villages or small cities—do exist here and there. Some places function periodically in the way Calhoun described: as inclusive of public spheres, filled with different associations and opportunities for varied in-person connections, in venues ranging from coffee shops to busy city streets and plazas. However, in general, residents of the Detroit region connect with difficulty across political, racial, and social barriers. From the regional perspective, if the political entities were people, Tonnies—who counseled that even nations should cultivate social bonds—might characterize them as atomized: "everyone is out for himself alone and living in a state of tension against everyone else." Although some cooperation exists among local governments and people, the overall picture is one of fragmentation.

A number of authors have explained these disconnections with regards to race. Sugrue (1996) described the role of white homeowners' associations and labor unions in fomenting racial discrimination and division in the region, and Freund (2007) explored the mindset of suburban Detroiters concerning real estate and racial change. Reynolds Farley, in *Detroit Divided* (Farley, Danziger, and Holzer 2000), showed that many Detroit-area whites avoided residential integration. Farley's decades-spanning research, based first in the 1970s on pictograms of hypothetical neighborhoods and most recently on videos shown to respondents of different races (Krysan, Cooper, Farley, and Forman 2009), showed that many white residents were unwilling to live in mixed black and white neighborhoods regardless of black families' income levels. Even though such unwillingness abated over time, its persistence remained a prime factor in the continued high racial segregation of the region. Thomas (2013) described urban renewal efforts to eliminate "slums" and protect key anchors, such as the CBD, Detroit Medical Center, and Wayne State University. Simultaneously, Thomas documented, city government failed to protect black residents' rights and to stabilize Detroit neighborhoods experiencing racial transition. Efforts since the 1960s to build interracial cooperation in the region have been omnipresent but only partially successful (Darden and Thomas 2013). All of these sources, and more, draw a picture of a region marked by historic race-related battles in the central city and in various suburban municipalities, in spite of gradual racial integration of those suburbs in recent years.

Divisions by political jurisdiction and socioeconomic status are important factors. Rusk (1995) revealed that Detroit metropolitan area has over 300 tax-levying units of government, a high degree of disaggregation compared to other metropolitan areas of comparable size. Orfield and Luce, in a report significantly subtitled "A Regional Agenda for Community and Prosperity in Michigan" (2003), suggested that many suburban localities were suffering because of the demands of providing municipal services amidst continual sprawl. Although this report showed that Detroit had a lower tax base and higher levels of poverty than many other municipalities in the region, it also showed that many suburbs were at risk for distress in terms of tax base or proportions of children in poverty. Southeast Michigan municipalities in distress or at risk included Highland Park, Hamtramck, River Rouge, Ecorse, and just about every municipality touching Detroit city boundaries, as well as exurban townships and small detached cities such as Adrian, Pontiac, Monroe, and Ypsilanti. The 2003 report pointed out the importance of sharing of resources in inner-ring suburbs, and it cited successful efforts to share regional tax base in the Minnesota twin cities of Minneapolis and St. Paul. This report had little visible effect, but the post-2007 economic downturn highlighted its prescience, as many small municipalities and school districts saw their tax revenues dry up as their expenses increased.

Both political and legislative barriers blocked necessary regional cooperation. Jacobs (2009) described the difficulties facing any efforts to overcome parochialism, showing that political fragmentation in metropolitan Detroit is embedded. He pointed to the stark contrasts between metropolitan Detroit and metropolitan Toronto in numbers of municipalities: metropolitan Detroit has more than ten times the number of local units of government. He reviewed the specific Michigan legislative acts that allowed the establishment of new cities with as few as 750 inhabitants and of homeland villages with only 150 people, as well as the high number of charter townships that state legislation enabled. His close comparison of these two metropolitan areas revealed that Detroit's fragmented system has caused many of its planning and economic development problems.

Boyle and Mohammed (2007) wrote about the fractured local government system in Michigan, discussing failed attempts to contain urban

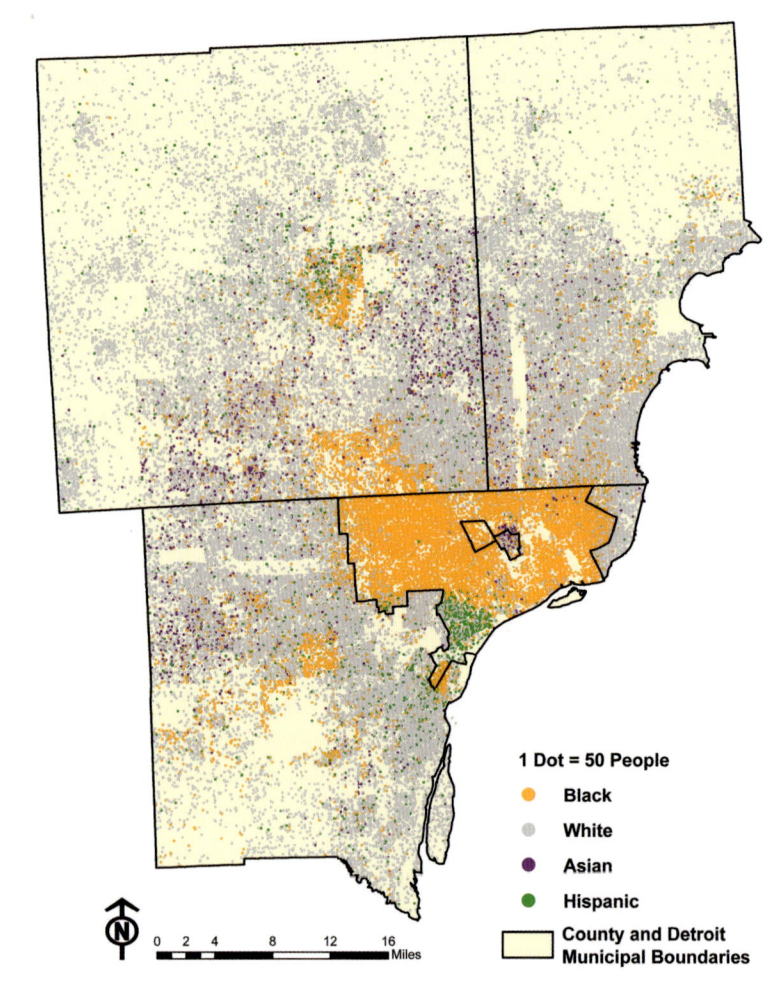

FIGURE 9.1 Dot density map of racial distribution in the Detroit tri-county area. Source: Data from U.S. Census Bureau, 2010. (Terra Reed, Map Editor)

(SEMCOG) and cooperative efforts led by the Michigan Suburbs Alliance. In their account of numerous missteps, these efforts and others largely failed to enhance regional cooperation because of political constraints and uneven commitment.

Figure 9.1 shows one illustration of the results. This particular map shows the political fragmentation and racial division in the three counties of Wayne, Oakland, and Macomb in 2010, but we could have presented a series of such maps to show income or educational levels; ethnicity; employment; and various indicators such as home ownership, age of housing, or tax base. Maps of larger portions of the region, including up to ten counties, show similar divisions for such variables. Because of the history of this region, we know that the apparent clustering of blacks is not due to voluntary action, and that they actually prefer mixed-race neighborhoods (Charles 2003; Farley, Danziger, and Holzer 2000). This is not necessarily the situation with other groups; for reasons of language, culture, and mutual support, many ethnic groups have deliberately formed geographically based ethnic enclaves.

Uneven distribution leads to differences in life-long opportunities for residents living in one municipality as opposed to another—a problem in several parts of the metropolis. Consider six different municipalities in metropolitan Detroit: Pontiac, Auburn Hills, and Bloomfield Township in Oakland County; and Detroit, Hamtramck, and Highland Park in Wayne County. Oakland County is relatively wealthy, with a median family income of $84,800, whereas Wayne County is less wealthy, with a median family income of $52,946 (U.S. Bureau of the Census 2010). Yet in Oakland County, Pontiac—a city that is much smaller than Detroit—echoes many of Detroit's difficulties, with a high level of individual poverty. Wayne County includes within its boundaries two suburbs (each surrounded completely by the city of Detroit): Highland Park and Hamtramck, both of which are experiencing some degree of distress. Yet, in

sprawl. They cited state-led efforts such as the bipartisan Michigan Land-Use Leadership Council, formed in 2002, which issued a report with fairly weak legislative recommendations (Thomas 2009), as well as regional planning initiatives such as Southeast Michigan Council of Governments

	OAKLAND COUNTY			WAYNE COUNTY		
	Auburn Hills/ Pontiac Township	Pontiac	Bloomfield Township	Detroit	Highland Park	Hamtramck
Population, 2000	21,412	59,515	41,070	713,777	11,1176	22,423
Population change percentage, 2000–10	7.9	−10.3	−4.5	−25.0	−29.7	−2.4
Population, 1950	6,210	73,681	3,851	1,849,568	46,393	43,555
Population change percentage, 1950–2010	244.8	−19.2	966.5	−61.4	−74.6	−48.5

TABLE 9.1 Population size and change for six metropolitan Detroit municipalities. *Source: Data from U.S. Census Bureau, 2010.*

some ways, Hamtramck neighborhoods have survived whereas Highland Park's have faltered. See Table 9.1 for a summary of population numbers for these six cities. Table 9.2 shows racial and poverty characteristics, which are also mapped in Figure 9.2.

The tables raise immediate questions. Starting with Oakland County, Auburn Hills and Bloomfield Township have grown considerably since the 1950s, although Bloomfield Township lost population between 2000 and 2010 (Table 9.1). Pontiac, the historic small central city in that county, has more people in poverty than its neighboring municipalities (Table 9.2). It also lost population, but not at rates as high as Detroit. Pontiac has faced numerous problems, including major diminishing of the economic importance of the Pontiac Silverdome when the Detroit Lions left it and moved to a new Detroit stadium in 2002. It also lost its namesake car brand and General Motors (GM) plant in 2009, saw official unemployment rise to 25 percent in 2009, and lost both city jobs and municipal services after the state appointed an emergency financial manager (Weigel 2011). Population dropped 10.3 percent between 2000 and 2010. Why has Pontiac faltered? Why has the population continued to grow in suburban Auburn Hills, while it has not in Bloomfield Township?

Wayne County presents bigger questions (see Tables 9.1 and 9.2). All three Wayne County communities selected had high poverty rates. Wayne County's Highland Park and Hamtramck, two conterminous small cities of approximately the same geographic size, had close to the same number of people in 1950. Both have lost population since then, but why was population loss relatively minor in Hamtramck from 2000 to 2010 but quite high in Highland Park? And what characteristics of inner-city Hamtramck attracted or kept whites and foreign-born residents, not present in great numbers in Highland Park, a city of similar size and location?

The fortunes of different municipalities within the same county and region can vary greatly. Oakland County's municipalities vary in part because of historical battles over desegregation. In the small central city of Pontiac, a federal court in 1970 ordered racial desegregation of the school

Percentages	OAKLAND COUNTY			WAYNE COUNTY		
	Auburn Hills/Pontiac Township	Pontiac	Bloomfield Township	Detroit	Highland Park	Hamtramck
Whites, 2010	66.3	34.4	82.3	10.6	3.2	53.6
Blacks, 2010	18.5	52.1	6.7	82.7	93.6	19.3
Asians, 2010	8.9	2.3	7.2	1.1	0.4	21.5
Hispanics, 2010	7.8	16.5	1.8	6.8	1.3	1.5
Foreign-born residents, 2010	14.9	8.1	13.6	6.5	1.2	42.3
People in poverty, 2005–09	11.3	28.0	3.3	33.2	42.5	38.4

TABLE 9.2 Racial and poverty characteristics for six metropolitan Detroit municipalities
Sources: Data from U.S. Census Bureau, 2010; and American Community Survey for 2005–09 estimates.

system through busing, leading to an enormous public uproar among whites and a spate of marches, demonstrations, and bus burnings. Until that time, black students and their families had remained segregated in the southern part of the city. The busing decree led to accelerated exodus by white families (Zacharias 1997). The repercussions were broader than this, however. What is now a city known as Auburn Hills was basically rural, suburban Pontiac Township in the 1970s, but in 1983 residents created Auburn Hills in order to avoid annexation by the city of Pontiac. Auburn Hills moved quickly to become an economic powerhouse. In the middle of the 1980s Auburn Hills attempted to annex land outside of the Pontiac school district, because two-thirds of its territory fell within the largely black Pontiac school district, and the city was having trouble attracting new residents. Auburn Hills planned to use the annexed land to attract new residential subdivisions while getting around court-ordered busing in those areas of the city falling within Pontiac's school district (DiGaetano and Klemanski 1991).

Auburn Hills did not depend on residential growth, however. It aimed to attract economic development to its vacant land, using the political backing of a local pro-growth coalition, which included leaders of tech-savvy Oakland University. Between 1984 and 1988, Auburn Hills land dedicated to commercial, office, or industrial use rose from 6.6 percent to 16 percent, while residential land use remained steady (DiGaetano and Klemanski 1991). By 2008, commercial, office, and industrial use took up fully 29.8 percent of the city's land (Oakland County, 2013). One of the most visible buildings constructed was the Auburn Hills Palace, opened in 1988 as home to the Detroit Pistons basketball team, but municipal efforts also attracted Oakland Technology Park and Chrysler's world headquarters as well as other industrial parks,

GM facilities, hotels, electronic firms, and various retail businesses. The city-led transformation was so astonishing and uncontested locally that one research team argued, using urban regime analysis as their theoretical basis, that the city illustrated a new type of suburban political economy, dedicated not to racial or class exclusion but rather to economic growth (DiGaetano and Klemanski 1991). Oakland County's Bloomfield Township, largely residential and home to a professional class of workers and five golf courses, had no comparable economic base or growth agenda but survived quite well as an upper-income suburb.

In a spread of effects, Chrysler abandoned Wayne County's city of Highland Park in order to move to suburban Auburn Hills, into a modernist building complex largely completed in 1991 and fully occupied a few years later. The city of Highland Park has never recovered from this blow, and, as Table 9.1 shows, its rate of population decline from 2000 to 2010 exceeded Detroit's.

Highland Park had long suffered from changes in the automobile industry. The city, 2.9 square miles of land embedded within the city of Detroit, nestled next to the similarly embedded Hamtramck, existed in large part because of the automobile industry; Henry Ford built a factory there in 1907–08 when his operations outgrew his original city of Detroit facilities. Residents incorporated Highland Park as a city in 1918 and they resisted subsequent attempts by the surrounding Detroit to annex it because the smaller city had exceptional public services and was "a desirable place to live" (City of Highland Park 2010, p. 6). The number of Ford jobs in Highland Park reached 36,000 by 1916, a significant number for a city that had 46,499 people in 1920. Unfortunately for Highland Park, Henry Ford started building the suburban River Rouge plant in the city of Dearborn in 1919, and he transferred production there in 1926 (City of Highland Park 2010, p. 5). At about the same time, in 1925, Chrysler established assembly operations as well as its world headquarters in Highland Park. Chrysler stayed there until it began its move to Auburn Hills in the

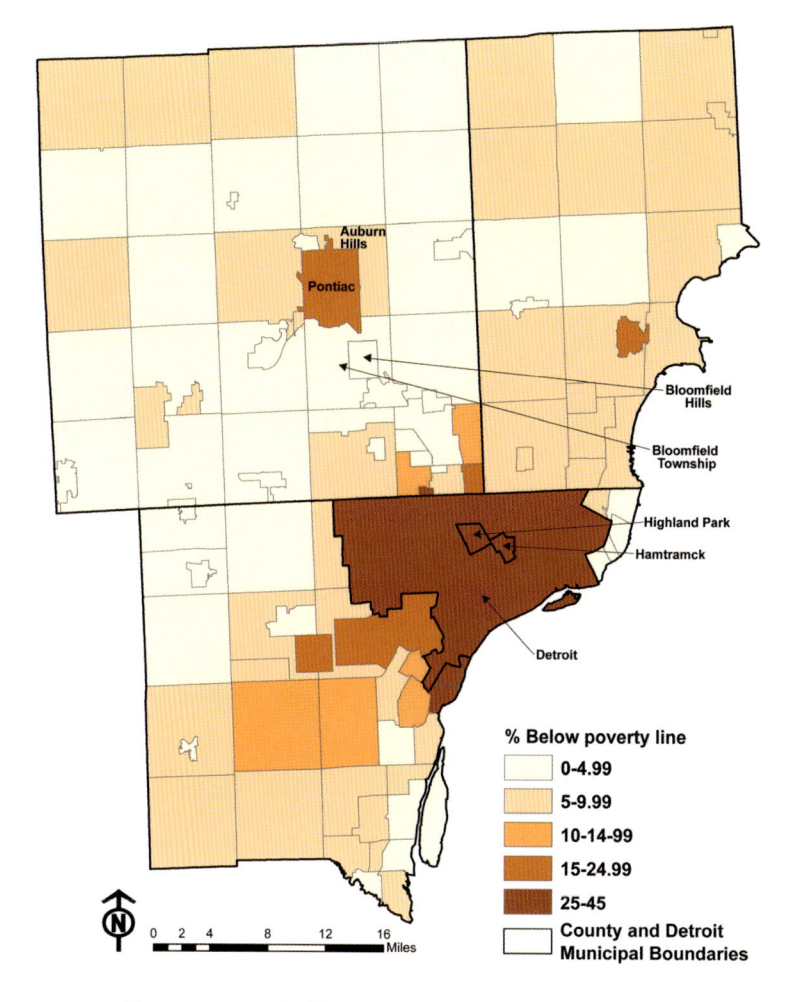

FIGURE 9.2 Poverty rates in the Detroit tri-county area.
Sources: Data from American Community Survey, 2005–09; U.S. Census Bureau, 2010. (Terra Reed and Michael Vos, Map Editors)

1980s, and this time no automobile company came to Highland Park to take its place. Chrysler took 5,000 jobs from the city in 1991 and 4,500 in 1992 (City of Highland Park 2010). Even before then, Highland Park had become a largely black city with diminished employment opportunities and a high poverty rate.

The state had passed legislation that sought to keep municipalities from raiding each other with tax abatements, but this had limited effectiveness. Chrysler paid Highland Park $44 million, the last payment arriving in 1993, so that Highland Park would grant Chrysler the exemption that it needed, according to state provisions, to accept Auburn Hills's offer of industrial tax abatement. Nevertheless, Highland Park experienced profound fiscal distress once the compensation payments from Chrysler ran out. The state appointed an emergency financial manager for Highland Park from 2001 to 2009, which led to the closing of countless public facilities and even less confidence in the city's future. Its 2010 plan noted that only 6.1 percent of local residents had a college degree, compared to 11.5 percent in Hamtramck and 17.2 percent in Wayne County. Hamtramck also had higher household income, higher family income, and less poverty than Highland Park.

Why did Hamtramck experience less population loss from 2000 to 2010 than Highland Park (and, by implication, than Detroit)? The two cities sit within the larger body of Detroit like small, conjoined twins, un-annexed progeny, each of them less than three square miles in area and Hamtramck barely more than two. In states with different annexation or incorporation laws, each would now exist as two or three Detroit neighborhoods instead of municipalities. Both have industrial histories, but in many ways Highland Park had certain advantages over Hamtramck, because of the presence of the Ford factory and then Chrysler's world headquarters; GM also had a presence in Hamtramck, but not quite as large during its developmental years. Hamtramck has contained mostly working-class people throughout its history, unlike Highland Park, where company executives built large brick homes. Hamtramck too has suffered fiscal distress and required an emergency financial manager for six years beginning in 2000, with major financial crises in 2011 and 2012 when the state cut revenue-sharing funds and GM and home-owner property tax revenues dropped (*Huffpost Detroit* 2012; Schimmel 2005). Yet it has retained larger shares of population and a semblance of community.

One way to look at Hamtramck's relative cohesion is simply to credit the impact of the automobile industry. In the early 1980s, a few years before Highland Park bid goodbye to Chrysler, GM negotiated with Detroit and Hamtramck to construct a new GM Detroit-Hamtramck assembly plant. The modern assembly plant, sited on the border between Detroit and Hamtramck, would supposedly put 6,000 people to work. (Actual direct employment figures varied but were usually much lower, depending on production and number of shifts.). The state passed special legislation that Detroit used to acquire the necessary properties more quickly than usual. Both cities applied for federal grants in order to entice GM to stay in the central portion of the region, and officials from both municipalities worked together with GM and with state government in order to build the plant and related infrastructure (Jones and Bachelor 1993). As this plant has picked up new car models and stayed in operation, it has been a major boon for Hamtramck. And so the answer to the question of why Hamtramck's population numbers remained relatively stable could simply be the continued presence of a large automobile assembly plant, albeit with faltering GM tax revenues in some years.

Another possible way to look at Hamtramck is to consider its history and social makeup as plausible factors in its relative ability to hold population. For much of its history, Hamtramck was a favored locale for Polish immigrants who came to the Detroit region to work in the automobile industry. During World War II, between 35 to 40 percent of workers at Hamtramck's Chevrolet Gear and Axle plant were of Polish descent. By 1970, much of the Polish population living in Hamtramck had moved to the suburbs, but many local Polish residents, businesses, and churches remained in the city. Interviews suggested that Polish workers involved in labor unions had strong religious affiliation, especially with the Catholic Church, which had a strong presence in Hamtramck, and that factory work was available for able-bodied Polish males. In the early 1980s, many laid-off auto workers in the Detroit area left for cities in the Sunbelt, but very few Polish-American workers left the region. The major reasons given during interviews included their high status as skilled workers and their desire to stay close to family, friends, and Polish people (Pilling 1990). Hamtramck had the restaurants, bakeries, churches, festivals, and other characteristics befitting a Polish enclave serving Polish auto workers and their families. Several nearby Detroit neighborhoods, quite similar in overall housing and neighborhood structure but located within the city of Detroit, lost population and did not have or retain these cultural amenities. This suggests that Hamtramck residents valued the local control of their small municipality.

Although it is difficult to compare racial and ethnic categories over time, because of changing definitions (Grieco and Cassidy, 2001), one source suggests that people of Polish origin made up 53 percent of Hamtramck's population in 1990 (Perkins 2010). By 2000, U.S. Census Bureau estimates showed that only 23 percent of the total population had Polish ancestry; the next largest group was Arab, at 9 percent. Hamtramck still received immigrant populations, however; 41 percent of its residents were foreign born, and three-fourths of those had arrived during the 1990s. The five-year estimates for 2006–10 showed that people with Polish ancestry had fallen to 20 percent of Hamtramck's population, and those of Arab ancestry had increased to 15 percent. Yet the proportion of residents who were foreign born remained the same, 41 percent, with a third of these having arrived in the previous ten years (U.S. Bureau of the Census 2000, 2010). Clearly Hamtramck still serves as a haven for recent immigrants, though they come from different parts of the world than before.

The U.S. Census characterizes people of Arab ancestry as white (Grieco and Cassidy 2001). This may partially answer the question of Hamtramck's relatively high proportion of whites in 2010 compared to Detroit or Highland Park, as noted in Table 9.2. But in addition to Polish and Arab residents, it also had people of Albanian, Dutch, English, German, Irish, Ukrainian, and Yugoslavian ancestry, as well as 19 percent blacks/African Americans, creating a polyglot of peoples. Its smallness and autonomy, along with its industrial base, seem to be parts of the answer to the puzzle of its relative survival. In an era when the ability to attract immigrants is important for localities (Florida 2004; New Economy Initiative of Southeast Michigan 2010), this small municipality offers instructive lessons about community and survival in the global economy.

REVISIONING COMMUNITY WITH PROPINQUITY

It is difficult to discuss community in the context of the Detroit region, because of its fragmentation and disunity. And yet certain places and organizations offer insights into the possibilities of supporting community. Hamtramck is small in geographic size and yet retains a sense of propinquity, or nearness, in striking contrast to the region's low-density suburbs, and, in its emptiest areas, low-density Detroit. Hamtramck's housing is modest but affordable for immigrants and native-born people as well. Its streets are reminiscent of working-class Detroit neighborhoods from the 1950s or the 1970s: the dense housing stock is similar, as are the main commercial strips. Hamtramck knows poverty, but much of this is the poverty of the newly arrived. Hamtramck is an important example not because it is a unified ethnic enclave, a village of homogeneous people such as one might find in rural societies, but rather because it is not. The considerable diversity that now characterizes the small city has led to conflicts that local residents have apparently managed to overcome.

For example, consider Hamtramck's debates over religion and values. The once heavily Catholic city now hosts people from Pakistan, Yemen, Bosnia, and Bangladesh, many of them Muslim or of other religious traditions.

In 2003, the al-Islah Islamic Center requested the city government's permission to amplify its mosque's five-time-a-day call to prayers, causing some annoyed protests from non-Muslim neighbors, but in the end a new noise ordinance regulated both calls to prayer and church bells (Kiser and Lubman, 2008). Five years later, some Hamtramck citizens supported a Human Rights Ordinance protecting alternative sexual orientations, a "liberal" cause. Conflict emerged when the local Muslim community refused to support the ordinance and formed oppositional alliances with Christian conservatives. This action outraged ordinance supporters, who had in many cases supported Muslims in their fight for amplified calls to prayer. But that outrage revealed lack of understanding of a people who saw themselves as Muslims rather than liberals or conservatives. In the end, the alliances shifted, but the parties reached an acceptable compromise (Perkins 2010). The give and take, even though it took place in heated rallies, was a great example of democracy in action in the public sphere. The scenario helps us recall Calhoun (1998), who suggested that interaction and debate are necessary for modern communities, and that density and contact with diverse peoples are essential ingredients. Complete separation into sanitized enclaves or subdivisions cannot generate the richness of culture now apparent in this small city.

The city of Detroit has neighborhood enclaves rich in diversity and heritage as well. These are embattled, spread apart, and not always acknowledged in official documents, but they do exist. Other affinity groupings range from block clubs (clusters of a few houses) to well-organized larger neighborhoods with fully functional community development corporations, to gardeners' networks and small-business associations. The rest of the region also has small, dense communities, bonded by ties of geography and perhaps culture or friendship, as in the older inner-ring suburbs. It is important to find these communities, support them, analyze them, and replicate them in any way possible. At times this replication will not be possible—having no jobs, few services, and no connectivity is a reality for many of these areas—but at times it might, as in the simple act of forming block clubs and fighting for attainable goals anchored by community assets.

Building any sense of community, cooperation, and mutual responsibility in the region as a whole, however, will continue to be a major struggle. Little progress in cooperation has taken place since Orfield and Luce wrote their *Michigan Metropatterns* report (2003). One book (Darden and Thomas 2013) offers a historical narrative of such efforts related to race relations; these range from the corporate sector, which came together to form the organization New Detroit, to faith-based organizations such as Focus: HOPE, which has created a food distribution program, revolutionized skilled-job training in the area, and supported neighborhood preservation as focal points for interracial cooperation. Other notable initiatives mentioned in the book are the Metropolitan Organization Strategy Enabling Strength (MOSES), the Michigan Roundtable for Diversity and Inclusion, the Michigan Suburbs Alliance, and a series of annual conferences on racial unity sponsored by the Baha'i religious community (Darden and Thomas 2013). But for every story of efforts to build linkages, we can recount a story of efforts to tear them down.

THE POSSIBILITIES

And yet it is important to think about potential. What might this be, in this context? No easy answer exists, and the long-hoped-for regional consciousness or tangible resource-sharing efforts apparent in metropolitan areas such as Toronto and Minneapolis/St. Paul, imperfect as these surely are, will not emerge soon in metropolitan Detroit. It is important to applaud the various efforts of the organizations that are struggling to build a regional identity or sphere of cooperation, and yet at the same time recognize that their task is daunting. In an era when state government fully enables local governments to act as atomized, self-interested entities, and when localities can screen new residents by socioeconomic status if not race or ethnicity, it is difficult to envision enhanced cooperation for anything more than surface conditions. However, several areas of endeavor could encourage enhanced cooperation in metropolitan Detroit.

Regional Transit

A number of people have worked for many years to promote improved regional transportation as a unified effort in metropolitan Detroit. Several efforts in the past to create a regional rail system faltered because of lack of coordination and cooperation between the municipalities and counties in the area. The most notable was a project that began in the mid-1970s. A plan that was supposed to make the downtown Detroit People Mover (a monorail system completed during Mayor Young's administration) the terminus of a complete system became instead a closed 2.9-mile loop that did not open until 1987 (Tadi and Dutta 1998).

SEMCOG continued to work on regional transportation issues by including these in its regional transportation plans. Its Regional Transit Coordinating Council (RTCC), for example, issued a 2008 report that offered a sensible array of strategies for regional transit in the area, including enhanced or arterial rapid transit (buses),[1] light rail, and commuter rail, all implemented in phases. Figure 9.3 shows the components this group anticipated coming into place by 2021–25. But it is hard to see the results of any such planning.

In 2011 local business leaders came together to propose and help finance a light rail system along Woodward Avenue. One of the most important outcomes of this discussion was the passage of state legislation, in the fall of 2012, establishing the Regional Transit Authority, which soon published bylaws (Regional Transit Authority 2013). Legislative efforts to establish such an authority had failed twenty-three times before (Helms 2013). Citizen-based groups, most notably Transportation Riders United, had persistently pressured the state legislature to create a regional authority, an effort aided in large part by the U.S.

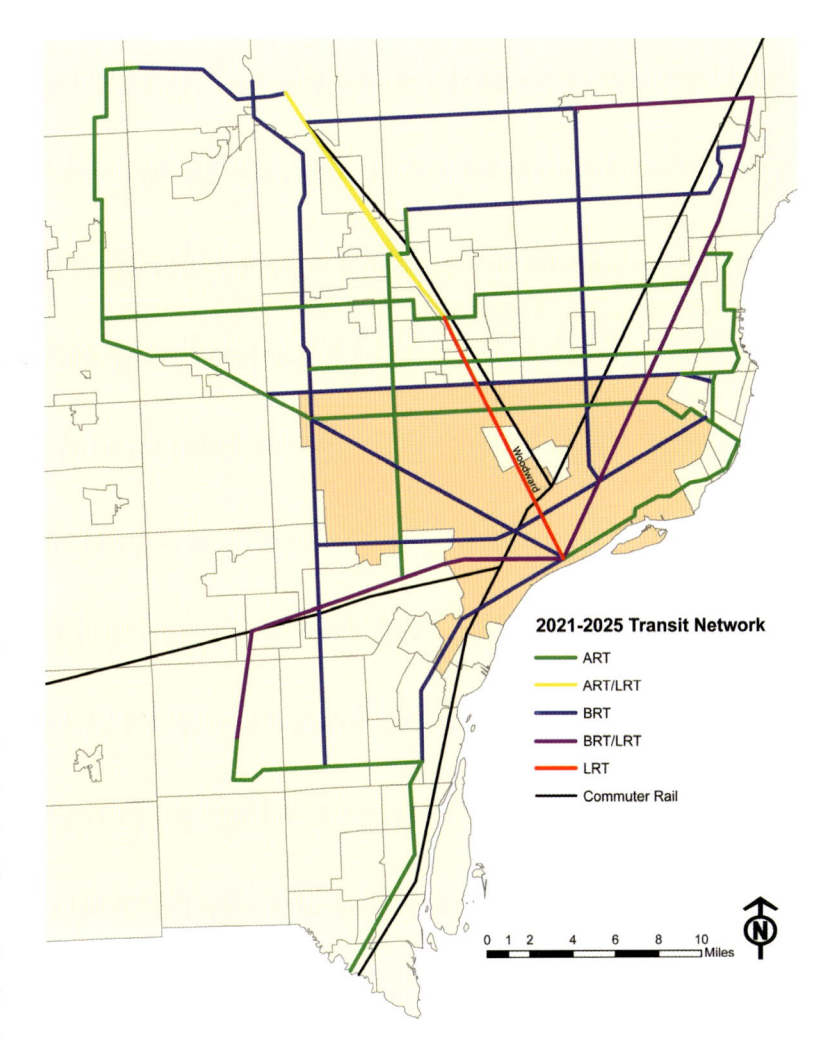

FIGURE 9.3 Proposed rapid transit corridors for 2021–25. This map shows 2008 plans for future transit. The key refers to Arterial Rapid Transit (ART, a few enhancements to buses including traffic light priority), Bus Rapid Transit (BRT, with more enhancements including dedicated transitways), Light Rail Transit (LRT), and Commuter Rail. *Sources: Data from U.S. Census Bureau, 2010; and City of Detroit, 2012. Based on SEMCOG map: Regional Transit Coordinating Council. (2008). Comprehensive Regional Transit Service Plan—Final Report. Detroit, MI: Southeast Michigan Council of Governments, p. 26. (Terra Reed, Map Editor)*

Department of Transportation's secretary, Ray LaHood, who at a critical point refused release of key federal transportation funds without the creation of such an authority. The new authority can help overcome the bifurcation of two different transit bus systems, one serving the suburbs with limited routes in the city, and the other serving the city. This travesty of inefficiency not only left many workers stranded, as discussed in chapter 5, but also created a segmented labor pool that shackled area-wide businesses with inefficiency as well.

Light rail systems, such as planned for a three-mile strip of Woodward Avenue, are only one aspect of potential regional transit improvements, but this component sometimes draws the most attention. Experiences in other cities and metropolitan areas have shown that such systems can fail without critical population density and sizeable operating subsidies. Also, in some metropolitan areas, rail systems have exacerbated class segregation, with professionals riding the light rail and the working class taking the bus. However, in other areas of the country and the world, the transit systems have gradually expanded to serve all classes of people. The task is to meet positive potential and simultaneously to reduce risks.

If the area's Regional Transit Authority can establish a viable regional transportation system, which would take years to build, the potential exists not only to improve accessibility for all but also to tie the region together more closely in physical, economic, and social spheres. The atomization aided by an automobile-dominated metropolis could gradually begin to abate, as could the inaccessibility that certain people, especially low-income workers, have experienced.

Municipal Service Consolidation

Another possible way to enhance regional community building would be to consolidate municipal services and, in some cases, to curtail localities' extension of public services as a check on sprawl. In the stories of Pontiac, Hamtramck, Auburn Hills, and Highland Park, we saw that municipalities in metropolitan Detroit exist in a competitive context that leaves some of them better off than others. Efforts to encourage cooperative service agreements, for example, have been tried in the past, and SEMCOG has long urged enactment of such agreements, as had other organizations, but the results thus far have not been encouraging (Holdsworth 2009; Southeast Michigan Council of Governments 2003).

Especially with recent economic woes, however, many previously prosperous municipalities have become stressed, as Orfield and Luce (2003) warned they would. Many of these stressors are taking years to emerge after the economic crisis of 2007 and beyond. For example, some small townships and municipalities, used to a culture of growth, borrowed money to pay for expensive infrastructure for planned new subdivisions—subdivisions that were never built due to the housing market collapse. Municipal bonds issued or money raised by borrowing against anticipated tax revenues to pay for roads, sewers, and water mains for anticipated new residential areas— now empty of residents— remained as debts. The atomized, individualistic, competitive behavior of area governments left many of these localities in the lurch. Falling tax revenues began to affect increasing numbers of localities as housing values rebounded more slowly than in other parts of the country. Faced with mounting crises, Michigan's Governor Rick Synder signed legislation in 2011 that removed many barriers to service agreements between municipalities in the state, a positive step forward in the movement to offer incentives for localities to share public services.

As it becomes obvious that society cannot continue to support existing segmentation at the scale evident in metropolitan Detroit, it is possible that small-scale consolidation of selected services will become increasingly popular. This would not be as grand as metropolitan consolidation, but rather more modest. Such efforts to encourage a meshing of the region would need to respect autonomy and yet offer municipal services in a way that does not burden regional residents or the state at large. It is ultimately the taxpayers who pick up the bill of municipal favors offered during competitive bidding wars—either through dedicated millages, reduced services, or increased taxes. Taxpayers also eventually pay directly or indirectly for economic losses incurred during fiscal emergencies or bankruptcies, such as Detroit's in 2013, or for the steady loss of viability caused by gradual decline of a region's central cities. Service cooperation and consolidation could help address the needs of obviously stressed places such as Detroit, Highland Park, and Pontiac, but also of less-obviously stressed places such as Oak Park, Hamtramck, and several of Wayne County's downriver suburbs. All of this, of course, would require negotiation and assurances of fair play; Detroit's city leaders rightfully distrust many past efforts to share city resources, for example—a wary attitude born of experience.

Decreased Social Distance

The third possible way to encourage greater regional community is a concept more difficult to describe than regional transportation or municipal service consolidation. The idea is to build on the concept of individual and neighborhood or municipal connections in order to more closely tie the people in the region to each other. Two primary strategies could help with this: one using public space and the other more private. Fragments of both strategies are already in place.

The public space strategy builds on Calhoun's idea but ties back as well to older theories about the role of urban space, which is, in part, to bring disparate people together. Several projects in the city of Detroit have become grounds for public encounters that would not take place in the private sphere. The most obvious of such places would be the hockey, football, and baseball arena and stadia, event venues in downtown Detroit that draw people from throughout the region, or the basketball arena in Auburn Hills. For the downtown Detroit venues, at least, the audience often includes large concentrations of suburbanites, identifiable by skin color. (It is unlikely that all whites living in the city choose to come out just for such events.) Venues where it is possible to see large concentrations of suburban Detroiters include musical venues such as the Detroit Opera House (depending on the production for that night). Such gatherings may take place because of genuine affection for particular sports or venues, but they also occur because concentrations of like-minded audience members bring feelings of security or camaraderie.

Other public spaces, some not so well established, are gradually coming into being; these allow for different kinds of encounters. One that is both established and new is Detroit Eastern Market, patronized by city and suburban dwellers alike and becoming increasingly popular in the wake of substantial rehabilitation. More intimate settings include the Dequindre Cut, the pedestrian/bikeway that links the riverfront with the area just south of the Detroit Eastern Market; the riverfront, an increasingly popular summer gathering place enhanced by the assiduous efforts of the Detroit Riverfront Conservancy; and Campus Martius Park, a downtown center of winter recreation that also serves as a haven for office workers. Also serving as crossroads, with regional millage support, are the Detroit Institute of Arts and the Detroit Zoo. Particularly since the state government has leased Belle Isle, the potential for historic institutions such as the newly reopened Belle Isle Aquarium is looking more promising. Continuing to seek opportunities to create such gathering places in the region could help to break up the barriers that stand like walls between races, neighborhoods, and localities.

The private strategy is more gossamer: it is reweaving the frayed fabric of the region at the individual, family, neighborhood, and organizational level. This is particularly important to overcome fragments of race and class. As described earlier in this book's introduction, the city lost 25 percent of its population from 2000 to 2010, including 16.5 percent of its black population, suggesting that at long last blacks were abandoning the city as had whites. The other side of that coin, however, is that these blacks were moving to Detroit's suburban areas and helping to break the hold of racial segregation in some of the suburbs, as housing there became more affordable because of the housing crisis. Simultaneously, small groups of whites, especially young adults and professionals, began to move into Detroit in limited numbers. Indices of dissimilarity show that regional racial segregation is still high, but they hide other more promising developments. Other researchers (Holloway, Wright, and Ellis 2011) have begun to measure residential racial diversity in new ways. By their measures, Detroit experienced a decided drop in "low diversity white" neighborhoods from 1990 to 2000 (as did other major metropolitan areas), as well as a small increase in "highly diverse" neighborhoods. Furthermore, in spite of the decreasing numbers of whites in the city overall, the number of young and professional whites moving to areas such as Midtown and the CBD has increased, at times because of company-sponsored incentive programs.

We have already mentioned the organizations credited with working for increased racial cooperation or the plight of the poor, such as MOSES, Focus: HOPE, and Transportation Riders United. Not often mentioned in such discussions on racial unity are the corporate leaders who have seen a good bargain in depressed CBD markets and moved all or a good chunk of their personnel to downtown Detroit. The most visible of these could be Dan Gilbert of Quicken Loans, through the umbrella corporation Rock Ventures, but others have supported such a return as well. Although theirs is a CBD strategy, based undoubtedly on investment goals, this approach also loosens barriers and forces people to encounter each other in new settings, turning the unfamiliar to the more familiar.

Unfortunately, the great American bringer-together of diverse peoples in past ages, the public school system, no longer serves that function in metropolitan Detroit (or in many other places), except in isolated instances. The battle now is to provide some rudimentary education to the children, many of them from low-income backgrounds, ghettoized into failing school systems. The Catholic parochial school system, a historic alternative, has also faltered as parish schools have shut down. The city's Detroit Public Schools has failed in many ways, although the system's call for volunteers in 2010 elicited an overwhelming output of volunteer tutors of all races and income levels from all over the region. Other strategies are also under way; for example, charter schools have grown in number and presence. Looking into the future, we might anticipate that some of the worst of the school-system failures will be mitigated, which would be a major step toward overcoming class barriers.

In the meantime, more purposeful encounters are needed to make personal connections at the level of individual, family, neighborhood, or organization. Some established Detroit neighborhoods serve this purpose internally, particularly the well-organized ones, which orchestrate encounters on several levels. More is needed on a regional basis: families can reach out to other families, individuals can arise as volunteer mentors and tutors, clubs or religious congregations can collaborate across municipal boundaries, organizations can merge people of disparate backgrounds, and corporations can move. If such actions did no more than remove entrenched prejudices, they would serve a purpose. An even more welcome result, however, would be an enhanced connectivity, and hence willingness among the electorate to make the hard decisions needed to improve the region, in areas ranging from public services to governance.

CONCLUSION: A FRAGMENTED REGION WITH POTENTIAL

Modern urbanity does not preclude community, which remains important in geographic space—even in a world filled with modern communication technology that helps us leap across space. Community, as defined here, means positive, mutual affirmation of humans bonded by locality, but can also mean a healthy encounter with strange others in the public sphere, as well as a collection of people who place the good of the whole above the good of the self. Community is not dependent on place, but geographic nearness can help create a special kind of community—in some ways fuller, more reflective of human diversity and potential than electronic linkages alone can become. *Gessellshaft,* the opposite of community, is a situation characterized by atomization; it describes, in many ways, the state of localities in the Detroit region. The region has experienced a high level of exodus from the city of Detroit and from other small cities that were historic urban centers and industrial locales; at the same time, it has endured a building up of multiple political entities largely concerned about their own well-being. Yet strong central cities are essential for the critical mass and centrality necessary for a functional democracy. Diverse peoples negotiating shared space can help create such centrality.

The current state of disunity in the region is long standing and hence entrenched and difficult to change. The two topics of racial division and political fragmentation reveal major fissures in the fabric of the region. Racial division may have abated in recent years—particularly with increasing mobility of black families—but historic patterns and political fragmentation have hardly budged, becoming, if anything, more calcified.

This chapter offered descriptions of Pontiac, Auburn Hills, Bloomfield Township, Highland Park, and Hamtramck to show that the peculiarities of metropolitan Detroit's political fragmentation are not disconnected from racial and socioeconomic inequality. Fragmentation is also strongly connected with economic change. The various movements of the automobile industry affected more than the city of Detroit; they also devastated centralized suburbs such as Highland Park and small detached cities such as Pontiac. Such places have experienced drops in population size, tax base, and employment centers, as have somewhat less stressed places such as Hamtramck. At the same time, competitive suburbs such as Auburn Hills have benefited from their economic development policies, setting up a winner-loser scenario with decisive benefits for winners who are under no obligation to share the spoils of victory with less fortunate localities.

Sprinkling the region are the municipalities left behind, sometimes laboring under the rule of emergency financial managers because they could no longer handle their finances in the face of fiscal collapse. High tax rates, low public services, and inferior schools are characteristic of such places. Not surprisingly, many households move to a more fortunate locale, exacerbating sprawl and increasing the level of fiscal distress in abandoned locales. Those residents who are unable or unwilling to move are left with reduced public services, less desirable residential and retail environments, and impoverished school systems. The true victims, under such circumstances, are the people left behind who do not have the financial and social resources to weather this environment without reduced quality of life.

The story of Hamtramck served as a respite to this composite tale. Here we see the long-yearned-for immigration that has kept so many other central cities afloat in other parts of the country. We also see evidence of negotiation across boundaries of religion, politics, and race, as various nationalities settled into this small city and learned to live together. Yet Hamtramck had an advantage other cities and parts of other cities did not; it managed to keep one large GM assembly plant. Hamtramck is a symbol of diverse urbanity in the modern, globalized world, but it has also experienced fiscal distress and lost population, and remains intact in large part because it serves as an isolated, politically autonomous haven embedded in the body of Detroit.

Three areas of intervention could offer new ways of reconnecting the region. The transportation approach is a tangible, feasible strategy to provide physical linkages. Specific plans already exist that could help to reduce spatial isolation and enhance connections. A second possible approach would be consolidation of municipal services, a simple way to reduce the costs of severe political fragmentation and sprawl. Finally, reducing social distance could assist residents to reengage with the region and overcome historic divisions. This last strategy would actually help the others because, with increased connection and empathy, regional voters' opposition to necessary initiatives could abate considerably.

A future to be hoped for in the region of Detroit is a binding up of the region as a whole: a gargantuan, more prosperous version of Hamtramck, with its affordable but intact neighborhoods, sense of propinquity, minimal or non-existing political barriers, and co-existing polyglot of diverse peoples. Gradually, the holes of vacancy in the region would be filled or put to good use, the connections would strengthen, and the fringes would stabilize.

NOTES

The author offers many thanks to this chapter's map editors, graduate assistants Terra Reed and Michael Vos. Graduate assistants Payton Heins and Pam Schaeffer also assisted with this chapter as they worked with the whole book. Graduate assistant Pete McGrath offered major contributions to this chapter's topic, particularly in helping to identify and collect data concerning the six municipalities, as well as helping to conceptualize how to write, in a new way, about the Detroit metropolitan area.

1. The report referred to Arterial Rapid Transit, which would have certain enhanced features for buses such as traffic signal priority and upgraded bus stops; Bus Rapid Transit, which would include these features plus others such as dedicated transit ways; Light Rail transit, with dedicated rail systems; and commuter rail, specifically from Detroit to Ann Arbor in this report, but possibly for other routes as well in later regional plans.

REFERENCES

Boyle, R., and Mohamed, R. (2007). State growth management, smart growth and urban containment: A review of the US and a study of the heartland. *Journal of Environmental Planning and Management, 50*(5), 677–697.

Calhoun, C. J. (1998). *Social theory and the politics of identity.* Oxford, UK: Blackwell.

Charles, C. Z. (2003). The dynamics of racial residential segregation. *Annual Review of Sociology, 29*(3), 167–207.

City of Highland Park (2010). *Master Plan 2010.* Draft retrieved from: http://www.highlandparkcity.us/GOVERNMENT/DOCS/2010MASTERPLANFINALEDITION.PDF

Darden, J., Hill, R., Thomas, J., and Thomas, R. (1987). *Detroit: Race and Uneven Development.* Philadelphia: Temple University Press.

Darden, J., and Thomas, R. W. (2013). *Detroit: Race riots, racial conflicts, and efforts to bridge the racial divide.* East Lansing: Michigan State University Press.

DiGaetano, A. and Klemanski, J. S. (1991), Restructuring the suburbs: Political economy of economic development in Auburn Hills, Michigan. *Journal of Urban Affairs,* 13: 137–158.

Farley, R., Danziger, S., and Holzer, H. J. (2000). *Detroit divided.* New York, NY: Russell Sage Foundation.

Fishman, R. (2012). Urban utopias in the twentieth century. In S. Fainstein and S. Campbell (Eds.), *Readings in planning theory* (3rd ed., pp. 27–53). Malden, MA: Wiley Blackwell.

Florida, R. L. (2004). *The rise of the creative class: And how it's transforming work, leisure, community and everyday life.* New York, NY: Basic Books.

Freund, D. M. (2007). *Colored property: State policy and white racial politics in suburban America.* Chicago, IL: University of Chicago Press.

Gans, H. (1962). *The urban villagers: Group and class in the life of Italian-Americans.* New York, NY: Free Press of Glencoe.

Glaeser, E. L. (2011). *Triumph of the city: How our greatest invention makes us richer, smarter, greener, healthier, and happier.* New York, NY: Penguin Press.

Grieco, E. M., and Cassidy, R. C. (2001). *Overview of race and Hispanic origin, 2000.* Washington, DC: U.S. Department of Commerce, Economics, and Statistics Administration, U.S. Census Bureau.

Helms, M. (2013, April 11). Transit advocates celebrate as regional authority gets to work. *Detroit Free Press.* Retrieved from www.freep.com/article/20130411/NEWS05/304110082Transit-advocates-celebrate-as-regional-authority-gets-to-work

Holdsworth, A. (2009). Selling stakeholders on interlocal cooperation. Working Group on Interlocal Services Cooperation, Paper 30. Retrieved from http://digitalcommons.wayne.edu/cgi/viewcontent.cgi?article=1031&context=interlocal_coop

Holloway, S. R., Wright, R., and Ellis, M. (2011). The racially fragmented city? Neighborhood racial segregation and diversity jointly considered. *The Professional Geographer, 64,* 63–82.

Huffpost Detroit. (2012, March 8). William Cooper, Hamtramck City Manager, fired as city faces payless paydays. *Huffington Post.* Retrieved from www.huffingtonpost.com/2012/03/08/william-cooper-hamtramck-city-manager-fired-payless-paydays_n_1331797.html

Jacobs, A. J. (2009). Embedded contrasts in race, municipal fragmentation, and planning: Divergent outcomes in Detroit and greater Toronto-Hamilton regions 1990–2000. *Journal of Urban Affairs, 31,* 147–72.

Jacobs, J. (1961). *The death and life of great American cities.* New York, NY: Random House.

Jones, B. D., and Bachelor, L. W. (1993). *The sustaining hand: Community leadership and corporate power.* Lawrence: University Press of Kansas.

Kiser, B. H., and Lubman, D. (2008, January 1). The soundscape of church bells-sound community or culture clash. *The Journal of the Acoustical Society of America, 123*(5), 3807.

Krysan, M., Couper, M. P., Farley, R., and Forman, T. A. (2009, September 1). Does race matter in neighborhood preferences? Results from a video experiment. *American Journal of Sociology, 115*(2), 527–59.

New Economy Initiative of Southeast Michigan. (2010, May 14). *Global Detroit: Short report.* Detroit, MI: New Economy Initiative.

Oakland County (2013). City of Auburn Hills 2013 land use statistics. Retrieved from: http://www.advantageoakland.com/ResearchPortal/Documents/Maps/sum_02.pdf

Orfield, M., and Luce, T. (2003). *Michigan metropatterns: A regional agenda for community and prosperity in Michigan.* Minneapolis, MN: Ameregis.

Perkins, A. (2010, April 1). Negotiating alliances: Muslims, gay rights and the Christian Right in a Polish-American city. *Anthropology Today, 26*(2), 19–24.

Pilling, P. L. (1990, April 1). The response of skilled Polish American automobile workers to job challenges in Hamtramck, Michigan, in the early 1980s. *Polish American Studies, 47*(1), 25–54.

Putnam, R. D. (2000). *Bowling alone: The collapse and revival of American community.* New York, NY: Simon & Schuster.

Regional Transit Authority. (2013). *By-laws of the Regional Transit Authority.* Retrieved from www.semcog.org/uploadedFiles/Programs_and_Projects/Transportation/RTA/BYLAWS%20(RTA)(21083403_2).pdf

Rusk, D. (1995). *Cities without suburbs.* Washington, DC: Woodrow Wilson Center Press. Distributed by Johns Hopkins University Press.

Sassen, S. (1991). *The global city: New York, London, Tokyo.* Princeton, NJ: Princeton University Press.

Schimmel, Jr., R. (2005, October 27). Hamtramck update: Will city thrive without emergency financial manager? *Inside Hamtramck.* Retrieved from www.insidehamtramck.com/2010/12/15/hamtramck-update-will-city-thrive-without-emergency-financial-manager-2005-article

Sennett, R. (1977). *The fall of public man.* New York, NY: Knopf.

Soja, E. W. (2010). *Seeking spatial justice.* Minneapolis: University of Minnesota Press.

Southeast Michigan Council of Governments. (2003, June). *Intergovernmental cooperation: A background paper.* Detroit, MI: SEMCOG.

Sugrue, T. J. (1996). *The origins of the urban crisis: Race and inequality in postwar Detroit.* Princeton, NJ: Princeton University Press.

Tadi, R., and Dutta, U. (1998). Detroit downtown people mover: Ten years after. In W. Sproule, E. Neumann, S. Lynch (Eds.), *Automated people movers VI: Creative access for major activity centers: Proceedings of the sixth international conference: Las Vegas, Nevada, April 9–12* (pp. 134–42). Reston, VA: American Society of Civil Engineers.

Thomas, J. M. (2009). Michigan's urban policies in an era of land use reform and creative-class cities. In R. Jelier and G. Sands (Eds.), *Sustaining Michigan: Metropolitan policies and strategies* (pp. 261–81). East Lansing: Michigan State University Press.

Thomas, J. M. (2013). *Redevelopment and race: Planning a finer city in postwar Detroit* (2nd ed.). Detroit, MI: Wayne State University Press.

Tonnies, F. (2001). *Community and civil society,* edited by Jose Harris, translated by Jose Harris and Margaret Hollis. Cambridge, UK, New York City, NY: Cambridge University Press.

U.S. Bureau of the Census. (2000). 2000 Summary Files 1, generated through Data Driven Detroit

U.S. Bureau of the Census. (2010). 2010 Summary Files 1, generated through Data Driven Detroit.

Webber, M. M. (1963, January 1). Order in diversity: Community without propinquity. In L. Wingo, Jr. (Ed.), *Cities and space* (pp. 23–56). Baltimore, MD: Johns Hopkins Press.

Weigel, D. (2011, November 23). Welcome to Austerityville: Can a technocrat save the Michigan city that democracy failed? *Slate.* Retrieved from www.slate.com/articles/news_and_politics/politics/2011/11/pontiac_mich_can_a_technocrat_succeed_where_democracy_failed_.html

Wirth, L. (1939, July). Urbanism as a way of life. *The American Journal of Sociology, 44*(1), 1–24.

Zacharias, P. (1997, May 4). Irene McCabe and her battle against busing. *Detroit News.* Retrieved from http://apps.detnews.com/apps/history/index.php?id=161

EPILOGUE

Detroit Future City

TONI L. GRIFFIN AND JUNE MANNING THOMAS

After the research and writing of most of the chapters in this book, an extraordinary event occurred in the history of Detroit's plans, necessitating an epilogue. A long-range planning team that had been working since 2010 issued a book-length, heavily illustrated report entitled *Detroit Future City: 2012 Detroit Strategic Framework Plan*, with an electronic version posted at its web page. This report release culminated a highly visible, collaborative initiative within the city.

Because of the considerable foundation support[1] that assisted this planning initiative, the long-range planning team had access to the expertise of numerous specialty consultant firms that generated a large amount of data, analysis, and mapping of current situations. As described in earlier chapters of this book, years passed between maps of Detroit in the past, and these representations were not only episodic but also individualistic. With the *Detroit Future City* project, however, the technology and concentrated expertise available during this process allowed for detailed analysis, mapping, and prescription. Furthermore, this work benefited from cooperation between community partners, public and quasi-public agencies, and private consultants, all vetted in public venues, and a purposeful citizen engagement and public education strategy carried out over a period of many months. This means that the recommendations come not just from a few researchers, but rather from a multi-dimensional strategic planning process.

In that sense, this epilogue differs somewhat from the rest of the book. The purpose of this epilogue is to summarize some of the key aspects of this award-winning[2] document, *Detroit Future City*. It is not an outside analysis or critique of the document or of the process that developed it. It is not an exploration of specific neighborhoods, histories, or urban systems, as are several earlier chapters. Nor is it an institutional or policy analysis.

Rather it is a current narrative, guided by the long-range team's lead planner (Griffin), describing what was unique about the *Detroit Future City* technical team's approach, and summarizing portions of what that project team (under the guidance of its citizen-, government-, and institution-based steering committee) found out and recommended concerning the city's present and future land use and related functions. This epilogue attempts to give some sense of the positive potential for Detroit's future from the vantage point of their findings and that planning process.

THE CHALLENGE

"What will Detroit look like?" After release of the *Detroit Future City* report (*Detroit Future City* 2012), this was often the first question reporters asked the team[3] that developed this document. Perhaps it is fair to assume that a discernible image of the city—some kind of visual representation of Detroit's future city—would emerge after three years of bringing the community together with some of best planners, urban designers, landscape architects, engineers, and economists to be found in Detroit and across the globe. After all, the perception of Detroit's central problem is linked to how it looks—its vacant land, abandoned homes, and relentless organic landscapes that have been taking root where residential life and mass production have ceased to exist. But Detroit's "problem" is about more than just its physical appearance. It is about how its people build and maintain a high quality of life that supports the development of families and young people; such quality of life enhances both the potential to create income and wealth and the ability to maintain community and civic pride. Understanding Detroit's problems involves understanding the social, economic, infrastructural, cultural, environmental, and political systems of Detroit and how these essential networks relate to one another.

Few cities have taken on the challenge of remapping the entire city's image in the context of long-standing population loss and abandonment.

To be sure, locally mandated comprehensive and master plans represent a municipality's intention to guide the physical development of the city, and many cities spend several years updating these important regulatory guides. However, these planning frameworks are often limited and constrained by scope, laws, and political time frames, and they do not involve reshaping the city's image in the context of abandonment. A few exceptions do exist. Within the last decade, Youngstown, Ohio, adopted the nation's first official "shrinking city" land use plan, and New Orleans adopted its first citywide master plan in the wake of sustained losses of people and place. Detroit also adopted and updated its Master Plan of Policies in 2009, but that plan did not offer a full embrace of the "smaller" city, and the city's staff planners had neither the resources nor the mandate to do this. Instead, the plan specified future land use that, for the most part, mirrored past uses. Even if this and Detroit's previous land use plans had addressed issues of vacancy and redefinition of land use, this would not have been enough.

Physical solutions alone are not sufficient at a time when problems with public safety, the quality of public education, access to jobs and health care, and the delivery of basic services threaten residents' quality of life. For this reason, instead of simply recording a typical land use plan for Detroit, a city facing extraordinary circumstances, the scope of work set out for this project was to remap the economic, land use, infrastructure and environmental systems of Detroit. The planning team also drew inspirational lessons from aspects of Daniel Burnham's 1909 *Plan of Chicago*. This may seem odd, because this is a very different era and city and because *Detroit Future City* did not put forward a rendered portrait of the new Motor City as Burnham and his colleagues did for the Windy City. For Burnham, the rendering—a common convention of the City Beautiful movement—helped the business and civic leadership imagine the transformation of the city. But if we look past the iconic paintings of Chicago's reimagined lakeshore and instead survey the entirety of the plan, we will find that Burnham was also very direct about proposing audaciously visionary frameworks for linked open space, revamped transportation networks, and reimagined streets and civic spaces. He wanted to do even more: "It should be clear that Burnham had hopes to change more than the city's face. So-called *'beautification'* was neither the sole nor the prime motivation for his comprehensive city plan: rather the provision of human services and the creation of a more humane environment, in concert with the development of a more convenient and efficient city structure, were his goals." (Schaffer 1993, p. xii.)

The remapping of early twentieth-century Chicago and 2013 Detroit differed in at least three important ways. Firstly, the 1909 plan offered reimaginations of Chicago during a time of beautification and growth, with a strong opportunity to position the city in the global marketplace. Conversely, Detroit's quest was to reclaim its national and global position at a time of population contraction, capital downsizing, and austerity; "making little plans" was the prevailing attitude. Secondly, the *Plan of Chicago* gave attention to economic and cultural concerns by using urban design that combined urban and natural public spaces, connected via transportation corridors. *Detroit Future City* also attends to economic and cultural concerns, but it does this by calling for reform of social as well as spatial systems, particularly those that address the growing challenges of income inequalities and racial segregation. Thirdly, the *Plan of Chicago* is a vision created by the city's business and civic leadership, whereas *Detroit Future City* tapped the voices of many via civic engagement tactics in order to reach the broadest constituency possible. In *Detroit Future City*, planners confronted the needs both to direct and shape what the city "looks like" and to improve how the city meets the daily needs of residents, workers, and visitors. Addressing the issues of place, performance, and quality of life demanded a comprehensive and ambitious scope for citywide transformation; specific to Detroit, the scope also required a confrontation with the city's (and region's) protracted issues of racial and economic disparities, political distrust, and fiscal insolvency.

Detroit Future City is an attempt to reclaim one of America's signature cities. Detroit's role in the American industrial age had a significant influence on the early standard for middle-class urban life, in which a person's hard work could provide a home and automobile in a safe neighborhood with access to high-quality education and amenities. Since the 1950s, that image of place has been on a steady decline. Following the recession of 2008, Detroit has become the poster child for the American city gone wrong. Sixty years of decline have produced a city image dominated by vacancy and disinvestment, conditions that have worsened in spite of sporadic city and federal government efforts to address such conditions (as discussed in chapter 3 and other chapters of this book).

However, despite the vacancy, a fierce civic pride keeps many lifelong Detroiters in the city. Detroit's strong brand identity is luring a new generation of urbanites and entrepreneurs to the city with the hopes of making a high quality of life for themselves. For example, the *7.2 Square Mile* report, commissioned by local civic leaders, documented emerging urban development trends in the downtown and midtown areas and surrounding neighborhoods—unique pockets of the city where commercial diversity and walkability were on the rise (Hudson-Webber Foundation 2013).

Nevertheless, Detroit as a whole is not back to viability, at least in the eyes of a majority of city residents, those who live and work outside the boundaries of the innermost center of the city. Optimism for reviving the traditional model of city life has not yet spread across the entire 139 square miles of the city. The Big Three automobile makers have recovered from their nadir, but the influence of their recovery is no longer shaping the physical form of the city or the quality of life in its neighborhoods as it once did a century ago. A new future is possible for Detroit, but this cannot rely on a single economic sector. It will be necessary to accept that a city of 600,000–700,000 residents (instead of 1.8 million) can still be a vibrant and productive city if more sustainable decisions are made about economic diversity, land use, and neighborhood quality of life. Significant changes must be made to alter land uses and related regulations, as well as to improve operation and investment practices. Detroiters are now recognizing that "business as usual" is no longer feasible, and they are ready to change the city's image of vacancy into an image informed by the new possibilities for productive land use and economic diversity.

DETROIT FUTURE CITY OVERVIEW

The Detroit Works Project (DWP) was launched in 2010; in 2011 it split into two initiatives: a city government-led short-term actions effort and a long-term planning initiative.[4] Overseeing the long-term planning effort was a steering committee appointed by the mayor and composed of twelve civic leaders from business, community, philanthropy, institutions, and government. The Detroit Economic Growth Corporation, a quasi-public agency oversaw the long-term portion of the DWP initiative, including the work of a planning and civic engagement team composed of a distinguished roster of local, national, and international consultants.[5]

The Detroit Works Project, Long-Term Planning initiative (DWPLTP) was a twenty-four-month planning and civic engagement process resulting in the document *Detroit Future City: 2012 Detroit Strategic Framework Plan* [*Detroit Future City*, also known in this epilogue as the Strategic Framework], a comprehensive and action-oriented blueprint for short-term and long-range decision making in several key areas. The Strategic Framework aimed to be (1) aspirational toward a physical vision for the city; (2) action oriented with strategies for new policies and implementation; and (3) accountable with assignment of implementation responsibilities. The DWPLTP process developed and used a careful methodology of gathering, integrating, and synthesizing anecdotal, qualitative, and quantitative data to inform the Strategic Framework's final recommendations. Community experts, including residents and private, public, nonprofit, institutional, and philanthropic stakeholders, along with a technical team and civic engagement team, collaborated to design and implement a series of meetings, allowing the initiative to blend research and data with residents' firsthand experiences, not usually captured in planning efforts of this scale. Together, the Detroit community and planning experts identified important core values, project goals, quality of life components, and imperative actions necessary to transform Detroit's liabilities into assets, and to build on the strengths that exist today in neighborhoods across the city.

Long before the Detroit Works Project, Detroiters have been anxious about the city's future. They have been concerned about the safety of their children and property, their increasing taxes, the quality of city services, access to jobs, home values, their ability to keep up with mortgage payments, and the growing vacancy and abandonment surrounding them. Residents and businesses alike have been concerned about whether utilities would be shut off in the more vacant parts of the city, whether families would be forced to move from their homes (as in the days of urban renewal), or whether some city departments or community facilities would be shut down permanently.

Although much speculation and fear emerged about possible planned actions that seemed unfair, unjust, or unacceptable, it became clear that "business as usual"[6] was no longer acceptable. Detroiters demand and deserve reliable city services, safe streets, and healthy environments. They also need access to healthy food, jobs, and public transit, and they deserve places to play, learn, and engage one's neighbor. Civic leaders in the public, private, nonprofit, grassroots, institutional, and philanthropic sectors understood that the city's sources of funding and service delivery mechanisms had to be realigned to achieve a better quality of life for residents, businesses, and visitors. A strategic approach to advancing this aspiration involved focusing on what the Strategic Framework calls "things we must do" to bring about change. This focus was captured in twelve imperatives, shown in Table E.1.

Bold and transformative moves needed to be undertaken to set the stage for managed growth. Such growth would have to occur in patterns that would support sustainable urban densities—much like the tenets of regional smart growth—with those densities connected by efficient public transit. To be clear, the Strategic Framework stops short of suggesting that the city's development pattern contract down to a handful of dense, walkable, mixed-use urban villages that function as mini cities within a city. To do so would naively fail to recognize the complexities and stigma of urban renewal, relocation, and gentrification. Instead, the team developed recommendations rooted in the realities of the current housing market, the pace of its recovery, and the urgent need for more reliable public services in the face of diminished resources. The team accepted the likelihood that the city's population would take another steep decline before it stabilized, despite a growing influx of young urban pioneers. The team was also acutely aware of the presence of the significant number of households and families of color whose options for residential mobility were limited.

Detroit Future City attempts to tackle these challenges head on, but it also aims high in the belief that Detroit can lead the way to a new set of innovative approaches to address the legacy problems caused by the disinvestment in many older, American post-industrial cities. It reinforces the city's physical and economic capital assets: Detroit is still Michigan's only true large urban city, serving as home to the largest concentration of workers, health, education, cultural and entertainment institutions; it is the busiest international border crossing in North America for international trade; and it is a destination for millions of annual tourists and visitors. Detroit's assets also include the resiliency, creativity, and ingenuity of its people and organizations, all contributing to human and social capital. Detroit's past and present include business leaders who forever

ECONOMIC GROWTH
We must reenergize Detroit's economy to increase job opportunities for Detroiters within the city and strengthen the tax base.
We must support our current residents and attract new residents.

LAND USE
We must use innovative approaches to transform and increase the value of vacant land.
We must use our open space to improve the health of all Detroit's residents.
We must promote a range of sustainable residential densities.

CITY SYSTEMS, INFRASTRUCTURE, AND THE ENVIRONMENT
We must re-align city systems to meet current needs efficiently and promote areas of economic potential, encouraging healthy and thriving communities.
We must re-size city systems for a smaller population in ways that are affordable now and that steadily lift the fiscal and environmental burdens of oversized networks.

NEIGHBORHOODS
We must promote a range of sustainable urban densities.

PUBLIC ASSETS
We must be strategic and coordinated in our use of land.

CIVIC ENGAGEMENT AND COLLABORATION
We must dedicate ourselves to implementing this framework for our future.
We must provide residents with meaningful ways to make change in their community and the city at large.
We must pursue a collaborative regional agenda that recognizes Detroit's strengths and the region's shared destiny.

TABLE E.1 The "things we must do" imperatives.
Source: Detroit Future City: 2012 Detroit Strategic Framework Plan, *p. 8.*

changed the culture of industrial production and music; creators who have pioneered new forms of transportation, infrastructure, and community food production; civic leaders who have organized community residents to exercise their voice and actively participate in the fate of their futures; and faith leaders who have supported Detroit communities by tending to their spiritual and human needs.

Detroit Future City puts forth five planning elements and a civic engagement element, each presented in a copiously illustrated chapter, to capture current conditions and proposed strategies for the future. The Economic Growth element tackles the need to support economic sectors but also provide equitable solutions for all Detroiters. The Land Use element suggests varied land use types possible within the framework of different land use typologies. We will discuss both of these elements in a section that follows. The City Systems element—covering such infrastructure topics as waste and water systems, transit, energy, lighting, and communication—concerns reforms needed for service delivery and offers a spatial framework for supporting these. The Neighborhood element elaborates upon the menu of different strategies that would strengthen and/or stabilize all areas of the city, and the Land and Buildings element offers options for better use of land and building assets that support other goals of the Strategic Framework. Finally, the Civic Engagement element articulates ways to enhance civic support for and participation in the implementation of the Strategic Framework as well as improvement in the city's overall civic capacity.

Within the five planning elements are three distinct approaches that guide the remapping of Detroit. Detroit's new economic maps emphasize economic diversity and advancing in-town business and job growth. Land use maps illustrate an approach toward a more sustainable redistribution of population and density and suggest how to redefine urban neighborhoods. Open space maps show how to transform vacancy and "weeds" into multi-functional infrastructure, recreation, and food production ventures.

In the sections that follow, we will summarize each of these three approaches and include a sampling of relevant maps.

ECONOMIC MAPPING: CREATING EQUITY AND ACCESS TO OPPORTUNITY

It is important to start with the economy. It can be difficult to conduct a planning process that focuses on a city's future when community stakeholders believe that their basic needs are not being met sufficiently. Early in the process, all sectors of the Detroit community unanimously agreed that Detroit's recovery and long-term prosperity require feeling safe, having better-educated youth and adults, and having access to jobs that pay at least a living wage. The fall in Detroit's population has been accompanied by a fall in the number of jobs in Detroit and the region; only one job exists for every four Detroit residents over 16 years old, a much lower proportion than in other major cities. Underemployment and unemployment, often the result of poor education and low skills, contribute to mental stresses that affect physical health, and they leave young adults few alternatives except for the informal economy. Remapping a stronger economic city requires moving beyond a monocentric city center, where downtown Detroit serves as the city's only concentration of employment, to a polycentric economic map. The planning team identified seven geographic districts with high potential for business and job growth. Reconfiguring Detroit to recognize and build on its seven employment districts is critical for three reasons.

First, the Southeast Michigan Council of Governments (SEMCOG) has projected Detroit city's job growth at only 5,000 jobs between 2010 to 2030 (2012, p. 53). This projection overlooks both the potential of Detroit's economic and infrastructure assets that cannot be replicated anywhere else in the region (such as educational institutions, medical institutions, and international port and border crossing infrastructure and employment) and the high percentage of the region's work force that resides in the city. The technical consultant team therefore thought these projection numbers could be boosted.

Second, four economic pillars have particularly high potential for Detroit: education/medical, industrial, digital/creative, and local entrepreneurship. The team estimated that 56 percent of the city's overall employment can be found within these economic pillars, and that these could be strengthened.

Third, within a region that is still heavily divided by race and class, the geography of where people work, and where they do not, reflects long-standing division and unequal opportunity. Transforming Detroit into a city with seven anchor-based employment districts, distributed throughout the city, helps to address the legacy economic inequalities present around race, class, access and mobility. *Detroit Future City* identifies employment opportunities in every quadrant of the city and allows for a diversity of skills, wages, ages, and gender. Figure E.1 maps the seven primary employment districts that the planning team proposed.

Detroit Future City discusses these conditions in the report's Economic Growth element chapter (*Detroit Future City*, 2012, pp. 32–89). In addition to identifying the seven primary employment districts, the chapter also identifies six secondary employment districts, each of which has potential to grow as well, such as the Upper Conner Creek and Lyndon districts.[7] Furthermore, the Strategic Framework proposes specific strategies designed to address historic inequities, such as encouraging local entrepreneurship and minority business ownership, skills building, and educational reform, and it describes specific steps needed for improving land regulations and encouraging private investment. For each of these strategies, the Strategic Framework suggests key actions. For example, under the heading of "Skills Building and Education Reform," one of the suggested steps is to expand innovative partnerships between jobs and training venues. This section points out experiences of organizations such as Focus: HOPE, a well-respected Detroit-based organization that offers social services such as food distribution but also trains local youth in fields such as machine tooling and information technologies. Such endeavors offer an important precedent, proving that such programs can succeed in Detroit. Other suggestions for skill building include linking workers with job sites via transportation, strengthening hiring of local residents for local jobs (Hire Detroit, *Detroit Future City*, 2012, p. 82), and improving efforts to coordinate development and training of the local workforce.

LAND USE MAPPING: CREATING A MORE SUSTAINABLE AND DIVERSE PALETTE OF NEIGHBORHOODS

The second major approach for remapping Detroit described in the Strategic Framework, land use, was particularly challenging. The city contains two-fifths of its peak population. Detroit's population has been in decline for decades, and this trend is expected to continue. SEMCOG's forecasts for Detroit predict that the population will fall from the 2010 census figure of 717,300 to 610,000 by 2030 (Southeast Michigan Council of Governments 2012, p. 53); this is a long way from the city's peak population of over 1.8 million in the early 1950s, but could still keep Detroit as one of the twenty largest cities in the United States.

The trends of population decline and job loss have had a devastating effect on the image of the city. In recent years, Detroit's urban identity has been defined more by its voids and vacant spaces than by the places and communities that still provide tangible indicators of the city's historic character. The city's estimated twenty square miles of total vacant land is roughly equal to the size of Manhattan. This singular characterization of Detroit is explained in recent years by high foreclosure rates, low house and property values, and an excess of vacant land and houses in areas for which not enough demand exists to

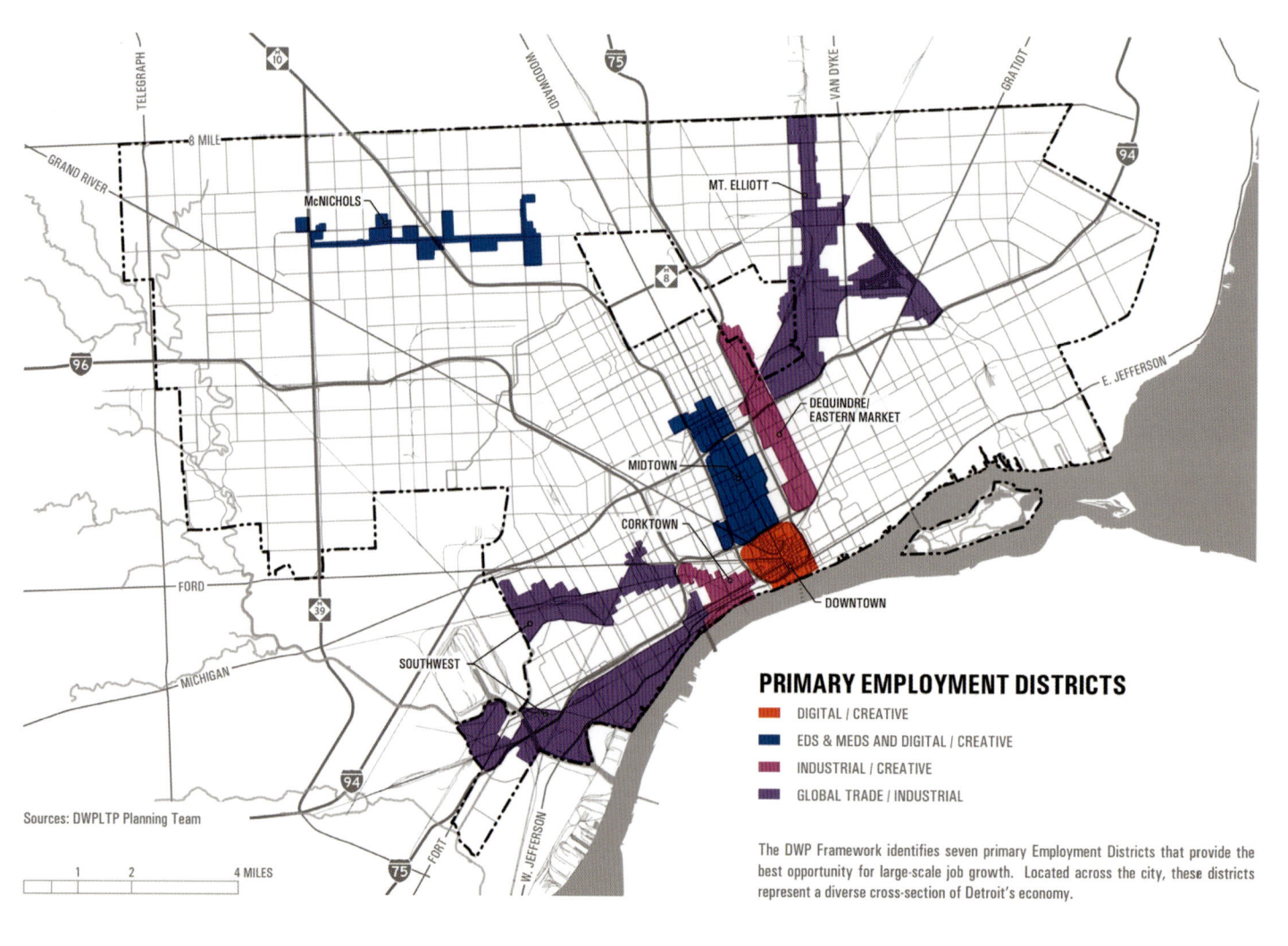

PRIMARY EMPLOYMENT DISTRICTS

- **DIGITAL / CREATIVE**
- **EDS & MEDS AND DIGITAL / CREATIVE**
- **INDUSTRIAL / CREATIVE**
- **GLOBAL TRADE / INDUSTRIAL**

The DWP Framework identifies seven primary Employment Districts that provide the best opportunity for large-scale job growth. Located across the city, these districts represent a diverse cross-section of Detroit's economy.

Sources: DWPLTP Planning Team

PRIMARY EMPLOYMENT DISTRICT DESCRIPTIONS AND LOCATIONS			
DIGITAL / CREATIVE	**EDS & MEDS / DIGITAL AND CREATIVE**	**INDUSTRIAL / CREATIVE**	**GLOBAL TRADE / INDUSTRIAL**
DESCRIPTION: Districts characterized by economic opportunities in information technology and creative businesses such as design & advertising.	Districts characterized by economic opportunities in education, healthcare, research, technology and creative enterprises.	Districts characterized by economic opportunities in industrial activity like food processing and automotive manufacturing as well as creative enterprises and local entrepreneurship.	Districts characterized by economic opportunities in global industrial activity including automotive, metals and logistics.
LOCATIONS: Downtown	Midtown McNichols	Dequindre-Eastern Market Corktown	Southwest Mt. Elliott

fill vacancies before rapid property deterioration sets in. Many homeowners in particular have seen housing and transportation expenses account for unsustainable portions of their monthly income while the value of their investment continues to decrease to a fraction of former market value.

Re-mapping Detroit around these chronic challenges requires a number of transformative ideas. We have already described one, which is to envision a number of employment districts that build on historic economic assets and also enable expansion for key economic clusters. A second major idea for transforming land use is to connect people to jobs and services by enhancing transportation systems; the section of the Strategic Framework devoted to city systems addresses needed changes in transportation as well as other portions of the city's infrastructure. A third idea is to transform vacant land into various kinds of landscapes that could contribute to human health and greener infrastructure, which we will discuss later in the "Open Space Mapping" section of this epilogue. Finally, a fourth transformative idea is to create a palette of livable neighborhoods of different types. Bringing these ideas into reality could have an enormous impact. As noted in *Detroit Future City,* "Detroit actually has the opportunity to lead the region in creating a new urban form, becoming a model for other North American cities. Here, in the midst of tremendous challenge, is the opportunity to transform the city's form and function in new and exciting ways" (2012, p. 93).

It will be easier to implement these ideas by taking deliberate approaches to innovation. Two key ideas presented in the Strategic Framework are (1) a strategic approach to investment and density, and (2) a broader and more innovative palette of land use options.

FIGURE E.1 Primary employment districts.
Source: Detroit Future City: 2012 Detroit Strategic Framework Plan, *p. 48. Courtesy of the Detroit Economic Growth Corporation.*

A Strategic Approach to Investment and Density

All areas of the city will require some level of investment to reinstate a healthy quality of life for all residents, and especially those with limited access to choice. However, the realities of obsolete land uses and depleted tax revenues suggest that not all areas of the city will return to their historic pattern of use or population. Similarly, trying to maintain adequate levels of service delivery across the entire 139 square miles, including areas where population densities have radically fallen, has increased the costs to city government and to home and business dwellers. As such, new interim and long-term ways to use land and a strategic investment approach are necessary to rebuild a more sustainable and affordable Detroit. Because no area of the city is completely without residential life, every area of the city will require some level of investment, whether it is maintaining the flow of essential (and legally required) water and electricity systems, or ensuring public safety by continuing to secure vacant and abandoned properties. However, what must change is the commitment to develop a more strategic approach to the types and levels of investment necessary given both an area's current condition and its potential to transition to a better and more sustainable land use in the future.

A number of local change agents, including the public sector, private citizens, foundations, and nonprofit organizations, must work with an informed understanding of current and anticipated uses of land in order to make more strategic and coordinated decisions about investment, whether in terms of money, time, or other resources. In order to do this, it is important to know where vacancy has already taken over large swaths of land, which areas have experienced recent investment, and what mechanism exists to measure the trending of these factors over time. This is a form of spatial knowledge best facilitated through data-driven spatial maps.

The way that *Detroit Future City* most succinctly helps to provide this information is through the framework zones map, illustrated in Figure

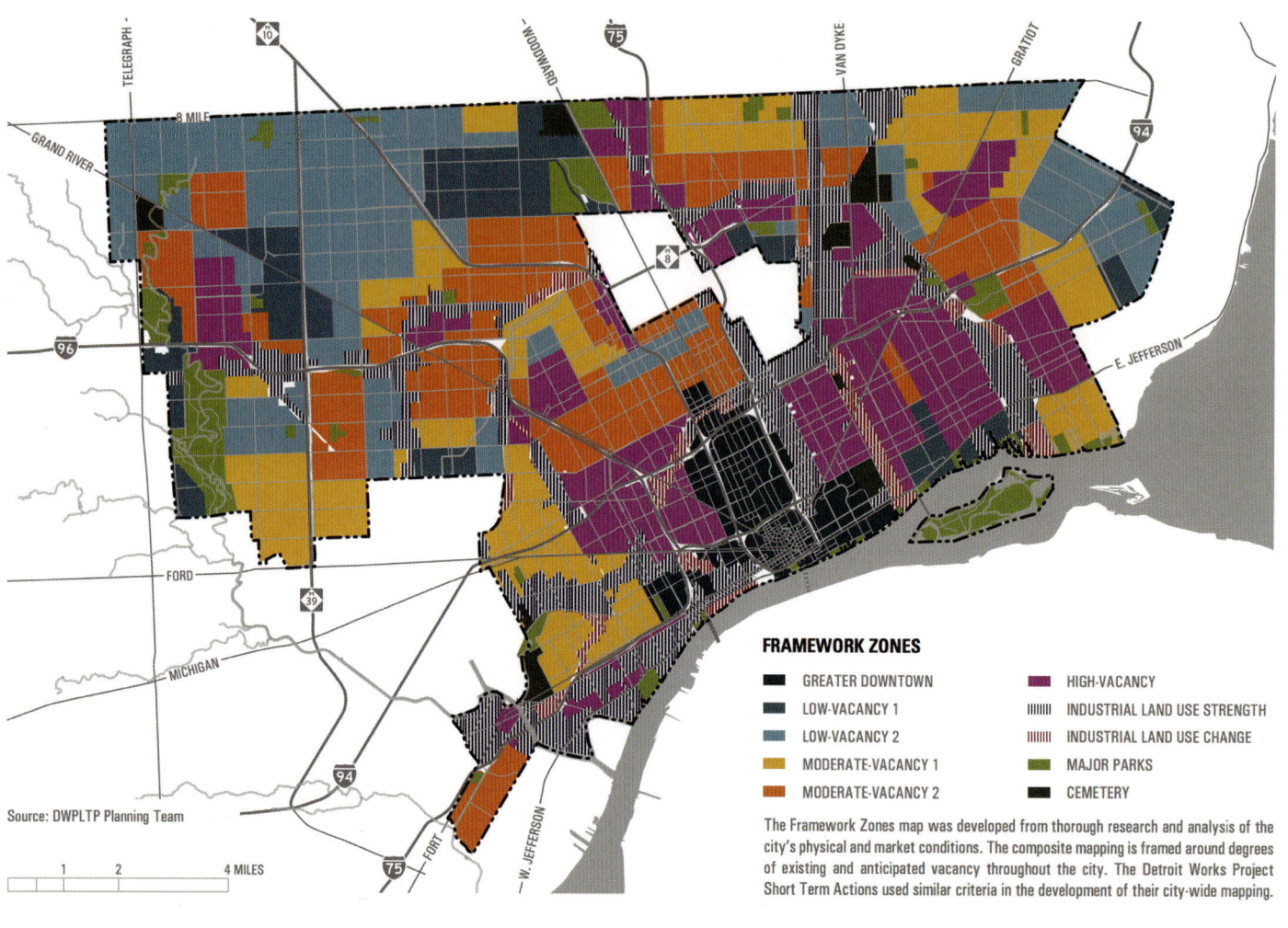

FRAMEWORK ZONES

- ■ GREATER DOWNTOWN
- ■ LOW-VACANCY 1
- ■ LOW-VACANCY 2
- ■ MODERATE-VACANCY 1
- ■ MODERATE-VACANCY 2
- ■ HIGH-VACANCY
- ||||| INDUSTRIAL LAND USE STRENGTH
- ||||| INDUSTRIAL LAND USE CHANGE
- ■ MAJOR PARKS
- ■ CEMETERY

Source: DWPLTP Planning Team

The Framework Zones map was developed from thorough research and analysis of the city's physical and market conditions. The composite mapping is framed around degrees of existing and anticipated vacancy throughout the city. The Detroit Works Project Short Term Actions used similar criteria in the development of their city-wide mapping.

ANALYSES THAT INFLUENCED THE FRAMEWORK FOR DECISION-MAKING			
	RESIDENTIAL PHYSICAL CONDITION ANALYSIS	**MARKET VALUE ANALYSIS**	**DWP SHORT TERM ACTIONS INTEGRATED ANALYSIS**
DESCRIPTION	Evaluation of prevailing physical conditions and household occupancy trends in residential areas across the city, identifying areas sharing common characteristics to inform decision making and strategy.	Evaluation of market factors and trends across the city, identifying areas sharing common market value characteristics to inform decision making and strategy.	Designation of general market types by the City of Detroit based on physical conditions and market value characteristics, articulating specific short-term governmental roles for intervention.
INDICATORS	Percent change in households 2000-2010; vacant land; vacant housing; housing condition	Median housing unit sales price 2009-2010; sales price coefficient of variance; percent residential properties in REO; subsidized rental stock; vacant lots; vacant, open, and dangerous buildings; foreclosures; commercial/residential ratio; owner occupancy	Residential Physical Condition Analysis; Market Value Analysis
SOURCES	Hamilton Anderson Associates; Data Driven Detroit; US Census 2000-2010	The Reinvestment Fund; Southeast Michigan Council of Governments (SEMCOG); US Census 2010; Data Driven Detroit; US Department of Housing and Urban Development (HUD); Wayne County Assessor's Office	Detroit Planning and Development Department; The Reinvestment Fund; Hamilton Anderson Associates

E.2. The long-term planning team undertook a comprehensive process of research and mapping of a number of factors, including both physical and market conditions of the city's land. Several organizations provided assistance to the team with data collection and analysis, including the city government's planning and development department, Data Driven Detroit, and The Reinvestment Fund; also helpful were data and analysis previously complied by the Community Development Advocates of Detroit (CDAD). Broad categories of vacancy proved to be a particularly important factor in creating the framework zones map, and boundaries were established using census tract data, neighborhood boundaries, natural features, and physical barriers. It is important to note that the mapping of different areas into framework zones categories was not intended to seal the long-term condition of any area, but instead to guide more productively what an area could become, identifying appropriate locations and strategies for future public and private investment, land use regulation, and service delivery.

The framework zones map uses four main categories to describe residential and commercial space in the city. The first category is the greater downtown, which contains vacant property but nevertheless has very strong market potential. As Figure E.2 shows, the greater downtown area is much larger than the traditional central business district and includes Midtown; Lafayette Park; and parts of the Corktown, Elmwood, New Center, East Riverfront, and Woodbridge neighborhoods. The other three categories are low-vacancy, moderate-vacancy, and high-vacancy areas of the city. Each of these three areas has different characteristics and potential. Figure E.3 summarizes maps and key statistics for three categories of neighborhood areas: low-, moderate-, and high-vacancy areas (*Detroit Future City,* 2012, pp. 106, 109).

FIGURE E.2 Framework zones.
Source: Detroit Future City: 2012 Detroit Strategic Framework Plan, *p. 22. Courtesy of the Detroit Economic Growth Corporation.*

Those areas with a high degree of vacancy, spreading to the northwest and northeast of the Greater Downtown, contain a large amount of vacant land with varied ownership and little to no productive use of the land, according to data collectors. Representing approximately 17 percent of the city in land mass, these areas contained 88,000 people in 2010. They also contain residential structures that are very isolated in surroundings of vacant land, and have housing vacancy rates that average 30 percent. Various public entities own approximately 39 percent of the land in this high-vacancy category. These high-vacancy areas, zoned predominately as residential, represent enormous opportunities for redefinition and improvement. One opportunity, for example, is for such land to accommodate job-producing uses, especially when these areas are adjacent to one of the seven major employment districts within the city. These areas could also offer significant environmental and ecological benefits to adjacent neighborhoods through landscape interventions that can improve land and air quality.

The next framework zone category is moderate-vacancy areas, located in the broad middle belt of Detroit's territory. These moderate-vacancy areas represent 33 percent of the total city land mass. The over 318,000 people who lived in these areas in 2010 experienced a wide range of housing vacancy and variation in market conditions in their neighborhoods, so strategies to stabilize and transform land use are particularly important. The average housing vacancy for standing structures was 26 percent, not as high as in high-vacancy neighborhoods but enough to make these communities more fragile and vulnerable than others. Innovative strategies for new neighborhood development patterns could make a very important difference in neighborhood stability by retaining population intensity within a broader range of housing types, including mid-rise developments.

The areas with comparatively low vacancy, making up 26 percent of city land mass, are clustered in the city's northwest, northeast, and east

LOW-VACANCY
- LOW-VACANCY 1
- LOW-VACANCY 2

MODERATE-VACANCY
- MODERATE-VACANCY 1
- MODERATE-VACANCY 2

HIGH-VACANCY
- HIGH-VACANCY

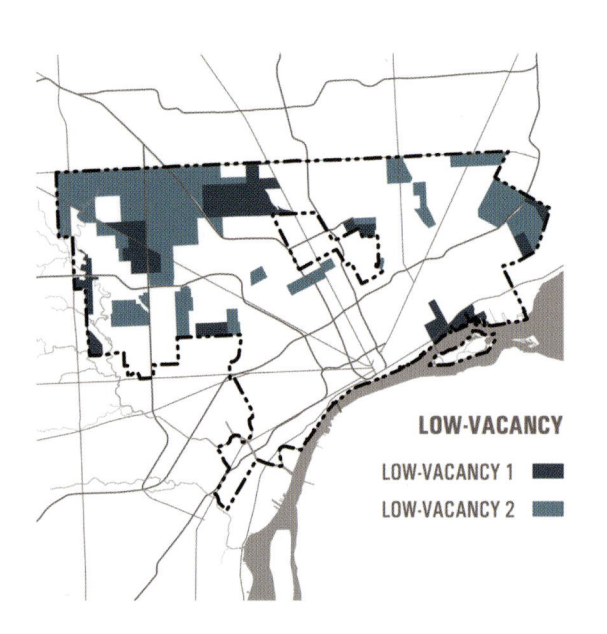

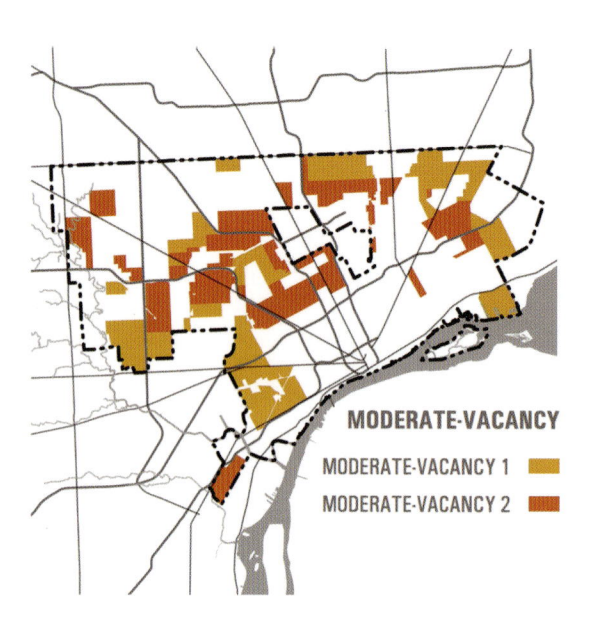

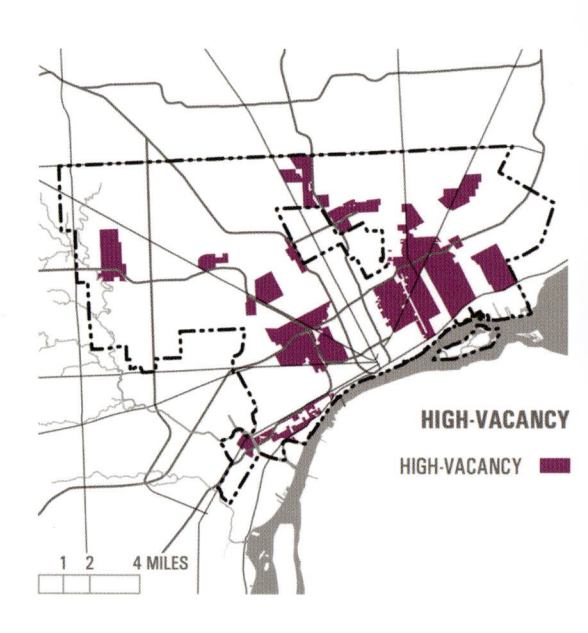

1 2 4 MILES

POPULATION: 254,260   MEAN INCOME: $48,509

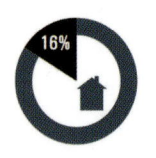

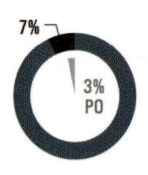

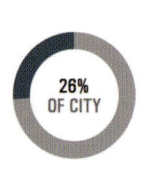

16% HOUSING VACANCY
7% / 3% PO — VACANT PARCELS: PUBLICLY OWNED
26% OF CITY — LAND AREA

POPULATION: 318,140   MEAN INCOME: $35,821

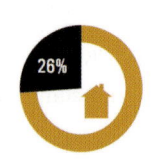

26% HOUSING VACANCY
22% / 15% PO — VACANT PARCELS: PUBLICLY OWNED
33% OF CITY — LAND AREA

POPULATION: 88,255   MEAN INCOME: $28,082

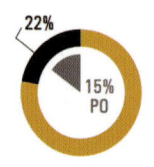

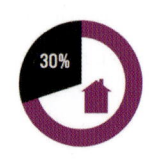

30% HOUSING VACANCY
56% / 39% — VACANT PARCELS: PUBLICLY OWNED
17% OF CITY — LAND AREA

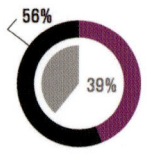

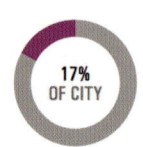

220   TONI L. GRIFFIN AND JUNE MANNING THOMAS

riverfront as illustrated in both Figure E.2 and E.3. As with moderately vacant areas, these sections of the city house a relatively large population: 254,000 in 2010. Housing vacancy drops to 16 percent in this category on average, with only 3 percent public ownership of land at the time data was collected. Appropriate strategies would aim to help stabilize the housing market and to prevent future problems by diminishing the number of foreclosures and improving neighborhood appearance. Focused strategies such as this could greatly enhance the viability and attractiveness of these neighborhoods for the region's residents.

A Broader and More Innovative Palette of Land Uses

The second key set of strategies involves creating options for land use, concerning neighborhoods, landscapes, industrial areas, and commercial areas. We will describe only a few of these options here, simply to illustrate the main idea, which is adaptation to existing conditions and flexibility of future development options. This means that actions should be flexible, depending on the actual characteristics of, and potential for, the land.

First we should note that work on the land use element took many months and required analysis of vast stores of data. The goal was to propose future land uses that met current needs but also optimized potential changes for the city's future. Using modeling scenarios, the team's approach identified specific geographic areas as appropriate locales for various strategies, all within the context of improving the overall quality of life, enhancing the quality of local businesses, and minimizing the cost of maintaining public services and utilities. Other considerations included the need to select strategies that required a minimal amount of capital

FIGURE E.3 Alternative locations and associated data for three different portions of the framework zones.
Source: Detroit Future City: 2012 Detroit Strategic Framework Plan, *pp. 108–9. Courtesy of the Detroit Economic Growth Corporation.*

costs to achieve but could help improve future revenue streams to local government. The end goal for all was to recognize current conditions in the framework zone and yet offer strategic ways to create positive changes in the future land use of the city.

This became clearer as the planning team considered several possible typologies of land use. Typically, land use plans and zoning ordinances divide uses in cities and other places by categorizing certain areas as appropriate for single-family housing, multi-family housing, industrial use, and so on. Aside from imposing regulations concerning spatial characteristics (such as minimum lot size) and allowable uses (such as no industrial use in single-family neighborhoods), these traditional categorizations give little guidance about how to guide growth and development. In contrast, the planning team used land use typologies to classify but also to suggest strategies, suggestions, and tools for enhancing the quality of life in these particular areas. *Detroit Future City* also geographically identifies these areas. It uses three main categories of land use typologies: neighborhood (both residential and mixed use), industrial, and landscape. Here we will describe only neighborhood (residential and mixed) and industrial uses, reserving the landscape typologies for the "Open Space Mapping" section of this epilogue.

Neighborhood Residential. Residential neighborhoods are the heart of life for many city dwellers. When these areas don't work for an individual or household, living in a city starts to become a less desirable option. Yet a lot of viable options exist for high-quality residential neighborhoods—even in a city with a high degree of vacancy. *Detroit Future City* suggests both traditional and "green" ways to think about residential neighborhoods. The traditional neighborhoods could be either low density or medium density. They may have some small amount of land vacancy, common throughout the city of Detroit, but they could also have predominately intact homes and large proportions of residents who are willing to commit to stay and improve their neighborhood.

The chapter of *Detroit Future City* that describes the Neighborhood element (2012, pp. 202–263) suggests many specific ways to strengthen and enhance such neighborhoods. These include focusing on density and stabilizing property values, as well as addressing issues related to safety, education, identity, and physical conditions. Such areas may provide a small amount of commercial retail space as well as public space such as parks. Green neighborhoods, defined as areas that are currently moderate or low vacancy, could become transformed in great part through landscape strategies. The Strategic Framework articulates different ways of thinking about residential densities for these neighborhoods. These areas may have seen increasing vacancy, but the most appropriate strategy could be to reconfigure housing and block patterns around new forms of productive landscapes, including blue infrastructure (planned landscapes, such as swales or retention ponds, which capture and clean stormwater), green infrastructure (landscapes that capture airborne pollutants), nontraditional recreational spaces, or urban agriculture. Despite its painful development legacy of displacement during the bygone urban renewal era, Lafayette Park offers an existing example of how a diverse arrangement of housing types within a landscape can create a sustainable urban density and sense of community. The key to developing successful green neighborhoods will be to allow a mix of building types that help to increase the overall density within the area.

Neighborhood Mixed Use. Neighborhood mixed use covers a number of different possible categories, some of which include economic activity. The Strategic Framework identifies four possibilities for neighborhood mixed use: neighborhood centers, district centers, the city center, and live + make. Of these, the first three are the most familiar. Neighborhood centers resemble hubs; they can include commercial and recreational activities as well as residential, and quite often they are associated with a specific residential neighborhood. They may also include public areas such as neighborhood parks or squares, as well as community anchors or places of worship. District centers are larger-scale mixed-use neighborhoods that have a higher proportion of mixed-use buildings and provide more retail amenities within the district. They are adjacent to residential areas. District centers may also contain an anchor such as a major commercial or institutional employer. The city center, more commonly known as the central business district (i.e., downtown), would form an important core for commercial and service employment mixed with retail and entertainment amenities, but may also include apartments and loft residential units that help to maintain a lively urban environment that is well used throughout days, evenings, and weekends. Prominent and often historic civic public spaces help to create a strong civic identity for the downtown and the city overall.

Live + make neighborhoods build on local entrepreneurship, one of the Strategic Framework's four economic pillars, as well as on Detroit's strong tradition of making things. These neighborhoods promote the integration of residential buildings and units with the spaces of cultural and industrial production. Although typically associated with artists living in lofts, such areas could also combine manufacturing, assembly, workshop, business incubators, and other small-scale economic or artistic activities with a range of housing and retail uses. These kinds of venues with a combination of purposes have already appeared in Detroit, such as in the Detroit Eastern Market area.

Industrial Use. We have already introduced the topic of industrial use by noting that some areas that provide places for people to live and work would indeed be considered small-scale industrial or manufacturing areas. But it is also necessary to consider more traditional ways of accommodating

FIGURE E.4 Existing land uses in Detroit.
Source: Detroit Future City: 2012 Detroit Strategic Framework Plan, *p. 118. Courtesy of the Detroit Economic Growth Corporation.*

EXISTING: CURRENT LAND USE

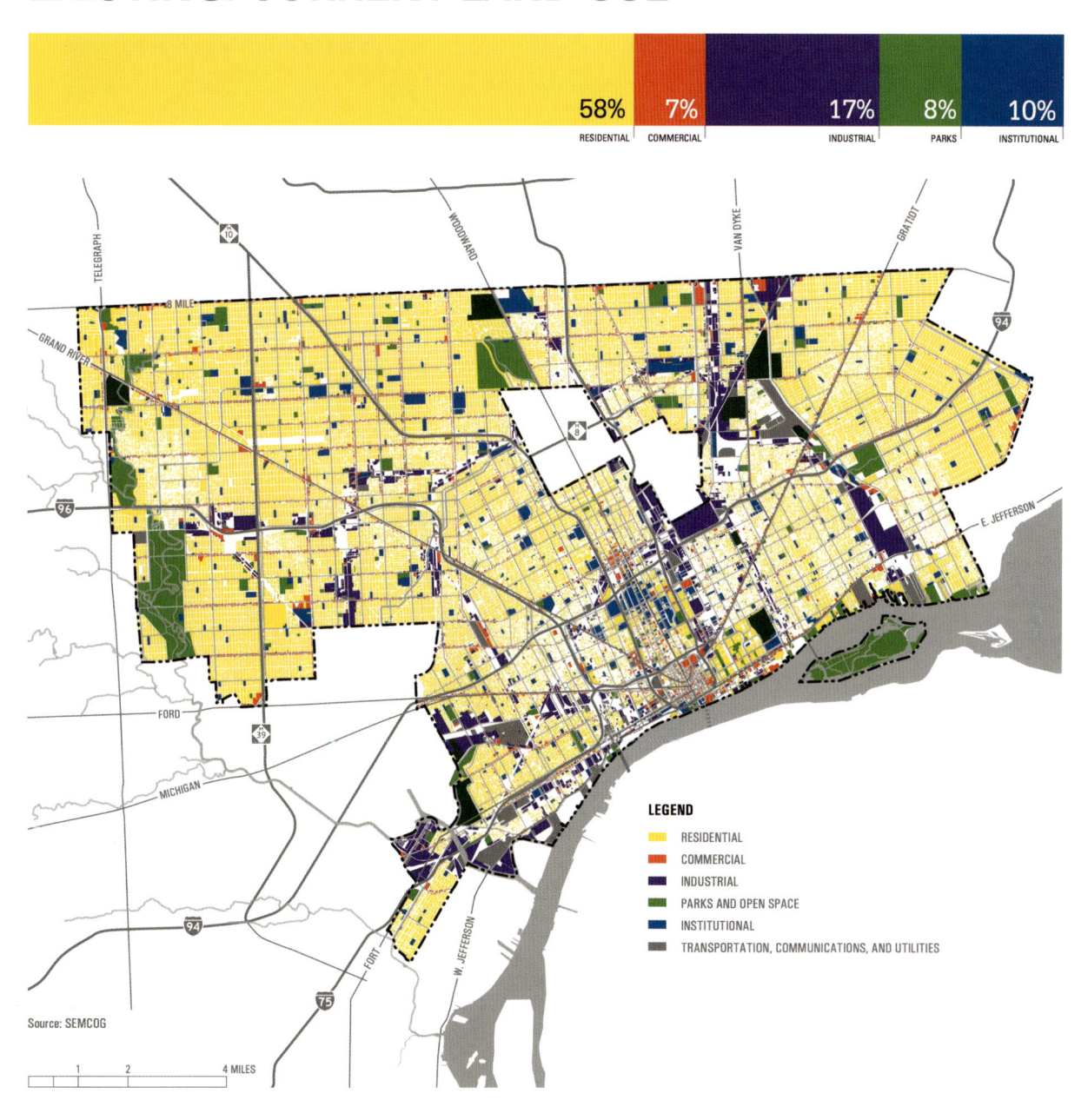

58% RESIDENTIAL | **7%** COMMERCIAL | **17%** INDUSTRIAL | **8%** PARKS | **10%** INSTITUTIONAL

LEGEND
- RESIDENTIAL
- COMMERCIAL
- INDUSTRIAL
- PARKS AND OPEN SPACE
- INSTITUTIONAL
- TRANSPORTATION, COMMUNICATIONS, AND UTILITIES

Source: SEMCOG

EPILOGUE: *Detroit Future City*

PROPOSED: 50-YEAR LAND USE SCENARIO

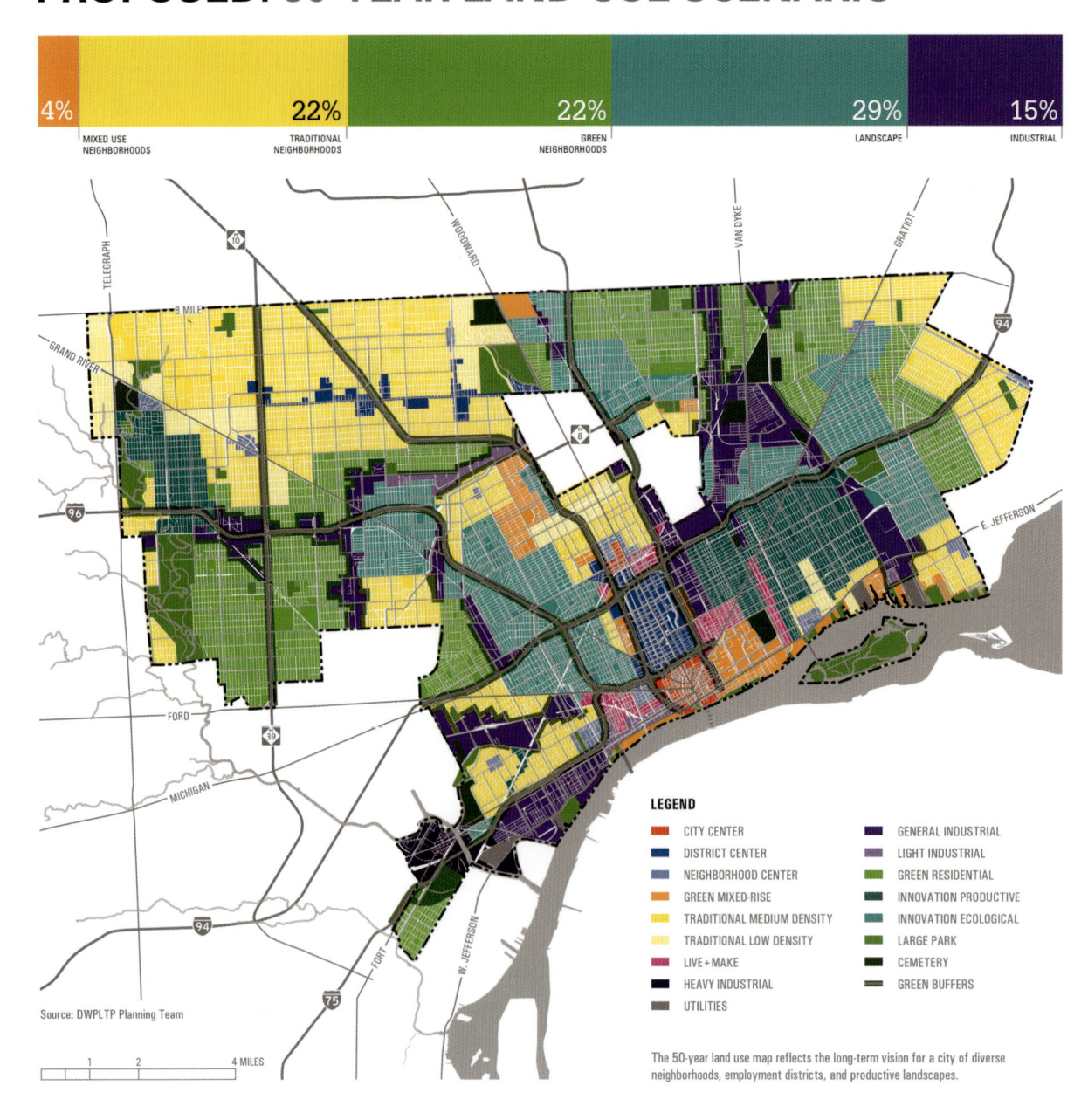

4%	22%	22%	29%	15%
MIXED USE NEIGHBORHOODS	TRADITIONAL NEIGHBORHOODS	GREEN NEIGHBORHOODS	LANDSCAPE	INDUSTRIAL

LEGEND

- CITY CENTER
- DISTRICT CENTER
- NEIGHBORHOOD CENTER
- GREEN MIXED-RISE
- TRADITIONAL MEDIUM DENSITY
- TRADITIONAL LOW DENSITY
- LIVE + MAKE
- HEAVY INDUSTRIAL
- UTILITIES
- GENERAL INDUSTRIAL
- LIGHT INDUSTRIAL
- GREEN RESIDENTIAL
- INNOVATION PRODUCTIVE
- INNOVATION ECOLOGICAL
- LARGE PARK
- CEMETERY
- GREEN BUFFERS

Source: DWPLTP Planning Team

The 50-year land use map reflects the long-term vision for a city of diverse neighborhoods, employment districts, and productive landscapes.

224 TONI L. GRIFFIN AND JUNE MANNING THOMAS

industrial land use. The major categories the planning team delineated were light industrial, general industrial, and heavy industrial. Such activity is very important for Detroit's economic growth, but future changes will have to be carefully planned in order to make the best use of existing industrial infrastructure while still protecting businesses and nearby neighborhoods. In some cases, it will be necessary to plan for cleaner and more sustainable forms of industrial use. It will also become important to think differently about the relationship between industrial uses and overall environmental health, which could include creating landscape buffers that protect nearby residents from industry. *Detroit Future City* offers illustrations in the Economic Growth element chapter of fairly isolated commercial/industrial centers that could still benefit from freeway carbon forests planted alongside the Chrysler (I-75) expressway; examples of such industrial centers include the Detroit Eastern Market, the Pepsi-Cola plant, the Greater Detroit Resource Recovery Authority plant, and the Russell Industrial Center, all in a consolidated Dequindre/Eastern Market district (p. 64).

Detroit's current land use map (Figure E.4) utilizes traditional land use classifications and highlights the predominance of land zoned for single-family residential use, much of which is vacant. Figure E.5 represents the Strategic Framework's proposal for a new future land use pattern that remaps the city by typologies of neighborhoods, landscapes, and industrial areas and employment districts.

OPEN SPACE MAPPING: MOVING FROM VACANCY TO MULTI-FUNCTIONAL LANDSCAPES

The third category we will summarize is open space. Many people consider open land to be a negative, but it actually offers much potential. Vacant

FIGURE E.5 Proposed 50-year land use scenario.
Source: Detroit Future City: 2012 Detroit Strategic Framework Plan, *p. 119. Courtesy of the Detroit Economic Growth Corporation.*

land is an asset that people in many cities would value highly (Bowman and Pagano 2004). Detroit has a lot of land available with which it can support a variety of new and innovative uses, particularly in terms of creating an environmentally sustainable city. Enhancing the Detroit landscape would offer an opportunity to develop an urban ecological system unmatched anywhere in the world (as described as well in chapter 8 of this book.) This landscape in the midst of settlement, a new urban form, would not simply be something to look at, or play in, but could actually become productive in other ways. Such productivity could lead to environmental benefits, such as cleaner air and water as well as enhanced soil and habitat for plant and animal wildlife. It could lead to economic benefits, such as purposeful use of the landscape to create jobs and produce tangible products such as food and wood products. It could also create social benefits: handling open space well could enhance recreation opportunities and increase property values, for example.

Traditionally, cities ensured that some sort of space was open to the public by establishing parks. As Figure E.6 shows, parks are distributed throughout Detroit, but their current locations are not always aligned with the population density necessary to support their size or programming. Maintaining them in the midst of fiscal crisis has proven to be difficult, if not impossible. Figure E.7 shows an alternative and more cost-effective way to integrate additional open space throughout the city. Establishing a broader range of landscape uses besides parks offers unique advantages for economic growth, neighborhoods, and the ecological network.

Landscapes for Economic Growth

Detroit's citizens are already using land for urban gardens, typically less than two acres. The potential for expanding on such production, however, has increased with land availability; the areas labeled in Figure E.7 as "innovation productive" show possible locations. Many more landscape applications are possible. These could provide job opportunities in the production of food, biomass for energy (as explained in chapter 8), trees for wood products; jobs would also be created by the construction and maintenance of the infrastructure systems needed for the landscape applications. Within these landscapes, closely situated and linked to employment districts, new and innovative technologies can be deployed for research that might aid in the further development of green industries related to the industrial, health-care, and construction sectors of Detroit's economy. Such landscapes could also facilitate cleaner air, soil, and water quality.

Landscapes for Neighborhoods

Residential and commercially zoned vacant lots that survive in traditional or green neighborhoods could also be put to new productive use within the neighborhood context. Dozens of communities and community organizations have already taken control of unused spaces for the purposes of stabilization and community building. These sites are being transformed into small-scale playgrounds, urban gardens, purposeful wetlands, and remediation meadows. Vacant lots repurposed as green spaces could serve a dual purpose by increasing recreation opportunities at the same time that they provide fresh food or clean air and water for communities. Other possible uses include capturing storm water and enhancing residential housing values by creating waterfront property. To the extent that these vacant areas begin to enhance the visible environment, rather than detract from it, such uses could help support other activities, leading to a stronger sense of community and attachment to the neighborhood.

Landscapes as Recreational and Ecological Networks

More traditional uses of the landscape, particularly as recreational spaces, continue to be important. The Strategic Framework calls for continued support of existing parks and other recreational land and buildings, but suggests that it is also possible to add other kinds of parks, such as ecological nature or storm-water parks, which would cost less to maintain. If networks can be created so that areas are not isolated, but rather linked by greenways and other means, the results could be particularly positive.

Landscapes as Transformative Infrastructures

Some of the most innovative ideas in *Detroit Future City* relate to transforming vacant land in ways that will support various city infrastructure systems. These are represented in Figure E.7. For example, the hard thick lines that outline the city's expressways represent carbon forests. As explained more fully in the Land and Buildings Assets element chapter (*Detroit Future City*, 2012, pp. 264–315; see especially page 301), the concept of carbon forests is to plant trees bordering the expressways and high traffic corridors to absorb airborne pollutants and improve overall air quality. Priority areas for planting trees that would grow into forest would include vacant land located within 500 feet of an interstate or major arterial highway. Lighter green lines in the same figure represent the same idea, except that these industrial buffers protect residential neighborhoods from industrial pollution. The report calls for a concerted effort by residents, businesses, and other institutions to construct and maintain such areas.

Detroit Future City also contains recommendations for blue infrastructure. Major streets and thoroughfares that allow for plantings could be used for enhanced retention of stormwater through the construction of landscape medians and swales located on the edges of overly wide streets. In addition, it is also possible to envision small surface lakes and wet buffers, which can be located throughout the city (2012, p. 133).

FIGURE E.6 Existing park system in Detroit.
Source: Detroit Future City: 2012 Detroit Strategic Framework Plan, *p. 134. Courtesy of the Detroit Economic Growth Corporation.*

CURRENT: EXISTING PARKS SYSTEM

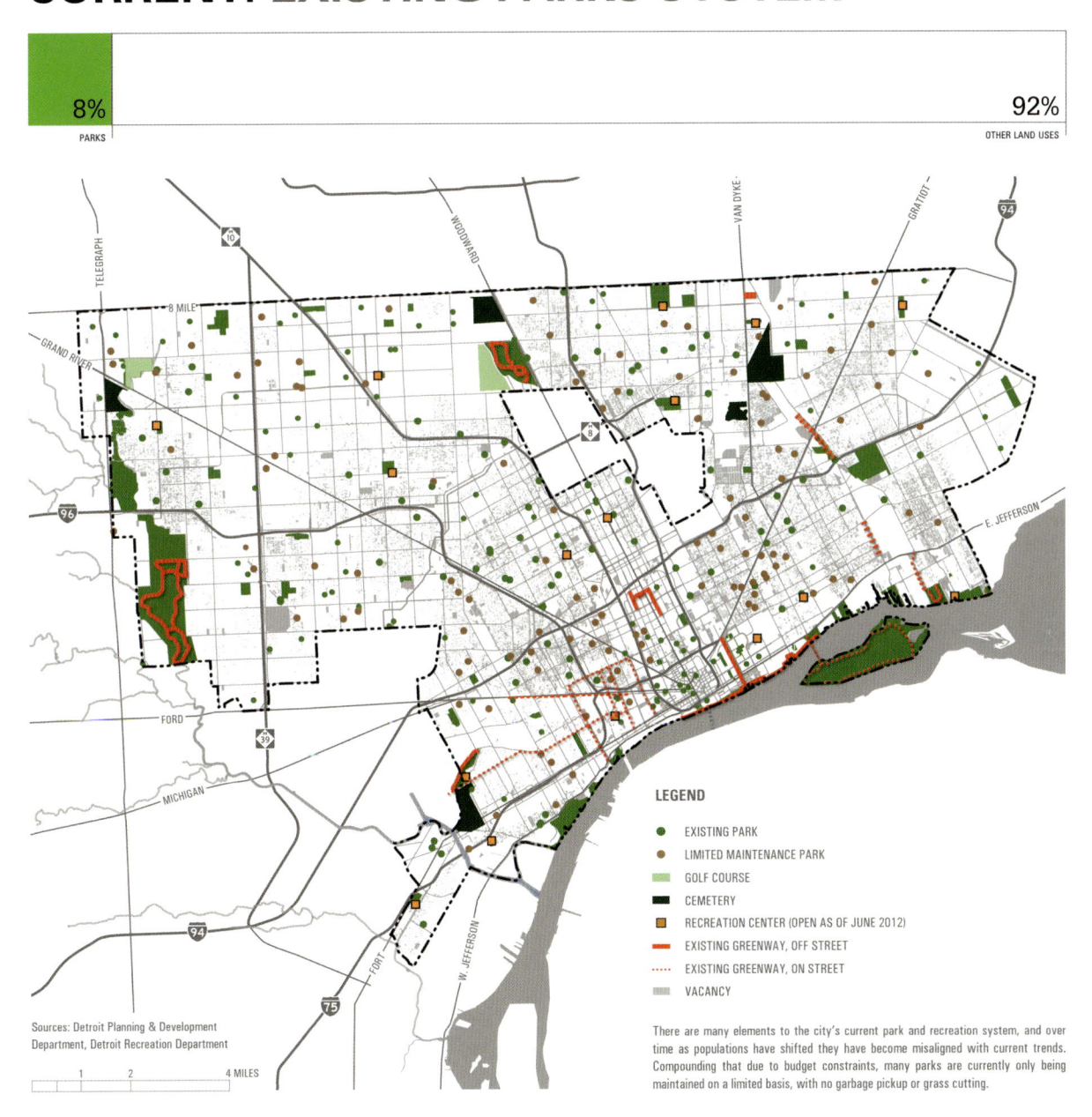

8% PARKS | **92% OTHER LAND USES**

LEGEND
- ● EXISTING PARK
- ● LIMITED MAINTENANCE PARK
- GOLF COURSE
- CEMETERY
- ■ RECREATION CENTER (OPEN AS OF JUNE 2012)
- — EXISTING GREENWAY, OFF STREET
- ⋯ EXISTING GREENWAY, ON STREET
- VACANCY

Sources: Detroit Planning & Development Department, Detroit Recreation Department

There are many elements to the city's current park and recreation system, and over time as populations have shifted they have become misaligned with current trends. Compounding that due to budget constraints, many parks are currently only being maintained on a limited basis, with no garbage pickup or grass cutting.

EPILOGUE: *Detroit Future City*

PROPOSED: FUTURE OPEN SPACE SYSTEM

7% PARKS | **29%** LANDSCAPE TYPOLOGIES | **64%** OTHER LAND USES

LEGEND
- CARBON FOREST
- INDUSTRIAL BUFFER
- BLUE INFRASTRUCTURE
- INNOVATION PRODUCTIVE
- INNOVATION ECOLOGICAL
- LARGE PARKS
- DISPERSED GREEN LANDSCAPES
- DISPERSED BLUE INFRASTRUCTURE

Sources: Detroit Recreation Department, DWPLTP Planning Team

The future open space network for Detroit will consist of a series of interlinked elements. These will not only include traditional parks but a series of newly repurposed parks, blue and green infrastructure, and large scale landscape typologies.

Another related transformative use that is evident in Figure E.7 is represented by land labeled as "innovation ecological." Also based in areas that already seem to be turning into high-vacancy areas, ecological areas could include forest, meadows, and other uses that are intended less for productivity than for land conservation and beautification. These would join with existing and new forms of parks to help create refuges for animals as well as wildflowers and other flora. Such ecological lands would require little to maintain.

CONCLUSION: A NEW APPROACH TO MAPPING DETROIT

A surprisingly radical move in *Detroit Future City* was its acknowledgment that Detroit's fate was to become a smaller city. This did not mean smaller in relevance or global impact, but rather smaller in its population and historic tax capture. The Strategic Framework embraces this reality and proposes a set of policy and implementation strategies designed to rebuild a sustainable and more affordable city of 600,000–800,000 residents. This is reasonable: cities such as Atlanta, Portland, and Denver have populations and land areas comparable to Detroit, and they frequently rank high on national polls of healthy economic and quality of life indicators.

With a clear and innovative vision, and with implementation of that vision shared by collaborative partners, Detroit can rewrite the book on the transformation of post-industrial cities in the United States and possibly abroad. But the economic and operational reforms needed to reposition the city will not happen in a day or even a year, but rather will be incremental over the course of years and decades. Most city planning frameworks produce a single long-range regulatory map, projecting a growth pattern twenty, thirty, or fifty years out, leaving the average resident or investor to speculate about what change might look like during the intervening years. Rather than a single long-range map, the *Detroit Future City* instead proposes three implementation horizons to chart and assess progress over time and to allow for adjustments in strategies based on both the planned and unplanned evolution of the city.

The implementation horizon maps (*Detroit Future City*, 2012, pp. 30–31, 146) represent three aspirational goals: (1) Stabilize and Improve (ten-year time frame); (2) Sustain (ten- to twenty-year frame); and (3) Transform (twenty- to fifty-year frame). The Stabilize and Improve plan builds on the existing and anticipated vacancy conditions of the framework zones map, and lays out the initial steps to stabilize neighborhoods and establish a long-term trajectory for sustainable growth. Critical components of the plan include establishing seven employment districts, putting reliable public transit in place along busy routes, stimulating market demand in strategic neighborhoods, reducing blight, initiating educational reform and workforce development, and introducing landscape-based productive land uses. During this period, it will also be important to set up an implementation framework that includes local and regional as well as national partners.

The Sustain plan builds on the first ten years, identifying areas to increase population density, but also allocating additional land to be repurposed for landscape-based reuse. By the twenty-year mark, city systems should be upgraded, renewed, reduced, or decommissioned to support target population densities across the city. The employment districts should be fully defined and connected through a regional and citywide transit system. A new environmentally sustainable open space network comprised of blue infrastructure, green industrial, highway buffers, and alternative productive land uses should be fully established within the fabric of the city. With careful implementation, public transit options will have been expanded by that time, and unemployment should have declined as the number of jobs per resident increases and educational reform takes hold.

FIGURE E.7 Proposed open space system.
Source: Detroit Future City: 2012 Detroit Strategic Framework Plan, *p. 135. Courtesy of the Detroit Economic Growth Corporation.*

The Transform land-use map (Figure E.5) represents the completed vision for land use transformation. The city would be composed of a diverse range of neighborhood types, each with a unique identity and each structured to accommodate sustainable densities. Strategic districts and neighborhoods would be established to receive future population growth in a rapidly urbanizing nation and world. Through the growth of the employment districts, the ratio of adult residents to jobs would be fiscally sustainable at two to one instead of its current four to one. A functional transportation network would connect job centers, residences, and the region. The city's identity would be internationally recognized for its integration of landscape and urban form as a twenty-first-century model of industrial reinvention and environmental sustainability, and the city would again become the major employment center for its region.

In this epilogue, we have summarized only a portion of the proposals, emphasizing in particular matters related to economic development, neighborhoods, and open space. The full version of *Detroit Future City*, however, includes a number of other necessary reforms, including improvements in educational and workforce development institutions, changes in the city's public transportation system, encouragement of minority businesses, purposeful handling of public land and buildings, and revision of local plans and regulations. Also recommended is a systematic engagement of the public in the implementation of all phases of the strategic planning framework over the next fifty years.

By the spring of 2013, Detroit leaders had begun implementation of the Strategic Framework. The Kresge Foundation pledged $150 million towards initiatives that would further the vision and strategies of *Detroit Future City*. Management of the implementation agenda is envisioned to be coordinated by an implementation consortium made of up key agencies, businesses, and organizations that had already played key roles in the planning and civic engagement elements of the Strategic Framework. Within this management structure, leaders plan to identify projects representative of each of the elements, which would then be implemented by a broad range of community, civic, nonprofit, business and public sector partners. The vision is that the hundreds and thousands of collective efforts of Detroiters and their community-based organizations and businesses would join with the larger efforts of lead institutions and governments to help bring about necessary positive change in a more coordinated fashion than has been the case before. All of this leads to the exciting prospect of the gradual but progressive transformation of today's Detroit into "Detroit Future City". All depends, of course, on concerted effort and strong leadership, consistently pursued and supported.

NOTES

1. These include most notably the Kresge Foundation, but also Ford Foundation, W. K. Kellogg Foundation, John S. and James L. Knight Foundation, Hudson Webber Foundation, Erb Family Foundation, and the Community Foundation for Southeast Michigan.
2. The document won the 2013 Daniel Burnham Award for a Comprehensive Plan from the Michigan Association of Planning, and the 2013 Honor Award in the Landscape Planning and Analysis division from the Michigan chapter of the American Society of Landscape Architects, 2013.
3. Toni L. Griffin, lead author for this epilogue, led the planning team. June Thomas, co-author, was not a major participant in the creation of *Detroit Future City*.
4. The reasons for the split are complicated, but hinged largely on difficulties involved in implementing the initiative and on the need to provide clear lines of authority and action for city staff and for consultants.
5. Toni L. Griffin was project director of the planning team. Firms making up the planning team included Hamilton Anderson Associates, for project management, land use, and neighborhoods; Stoss Landscape Urbanism, for landscape, and ecology and environment; Initiative for a Competitive Inner City, for economic growth; Mass Economics, for economic growth; Interface Studio, for economic growth; Happold Consulting, for city systems; Center for Community Progress, for land and buildings assets; Carlisle Wortman, for zoning; AECOM, for landscape, and ecology and environment audit; Skidmore Owings

and Merrill, LLP, for urban design audit; and HR&A Advisors, for public land audit. The civic engagement team included Detroit Collaborative Design Center, co-director; Michigan Community Resources, co-director; and Grassroots Solutions, advisor.
6. See *Detroit Future City* (e.g., pp. 7, 11).
7. Others include the I-96 corridor just west of the Southfield Expressway, Westfield, Livernois, and Lower Conner Creek districts. See *Detroit Future City,* p. 74.

REFERENCES

Bowman, A., and Pagano, M. (2004). *Terra incognita: Vacant land and urban strategies.* Washington, DC: Georgetown University Press.

Community Development Advocates of Detroit. (2012, Spring). *Neighborhood revitalization strategic framework process guide.* Retrieved from http://cdad-online.org/wp-content/uploads/2012/01/CDAD_Process_Guide_2012.pdf

Community Development Advocates of Detroit. (2013). *Neighborhood revitalization strategic framework.* Retrieved from http://cdad-online.org/wp/wp-content/uploads/2012/01/Strategic-Framework-Overview.pdf

Detroit future city: 2012 Detroit strategic framework plan. (2012). Detroit, MI.

Hudson-Webber Foundation, Detroit Economic Growth Corporation, and partners. (2013). *7.2 sq. miles: A report on greater downtown Detroit.* Retrieved from www.detroitsevenpointtwo.com

Schaffer, K. (1993). New introduction to D. H. Burnham and E. H. Bennett, *The Plan of Chicago,* originally published by the Commercial Club of Chicago, 1909. New York, NY: Princeton Architectural Press.

Southeast Michigan Council of Governments. (2012, April). *Southeast Michigan 2040 forecast summary.*

CONTRIBUTORS

MARÍA ARQUERO DE ALARCÓN is an assistant professor of architecture and urban planning at Taubman College of Architecture and Urban Planning at the University of Michigan. Her research and teaching focus on the design, representation, and use of public space, both as environmental infrastructure and as a field of experimentation to devise new forms of civic engagement. Other academic endeavors include the use of visual representation as a mode of inquiry and the use of spatial thinking for design synthesis across geographies, scales, and disciplines. Arquero is a founding partner of MAde Studio. She brings to this partnership her experience and professional practice through interdisciplinary collaborations in Europe, Asia, the Americas, and the Middle East.

HENCO BEKKERING is a professor emeritus of urban design at the School of Architecture at Delft University of Technology in the Netherlands. He served as the chair of urban design for over twenty years, overseeing work in the design of cities and urban projects, public space and infrastructure, pedestrian behavior and GPS tracking, and the meaning of history and historical continuity for design. Bekkering was Netherlands Visiting Professor at Taubman College of Architecture and Urban Planning at the University of Michigan in 2009 and Visiting Scholar at Tsinghua University in Beijing in 2010. Until 2009, he combined teaching with a private practice, doing urban planning and design at HKB stedenbouwkundigen/urbanists Groningen and Rotterdam in the Netherlands.

MARGARET DEWAR is a professor of urban and regional planning at Taubman College of Architecture and Urban Planning at the University of Michigan. Her research addresses urban economic development, environmental planning, and land use, particularly in cities facing disinvestment and property abandonment. Her most recent book is *The City after Abandonment* (University of Pennsylvania Press, 2012), co-edited with June Manning Thomas.

BRIAN LEIGH DUNNIGAN is the associate director and curator of maps at the William L. Clements Library at the University of Michigan. His research and cartographic interests involve the military maps and plans of the eighteenth and nineteenth centuries, town and fortification plans, and the mapping of the Great Lakes. His publications include *A Picturesque Situation: Mackinac before Photography, 1615–1860* (Wayne State University Press, 2008); *Frontier Metropolis: Picturing Early Detroit, 1701–1838* (Wayne State University Press, 2001); and articles on the history of the Great Lakes, particularly the Detroit, Niagara, and Straits of Mackinac regions.

ROBERT FISHMAN is a professor of architecture and urban planning at Taubman College of Architecture and Urban Planning at the University of Michigan. An expert in the areas of urban history and urban policy and planning, he has authored several books on the history of cities and urbanism, including *Bourgeois Utopias: The Rise and Fall of Suburbia* (Basic Books, 1987) and *Urban Utopias in the Twentieth Century: Ebenezer Howard, Frank Lloyd Wright, and Le Corbusier* (MIT Press, 1977). His honors include the 2009 Laurence Gerckens Prize for Lifetime Achievement from the Society for City and Regional Planning History, the 2010 Walker Ames Lectureship from the University of Washington in Seattle, and the Emil Lorch Professorship at Taubman College for 2006 through 2009.

LARS GRÄBNER is an assistant professor of practice and teaches architecture, urban design, and construction methods at Taubman College of Architecture and Urban Planning at the University of Michigan. In 2004, he co-founded VolumeOne, an architectural practice based in Detroit and Berlin. Gräbner focuses on urban design and innovative housing. He has undertaken public projects at various scales, exploring the built environment under social considerations and the advancement of building performance, especially with regard to sustainability. In addition to Detroit and Berlin, his teaching and practice have taken him to The Netherlands, Austria, Switzerland, and China.

JOE GRENGS is an associate professor of urban and regional planning at Taubman College of Architecture and Urban Planning at the University of Michigan. His research focuses on transportation planning and how metropolitan urban form contributes to uneven economic development and social disparities. Recent publications include "Job Accessibility and the Modal Mismatch in Detroit," published by the *Journal of Transport Geography* (2010), and "Intermetropolitan Comparison of Transportation Accessibility: Sorting Out Mobility and Proximity in San Francisco and Washington, D.C.," published in the *Journal of Planning Education and Research* (2010). Grengs is a certified planner and a registered professional engineer with work experience in both the private and public sectors and in international settings.

TONI L. GRIFFIN is a professor and the director of the J. Max Bond Center for Architecture at the Spitzer School of Architecture at the City College of New York. She maintains a private practice, Urban Planning and Design for the American City, where she was the project director for the long-range planning process that produced the *Detroit Future City* Strategic Framework. She has also worked in public planning organizations in Newark, New Jersey; Washington, D.C.; and New York City.

LARISSA LARSEN is an associate professor of urban and regional planning at Taubman College of Architecture and Urban Planning at the University of Michigan, where she also holds an appointment in the School of Natural Resources and the Environment. Her research focuses on identifying inequalities in the built environment and advancing issues of urban sustainability and social justice. She is also a registered landscape architect and has practiced in Chicago, Illinois.

ROBERT LINN is an urban planner and data analyst with the Southwest Detroit Business Association, and previously worked for Data Driven Detroit. He is co-editor of *Belle Isle to 8 Mile: An Insider's Guide to Detroit* (City Bird or Nest, 2012), along with Andy Linn and Emily Linn. His research specialties include urban land use planning, economic development, vacant property re-use, and spatial and numeric data analysis. Linn holds a Master's degree in urban planning from Taubman College of Architecture and Urban Planning at the University of Michigan.

YANJIA LIU is a chief investment officer with Country Garden, a public listed company in Hong Kong and one of China's top five developers. He recently graduated from the Master's in real estate development program at the Massachusetts Institute of Technology. Prior to MIT, Liu worked as an urban designer and planner in Switzerland, San Francisco, New York, and Boston. His real estate development work spanned a broad range of asset types, with a specialization on sustainable projects. He holds a Master's degree in urban planning from Taubman College of Architecture and Urban Planning at the University of Michigan, and he is a LEED accredited professional and a member of the American Institute of Certified Planners.

JUNE MANNING THOMAS is Centennial Professor of Urban and Regional Planning at Taubman College of Architecture and Urban Planning at the University of Michigan. Her books include the co-edited *Urban Planning and the African American Community: In the Shadows* (Sage, 1996), *Redevelopment and Race: Planning a Finer City in Postwar Detroit*, 2nd edition (Wayne State University Press, 2013), *Planning Progress: Lessons from Shoghi Effendi* (Association for Baha'i Studies, 1999), and the co-edited *The City after Abandonment* (University of Pennsylvania Press, 2012, with Margaret Dewar), as well as many articles. She is a Fellow in the American Institute of Certified Planners.

INDEX

Figures and tables are denoted by the letter *f* or *t* (respectively) following page numbers.
The letters *ch* following page ranges indicate a chapter in this volume.

abandonment, 4, 5, 32, 67, 70, 175; Brightmoor, 145–50, 159; neighborhood, 144–45; racial, 4, 97, 148, 204
accessibility, 101–14, 189; definition, 101, 110; employment, 104f, 105, 106f, 107, 107f, 108f; household, 107–8, 108f; index, scores, 103, 104; mapping, 106, 111; non-work, 108–11, 109f, 110f; patterns, 103–11; public transit, 103, 108; race, by, 106–8, 107f, 108f; social equity, 101–3, 111; transportation, 101–14
adjacent lots, 145, 150; definition, 163n3; informal use, 150
Allied Chemical. *See* Solvay Process Company
Ambassador Bridge, 21, 123, 127, 136
American Dream, 92, 93; reverse 27
anarerobic digestion, 183, 187n4
annexation, 3–4, 43, 95, 121, 145, 190, 196, 197, 198

Archer, Dennis, 52, 64, 67, 133; Mayor's Land Use Task Force, 66. *See also* Community Reinvestment Strategy (CRS)
archipelago, 169–88; creating, 180; neighborhood typologies, 185–86; urban district islands, 180–81, 182, 184–86
arpent, 25n1
Arquero, María A. de Alarcón, 10–11, 115–42ch
Arsenal of Democracy, 81, 115. *See also* war production
Art Center, 57, 68
assembly line, 87; citywide, 87, 91
Atlas of Shrinking Cities, 6
Auburn Hills, MI, 194–99, 195t, 196t, 205; Chrysler, 197
automobile: affordability, 8; factory outplacement, 28–30; household access to, 103; industry, 28, 30, 205; industry leaving central city, 58; industry market share, 64; industry spatial spread, 32–3; manufacturing, 77–99; manufacturing crisis, 4–5, manufacturing decline, 172, 190, manufacturing dependency, 3

Baha'i religious community, 200
bankruptcy, 71
Behrens, Peter: AEG Turbine Factory, 81
Bekkering, Henco, 10, 1–13ch, 27–50ch
Bell, Daniel, 92–93
Belle Isle, 21, 203
Big Three (GM, Ford, Chrysler), 30, 58, 88, 92, 95, 97, 211; central business district, 57
Bing, David, 67, 70, 171
Biocrops, biofuels, 182, 187n3
black ghetto, 55, 57
Blessing, Charles, 127–28
Blessing, Hedrich, 98n1

INDEX 237

blight, 4, 52, 54–61, 57, 71, 72n1, 161
Blitz, Louis, 119
Bloomfield Township, MI, 194–99, 195t, 196t, 205
blots, 150–53, 152f, 153f
Blue Cross and Blue Shield (BCBS). *See* Michigan Blue Cross and Blue Shield
blue infrastructure, 222, 226
Book Cadillac Hotel (Westin), 65, 67, 69
Brewster Homes, 53, 54
Brightmoor Alliance, 155, 163n1
Brightmoor neighborhood, 143–65; adjacent lots, 150–53 151f, 152f, 153f; affordable housing, 152; Appalachia, 145, 146; boundaries, 145, 146f; future, 157–59; government owned, 159–61; household tenure, 148; nonprofit developers, 151, 152–53, 158f; outside investors, 157–58, 159f; pedestrian trails, 155; planning, 160; population profile, 149–50; reuse land patterns, 150; urban gardens, 154, 155f; vacant lots, 148f, 149f
Burnham, Daniel, 210–11
busing, 61, 196

Cadillac car, 88
Cadillac, Antoine Laumet de la Mothe, 18, 21–22, 25
Cadillac Place 30
Calhoun, Craig Jackson, 192, 200, 203
Campus Martius Park, 37, 39, 69, 203
carbon forests, 226
cartographic: accuracy, foundation, 23–25; record, 18, 23–25
Catholic parochial school system, 5, 204
central business district, 3, 6, 9, 30, 52, 55, 57, 71, 103, 124, 175, 204, 219, 222; accessibility, 105, 108; redevelopment projects, 54–57, 61, 62t, 63–64, 67, 68–69, 193

Chevrolet, 28, 88
Chicago, IL 84; 1909 Plan of Chicago, 210–11
Chrysler, Walter P., 88, 89
Chrysler Corporation, 28, 87, 88, 89, 190, 196–98; Jefferson Avenue assembly plants, 63f, 64, 87, 89
CIAM, American (International Congress of Modern Architecture), 82
citizen district councils, 61, 62t
city: blight citations, 158; collapse, 9; government distrust, 64; regulation enforcement, 154, 156, 161; urban agriculture, 175
city of holes, 1, 27–50, 30, 32, 43, 46; holes in urban fabric, 42f
civil disorders 1960s, 4, 58, 61
Clark Street plant. *See under* General Motors
Cleveland, OH, 7–8, 7t, 8t, 170; Model Neighborhoods, 60
Cobo, Albert, 53
Cockrel, Kenneth Jr., 67
co-generation, 182, 183
Comerica Park, 68
commercial vacancy, 175
community, 204–5; definition, 191; density, 200; propinquity, 191–92, 199–200; sense of, 190; virtual, 192
Community Benefits Agreement, 137
Community Benefits Coalition, 136
Community Development Advocates of Detroit (CDAD) framework, 173, 219
Community Reinvestment Strategy (CRS), 66–67
concentration of suppliers, 87, 88
Corktown, 55, 57, 62, 69, 219
Cultural Center, 57, 59, 62

Data Driven Detroit, 32

day-lighting streams, 177–80; benefits, 177–78, 181
DDOT. *See* Detroit Department of Transportation
Dearborn, MI, 84
decentralization, 2, 8, 9, 192; of employment, 103; of industrial, 2, 30, 58, 89, 95; of residential, 58, 95
Delray neighborhood, 115–42; boundaries, 116f, 117; environmental conditions, 133, 136; highway, 126–27; Hispanic and Latino residents, 132; industrial landscape, 119–21, 125–27, 138f, 139f; planning process, 133; poverty, 132, 134; residential, 121–23, 133, 135f
demolition, 4, 67, 68, 143, 174
Dequindre Cut Greenway, 69, 176, 203
desegregation, 195–96
desire paths, 155. *See also* pedestrian trails
Detroit, early years, 17–25
Detroit Agriculture Network, 174
Detroit City Glass Works, 119
Detroit Data Collaborative, 32
Detroit Department of Transportation (DDOT), 103
Detroit Eastern Market, 69, 176, 203
Detroit Economic Growth Corporation (DEGC), 69, 212
Detroit Edison, 123
Detroit Future City, x, 2, 8, 11, 70, 71, 72n1, 140n4, 160, 187n1n2, 209–31; aims, 212; civic engagement, 214; density, 217–21; economic mapping, 214–15; employment districts, 214, 215, 216f, 217; employment opportunities, 215; framework zones, 217–19, 218f, 220f; greater downtown framework zone, 219; high-vacancy framework zone, 219, 229; imperatives, 213, 213t; implementation, 229–30; investment, 217–21; land use mapping, 215–25,

223f, 224f; low-vacancy framework zone, 219–20, 222; mapping industrial use, 222–5, mapping neighborhood mixed use, 222, mapping neighborhood residential 221–22; mapping open space, 225–29, 228f; moderate-vacancy framework zone, 219–20, 222; planning elements, 214; planning process, 209, 212; remap systems, 210
Detroit Housing Commission, 54
Detroit Institute of Art, 57, 203; tax millage, 68
Detroit International Exposition, 117, 118f, 120
Detroit Land Bank. *See under* land bank
Detroit Master Plans and reports: 1951 Master Plan, 58, 125, 129; 1956 Industrial Renewal report, 125; 1973 Master Plan, 129–30; 1985 Master Plan, 130–31; 1992 Master Plan of Policies, 61, 64, 133; 2009 Master Plan of Policies, 67, 70, 133, 210
Detroit Medical Center, 52, 57, 59, 62, 68
Detroit Midtown, Inc., 68
Detroit Opera House, 203
Detroit People Mover, 3, 112n2, 201
Detroit Public School, 204
Detroit Residential Parcel Survey, 32
Detroit River, 18, 115; spatial system, 39
Detroit Riverfront Conservancy, 69, 175, 203
Detroit Salt Company, 121, 140n2
Detroit Tank Arsenal, 81, 89, 91, 91f, 96
Detroit Terminal Railroad, 86–89, 87f
Detroit Vacant Property Campaign, 162
Detroit Waste Water Treatment Plant, 123, 125f, 140n3
Detroit Works Project (DWP), 70, 71 171, 212; long-term initiative (DWPLTP), 212; short-term actions, 212. See also *Detroit Future City*
Detroit Zoo, 203
Dewar, Margaret, 11, 143–65ch

dissimilarity index, 204
Dodge plants: Main plant, 87–89, 130; Truck plant, 81, 89, 91f, 96
double *patte d-oie*, 37, 39
Douglass Homes, 54
Doxiadis, Constantinos, ix, 27, 44, 45f, 49n2
Dresden, Germany, 170
Duggan, Mike, 70, 72n1
dumping, 153, 155, 156f, 157f, 162
Dunnigan, Brian Leigh, 10, 12, 17–26ch, 30
DWPLTP. *See under* Detroit Works Project

ecological: restoration, 179; stabilization, 184
economic recession: 1970s, 61; 2007, 67
1805 fire. *See* fire of 1805
Eliza Howell Park, 147, 154
Elmwood, 57, 59, 61, 219
Elmwood III, 55, 62; Community Development Block Grant, 61; citizen-driven plans 59; McDougall-Hunt neighborhood, 59
emergency fiscal manager, 5, 71n1, 205; Hamtramck, 198; Highland Park, 198
employment: Model Neighborhoods, 59; opportunity, 215; systems, 3
Empowerment Zones (EZ). *See under* federal policy and agencies
Emscher (Landscape) Park, Germany, 184
energy: landscape, 182–84; production, 182–84, 186; use reduction, 182
environmental: justice, 116; rankings, 172; remediation, 133
Erie Canal, 117
ethnic enclaves: Hispanic and Latino, 123, 132; Hungarian, 115, 119, 122, 123f; Polish, 198–99
equity: for blacks, 57; employment, 96–97; housing, 97; inequity, 215; transportation, 101–3, 111

exodus: from central city, 190; middle-class, 4; from Pontiac, 196
EZ. *See under* federal policy and agencies

factory zone, 84, 89
Fair Housing Act (1968). *See under* federal policy and agencies
fallow land, 30, 169, 173, 174–75, 186
federal policy and agencies 2–3, 59, 190; Community Development Block Grant (CDBG), 52, 61, 63, 63f, 66, 70; CDBG Neighborhood Opportunity Fund (NOF), 63; Demonstration Cities and Metropolitan Development Act (1966), 54; Department of Housing and Development (HUD), 53; Department of Transportation, 202; Empowerment Zone (EZ), 52, 64–70, 64f, 65f, 133; Enterprise Communities, 133; Fair Housing Act (1968), 95; Federal Highway Act (1956), 3, 126, 190; Federal Housing Administration (FHA), 2, 80–81, 92, 93, 96; HOPE VI, 54; Housing Act (1949), 54; Housing Act (1949), and redevelopment projects, 55; Housing Act (1954), 54; HUD voucher program, 54; Low Income Housing Tax Credits (LIHTC), 54, 55, 61, 67–68, 157; Model Cities, 52, 54, 58f, 59; Model Neighborhoods, 52, 59, 60f, 61; Model Neighborhoods local resident involvement, 59–60; Model Neighborhoods racial conflict calming, 60; Neighborhood Stabilization Program (NSP), 67–68, 67f, 68f, 160; Office of War Information (OWI) photographers, 92, 95; Renewal Community, 65, 66, 66f; Revenue Act (1913), 2; Veterans' Administration, 2
Federal Housing Administration. *See under* federal policy and agencies
FHA. *See under* federal policy and agencies

INDEX 239

fire of 1805, 22, 34; after, 22–23, 36; impact, 23
fiscal emergency, 203
Fisher Body Plant, 175
Fisher Building, 30
Fishman, Robert, 3, 10, 77–100ch
Fleetwood plant. *See under* General Motors
Flint, MI, 32, 88, 170
Focus:HOPE, 200, 204, 215
foreclosure, 5, 32, 67, 160
Ford Field, 68
Ford, Henry, 17, 58, 84–88, 197
Ford, Henry III, 58
Ford Motor Company, 3, 28, 87
Forest Park, 59
Fort Detroit, 22, 23, 35f, 36f
Fort Lernoult, 21, 22, 23f
Fort Pontchartrain, 30, 35
Fort Shelby, 22–23
Fort Wayne, 117, 119f, 140n1
fortifications, 18, 21, 22, 39
foundation initiatives, 71. *See also* Skillman Foundation; Kresge Foundation
French: agricultural, trade activity, 17, 18; colonial period, 18–22, 25; settlers, 117
Frontier Metropolis: Picturing Early Detroit, 1701–1838, 18, 23, 24, 30, 42, 47–48

Gemeinshaft, 190–92, 205; definition, 191
General Motors, 28, 30, 69, 81, 88, 92–93, 95, 130, 131, 133, 172, 190, 195, 198; Clark Street and Fleetwood plants, 131–32; Detroit-Hamtramck Assembly Plant, 30, 63f, 64, 130, 198
Genesee County Land Bank. *See under* land bank
gentrification, 69, 213
Gessellshaft, 190–91, 192–93, 205; definition, 191
Gilbert, Dan, 69, 71, 204
Glasgow, Scotland, 7

GM. *See* General Motors
Gomon, Josephine, 53
Gräbner, Lars, 11, 169–88ch
greenway networks, 176–77
Grengs, Joe, 10, 101–14ch
Griffin, Toni, 12, 209–31ch
Groesbeck Highway linear city, 79, 79f, 89
Gropius, Walter: Fagus Shoe Factory, 81

Habitat for Humanity, 68, 152–53, 157
Hamtramck, MI, 46, 87, 93, 130, 194–95, 195t, 196t, 205; Arab ancestry, 199; density and diversity, 199; emergency financial manager, 198; General Motors, 198, 205; immigrants, 198–99, 205
Hastings Street, 40
Heidelberg Project, 59
Highland Park, MI, 46, 93, 194–99, 195t, 196t, 205; Chrysler, 197; emergency financial manager, 198; Ford Motor Company, 197
Highland Park plant, 28, 84–89, 86f, 197; proto linear city, 84, 88
highways: Davison Expressway, 93, 95; Fisher Freeway, 126–27; interstate highways and freeways, 3, 43, 93, 95, 103, 126–27; spatial system, 39–40; state highways, 103
home rule, 190
homesteads, 150
housing, 91–93, 95–96; affordable, 53–54, 152; equal, 97; new construction, 68; public, 52, 53, 54f; and segregation, 95–96, 98; single-family tract, 93, 98. *See also* worker housing
Hungarian enclave, 115, 119, 122, 123f
hydrologic systems, 169, 178, 178f; restore 181

Illitch family, 69, 71
image of the city, 210; decline, 211; remapping, 210

Indian trails, 34, 35
industrial: closings, 127; jobs, 3, 9, 58; redevelopment, 130; relocation, 124, 205; spatial spread, 28–30, 32–33, 95, 190; vacancy, 175
infrastructure, 171–72; blue, 222, 226; excess, 173; green, 222; landscape, 226
inner-ring suburb, 8, 103, 193; black movement into, 9
international bridge, 115, 117, 136; community benefits, 117, 136–37
interracial cooperation, 193, 200
interstate freeways. *See* highways

Jefferson-Chalmers neighborhood, 61, 62, 66–67
Jefferson Grid, 34, 49n3; spatial system, 39
Jeffries Homes, 53
job changes, 9, 58, 214–15
Joe Louis Arena, 63

Kahn, Albert, 28, 30, 81, 84, 89
Kilpatrick, Kwame, 67
Kramer Homes, 96, 96f
Kresge Foundation, 70, 230

labor union, 92–93; equal employment, 96–97; non-union, 97; racial segregation, 3
Lafayette Park, 55–56, 57, 59, 61, 62, 69, 219, 222
land bank, 32; Detroit, 32, 71, 160; Genesee County, 32; Wayne County, 32
land ownership, 143; city-owned, 153, 159–61, 173f
landscape: buffers, 225; ecology and economy, 170; economic growth, 225–26; infrastructure, 226; neighborhood, 226; park, 175, 179, 182, 184; productive, 170, 181f, 182, 186, 222, 225; recreational and ecological, 226; types 215; urbanism, 170

land usage, 1, 4; challenges, 9; definition, 2, 12n2; dilemma, 5
land use, 170; communal, 162; definition, 12n2; ecologically based, 170, 229; existing, 223f; industrial, 222–25; low density, 160; official (Delray), 125–27; productive, 160, 222, 225; patterns, 171f; planning, 70, 210, 217, 225f; redesign and reuse, 170, 176; residential, green, and neighborhood, 160, 221–22; transportation, 102, 109; vacancy, 210
Larsen, Larissa, 10–11, 115–42ch
Le Corbusier, 77–79, 78f, 84, 91–92, 94f, 98
legacy city, 2; definition, 12n1; problems, 213
Leipzig, Germany, 184
L'Enfant Plan (Pierre-Charles), 36–37, 37f
light rail, 202
LIHTC. *See under* federal policy and agencies
linear city, 77–99, 189; analysis, 95–98; definition, 77; equal employment, 96–97; Groesbeck, 79, 79f, 89; Livonia, 79, 94f, 95–96; Lynch Road, 89, 90f; Mound Road, 78, 79f, 80f, 81, 89, 91, 92, 93f, 95–96, 96f; proto linear city, 84, 88; worker housing, 77, 79
Linn, Robert, 11, 143–65ch
Liu, Yanjia, 10, 27–50ch
Livonia linear city, 79, 94f, 95
Lynch Road plant, 89, 90f

Macomb County, MI, 89, 95, 97, 102
manufacturing: automobile, 77–99; automobile crisis, 4–5; automobile decline, 172, 190; new products, 172
mapping potential, 177–80
McDougall-Hunt neighborhood, 59, 62t
McMillan, James, 119
McMillan, William C., 119, 127f

metropolitan: area, 43–44, 44f, 189–207; boundaries, 43; context, 9, 52; economy, 190; fragmentation, 193; growth, 43–44; overflow, 46
Metropolitan Organization Strategy Enabling Strength (MOSES), 200, 204
Michigan, State of: Belle Isle, 203; home-rule, 43; local government system, 193–94; municipalities, 193; municipal service agreements, 202; Neighborhood Enterprise Zone Act, 66; regional transit authority, 201; Renaissance Zone Act, 66
Michigan Blue Cross and Blue Shield, 57
Michigan Central Depot, 30, 175
Michigan Community Resources, 162
Michigan Land-Use Leadership Council, 194
Michigan Roundtable for Diversity and Inclusion, 200
Michigan State Fair (1880's), 117
Michigan Suburbs Alliance, 194, 200
Midtown, 5, 6, 9, 52, 68–69, 204, 219
Mies van der Rohe, Ludwig, 55
migration: outward, 169
Miliutin, Nikolai, 77–79, 78f, 84, 91–92, 94f, 98
Millender Center, 63
Milwaukee Junction, 57, 59
mobility: definition of, 101; racial, 58, 203–4, 205; residential, 213; and transportation, 101–2, 134; urban sprawl, 102; vs. accessibility, 101
Model Cities. *See under* federal policy and agencies
Model Neighborhoods. *See under* federal policy and agencies
mortgages, 58, 160
Mound Road linear city, 78, 79f, 80f, 81, 89, 91, 92, 93f, 95–96, 96f; Detroit Tank Arsenal, 81, 89, 91, 91f, 96; Dodge Truck, 81, 89, 91f, 96; equal employment, 96–97; housing, 92, 92f,

95–96, 96f; Hudson Naval Ordinance plant, 81, 89, 96; Tech Center, 95

Native American: assaults, 22; villages, 18
Naval Ordinance plant (Hudson), 81, 89, 96
Neighborhood Opportunity Fund (NOF). *See under* federal policy and agencies; Community Development Block Grant
Neighborhood Stabilization Program (NSP). *See under* federal policy and agencies
Neighbors Building Brightmoor, 154–56
networks: community, 203; creative 95; essential, 210; highways, 3, 93, 95; interconnected use of, 176; railways, 83, 84, 98, 117; recreational and ecological, 226; suppliers, 87, 88; water, 117
Neutra, Richard, 82
New Center, 28, 30, 43, 71, 219
New Detroit, 200
New International Trade Crossing (NITC). *See* international bridge
New Orleans, LA master plan, 210
Next Detroit Neighborhood Initiative (NDNI), 67
nonprofit institutions, 57, 68
Northwest Detroit Neighborhood Development (NDND), 151–53, 157, 158

Oakland County, MI, 102, 194–95
Orfield, Myron and Luce, Thomas, 193, 200, 202
Orr, Kevin, 71n1
outer-ring suburb, 103; predominately white 9

Packard Motors, 28; plant, 30, 84, 175
parks. *See under* public, parks
pedestrian trails, 155, 156f, 163n5

INDEX 241

Petit Atlas Maritime, Le, 25
planning: Brightmoor community, 145, 160; citizen-driven in Model Neighborhoods, 59; Delray public process, 133; growth-centered, 170; informal, 145; land use, 70; place-based, 170
Plunz, Richard, 27
Plymouth (auto), 89
Pontiac, Chief, 19f, 20f, 22
Pontiac, MI, 194–99, 195t, 196t, 205; busing, 196
population decline, 1–2, 6, 7t, 8t, 9, 30, 52, 57, 61, 64, 70, 147, 203, 213, 215
poverty rates, 9, 197f
productive landscape, 170, 181f, 182–3, 186. *See also Detroit Future City*
pro-growth coalition, 51, 55, 69, 71; Auburn Hills, 196; fragmented, 52; nonprofit institutions, 57
propinquity, 191–2, 199–200; Hamtramck, 199
public: health in Model Neighborhoods, 59; housing, 53, 54f; housing era 52; housing maintenance funds 53; housing racial segregation 53; incentives, 190; infrastructure in Delray, 123–26; parks, 225, 227f; safety, 4; schools in Model Neighborhoods, 59; school system, 5, 204; services, 70, 212, 213; space, 144, 203; sphere, 192, 205; transit, 103, 108, 111
public housing projects: Brewster Homes, 53, 54; Douglass Homes, 54; Jeffries Homes, 53; Sojourner Truth, 53

Quicken Loans, 204

radial avenues spatial system, 39
race and: employment, 96–97; housing, 95–96, 98; transportation accessibility, 106–8
race riots (1943), 53
racial: conflict, 52, 58, 60, 70; cooperation, 193, 203–4; disunity and division, 4, 9, 53, 193–94, 194f, 205; diversity, 12n5; diversity measurement, 3, 53, 204; housing discrimination, 58; population density, 194f; segregation, 3, 53;
railways, 83, 98, 117; Detroit Terminal Railroad, 86–89; Grand Trunk Railway, 89; Michigan Central, 84, 89, 91; spatial system, 39
Rapid Transit Commission of Detroit, 83, 83f, 84
rapid transit system, 83, 103, 201f
Ravitz, Mel, 58
real estate owned, 160f, 161
recreational spaces, 222
redevelopment, 51–74; agenda, 51, 70; areas, 56f; major periods of, 52; spatial system, 40
regional: context, 189–207; cooperation, 193–94, 200; fragmentation, 8, 61, 70, 189–90, 192–93, 205; growth management, 190; hub, 83; identity, 83, 200, 203; landscape, 181, 184; millage, 68, 203; service coordination, 202–3, 205; transit, 41, 201–2, 205; transit accessibility, 108, 202; transit fragmentation 202. *See also* southeast Michigan municipalities; *names of individual cities*
Regional Transit Authority, 41, 103, 201–2
relocation, 213
remediation of soil. *See* soil remediation
Renaissance Center, 58, 69
REO. *See* real estate owned
replatting, de facto, 150, 153, 154
residential: neighborhood fate, 69; suburbanization, 190; turmoil, 58
Reuther, Walter, 92, 96
ribbon farms, 21, 21f, 23, 35, 42, 117; definition, 21; spatial system, 39
right sizing, 170
River Rouge plant, 84, 86, 88, 123
Rock Ventures, 69, 71, 204
Ruhr Valley, Germany, 170; industrial region, 170; Emscher Landscape Park, 184

ruins voyeurism, 143, 145
Rundell Ernstberger Associates, 39

Saarinen, Eero, 79, 95, 96, 98
salt deposits, tunnels, 120, 121, 140n2
satellite cities, 84, 88
Schumack, Riet, 154, 155
segregation: accessibility, 110–11; housing, 2–3, 95–96, 98; labor, 96; residential, 103
SEMCOG. *See* Southeast Michigan Council of Governments
7.2 Square Mile report, 69, 211
shrinkage, 64–70, 169, 170, 186; right sizing, 170
shrinking cities, 170, 210; *Atlas of Shrinking Cities,* 6
Skillman Foundation, 67
Sloan, Alfred P., 87, 88, 95
slums, 52, 54–61, 55, 57
SMART *See* Suburban Mobility Authority for Regional Transit
Smets, Marcel, 27
Snyder, Rick, 71n1, 202
social context: *Gemeinshaft*, 190; *Gessellshaft*, 190
social distance, 70, 203–4, 205
social equity. *See* equity
soil remediation, 175, 182, 183
Sojourner Truth housing project, 53
solar energy projects, 184
Solvay Process Company, 120, 120f, 127; General Hospital, 120, 120f; Lodge, 121
Soria y Mata, Arturo, 77
Southeast Michigan Council of Governments (SEMCOG), 194, 201, 202, 214
southeast Michigan municipalities, 193; connections, 203, 204; fragmentation, 3–4; economic stress, 202–3; service coordination, 202–3, 205

Southern Automotive Corridor, 97, 98
spatial: mismatch, 102, 111; justice, 190
spatially based compensation, 117
spatial systems, 39–41, 40f
St. Louis, MO, 7–8, 7t, 8t, 170
state policies, 190. *See also* Michigan, State of
stormwater, 173, 177
Strategic Framework. See *Detroit Future City*
streetcar system, 39–40, 41f
suburban: federal favor, 2–3; housing, 92, 93, 98; jobs, 93; migration, 128; postwar subdivision, 92; segregation, 95–96, 204; shopping mall, 3, 4;
suburbanization, 52, 190, 192; racially exclusionary, 61
Suburban Mobility Authority for Regional Transit (SMART), 103
Syracuse, NY, 110, 120

targeting, 54, 173; black communities, 54; development resources, 52, 54–61; Neighborhood Stabilization Program, 67–8, 67f, 68f; Skillman Foundation, 67
Taylor homes and lots, 145–46, 146f, 148, 152
TAZ. *See* transportation analysis zones
Tech Town, 172
Ten Thousand Acre Grid, 33, 34, 34f, 35, 49n3; spatial system, 39
Thomas, June Manning, 10, 11, 12, 1–13ch, 40, 51–74ch, 189–207ch, 209–31ch
Tonnies, Ferdinand, 191, 192
Transit Windsor, 112n2
transportation: analysis zones (TAZ), 105; freight, 131; international, 123; systems, 3, 217; territorial roads, 117; water, 117, 131. *See also* accessibility; mobility
Transportation Riders United, 201, 204

Treaty of Detroit, 92, 95, 97

UAW. *See* United Auto Workers
United Auto Workers (UAW), 92, 96–97
urban: agriculture, 154, 155f, 174–75, 222, 225; ecological system, 225; fabric, 1, 42f; interventions, 169, 181f; islands, 180–81, 182; landscape park, 175, 179, 182, 184; morphology, 28; prairie, 32; public sphere, 192; regimes, 51, 52, 57; restructuring, 170, 177, 186; sprawl, 102, 177, 193–94
urban renewal, 52, 54, 55, 59, 70, 134, 193, 213; areas, 56–57, 56f, 61, 144; areas vs. Empowerment Zones, 65; nonprofit institutions, 57
urban renewal projects: Corktown, 55, 57; Elmwood (I, II, III), 55; Gratiot (Lafayette Park), 55; Milwaukee Junction, 57
urbanism, landscape, 170
urbanization and social disorganization, 191

vacancy, 4, 143; commercial, 175; concentration, 42; housing, 31–33, 65f; industrial, 30, 175; land use plan, 210; rates, 171f; survey, 31; tourism, 143
vacant: building clearance, 32, 68; fallow land, 169, 174; fragmented parcels, 175; houses, 4, 156; land, 143, 147, 154–56, 170, 171; land area, 215; land maintenance, 174; land studies, 181; lot improvement, 174; lots, 1, 31, 31f, 32; residential lots, 30, 143, 148f, 154, 174; structures, 172f; urban renewal sites, 55
voucher program (HUD), 54

Waldopolenz Solar Park, 184
war production, 89, 123
Warren, MI, 8, 89, 95–96
Washington, DC plan, 36–37, 37f

Wayne County, MI, 102, 194–95
Wayne County Land Bank. *See under* land bank
Wayne State University, 56, 57, 59, 62, 68, 172, 193
Weaver, Robert, 79, 96, 98
Webber, Melvin, 192
Weston Book Cadillac Hotel. *See* Book Cadillac Hotel
wetlands, 177, 180f, 181; restoration, 182
Wider Woodward Association, 53
Willow Run Plant, 3
Windsor, Ontario, 136
Woodward, Augustus, 22
Woodward Avenue, 28, 34; light rail (M1), 69, 202
Woodward Plan, 22, 23, 36–37; radial pattern, 38
Woodward Trace. *See* Woodward Plan
worker housing, 77, 79, 91–92, 96
Wright, Frank Lloyd, 79, 96, 97f, 98, 191

Young, Coleman, 52, 61, 64, 79, 97, 98, 133, 190; built-environment legacy, 64; public housing policy, 53
Youngstown, OH, 170; land use plan, 201

zoning ordinance: Delray, 122–23, 124f, 125; enforcement, 153; lot size, 145, 152, 153; typical, 221
Zug Island, 119